JOHN DONNE'S POETRY

AUTHORITATIVE TEXTS
CRITICISM

SECOND EDITION

W. W. NORTON & COMPANY, INC.
Also Publishes

THE NORTON ANTHOLOGY OF AFRICAN AMERICAN LITERATURE
edited by Henry Louis Gates Jr. and Nellie Y. McKay et al.

THE NORTON ANTHOLOGY OF AMERICAN LITERATURE
edited by Nina Baym et al.

THE NORTON ANTHOLOGY OF CONTEMPORARY FICTION
edited by R. V. Cassill and Joyce Carol Oates

THE NORTON ANTHOLOGY OF ENGLISH LITERATURE
edited by M. H. Abrams and Stephen Greenblatt et al.

THE NORTON ANTHOLOGY OF LITERATURE BY WOMEN
edited by Sandra M. Gilbert and Susan Gubar

THE NORTON ANTHOLOGY OF MODERN AND CONTEMPORARY POETRY
edited by Jahan Ramazani, Richard Ellmann, and Robert O'Clair

THE NORTON ANTHOLOGY OF POETRY
edited by Margaret Ferguson, Mary Jo Salter, and Jon Stallworthy

THE NORTON ANTHOLOGY OF SHORT FICTION
edited by R. V. Cassill and Richard Bausch

THE NORTON ANTHOLOGY OF THEORY AND CRITICISM
edited by Vincent B. Leitch et al.

THE NORTON ANTHOLOGY OF WORLD LITERATURE
edited by Sarah Lawall et al.

THE NORTON FACSIMILE OF THE FIRST FOLIO OF SHAKESPEARE
prepared by Charlton Hinman

THE NORTON INTRODUCTION TO LITERATURE
edited by Jerome Beaty, Alison Booth, J. Paul Hunter, and Kelly J. Mays

THE NORTON INTRODUCTION TO THE SHORT NOVEL
edited by Jerome Beaty

THE NORTON READER
edited by Linda H. Peterson, John C. Brereton, and Joan E. Hartman

THE NORTON SAMPLER
edited by Thomas Cooley

THE NORTON SHAKESPEARE, BASED ON THE OXFORD EDITION
edited by Stephen Greenblatt et al.

For a complete list of Norton Critical Editions, visit
www.wwnorton.com/college/english/nce_home.htm

A NORTON CRITICAL EDITION

JOHN DONNE'S POETRY

AUTHORITATIVE TEXTS
CRITICISM

SECOND EDITION

Selected and Edited by

ARTHUR L. CLEMENTS

HARPUR COLLEGE, BINGHAMTON UNIVERSITY

W · W · NORTON & COMPANY · *New York* · *London*

Printed in the United States of America.
The text of this book is composed in Electra,
with the display set in Bernhard Modern.
Composition by Vail Composition.
Manufacturing by Maple-Vail.
Book design by Antonnia Krass.
Library of Congress Cataloging-in-Publication Data
Donne, John, 1572–1631.
[Poems. Selections]
John Donne's poetry : authoritative texts, criticism / selected
and edited by Arthur L. Clements.—2nd ed.
p. cm.—(A Norton critical edition)
Includes bibliographical references.
1. Donne, John, 1572–1631—Criticism and interpretation.
I. Clements, Arthur L. II. Title.
PR2246.C57 1991
821'.3—dc20 90-21390

ISBN 0-393-96062-5

W. W. Norton & Company, Inc., 500 Fifth Avenue, New York, N.Y. 10110
W. W. Norton & Company, Ltd., Castle House, 75/76 Wells Street,
London W1T 3QT

7 8 9 0

Contents

Criticism

Preface to the Second Edition

For this second edition, I have had the help of my colleague and friend Philip Brady of Youngstown State University. We have shared various editorial tasks in the following ways. I selected the poems to be added and the criticism to be added or dropped. Professor Brady edited, updated, and annotated the poems and prepared textual notes. I checked, confirmed, or modified the text, glosses, and notes. He prepared the indexes of titles and first lines. I edited and arranged the criticism and compiled the Selected Bibliography. We shared or divided various routine tasks. For this revision of *John Donne's Poetry* he therefore deserves much of the credit.

We have added nineteen poems with glosses and textual notes, seven new essays in criticism, a much-expanded Selected Bibliography, and indexes of titles and first lines, all while managing not to exceed by too very much the page limitations suggested by the publisher. The additional poems include five Elegies, four Satires (so that all five Satires, recently regarded by critics as a sequence, are now available), six Verse Letters, and four Divine Poems. The text of all the poems in this second edition, as in the first, is based upon the first seventeenth-century Donne edition of each poem or (in the case of "Elegy XX. Love's War," and three Holy Sonnets) upon the Westmoreland manuscript. This means that the primary text for most of the poems remains that of the 1633 edition. Exceptions are individually noted in the Textual Notes. The principles for the editing, updating, and annotating of the text, and for the preparing of the Textual Notes have also remained the same as those articulated in the Preface to the first edition and in the Textual Notes. The reliability and usefulness of this second edition for the student and general reader have continued to be principal criteria. These criteria could be served when the first edition was published in 1966 largely because the important editions of Donne by such scholars as Sir Herbert Grierson, Dame Helen Gardner, and Frank Manley were then helpfully available. Since that time, major texts of value and help for this second edition have been published, especially the work of W. Milgate, C. A. Patrides, John Shawcross, and A. J. Smith, to whom we are indebted. Any further improvements await publication of the *Variorum Edition of the Poetry of John Donne*, now being prepared by a group of scholars, some of whom have already raised and published questions regarding previous textual assumptions and authority.

The reasons for choosing criticism for reprinting here continue to include, among other considerations, the importance and usefulness of the selection and its relevance to other selections. Instead of the original three sections of criticism, there are now five. The first section, Donne and Metaphysical Poetry, containing historical and famous works, remains unchanged. Partly out of space considerations, the second section, Donne's Love Poetry, now omits C. S. Lewis's essay, which no longer holds currency in Donne studies and is, in any event, more than adequately answered by Joan Bennett's essay. This section adds an excerpt from my recently published *Poetry of Contemplation (1990)*, "[Eros in the *Songs and Sonnets*]," which in various ways is responsive to the preceding essays on Donne's love poetry by Cleanth Brooks, Clay Hunt, and R. A. Durr, and which, since it concerns contemplation, complements the subsequent discussions by Helen Gardner, Louis Martz, and Stanley Archer on meditation in the Divine Poems. The next section, Satires, Verse Letters, and *The Anniversaries*, includes from the first edition Frank Manley's discussion of *The Anniversaries*, focusing on the poem's central symbol of the essential Godlike self as formulated in the traditional concept of Wisdom, plus new essays on the Satires, by John R. Lauritsen, and on the Verse Letters, by David Aers and Gunther Kress. These two new essays, originally published in 1976 and 1981, both begin by noting how relatively little criticism exists on the poems that are the essays' subjects. Like other critics, Lauritsen regards the Satires as a sequence, and, in particular, he discusses them as a progress of self-discovery. In their article, Aers and Kress attempt to construct a framework by which to describe and account for versions of the self in the Verse Letters. Like Manley's important work, the work of these and other critics is helping to provide and stimulate more of the attention that the poems of their studies deserve.

Whereas, in the past, critics have argued for or against the influence of Ignatian meditation on Donne's divine poems, current criticism has been divided on the question of Catholic and Protestant influences. In a perceptive essay, "Donne's Holy Sonnets and the Theology of Grace," now included in the fourth section, Donne's Divine Poems, R. V. Young restores balance to recent discussions, concluding that Donne and other seventeenth-century Protestant poets are not "so much militant proponents of the Reformation as Christians confronting God," drawing "upon a number of Christian resources—Catholic and Protestant, Medieval and Renaissance." Again partly out of space considerations, I have dropped from the last section my article on "Batter my heart," though I still stand by its reading; it is now available, slightly expanded, in *Poetry of Contemplation* and is, in any case, referred to by other readings of this Holy Sonnet, including the new ones by R. D. Bedford and Raymond-Jean Frontain, here reprinted. "Holy Sonnet 10 (XIV)" is one of the most discussed of Donne's poems, there being anywhere from five to ten to twenty times more critical treatments of it than of any one of the other

Holy Sonnets. Most of the recent articles on it refer to some or all of the readings reprinted in the first edition. And while some of the later discussions are merely repetitious or minimally valuable, others supplement, clarify, or otherwise improve previous critical understanding and appreciation of the poem—which is, of course, the task of criticism. As in the first edition, the sections of criticism, interweaving and resonating themes and subjects in various ways, contain or refer to controversy and varying opinions, yet also display continuity and development of critical ideas about Donne's poetry. The even greater abundance of valuable writing on Donne in the past twenty-five years makes it utterly impossible to represent here every deserving point of view, but the much expanded Selected Bibliography may better direct the reader to sources helpful in the further study of Donne. Particularly because not all of the many worthy studies of Donne can adequately be represented here, the sections of criticism are rounded off by John R. Roberts's excellent overview of a half-century of Donne criticism, an overview that concludes with the hope that Donne's poetry will become more accessible to an even wider audience, a hope that the editor trusts may be served by this second edition of *John Donne's Poetry*.

July 1990 ARTHUR L. CLEMENTS

Preface to the First Edition

> "If you would teach a scholar in the highest form how to *read*, take Donne . . . When he has learnt to read Donne, with all the force and meaning which are involved in the words, then send him to Milton, and he will stalk on like a master *enjoying* his walk."
>
> SAMUEL TAYLOR COLERIDGE

Excepting the few poems published in Donne's lifetime, the first edition of his poetry appeared in 1633, two years after his death. Six other editions were printed in the seventeenth century. Of all of these, modern scholars, following Sir Herbert Grierson's monumental work and Helen Gardner's valuable edition of *The Divine Poems*, are generally agreed that the edition of 1633 is the most reliable. Though subject to some correction from the other editions and the manuscripts, it provides, they believe, a better text than could be provided by any single extant manuscript or than could be constructed by taking the extant manuscripts together; and they agree that it must be the basis of any critical edition. The edition of 1635 adds some new poems by Donne, rearranges the order of the poems more satisfactorily, and makes many changes in the 1633 text. Although the 1635 edition does not have greater authority, it is especially useful for its new poems (nine of which are included in this volume), for its order, and for its corrections of the misprints and some of the punctuation of the 1633 edition. Of the remaining seventeenth-century editions, which are significant mainly for their new poems, only the 1650 and 1669 editions are here notable. The 1650 edition is the text for two of the Songs and Sonnets: "Sonnet. The Token" and "Self-Love," poems that only doubtfully can be ascribed to Donne. (Although "Sonnet. The Token" was first printed in 1649, the texts of the poem in 1649 and 1650 are identical; it appears that the edition of 1649 was not actually issued and that the sheets of most of the copies were incorporated in the 1650 volumes, edited by the younger John Donne.) The 1669 edition is, as Grierson says, "the last which affords evidence of access to independent manuscript sources"; it adds two elegies, one of which, Elegy XIX, considerably corrected by the manuscripts, is included in this selection. The Westmoreland manuscript, now in the New York Public Library, and of high textual value, is the sole authority for several poems not printed in the early editions, most notably Holy Sonnets XVII, XVIII, and XIX. Of the poems printed in Donne's lifetime, the most significant are *The Anniversaries*, published in 1611 and 1612. Recently, Frank Manley has demonstrated that the 1611 edition, which Donne may have seen through the press, furnishes, with some correction from 1633 and from the 1612 edition with its "unique" errata slip, the only authoritative text of *The First Anniversary*.

The text of this edition, therefore, is substantially that of 1633; sixteen poems are included for which the Westmoreland manuscript and the editions of 1611, 1635, 1650 and 1669 have authority. That is, the text is based upon the first edition of each poem or, in the case of three Holy Sonnets, upon the Westmoreland manuscript. Effort has been made throughout to take into account the many important contributions of modern scholars and editors of Donne. For example, while retaining in parentheses Grierson's numbering of the Holy Sonnets, by which they are usually referred to, this volume adopts the sequence suggested by Helen Gardner, based on her study of the editions and manuscripts. The annotations are intended chiefly to compensate for some of the changes in language and knowledge effected by the passage of more than three centuries and to suggest some of the rewarding complexities of Donne's poetry. On occasion, the annotations also refer the reader to helpful critical articles and record some of the editor's debts. Accidentals of spelling, capitalization, and punctuation have been carefully updated; when the updating might obscure a possible alternative reading, I have printed the original or have indicated editorial changes in the Textual Notes, which contain further prefatory remarks on my principles for updating. The Notes also record substantive departures from the authoritative text (as corrected by the other editions and manuscripts) and significant variants. The aim throughout has been reliability.

The essays in criticism range from the seventeenth century to the twentieth century, from sharply critical accounts to highly favorable evaluations, from close analyses of individual poems to general considerations of Donne and metaphysical poetry. The division of the essays into three sections should be almost self-explanatory. The first section, "Donne and Metaphysical Poetry," contains introductory and background material and provides an historical range of opinion by outstanding critics. The second section, "Donne's Love Poetry," begins with the dispute between C. S. Lewis and Joan Bennett; and Theodore Redpath continues and elaborates the discussion of critical issues raised. The articles by Cleanth Brooks, Clay Hunt, and R. A. Durr not only present sensitive, illuminating explications, but also afford some transition from the love poetry to the divine poems. In the third section, "Donne's Divine Poems and *The Anniversaires*," Helen Gardner offers some comprehensive considerations of Donne's religious poetry. Helen Gardner, in the second part of her essay, and Louis Martz discuss the meditative element in the Holy Sonnets and in "Good Friday, 1613," and Stanley Archer raises objections to their approach. The short "Readings of Holy Sonnet 10 (XIV)" provide, again, differing views and yet also illustrate how criticism may contribute, over a period of time, to a fuller and more exact understanding of literature. Finally, Frank Manley summarizes criticism of *The Anniversaries* over the centuries and then considers these poems in terms of the complex and inchoate Renaissance tradition of Wisdom. Thus, each of these interrelated sections contains controversy and varying and divergent opinions, yet also displays some continuity and development of particular critical ideas on Donne's poetry. The abundance of excellent writing on Donne makes it impossible to represent here every point of view, but the Selected Bibliography at the end of this book will direct the reader to sources helpful in the further study of Donne.

Indeed, the abundance of excellent work on Donne in this century puts any modern editor of Donne under heavy debt. I am especially conscious of indebtedness to Sir Herbert Grierson, Helen Gardner, and Frank Manley, all of whom have contributed greatly to establishing and illuminating the text of Donne's poetry. Special expression of my gratefulness must go also to the other scholars whose work is represented in the critical essays of this book. I am grateful also to Professor John Hagopian, who generously put in my hands his published and unpublished materials on Donne; to Professor David Novarr, who offered many thoughtful suggestions, some of which I have incorporated; to Mr. Josiah Newcomb, Director of Libraries, State University of New York at Binghamton, who helped me to obtain the numerous books, photostats, and microfilms I needed; and to members of the staffs of the Huntington Library, the New York Public Library, Princeton University Library, and Yale University Library, who extended many courtesies.

A. L. CLEMENTS

The Texts of THE POEMS

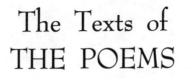

Songs and Sonnets

The Good-Morrow

I wonder, by my troth, what thou and I
Did, till we loved? were we not weaned till then?
But sucked on country pleasures, childishly?
Or snorted we in the Seven Sleepers' den?[1]
'Twas so; but this,[2] all pleasures fancies be.
If ever any beauty I did see,
Which I desired, and got, 'twas but a dream of thee.

And now good-morrow to our waking souls,
Which watch not one another out of fear;
For love, all love of other sights controls,
And makes one little room an everywhere.
Let sea-discoveres to new worlds have gone,
Let maps to others, worlds on worlds have shown,[3]
Let us possess one world, each hath one, and is one.[4]

My face in thine eye, thine in mine appears,
And true plain hearts do in the faces rest;
Where can we find two better hemispheres,
Without sharp north, without declining west?
Whatever dies was not mixed equally;[5]
If our two loves be one, or, thou and I
Love so alike that none do slacken, none can die.

Song

Go and catch a falling star,
    Get with child a mandrake root,[6]

1. Legend tells of seven Christian youths who, fleeing from Roman persecution, took refuge in a cave and slept unharmed for two centuries.
2. Except for this.
3. Let maps reveal to other people many worlds.
4. According to the theory of Donne's time, every man was thought to be a little world in himself, a microcosm, parallelling the great world, the macrocosm.
5. Scholastic doctrine held that decay will eventually occur when a thing is composed of unequal or dissimilar elements.
6. The mandrake root's forked shape roughly resembles the human body. But the mandrake was also thought to be a soporific, an aphroidisiac, and a cause of fruitfulness in women. See D. C. Allen, *Modern Language Notes* 74 (1959): 393–97, and cf. "Twickenham Garden," line 17.

Tell me where all past years are,
  Or who cleft the Devil's foot,
Teach me to hear mermaids singing,
  Or to keep off envy's stinging,
    And find
    What wind
Serves to advance an honest mind.

If thou be'st born to strange sights,
  Things invisible to see,
Ride ten thousand days and nights,
  Till age snow white hairs on thee,
Thou, when thou return'st, wilt tell me
  All strange wonders that befell thee,
    And swear
    Nowhere
Lives a woman true, and fair.

If thou findst one, let me know,
  Such a pilgrimage were sweet.
Yet do not; I would not go,
  Though at next door we might meet;
Though she were true, when you met her,
  And last, till you write your letter,
    Yet she
    Will be
False, ere I come, to two, or three.

Woman's Constancy

Now thou hast loved me one whole day,
Tomorrow when thou leav'st, what wilt thou say?
Wilt thou then antedate some new-made vow?
    Or say that now
We are not just those persons which we were?
Or, that oaths made in reverential fear
Of Love, and his wrath, any may forswear?
Or, as true deaths true marriages untie,
So lovers' contracts, images of those,
Bind but till sleep, death's image, them unloose?
    Or, your own end to justify,
For having purposed change, and falsehood, you
Can have no way but falsehood to be true?
Vain lunatic,[7] against these 'scapes I could

7. Under sway of the moon, and thus changeable, inconstant, as well as madly foolish person; " 'scapes" means "excuses," "evasions."

Dispute, and conquer, if I would,
Which I abstain to do,
For by tomorrow, I may think so too.

The Undertaking

I have done one braver thing
Than all the Worthies[8] did,
And yet a braver thence doth spring,
Which is, to keep that hid.

It were but madness now to impart
The skill of specular stone,[9]
When he which can have learned the art
To cut it can find none.

So, if I now should utter this,
Others (because no more
Such stuff to work upon there is)
Would love but as before.

But he who loveliness within
Hath found, all outward loathes,
For he who color loves, and skin,
Loves but their oldest clothes.

If, as I have, you also do
Virtue attired in woman see,
And dare love that, and say so too,
And forget the He and She,

And if this love, though placed so,
From profane men you hide,
Which will no faith on this bestow,
Or, if they do, deride:

Then you have done a braver thing
Than all the Worthies did.
And a braver thence will spring
Which is, to keep that hid.

8. Outstanding heroes of antiquity.
9. The technique or craft of cutting old selenite, an ancient transparent material used for glazing, but no longer available in Donne's time.

The Sun Rising

Busy old fool, unruly sun,
Why dost thou thus,
Through windows, and through curtains, call on us?
Must to thy motions lovers' seasons run?
Saucy pedantic wretch, go chide
Late schoolboys, and sour prentices,
Go tell court-huntsmen that the King will ride,
Call country ants to harvest offices;
Love, all alike, no season knows, nor clime,
Nor hours, days, months, which are the rags of time.

Thy beams, so reverend and strong
Why shouldst thou think?
I could eclipse and cloud them with a wink,
But that I would not lose her sight so long:
If her eyes have not blinded thine,
Look, and tomorrow late, tell me
Whether both the Indias of spice and mine[1]
Be where thou leftst them, or lie here with me.
Ask for those kings whom thou saw'st yesterday,
And thou shalt hear, All here in one bed lay.

She's all states, and all princes I,
Nothing else is.
Princes do but play us; compared to this,
All honor's mimic, all wealth alchemy.[2]
Thou, sun, art half as happy as we,
In that the world's contracted thus;
Thine age asks[3] ease, and since thy duties be
To warm the world, that's done in warming us.
Shine here to us, and thou art everywhere;
This bed thy center is, these walls thy sphere.

The Indifferent

I can love both fair and brown,
Her whom abundance melts, and her whom want betrays,
Her who loves loneness best, and her who masks and plays,
Her whom the country formed, and whom the town,
Her who believes, and her who tries,
Her who still weeps with spongy eyes,
And her who is dry cork, and never cries;
I can love her, and her, and you, and you,
I can love any, so she be not true.

1. The East Indies, source of spices, and the West Indies, source of precious metals.
2. Alchemy was often regarded as a fraud.
3. Requires.

Will no other vice content you?
Will it not serve your turn to do as did your mothers?
Or have you all old vices spent, and now would find out others?
Or doth a fear, that men are true, torment you?
Oh we are not, be not you so;
Let me, and do you, twenty know.
Rob me, but bind me not, and let me go.
Must I, who came to travail[4] thorough[5] you,
Grow your fixed subject, because you are true?

Venus heard me sigh this song,
And by love's sweetest part, variety, she swore
She heard not this till now; and that it should be so no more.
She went, examined, and returned ere long,
And said, "Alas, some two or three
Poor heretics in love there be,
Which think to 'stablish[6] dangerous constancy.
But I have told them, 'Since you will be true,
You shall be true to them who are false to you.' "

Love's Usury

For every hour that thou wilt spare me now,
I will allow,
Usurious God of Love, twenty to thee,
When with my brown, my gray hairs equal be;
Till then, Love, let my body reign, and let
Me travel, sojourn, snatch, plot, have, forget,
Resume my last year's relict:[7] think that yet
We'd never met.

Let me think any rival's letter mine,
And at next nine[8]
Keep midnight's promise; mistake by the way
The maid, and tell the lady of that delay;
Only let me love none, no, not the sport;
From country grass, to comfitures of Court,
Or city's quelque-choses, let report
My mind transport.[9]

This bargain's good: if, when I'm old, I be
Inflamed by thee,
If thine own honor, or my shame, or pain,
Thou covet, most at that age thou shalt gain.

4. Hardship, suffering; labor; with a pun on travel (as a verb).
5. "Thorough": "through."
6. Establish.
7. The woman loved and left behind last year.
8. Nine A.M.
9. Let reports about the different kinds of women—"country grass"; "comfitures" (literally, "sweetmeats"); "quelque-choses" (literally, "fancy dishes")—turn my fancy from one to the other.

Do thy will then, then subject and degree
And fruit of love, Love, I submit to thee;
Spare me till then, I'll bear it, though she be
One that loves me.

The Canonization

For God's sake, hold your tongue, and let me love,
Or chide my palsy, or my gout,
My five gray hairs, or ruined fortune flout,
With wealth your state, your mind with arts improve,
Take you a course, get you a place,[1]
Observe his honor, or his grace,
Or the King's real, or his stamped[2] face
Contemplate; what you will, approve,[3]
So you will let me love.

Alas, alas, who's injured by my love?
What merchant's ships have my sighs drowned?
Who says my tears have overflowed his ground?
When did my colds a forward spring remove?
When did the heats which my veins fill
Add one more to the plaguy bill?[4]
Soldiers find wars, and lawyers find out still
Litigious men, which quarrels move,
Though she and I do love.

Call us what you will, we are made such by love;
Call her one, me another fly,
We're tapers too, and at our own cost die,[5]
And we in us find the eagle and the dove.[6]
The phoenix riddle hath more wit
By us; we two being one, are it.
So, to one neutral thing both sexes fit.
We die and rise the same, and prove
Mysterious by this love.[7]

We can die by it, if not live by love,
And if unfit for tombs and hearse
Our legend be, it will be fit for verse;
And if no piece of chronicle we prove,

1. Take a course of action, get yourself a position.
2. Stamped on coins.
3. Try, experience.
4. A list of people who died of the plague.
5. Flies or moths, symbols of the ephemeral and lustful, are attracted to and burned by candles ("tapers"), which are self-consuming. In Donne's time, to "die" was slang for consummating the sexual act, and it was believed that this act reduced one's life span.
6. Symbols of strength and of meekness.
7. Just as the phoenix, a unique mythological bird, is consumed by its own funeral fire, yet rises reborn from the ashes, so the lovers, made one by love, are consumed in their fire of passion but revive; "wit" means "sense," "meaning."

We'll build in sonnets pretty rooms;[8]
As well a well-wrought urn becomes
The greatest ashes, as half-acre tombs,
And by these hymns, all shall approve
Us *canonized* for Love.

And thus invoke us: "You, whom reverend love
Made one another's hermitage;
You, to whom love was peace, that now is rage;
Who did the whole world's soul extract, and drove[9]
Into the glasses of your eyes
(So made such mirrors, and such spies,
That they did all to you epitomize)
Countries, towns, courts: beg from above
A pattern of your love!"

The Triple Fool

I am two fools, I know,
For loving, and for saying so
In whining poetry;
But where's that wiseman, that would not be I,
If she would not deny?
Then, as the earth's inward narrow crooked lanes
Do purge sea-water's fretful salt away,
I thought, if I could draw my pains
Through rhyme's vexation, I should them allay.
Grief brought to numbers[1] cannot be so fierce,
For he tames it that fetters it in verse.

But when I have done so,
Some man, his art and voice to show,
Doth set[2] and sing my pain,
And, by delighting many, frees again
Grief, which verse did restrain.
To love and grief tribute of verse belongs,
But not of such as pleases when 'tis read;
Both are increased by such songs:
For both their triumphs so are published,
And I, which was two fools, do so grow three;
Who are a little wise, the best fools be.

8. Donne uses "sonnets" loosely to mean "love poems"; "stanza" in Italian means "room."
9. Crammed. "Countries, towns, courts" (line 44) are objects of the verb "drove."
1. Verse.
2. To music.

Lovers' Infiniteness

If yet I have not all thy love,
Dear, I shall never have it all;
I cannot breathe one other sigh to move,
Nor can entreat one other tear to fall;
And all my treasure, which should purchase thee,
Sighs, tears, and oaths, and letters, I have spent.
Yet no more can be due to me,
Than at the bargain made was meant,
If then thy gift of love were partial,
That some to me, some should to others fall.
  Dear, I shall never have thee all.

Or if then thou gavest me all,
All was but all which thou hadst then;
But if in thy heart, since, there be or shall
New love created be, by other men,
Which have their stocks entire, and can in tears,
In sighs, in oaths, in letters, outbid me,
This new love may beget new fears,
For this love was not vowed by thee.
And yet it was, thy gift being general,
The ground, thy heart, is mine; whatever shall
  Grow there, dear, I should have it all.

Yet I would not have all yet;
He that hath all can have no more.
And since my love doth every day admit
New growth, thou shouldst have new rewards in store;
Thou canst not every day give me thy heart;
If thou canst give it, then thou never gavest it:
Love's riddles are, that though thy heart depart,
It stays at home, and thou with losing savest it:
But we will have a way more liberal
Than changing hearts, to join them, so we shall
  Be one, and one another's All.

Song

Sweetest love, I do not go
  For weariness of thee,
Nor in hope the world can show
  A fitter love for me;
    But since that I
Must die at last, 'tis best

To use myself in jest,
  Thus by feigned deaths to die.[3]

Yesternight the sun went hence,
  And yet is here today;
He hath no desire nor sense,
  Nor half so short a way:
    Then fear not me,
But believe that I shall make
Speedier journeys, since I take
  More wings and spurs than he.

O how feeble is man's power,
  That if good fortune fall,
Cannot add another hour,
  Nor a lost hour recall!
    But come bad chance,
And we join to it our strength,
And we teach it art and length,
  Itself o'er us to advance.

When thou sigh'st, thou sigh'st not wind,
  But sigh'st my soul away;
When thou weep'st, unkindly kind,
  My life's blood doth decay.[4]
    It cannot be
That thou lov'st me, as thou say'st,
If in thine my life thou waste;
  Thou art the best of me.

Let not thy divining heart
  Forethink me any ill;
Destiny may take thy part,
  And may thy fears fulfill;
    But think that we
Are but turned aside to sleep;
They who one another keep
  Alive, ne'er parted be.

The Legacy

When I died last (and, dear, I die
  As often as from thee I go),
  Though it be but an hour ago,
And lovers' hours be full eternity,

3. To accustom myself to death by playing at it through "feigned deaths," i.e., absences.

4. Every sigh or tear was supposed to shorten life a little.

I can remember yet, that I
   Something did say, and something did bestow;
Though I be dead, which sent me, I should be
Mine own executor and legacy.

I heard me say, Tell her anon,
   That my self (that is you, not I)
   Did kill me, and when I felt me die,
I bid me send my heart, when I was gone,
But I alas could there find none,
   When I had ripped me, and searched where hearts did lie;
It killed me again, that I who still was true
In life, in my last will should cozen you.

Yet I found something like a heart,
   But colors it, and corners had;[5]
   It was not good, it was not bad,
It was entire to none, and few had part.
As good as could be made by art
   It seemed; and therefore, for our losses sad,
I meant to send this heart instead of mine,
But oh, no man could hold it, for 'twas thine.

A Fever

Oh do not die, for I shall hate
   All women so, when thou art gone,
That thee I shall not celebrate,
   When I remember, thou wast one.

But yet thou canst not die, I know;
   To leave this world behind, is death,
But when thou from this world wilt go,
   The whole world vapors[6] with thy breath.

Or if, when thou, the world's soul, goest,
   It stay, 'tis but thy carcass then,
The fairest woman, but thy ghost,
   But corrupt worms, the worthiest men.

O wrangling schools,[7] that search what fire
   Shall burn this world, had none the wit
Unto this knowledge to aspire,
   That this her fever might be it?

5. It was painted and thus not plain and true; it had corners and thus was imperfect, the circle being a symbol of perfection.
6. Evaporates.
7. Writers of various philosophical and religious schools of thought had written and disputed about the final conflagration that would destroy the world.

And yet she cannot waste by this,
  Nor long bear this torturing wrong,
For much corruption needful is,
  To fuel such a fever long.

These burning fits but meteors[8] be,
  Whose matter in thee is soon spent.
Thy beauty and all parts which are thee
  Are unchangeable firmament.

Yet 'twas of my mind, seizing thee,
  Though it in thee cannot persever:
For I had rather owner be
  Of thee one hour, than all else ever.

Air and Angels

Twice or thrice had I loved thee,
Before I knew thy face or name;
So in a voice, so in a shapeless flame
Angels affect us oft, and worshipped be;
  Still when, to where thou wert, I came,
Some lovely glorious nothing I did see.
  But since my soul, whose child love is,
Takes limbs of flesh, and else could nothing do,
  More subtle than the parent is
Love must not be, but take a body too;
  And therefore what thou wert, and who,
    I bid Love ask, and now
That it assume thy body, I allow,
And fix itself in thy lip, eye, and brow.

Whilst thus to ballast love, I thought,
And so more steadily to have gone,
With wares which would sink admiration
I saw I had love's pinnace overfraught;[9]
  Every thy hair[1] for love to work upon
Is much too much, some fitter must be sought;
  For, nor in nothing, nor in things
Extreme, and scatt'ring[2] bright, can love inhere;
  Then as an angel, face, and wings
Of air, not pure as it, yet pure doth wear,[3]

8. I.e., passing foreign bodies that will soon burn themselves out and disappear.
9. I had overloaded love's small, light vessel; the pinnace was often used as a scout and the word also meant "a woman" in Donne's time; also, there is a possible pun on "pinnace."
1. Each one of your hairs and even your least hair.
2. Dazzlingly.
3. According to scholastic doctrine, angels, in order to appear to men, assumed bodies of air, which were pure but not as pure as the angelic essence.

So thy love may be my love's sphere;[4]
Just such disparity
As is 'twixt air and angels' purity,
'Twixt women's love and men's will ever be.

Break of Day[5]

'Tis true, 'tis day; what though it be?
Oh wilt thou therefore rise from me?
Why should we rise because 'tis light?
Did we lie down because 'twas night?
Love, which in spite of darkness brought us hither,
Should in despite of light keep us together.

Light hath no tongue, but is all eye;
If it could speak as well as spy,
This were the worst that it could say,
That being well, I fain would stay,
And that I loved my heart and honor so,
That I would not from him, that had them, go.

Must business thee from hence remove?
Oh, that's the worst disease of love;
The poor, the foul, the false, love can
Admit, but not the busied man.
He which hath business, and makes love, doth do
Such wrong, as when a married man doth woo.

The Anniversary

All kings, and all their favorites,
All glory of honors, beauties, wits,
The sun itself, which makes times,[6] as they pass.
Is elder by a year, now, than it was
When thou and I first one another saw:
All other things to their destruction draw,
Only our love hath no decay;
This, no tomorrow hath, not yesterday;
Running it never runs from us away,
But truly keeps his first, last, everlasting day.

4. Each celestial sphere was thought to be inhabited and governed by an angel.

5. The speaker of this poem is a woman. In the 1669 edition and some MSS., a stanza (in a different meter, spoken by a man, and probably not wirtten by Donne) precedes the three stanzas of this poem. See Grierson's *Poems of John Donne*, I. 432.

6. Days, years; "they" probably refers to "times" rather than to "kings," "favorites," etc.

Two graves must hide thine and my corse;[7]
If one might, death were no divorce:
Alas, as well as other princes, we
(Who prince enough in one another be)
Must leave at last in death, these eyes, and ears,
Oft fed with true oaths, and with sweet salt tears;
But souls where nothing dwells but love
(All other thoughts being inmates[8]) then shall prove
This, or a love increased there above,[9]
When bodies to their graves, souls from their graves remove.

And then we shall be throughly[1] blest,
But we no more than all the rest;
Here upon earth, we're kings, and none but we
Can be such kings, nor of such subjects be;
Who is so safe as we, where none can do
Treason to us, except one of us two?
True and false fears let us refrain,
Let us love nobly, and live, and add again
Years and years unto years, till we attain
To write threescore, this is the second of our reign.

A Valediction: Of My Name, in the Window

My name engraved herein
Doth contribute my firmness to this glass,
Which, ever since that charm, hath been
As hard as that which graved it was;
Thine eye will give it price enough to mock
The diamonds of either rock.[2]

'Tis much that glass should be
As all-confessing, and through-shine[3] as I;
'Tis more, that it shows thee to thee,
And clear reflects thee to thine eye.
But all such rules, love's magic can undo,
Here you see me, and I am you.[4]

As no one point, nor dash,
Which are but accessories to this name,
The showers and tempests can outwash,
So shall all times find me the same;

7. Corpse.
8. Only temporary lodgers; "prove" means "learn," "discover."
9. In heaven.
1. Thoroughly.
2. Your looking at it will give the glass (on which the speaker has engraved his name with a diamond) a value superior to the diamonds of either India or South America.
3. Transparent.
4. Because lovers are one.

You this entireness better may fulfill,
Who have the pattern with you still.[5]

Or if too hard and deep
This learning be, for a scratched name to teach,
It as a given death's head[6] keep,
Lovers' mortality to preach,
Or think this ragged bony name to be
My ruinous anatomy.[7]

Then, as all my souls[8] be
Emparadised in you (in whom alone
I understand, and grow, and see),
The rafters of my body, bone,[9]
Being still with you, the muscle, sinew, and vein,
Which tile this house, will come again.

Till my return, repair
And recompact my scattered body so.
As all the virtuous powers which are
Fixed in the stars, are said to flow
Into such characters as graved be
When these stars have supremacy:

So since this name was cut
When love and grief their exaltation had,
No door 'gainst this name's influence shut;
As much more loving, as more sad,
'Twill make thee; and thou shouldst, till I return,
Since I die daily,[1] daily mourn.

When thy inconsiderate hand
Flings ope this casement, with my trembling name,
To look on one, whose wit or land
New batt'ry to thy heart may frame,
Then think this name alive, and that thou thus
In it offend'st my Genius.[2]

And when thy melted maid,
Corrupted by thy lover's gold, and page,
His letter at thy pillow hath laid,
Disputed it,[3] and tamed thy rage,

5. You may complete this unchanging love by also loving wholeheartedly, and you may do so more easily for you have the "pattern" (example) of my enduring name always with you.
6. A skull, a reminder of mortality.
7. My skeleton.
8. The intellectual ("understand"), vegetative ("grow"), and sensitive ("see") faculties of the soul.
9. Skeleton, i.e., the name.
1. By being absent.
2. Spirit.
3. Argued in its favor.

And thou begin'st to thaw towards him, for this,
May my name step in,[4] and hide his.

And if this treason go
To an overt act, and that thou write again,
In superscribing, this name flow[5]
Into thy fancy, from the pane.
So, in forgetting, thou rememb'rest right,
And unaware to me shalt write.

But glass and lines must be
No means our firm substantial love to keep;
Near death inflicts this lethargy,
And this I murmur in my sleep;
Impute this idle talk to that I go,
For dying men talk often so.

Twickenham Garden[6]

Blasted with sighs, and surrounded with tears,
Hither I come to seek the spring,[7]
And at mine eyes, and at mine ears,
Receive such balms as else cure everything;
But oh, self-traitor, I do bring
The spider[8] love, which transubstantiates all,
And can convert manna to gall;
And that this place may thoroughly be thought
True Paradise, I have the serpent[9] brought.

'Twere wholesomer for me, that winter did
Benight the glory of this place,
And that a grave frost did forbid
These trees to laugh, and mock me to my face;
But that I may not this disgrace
Endure, nor leave this garden, Love, let me
Some senseless piece of this place be;
Make me a mandrake,[1] so I may groan here,
Or a stone fountain weeping out my year.

Hither with crystal vials, lovers, come,
And take my tears, which are love's wine,

4. Perhaps by the sunlight's reflecting the name from the window onto the rival's letter.
5. In addressing your reply to the other lover, may the name in the window flow.
6. Twickenham was the home of Lucy, countess of Bedford, a patroness and friend of Donne.
7. The season; healing waters; the source or cause of the sighs and tears.
8. Believed to be poisonous.
9. The tempter. The serpent is also often a symbol of envy or jealousy; cf. lines 26–27.
1. A plant whose forked shape roughly resembles the human body; it was supposed to shriek or groan when uprooted and was thought to be an aphrodisiac. If he were a mandrake or a fountain, he could groan his sighs or weep his tears inconspicuously.

And try your mistress' tears at home,
For all are false, that taste not just like mine;
Alas, hearts do not in eyes shine,
Nor can you more judge woman's thoughts by tears,
Than by her shadow, what she wears.
O perverse sex, where none is true but she,
Who's therefore true, because her truth kills me.

A Valediction: Of the Book

I'll tell thee now, dear love, what thou shalt do
To anger destiny, as she doth us,
How I shall stay, though she eloign[2] me thus,
And how posterity shall know it too,
How thine may out-endure
Sibyl's glory, and obscure
Her who from Pindar could allure,
And her, through whose help Lucan is not lame,
And her, whose book (they say) Homer did find, and name.[3]

Study our manuscripts, those myriads
Of letters, which have past 'twixt thee and me,
Thence write our annals, and in them will be,
To all whom love's subliming[4] fire invades,
Rule and example found;
There, the faith of any ground[5]
No schismatic will dare to wound,
That sees how Love this grace to us affords,
To make, to keep, to use, to be these his records.

This book, as long-lived as the elements,
Or as the world's form, this all-graved tome
In cypher writ, or new-made idiom;
We for Love's clergy only are instruments,
When this book is made thus,
Should again the ravenous
Vandals and Goths inundate us,
Learning were safe; in this our universe
Schools might learn sciences, spheres music,[6] angels verse.

Here Love's divines (since all divinity
Is love or wonder) may find all they seek,
Whether abstract spiritual love they like,

2. Remove far off.
3. The Cumaean Sibyl was a legendary prophetess and authoress; Corinna was a poetess who five times defeated the Greek poet Pindar in competition; the wife of the Latin poet Lucan assisted him with his poetry; the mythical Egyptian poetess Phantasia was reputed to have been Homer's source.
4. Purifying.
5. Basic tenet.
6. The movement of the heavenly spheres was said to produce music.

Their souls exhaled[7] with what they do not see,
Or, loath so to amuse[8]
Faith's infirmity, they choose
Something which they may see and use;
For, though mind be the heaven, where love doth sit,
Beauty a convenient type may be to figure[9] it.

Here, more than in their books, may lawyers find
Both by what titles mistresses are ours
And how prerogative these states devours,
Transferred from Love himself, to womankind,
Who, though from heart, and eyes,
They exact great subsidies,
Forsake him who on them relies,
And for the cause, honor, or conscience, give—
Chimeras, vain as they, or their prerogative.

Here statesmen (or of them, they which can read)
May of their occupation find the grounds:
Love and their art alike it deadly wounds,
If to consider what 'tis, one proceed;
In both they do excel
Who the present govern well,
Whose weakness none doth or dares tell;
In this thy book, such will their nothing see,
As in the Bible some can find out alchemy.

Thus vent thy thoughts; abroad I'll study thee,[1]
As he removes far off, that great heights takes;
How great love is, presence best trial makes,
But absence tries how long this love will be;
To take a latitude,
Sun, or stars, are fitliest viewed
At their brightest, but to conclude
Of longitudes, what other way have we,
But to mark when and where the dark eclipses be?

Community

Good we must love, and must hate ill,
For ill is ill, and good good still,
But there are things indifferent,
Which we may neither hate, nor love,
But one, and then another prove,[2]
As we shall find our fancy bent.

7. Drawn out.
8. Bewilder.
9. Represent.
1. Thus express your thoughts; while I'm away I'll read what you have written.
2. Try, experience.

If then at first wise Nature had
Made women either good or bad,
  Then some we might hate, and some choose;
But since she did them so create,
That we may neither love, nor hate,
  Only this rests:[3] All, all may use.

If they were good it would be seen,
Good is as visible as green,
  And to all eyes itself betrays;
If they were bad, they could not last,
Bad doth itself, and others, waste;
  So, they deserve nor blame, nor praise.

But they are ours as fruits are ours,
He that but tastes, he that devours,
  And he that leaves all, doth as well;
Changed loves are but changed sorts of meat,
And when he hath the kernel eat,
  Who doth not fling away the shell?

Love's Growth

I scarce believe my love to be so pure
    As I had thought it was,
    Because it doth endure
Vicissitude, and season, as the grass;
Methinks I lied all winter, when I swore
My love was infinite, if spring make it more.

But if this medicine, love, which cures all sorrow
With more, not only be no quintessence,[4]
But mixed of all stuffs paining soul or sense,
And of the sun his working vigor borrow,
Love's not so pure, and abstract, as they use
To say, which have no mistress but their muse,
But as all else, being elemented[5] too,
Love sometimes would contemplate, sometimes do.

And yet no greater, but more eminent,[6]
    Love by the spring is grown;
    As, in the firmament,
Stars by the sun are not enlarged, but shown,[7]

3. Remains.
4. A pure essence, which could cure all ills.
5. Composed of various elements; i.e., not a pure essence.
6. I.e., outstanding, perceptible; etymologically, standing out, projecting.
7. Referring to the phenomenon that as the sun rises and the sky becomes lighter the definite dark background of the sky gradually recedes and the stars thus gradually *seem* larger. Such a "growing" appearance is similar to the gradual budding out of a blossom.

Gentle love deeds, as blossoms on a bough,
From love's awakened root do bud out now
If, as in water stirred more circles be
Produced by one, love such additions take,
Those, like so many spheres, but one heaven make,
For they are all concentric unto thee;[8]
And though each spring do add to love new heat,
As princes do in times of action get
New taxes, and remit them not in peace,
No winter shall abate the spring's increase.

Love's Exchange

Love, any devil else but you
Would for a given soul give something too.
At Court your fellows every day
Give the art of rhyming, huntsmanship, or play,[9]
For them which were their own before;
Only I have nothing which gave more,
But am, alas, by being lowly, lower.

I ask no dispensation now
To falsify a tear, or sigh, or vow,
I do not sue from thee to draw
A *non obstante*[1] on nature's law;
These are prerogatives, they inhere
In thee and thine; none should forswear
Except that he Love's minion were.

Give me thy weakness, make me blind,
Both ways, as thou and thine, in eyes and mind;
Love, let me never know that this
Is love, or, that love childish is.
Let me not know that others know
That she knows my pains, lest that so
A tender shame make me mine own new woe.

If thou give nothing, yet thou art just,
Because I would not thy first motions[2] trust;
Small towns which stand stiff till great shot[3]
Enforce them, by war's law *condition* not.[4]
Such in love's warfare is my case;

8. According to Ptolemaic astronomy, the heavenly spheres were concentric to the earth. By "love's growth," Donne might also be referring to the physical appearance of a woman's pregnancy; esp. cf. lines 15–20. If so, the asymmetrical, "growing" stanzas of the editions and some MSS. may have an added significance and may have been quite deliberate.

9. Gambling.

1. Exception.

2. Impulses.

3. Heavy artillery.

4. I.e., they must surrender unconditionally.

I may not article[5] for grace,
Having put Love at last to show this face—

This face, by which he could command
And change the idolatry of any land;
This face, which, wheresoe'er it comes,
Can call vowed men from cloisters, dead from tombs,
And melt both poles at once, and store
Deserts with cities, and make more
Mines in the earth, than quarries were before.

For this,[6] Love is enraged with me,
Yet kills not. If I must example be
To future rebels, if the unborn
Must learn by my being cut up and torn,
Kill, and dissect me, Love; for this
Torture against thine own end is:
Racked carcasses make ill anatomies.[7]

Confined Love

Some man unworthy to be possessor
Of old or new love, himself being false or weak,
Thought his pain and shame would be lesser,
If on womankind he might his anger wreak;
And thence a law did grow,
One might but one man know;
But are other creatures so?

Are sun, moon, or stars by law forbidden
To smile where they list, or lend away their light?
Are birds divorced, or are they chidden
If they leave their mate, or lie abroad a night?
Beasts do no jointures[8] lose
Though they new lovers choose,
But we are made worse than those.

Who e'er rigged fair ship to lie in harbors,
And not to seek new lands, or not to deal withal?[9]
Or built fair houses, set trees, and arbors,
Only to lock up, or else to let them fall?
Good is not good, unless
A thousand it possess,
But doth waste with greediness.

5. Negotiate, arrange.
6. See esp. lines 23, 28.
7. Tortured bodies make bad corpses for dissection.
8. Joining, union; also, joint holding of an estate by husband and wife for life.
9. Trade with.

The Dream

Dear love, for nothing less than thee
Would I have broke this happy dream;
        It was a theme
For reason, much too strong for phantasy,
Therefore thou wak'dst me wisely; yet
My dream thou brok'st not, but continued'st it,
Thou art so truth, that thoughts of thee suffice
To make dreams truths, and fables histories;
Enter these arms, for since thou thought'st it best
Not to dream all my dream, let's do the rest.

As lightning, or a taper's light,
Thine eyes, and not thy noise, waked me;
        Yet I thought thee
(For thou lovest truth) an angel, at first sight,
But when I saw thou sawest my heart,
And knew'st my thoughts, beyond an angel's art,[1]
When thou knew'st what I dreamt, when thou knew'st when
Excess of joy would wake me, and cam'st then,
I must confess, it could not choose but be
Profane to think thee anything but thee.

Coming and staying showed thee, thee,
But rising makes me doubt,[2] that now
        Thou art not thou.
That love is weak, where fear's as strong as he;
'Tis not all spirit, pure, and brave,
If mixture it of *fear*, *shame*, *honor* have.
Perchance, as torches which must ready be,
Men light and put out, so thou deal'st with me,
Thou cam'st to kindle, goest to come; then I
Will dream that hope again, but else would die.[3]

A Valediction: Of Weeping

        Let me pour forth
My tears before thy face, whilst I stay here,
For thy face coins them, and thy stamp they bear,
And by this mintage they are something worth,
        For thus they be
        Pregnant of thee;
Fruits of much grief they are, emblems of more,

1. Church doctrine held that only God, not angels, could see into the heart and thoughts of man.
2. Fear.
3. With a possible play on the slang meaning of "die": to consummate the sexual act.

When a tear falls, that thou falls which it bore,[4]
So thou and I are nothing then, when on a diverse shore.

On a round ball
A workman that hath copies by, can lay
An Europe, Afric, and an Asia,
And quickly make that, which was nothing, *All;*[5]
So doth each tear
Which thee doth wear,[6]
A globe, yea world, by that impression grow,
Till thy tears mixed with mine do overflow
This world, by waters sent from thee, my heaven dissolved so.

O more than Moon,
Draw not up seas to drown me in thy sphere,
Weep me not dead, in thine arms, but forbear
To teach the sea what it may do too soon;
Let not the wind
Example find
To do me more harm than it purposeth;
Since thou and I sigh one another's breath,
Who'er sighs most is cruellest, and hastes the other's death.[7]

Love's Alchemy

Some that have deeper digged love's mine than I,
Say, where his centric happiness doth lie:
I have loved, and got, and told,
But should I love, get, tell, till I were old,
I should not find that hidden mystery;
Oh, 'tis imposture all:
And as no chemic yet the elixir got[8]
But glorifies his pregnant pot,[9]
If by the way to him befall
Some odoriferous thing, or medicinal,
So, lovers dream a rich and long delight,
But get a winter-seeming summer's night.

Our ease, our thrift, our honor, and our day,
Shall we for this vain bubble's shadow pay?
Ends love in this, that my man[1]

4. The imminent separation of the lovers causes the speaker's tears, in which the woman's face is reflected; hence when a tear falls the woman's image (the "thou" that the tear bore) also falls.
5. By pasting his maps onto a blank globe ("round ball"), a mapmaker makes "that which was nothing" (the blank globe) into (a representation of) "All" the world.
6. I.e., which bears your image.
7. Sighing was thought to shorten life.
8. As no alchemist has yet obtained the panacean elixir of life.
9. Fruitful crucible.
1. Servant.

Can be as happy as I can, if he can
Endure the short scorn of a bridegroom's play?
That loving wretch that swears
'Tis not the bodies marry, but the minds,
Which he in her angelic finds,
Would swear as justly, that he hears,
In that day's rude hoarse minstrelsy, the spheres.[2]
Hope not for mind in women; at their best
Sweetness and wit, they're but *Mummy*, possessed.[3]

The Flea

Mark but this flea, and mark in this
How little that which thou deny'st me is;
It sucked me first, and now sucks thee,
And in this flea our two bloods mingled be;
Thou know'st that this cannot be said
A sin, nor shame, nor loss of maidenhead,
Yet this enjoys before it woo,
And pampered swells with one blood made of two,[4]
And this, alas, is more than we would do.

Oh stay, three lives in one flea spare,
Where we almost, yea more than married are.
This flea is you and I, and this
Our marriage bed, and marriage temple is;
Though parents grudge, and you, we're met
And cloistered in these living walls of jet.
Though use[5] make you apt to kill me,
Let not to that, self-murder added be,
And sacrilege, three sins in killing three.

Cruel and sudden, hast thou since
Purpled thy nail in blood of innocence?
Wherein could this flea guilty be,
Except in that drop which it sucked from thee?
Yet thou triumph'st, and say'st that thou
Find'st not thyself, nor me, the weaker now;
'Tis true; then learn how false, fears be;
Just so much honor, when thou yield'st to me,
Will waste, as this flea's death took life from thee.

2. In the wedding day's raucous music, the heavenly music of the celestial spheres.

3. The punctuation of lines 23–24 is uncertain. Among possible meanings: even the sweetest and wittiest women are merely dead flesh possessed or animated by an evil demon; or are, when a man possesses them, merely bodies without minds. *Mummy* was also a reputed panacea made from mummies.

4. Medical theory of Donne's time held that in sexual intercourse blood was literally mingled, leading to procreation. The flea symbolizes this mingling.

5. Habit.

The Curse

Whoever guesses, thinks, or dreams he knows
Who is my mistress, wither by this curse:
His only, and only his purse
May some dull heart to love dispose,[6]
And she yield then to all that are his foes;
May he be scorned by one, whom all else scorn,
Forswear[7] to others, what to her he hath sworn,
With fear of missing, shame of getting, torn:

Madness his sorrow, gout his cramp, may he
Make by but thinking who hath made him such:
And may he feel no touch
Of conscience, but of fame,[8] and be
Anguished, not that 'twas sin, but that 'twas she:
In early and long scarceness may he rot,
For land which had been his, if he had not
Himself incestuously an heir begot:

May he dream treason, and believe that he
Meant to perform it, and confess, and die,
And no record tell why:
His sons, which none of his may be,
Inherit nothing but his infamy:
Or may he so long parasites have fed,
That he would fain be theirs, whom he hath bred,
And at the last be circumcised for bread:

The venom of all stepdames, gamesters' gall,
What tyrants and their subjects interwish,
What plants, mines, beasts, fowl, fish
Can contribute, all ill which all
Prophets or poets spake; and all which shall
Be annexed in schedules[9] unto this by me,
Fall on that man; for if it be a she,
Nature beforehand hath out-cursed me.

The Message

Send home my long-strayed eyes to me,
Which oh too long have dwelt on thee;
Yet since there they have learned such ill,
Such forced fashions,

6. May his only purse, and nothing but his purse, incline some dull woman to love him.
7. Strongly deny.
8. Public report, reputation.
9. Appended supplementary papers.

And false passions,
That they be
Made by thee
Fit for no good sight, keep them still.

Send home my harmless heart again,
Which no unworthy thought could stain;
But if it be taught by thine
To make jestings
Of protestings,
And cross[1] both
Word and oath,
Keep it, for then 'tis none of mine.

Yet send me back my heart and eyes,
That I may know and see thy lies,
And may laugh and joy, when thou
Art in anguish
And dost languish
For some one
That will none,[2]
Or prove as false as thou art now.

A Nocturnal upon St. Lucy's Day, Being the Shortest Day

'Tis the year's midnight, and it is the day's,
Lucy's, who scarce seven hours herself unmasks;[3]
The sun is spent, and now his flasks[4]
Send forth light squibs,[5] no constant rays;
The world's whole sap is sunk;
The general balm the hydroptic earth hath drunk,[6]
Whither, as to the bed's-feet, life is shrunk,
Dead and interred; yet all these seem to laugh,
Compared with me, who am their epitaph.

Study me then, you who shall lovers be
At the next world, that is, at the next spring:
For I am every dead thing,
In whom love wrought new alchemy.
For his art did express[7]
A quintessence even from nothingness,
From dull privations, and lean emptiness;

1. Cancel, break.
2. Will have none of you.
3. St. Lucy's feast day, December 13, thought to be the shortest day of the year in the old calendar.
4. Powder flasks; possibly the stars are intended here.
5. A kind of fireworks, terminated by a slight explosion.
6. The thirsty earth has consumed the general balm, i.e., the healing ointment or the vital sap of all things.
7. Press out.

He ruined me, and I am re-begot
Of absence, darkness, death; things which are not.

All others, from all things, draw all that's good,
Life, soul, form, spirit, whence they being have;
I, by love's limbeck,[8] am the grave
Of all that's nothing. Oft a flood
Have we two wept, and so
Drowned the whole world, us two; oft did we grow
To be two chaoses, when we did show
Care to aught else; and often absences
Withdrew our souls, and made us carcasses.

But I am by her death (which word wrongs her)
Of the first nothing the elixir[9] grown;
Were I a man, that I were one
I needs must know; I should prefer,
If I were any beast,
Some ends, some means; yea plants, yea stones detest,
And love; all, all some properties invest;
If I an ordinary nothing were,
As shadow, a light and body must be here.[1]

But I am none; nor will my Sun renew.
You lovers, for whose sake the lesser sun
At this time to the Goat[2] is run
To fetch new lust, and give it you,
Enjoy your summer all;
Since she enjoys her long night's festival,
Let me prepare towards her, and let me call
This hour her Vigil, and her Eve, since this
Both the year's, and the day's deep midnight is.

Witchcraft by a Picture

I fix mine eye on thine, and there
Pity my picture burning in thine eye;
My picture drowned in a transparent tear,
When I look lower I espy;
Hadst thou the wicked skill
By pictures made and marred, to kill,[3]
How many ways mightst thou perform thy will!

8. Still, retort.
9. The quintessence of the nothing out of which God created the world.
1. If I were an ordinary nothing, such as a shadow, a light and body must exist to produce it.
2. The zodiacal sign called Capricorn. Goats were reputed to be lustful.
3. One reputed practice of witchcraft was the killing of a person by making and then destroying a picture of him.

But now I have drunk thy sweet salt tears,
  And though thou pour more I'll depart;
My picture vanished, vanish fears
  That I can be endamaged by that art;
    Though thou retain of me
One picture more, yet that will be,
Being in thine own heart, from all malice free.

The Bait[4]

Come live with me, and be my love,
And we will some new pleasures prove
Of golden sands, and crystal brooks:
With silken lines, and silver hooks.

There will the river whispering run
Warmed by thy eyes, more than the sun.
And there the enamored fish will stay,
Begging themselves they may betray.

When thou wilt swim in that live bath,
Each fish, which every channel hath,
Will amorously to thee swim,
Gladder to catch thee, than thou him.

If thou to be so seen be'st loath
By sun, or moon, thou dark'nest both,
And if myself have leave to see,
I need not their light, having thee.

Let others freeze with angling reeds,
And cut their legs with shells and weeds,
Or treacherously poor fish beset,
With strangling snare or windowy net:

Let coarse bold hands, from slimy nest
The bedded fish in banks out-wrest;
Or curious traitors, sleave-silk[5] flies,
Bewitch poor fishes' wand'ring eyes.

For thee, thou need'st no such deceit,
For thou thyself art thine own bait;
That fish that is not catched thereby,
Alas, is wiser far than I.

4. One of many replies to Marlowe's "The Passionate Shepherd to his Love."

5. Untwisted silk.

The Apparition

When by thy scorn, O murd'ress, I am dead,
    And that thou thinkst thee free
From all solicitation from me,
Then shall my ghost come to thy bed,
And thee, fained vestal,[6] in worse arms shall see;
Then thy sick taper will begin to wink,[7]
And he, whose thou art then, being tired before,
Will, if thou stir, or pinch to wake him, think
    Thou call'st for more,
And in false sleep will from thee shrink,
And then, poor aspen[8] wretch, neglected thou
Bathed in a cold quicksilver sweat wilt lie,
    A verier ghost than I;
What I will say, I will not tell thee now,
Lest that preserve thee; and since my love is spent,
I had rather thou shouldst painfully repent,
Than by my threatnings rest still innocent.

The Broken Heart

He is stark mad, who ever says
  That he hath been in love an hour,
Yet not that love so soon decays,
  But that it can ten in less space devour;
Who will believe me, if I swear
That I have had the plague a year?
  Who would not laugh at me, if I should say
  I saw a flask of powder burn a day?

Ah, what a trifle is a heart,
  If once into love's hands it come!
All other griefs allow a part
  To other griefs, and ask themselves but some;
They come to us, but us Love draws,
He swallows us, and never chaws:[9]
  By him, as by chained shot, whole ranks do die;
  He is the tyrant pike, our hearts the fry.[1]

If 'twere not so, what did become
  Of my heart, when I first saw thee?
I brought a heart into the room,
  But from the room I carried none with me;
If it had gone to thee, I know

6. Willing, eager (with a pun on "feigned") virgin.
7. Flicker.
8. Figuratively, tremulous; timorous.
9. Chews.
1. Small fish (which the pike devours).

Mine would have taught thine heart to show
  More pity unto me: but Love, alas,
  At one first blow did shiver it as glass.

Yet nothing can to nothing fall,
  Nor any place be empty quite,
Therefore I think my breast hath all
  Those pieces still, though they be not unite;
And now, as broken glasses[2] show
A hundred lesser faces, so
  My rags of heart can like, wish, and adore,
  But after one such love, can love no more.

A Valediction: Forbidding Mourning[3]

As virtuous men pass mildly away,
  And whisper to their souls to go,
Whilst some of their sad friends do say,
  "The breath goes now," and some say, "No,"

So let us melt, and make no noise,
  No tear-floods, nor sigh-tempests move;
'Twere profanation of our joys
  To tell the laity our love.

Moving of the earth[4] brings harms and fears,
  Men reckon what it did and meant;
But trepidation of the spheres,
  Though greater far, is innocent.[5]

Dull sublunary[6] lovers' love
  (Whose soul is sense) cannot admit
Absence, because it doth remove
  Those things which elemented[7] it.

But we, by a love so much refined
  That our selves know not what it is,
Inter-assured of the mind,
  Care less, eyes, lips, and hands to miss.

Our two souls therefore, which are one,
  Though I must go, endure not yet
A breach, but an expansion,
  Like gold to airy thinness beat.

2. Mirrors.
3. Izaak Walton says that Donne wrote this poem for his wife before he left for France in 1611.
4. Earthquakes.
5. The oscillatory movement of the celestial spheres, though far greater than earthquakes, "is innocent," i.e., causes no "harms and fears."
6. Under the moon, and thus earthly and changeable.
7. Composed.

If they be two, they are two so
  As stiff twin compasses are two:
Thy soul, the fixed foot, makes no show
  To move, but doth, if the other do;

And though it in the center sit,
  Yet when the other far doth roam,
It leans, and hearkens after it,
  And grows erect, as that comes home.

Such wilt thou be to me, who must,
  Like the other foot, obliquely run;
Thy firmness makes my circle just,
  And makes me end where I begun.

The Ecstasy

Where, like a pillow on a bed,
  A pregnant bank swelled up, to rest
The violet's reclining head,
  Sat we two, one another's best.

Our hands were firmly cemented
  With a fast balm, which thence did spring;
Our eye-beams twisted, and did thread
  Our eyes, upon one double string;[8]

So to intergraft our hands, as yet
  Was all the means to make us one,
And pictures in our eyes to get[9]
  Was all our propagation.

As, 'twixt two equal armies, Fate
  Suspends uncertain victory,
Our souls (which to advance their state
  Were gone out) hung 'twixt her and me.

And whilst our souls negotiate there,
  We like sepulchral statues lay;
All day, the same our postures were,
  And we said nothing, all the day.

If any, so by love refined
  That he souls' language understood,

8. According to Renaissance theory of perception, the eyes sent out invisible beams, which then carried the object's image back to the spectator. Thus the lovers are united by their gazing into one another's eyes as well as by their holding hands.
9. Beget.

And by good love were grown all mind,
  Within convenient distance stood,

He (though he knew not which soul spake,
  Because both meant, both spake the same)
Might thence a new concoction[1] take,
  And part far purer than he came.

This Ecstasy doth unperplex,
  We said, and tell us what we love;
We see by this it was not sex;
  We see we saw not what did move:[2]

But as all several[3] souls contain
  Mixture of things, they know not what,
Love these mixed souls doth mix again,
  And makes both one, each this and that.

A single violet transplant,
  The strength, the color, and the size,
(All which before was poor, and scant)
  Redoubles still, and multiplies.

When love, with one another so
  Interinanimates two souls,
That abler soul, which thence doth flow,
  Defects of loneliness controls.

We then, who are this new soul, know
  Of what we are composed, and made,
For the atomies[4] of which we grow
  Are souls, whom no change can invade.

But oh, alas, so long, so far
  Our bodies why do we forbear?
They're ours, though they're not we, we are
  The intelligences, they the sphere.[5]

We owe them thanks because they thus
  Did us to us at first convey,
Yielded their forces, sense, to us,
  Nor are dross to us, but allay.[6]

1. Purified, perfected state.
2. We now see that we did not before understand what was the cause and source of our love.
3. Separate.
4. Atoms.
5. The celestial spheres were thought to be governed by angels or intelligences. So the body is governed by the soul or essential self.
6. Alloy; "dross" is the weakening impurity that is discarded in the process of refining a metal.

On man heaven's influence works not so,
But that it first imprints the air;[7]
So soul into the soul may flow,
Though it to body first repair.

As our blood labors to beget
Spirits[8] as like souls as it can,
Because such fingers need to knit
That subtle knot which makes us man:

So must pure lovers' souls descend
To affections, and to faculties,
Which sense may reach and apprehend,
Else a great Prince in prison lies.

To our bodies turn we then, that so
Weak men on love revealed may look;
Love's mysteries in souls do grow,
But yet the body is his book.

And if some lover, such as we,
Have heard this dialogue of one,
Let him still mark us, he shall see
Small change, when we're to bodies gone.

Love's Deity

I long to talk with some old lover's ghost,
Who died before the god of love was born:
I cannot think that he who then loved most
Sunk so low as to love one which did scorn.
But since this god produced a destiny,
And that vice-nature,[9] custom, lets it be,
I must love her that loves not me.

Sure, they which made him god meant not so much,
Nor he, in his young godhead, practised it.
But when an even flame two hearts did touch,
His office was indulgently to fit
Actives to passives.[1] Correspondency
Only his subject was; it cannot be
Love, till I love her that loves me.

7. Astrology held that the stars influenced man through their effect on the air.
8. Vapors produced by the blood and forming a link between body and soul.
9. Substitute for nature.
1. To join male lovers to corresponding female lovers.

But every modern god will[2] now extend
  His vast prerogative, as far as Jove.
To rage, to lust, to write to, to commend,
  All is the purlieu of the god of love.
Oh were we wakened by this tyranny
To ungod this child again, it could not be
  I should love her who loves not me.

Rebel and atheist too, why murmur I,
  As though I felt the worst that love could do?
Love might make me leave loving, or might try
  A deeper plague, to make her love me too,
Which, since she loves before,[3] I'm loth to see;
Falsehood is worse than hate; and that must be,
  If she whom I love should love me.

Love's Diet

To what a cumbersome unwieldiness
And burdenous corpulence my love had grown,
    But that I did, to make it less,
    And keep it in proportion,
Give it a diet, made it feed upon
That which love worst endures, *discretion*.

Above one sigh a day I allowed him not,
Of which my fortune and my faults had part;[4]
    And if sometimes by stealth he got
    A she-sigh from my mistress' heart,
And thought to feast on that, I let him see
'Twas neither very sound, nor meant to me.[5]

If he wrung from me a tear, I brined[6] it so
With scorn or shame, that him it nourished not;
    If he sucked hers, I let him know
    'Twas not a tear which he had got,
His drink was counterfeit, as was his meat;[7]
For eyes which roll towards all, weep not, but sweat.

Whatever he would dictate, I writ that,
But burnt my letters; when she writ to me,
    And that that favor made him fat,[8]
    I said, if any title be

2. Wants to.
3. Already loves someone else.
4. And a part of that sigh was owing to my own bad fortune and faults.
5. Neither genuine nor meant for me.
6. Salted.
7. I.e., his sighs.
8. When she wrote to me, and wrote (understood repetition of the preceding verb) that that favor (of writing) made love grow. (See J. V. Hagopian, *Explicator* XVII:5.)

Conveyed by this, ah, what doth it avail
To be the fortieth name in an entail?[9]

Thus I reclaimed my buzzard[1] love, to fly
At what, and when, and how, and where I choose;
Now negligent of sport I lie,
And now, as other falconers use,[2]
I spring[3] a mistress, swear, write, sigh and weep:
And the game killed, or lost, go talk, and sleep.

The Will

Before I sigh my last gasp, let me breathe,
Great Love, some legacies: Here I bequeath
Mine eyes to Argus,[4] if mine eyes can see;
If they be blind, then, Love, I give them thee;
My tongue to Fame;[5] to ambassadors mine ears;
To women or the sea, my tears.
Thou, Love, hast taught me heretofore
By making me serve her who had twenty more,
That I should give to none but such as had too much before.

My constancy I to the planets give;
My truth to them who at the Court do live;
Mine ingenuity[6] and openness,
To Jesuits; to buffoons my pensiveness;
My silence to any who abroad hath been;
My money to a Capuchin.[7]
Thou, Love, taught'st me, by appointing me
To love there where no love received can be,
Only to give to such as have an incapacity.

My faith I give to Roman Catholics;
All my good works unto the Schismatics
Of Amsterdam;[8] my best civility
And courtship to an University;
My modesty I give to soldiers bare;
My patience let gamesters share.
Thou, Love, taught'st me, by making me
Love her that holds my love disparity,[9]
Only to give to those that count my gifts indignity.

9. The fortieth person named in an order of succession for inheriting an estate.
1. A useless species of hawk and a worthless, stupid person. "Reclaim" means "to reduce to obedience, tame."
2. Habitually do.
3. Start, flush (an animal).
4. The mythological figure who had a hundred eyes.
5. Also meaning rumor and evil repute.
6. Frankness; and perhaps also nobility of character.
7. A Franciscan monk, vowed to poverty.
8. Extreme Puritans, who believed in salvation through faith only, not good works.
9. Of unequal or inferior quality.

I give my reputation to those
Which were my friends; mine industry to foes;
To Schoolmen[1] I bequeath my doubtfulness;
My sickness to physicians, or excess;[2]
To Nature, all that I in rhyme have writ;
And to my company my wit.
Thou, Love, by making me adore
Her who begot this love in me before,
Taught'st me to make as though I gave, when I do but restore.

To him for whom the passing bell next tolls,
I give my physic[3] books; my written rolls
Of moral counsels, I to Bedlam[4] give;
My brazen medals, unto them which live
In want of bread; to them which pass among
All foreigners, mine English tongue.
Thou, Love, by making me love one
Who thinks her friendship a fit portion
For younger lovers, dost my gifts thus disproportion.

Therefore I'll give no more; but I'll undo
The world by dying, because love dies too.
Then all your beauties will be no more worth
Than gold in mines where none doth draw it forth,
And all your graces no more use shall have
Than a sun-dial in a grave.
Thou, Love, taught'st me, by making me
Love her who doth neglect both me and thee,
To invent, and practise, this one way to annihilate all three.

The Funeral

Whoever comes to shroud me, do not harm
Nor question much
That subtle wreath of hair, which crowns my arm;
The mystery, the sign, you must not touch,
For 'tis my outward Soul,
Viceroy to that, which then to heaven being gone,
Will leave this to control,
And keep these limbs, her provinces, from dissolution.

For if the sinewy thread[5] my brain lets fall
Through every part
Can tie those parts, and make me one of all,

1. Medieval philosophers of the universities.
2. Intemperance, a cause of sickness.
3. Medical.
4. The London insane asylum.
5. The spinal cord and nervous system.

These hairs, which upward grew, and strength and art
Have from a better brain,
Can better do it; except she meant that I
By this should know my pain,
As prisoners then are manacled, when they're condemned to die.

Whate'er she meant by it, bury it with me,
For since I am
Love's martyr, it might breed idolatry,
If into others' hands these relics came;
As 'twas humility
To afford to it all that a soul can do,
So, 'tis some bravery,[6]
That since you would save none of me, I bury some of you.

The Blossom

Little think'st thou, poor flower,
Whom I have watched six or seven days,
And seen thy birth, and seen what every hour
Gave to thy growth, thee to this height to raise,
And now dost laugh and triumph on this bough,
Little think'st thou
That it will freeze anon, and that I shall
Tomorrow find thee fal'n, or not at all.

Little think'st thou, poor heart,
That labor'st yet to nestle thee,
And think'st by hovering here to get a part
In a forbidden or forbidding tree,
And hop'st her stiffness by long siege to bow,
Little think'st thou
That thou tomorrow, ere that Sun[7] doth wake,
Must with this sun and me a journey take.

But thou which lov'st to be
Subtle to plague thyself, wilt say,
"Alas, if you must go, what's that to me?
Here lies my business, and here I will stay:
You go to friends, whose love and means present
Various content
To your eyes, ears, and tongue, and every part.
If then your body go, what need you a heart?"

Well then, stay here; but know,
When thou hast stayed and done thy most,

6. Bravado.

7. The lady.

A naked thinking heart, that makes no show,
Is to a woman but a kind of ghost;
How shall she know my heart; or, having none,
Know thee for one?
Practice may make her know some other part,
But take my word, she doth not know a heart.

Meet me at London, then,
Twenty days hence, and thou shalt see
Me fresher, and more fat, by being with men,
Than if I had stayed still with her and thee.
For God's sake, if you can, be you so too:
I would give you
There, to another friend, whom we shall find
As glad to have my body, as my mind.

The Primrose

Upon this primrose hill
Where, if Heav'n would distil
A shower of rain, each several[8] drop might go
To his own primrose, and grow manna so;
And where their form, and their infinity
Make a terrestrial galaxy,
As the small stars do in the sky,
I walk to find a true love;[9] and I see
That 'tis not a mere woman that is she,
But must or more or less than woman be.

Yet know I not, which flower
I wish; a six, or four;[1]
For should my true-love less than woman be,
She were scarce anything; and then, should she
Be more than woman, she would get above
All thought of sex, and think to move
My heart to study her, and not to love;
Both these were monsters; since there must reside
Falsehood in woman, I could more abide
She were by art, than Nature, falsified.

Live, Primrose, then, and thrive
With thy true number, five;
And women, whom this flower doth represent,
With this mysterious number be content;
Ten is the farthest number;[2] if half ten

8. Separate.
9. Also, "true love" is another name for the primrose.
1. I.e., six- or four-petaled.
2. Highest number; it contains the elements of all other numbers and is thus symbolic of all life.

Belong unto each woman, then
Each woman may take half us men;
Or, if this will not serve their turn, since all
Numbers are odd, or even, and they fall
First into this five, women may take us all.

The Relic

When my grave is broke up again
Some second guest to entertain[3]
(For graves have learned that woman-head,[4]
To be to more than one a bed)
And he that digs it spies
A bracelet of bright hair about the bone,
Will he not let us alone,
And think that there a loving couple lies,
Who thought that this device might be some way
To make their souls, at the last busy day,[5]
Meet at this grave, and make a little stay?

If this fall in a time, or land,
Where mis-devotion doth command,
Then he that digs us up will bring
Us to the Bishop and the King
To make us relics; then
Thou shalt be a Mary Magdalen, and I
A something else thereby;
All women shall adore us, and some men;
And, since at such time miracles are sought,
I would have that age by this paper taught
What miracles we harmless lovers wrought.

First, we loved well and faithfully,
Yet knew not what we loved, nor why;
Difference of sex no more we knew,
Than our guardian angels do;
Coming and going, we
Perchance might kiss,[6] but not between those meals;
Our hands ne'er touched the seals
Which nature, injured by late law,[7] sets free.
These miracles we did; but now, alas,
All measure, and all language, I should pass,
Should I tell what a miracle she was.

3. Alludes to the reuse of burial ground.
4. Characteristic of women.
5. Judgment Day, when the risen body must go first to wherever it lost or left a part of itself in order to retrieve it and be whole.
6. The customary kiss of salutation and parting.
7. By the law that came later than nature.

The Damp

When I am dead, and doctors know not why,
And my friends' curiosity
Will have me cut up to survey each part,
When they shall find your picture in my heart,
You think a sudden damp[8] of love
Will through all their senses move,
And work on them as me, and so prefer[9]
Your murder to the name of massacre.

Poor victories! but if you dare be brave,
And pleasure in your conquest have,
First kill the enormous giant, your *Disdain*,
And let the enchantress *Honor* next be slain,
And like a Goth and Vandal rise,
Deface records, and histories,
Of your own arts and triumphs over men,
And without such advantage kill me then.

For I could muster up as well as you
My giants, and my witches too,
Which are vast *Constancy*, and *Secretness*,
But these I neither look for, nor profess;
Kill me as woman, let me die
As a mere man; do you but try
Your passive valor, and you shall find than,[1]
Naked you've odds enough of any man.

The Dissolution

She's dead; and all which die
To their first elements resolve;
And we were mutual elements to us,
And made of one another.
My body then doth hers involve,
And those things whereof I consist, hereby
In me abundant grow, and burdenous,
And nourish not, but smother.
My fire of passion, sighs of air,
Water of tears, and earthly[2] sad despair,
Which my materials be
(But near worn out by love's security),
She, to my loss, doth by her death repair;[3]
And I might live long wretched so,

8. Vapor, mist.
9. Promote.
1. Then.
2. Earthy.
3. Restore.

But that my fire doth with my fuel grow,
Now, as those active kings
Whose foreign conquest treasure brings,
Receive more, and spend more, and soonest break:
This (which I am amazed that I can speak)
This death, hath with my store
My use increased.
And so my soul, more earnestly[4] released,
Will outstrip hers; as bullets flown before
A latter bullet may o'ertake, the powder being more.

A Jet Ring Sent

Thou art not so black as my heart,
Nor half so brittle as her heart, thou art;
What wouldst thou say? Shall both our properties by thee be spoke,
Nothing more endless, nothing sooner broke?

Marriage rings are not of this stuff;
Oh, why should aught less precious or less tough
Figure our loves? Except in thy name thou have bid it say,
"I'm cheap, and naught but fashion, fling me away."[5]

Yet stay with me since thou art come,
Circle this finger's top, which didst her thumb.
Be justly proud, and gladly safe, that thou dost dwell with me,
She that, oh, broke her faith, would soon break thee.

Negative Love[6]

I never stooped so low, as they
Which on an eye, cheek, lip, can prey;
Seldom to them,[7] which soar no higher
Than virtue or the mind to admire,
For sense and understanding may
Know what gives fuel to their fire.
My love, though silly,[8] is more brave,
For may I miss, whene'er I crave,
If I know yet, what I would have.

If that be simply perfectest
Which can by no way be expressed

4. Eagerly.
5. Donne puns on "jet" and the French "*jette*" (throw away).
6. Some MSS. give "The Nothing" as title; some give both titles.
7. I.e., seldom stooped to them.
8. Plain, unsophisticated.

But *Negatives*,[9] my love is so.
To All, which all love,[1] I say no.
If any who deciphers best
What we know not, our selves, can know,
Let him teach me that nothing; this
As yet my ease and comfort is:
Though I speed not, I cannot miss.[2]

The Prohibition

Take heed of loving me;
At least remember, I forbade it thee;
Not that I shall repair[3] my unthrifty waste
Of breath and blood, upon[4] thy sighs and tears,
By being to thee then what to me thou wast;
But so great joy our life at once outwears.
Then, lest thy love, by my death, frustrate be,
If thou love me, take heed of loving me.

Take heed of hating me,
Or too much triumph in the victory;
Not that I shall be mine own officer,[5]
And hate with hate again retaliate;
But thou wilt lose the style[6] of conqueror,
If I, thy conquest, perish by thy hate.
Then, lest my being nothing lessen thee,
If thou hate me, take heed of hating me.

Yet, love and hate me too,
So, these extremes shall neither's office do;
Love me, that I may die the gentler way;
Hate me, because thy love's too great for me;
Or let these two, themselves, not me, decay;
So shall I live thy stage,[7] not triumph be.
Then, lest thy love, hate, and me thou undo,
Oh let me live, yet love and hate me too.

9. Alluding to the idea of the *via negativa* that the perfect Godhead cannot be named, can only be expressed by negative terms, and is therefore an essential Nothing; see line 16.
1. To all positive things, which everybody else loves.
2. I.e., though I succeed not, I cannot fail.
3. Recover.
4. By drawing upon.
5. Agent.
6. Name.
7. For your repeated conquests (rather than a single, unrepeatable triumph).

The Expiration[8]

So, so, break off this last lamenting kiss,
Which sucks two souls, and vapors both away;[9]
Turn thou, ghost, that way, and let me turn this,
And let ourselves benight our happiest day;
We asked none leave to love; nor will we owe
Any so cheap a death as saying, "Go";

"Go"; and if that word have not quite killed thee,
Ease me with death by bidding me go too.
Or, if it have, let my word work on me,
And a just office on a murderer do,
Except[1] it be too late to kill me so,
Being double dead, going, and bidding go.

The Computation

For the first twenty years, since yesterday,
I scarce believed thou couldst be gone away;
For forty more, I fed on favors past,
And forty on hopes, that thou wouldst they might last.
Tears drowned one hundred, and sighs blew out two;
A thousand, I did neither think, nor do,
Or not divide, all being one thought of you;
Or, in a thousand more, forgot that too.
Yet call not this long life; but think that I
Am, by being dead, immortal; can ghosts die?

The Paradox

No lover saith, "I love," nor any other
Can judge a perfect lover;
He thinks that else none can, nor will agree
That any loves but he:
I cannot say I loved, for who can say
He was killed yesterday?[2]
Love with excess of heat, more young, than old,
Death kills with too much cold;
We die but once, and who loved last did die,
He that saith twice, doth lie:
For though he seem to move, and stir a while,
It doth the sense beguile.

8. Entitled "Valediction" in some manuscripts.
9. Causes both to pass away in the form of a vapor.
1. Unless.
2. Here and subsequently, Donne may be playing upon the sexual meaning of "die" and "kill."

Such life is like the light which bideth yet
When the light's life[3] is set,
Or like the heat, which fire in solid matter
Leaves behind, two hours after.
Once I loved and died; and am now become
Mine epitaph and tomb.
Here dead men speak their last, and so do I:
Love-slain, lo, here I lie.[4]

Farewell to Love

Whilst yet to prove,[5]
I thought there was some deity in love,
So did I reverence, and gave
Worship; as atheists at their dying hour
Call, what they cannot name, an unknown power,
As ignorantly did I crave:
Thus when
Things not yet known are coveted by men,
Our desires give them fashion,[6] and so
As they wax lesser, fall, as they size,[7] grow.

But, from late fair
High Highness sitting in a golden chair[8]
Is not less cared for after three days
By children, than the thing which lovers so
Blindly admire, and with such worship woo;
Being had, enjoying it decays:
And thence,
What before pleased them all, takes but one sense,[9]
And that so lamely, as it leaves behind
A kind of sorrowing dullness to the mind.

Ah, cannot we,
As well as cocks and lions, jocund be
After such pleasures? Unless wise
Nature decreed (since each such act, they say,
Diminisheth the length of life a day)
This; as she would man should despise
The sport,
Because that other curse of being short,
And only for a minute made to be
Eagers desires to raise posterity.[1]

3. Sun.
4. I.e., lie prone, dead, and tell a lie.
5. While still inexperienced.
6. Form.
7. Subside, as they increase.
8. I.e., a toy bought at a recent fair.
9. What before pleased all the senses, now pleases only one sense.
1. Various emendations and interpretations have been suggested for these most difficult lines. Sir Herbert Grierson originally emended "Eager, desires" to "Eagers desire". K. T. Emerson sug-

Since so, my mind
Shall not desire what no man else can find;
I'll no more dote and run
To pursue things which had endamaged me.
And when I come where moving beauties be,
As men do when summer's sun
Grows great,
Though I admire their greatness, shun their heat;
Each place can afford shadows. If all fail,
'Tis but applying wormseed[2] to the tail.

1635

A Lecture upon the Shadow

Stand still, and I will read to thee
A lecture, love, in love's philosophy.
These three hours that we have spent
In walking here, two shadows went
Along with us, which we ourselves produced;
But, now the sun is just above our head,
We do those shadows tread;
And to brave[3] clearness all things are reduced.
So whilst our infant loves did grow,
Disguises did, and shadows, flow
From us, and our cares; but now 'tis not so.

That love hath not attained the high'st degree,
Which is still diligent lest others see.

Except our loves at this noon stay,
We shall new shadows make the other way.
As the first were made to blind
Others, these which come behind[4]
Will work upon ourselves, and blind our eyes.
If our loves faint, and westwardly decline,
To me thou, falsely, thine,
And I to thee mine actions shall disguise.
The morning shadows wear away,
But these grow longer all the day,
But oh, love's day is short, if love decay.

gests: the brevity of the sex act sharpens man's desire to repeat the act—"to raise posterity" being a cynical euphemism for "to engage in sexual intercourse." *Modern Language Notes* 72 (1957): 94.

2. A plant used medically against intestinal worms. M. Morillo argues that in an ironic reversal Donne plays upon the bawdy connotations of the last line and that lines 39–40 mean: "if, in spite of my resolution to avoid sex, I succumb, then I shall console myself with the rationalization that the act is commited with purely curative intent." *Tulane Studies in English* 13 (1963): 39–40. On the other hand, wormseed was also a reputed anaphrodisiac, and "tail" is Latin for "penis."

3. Splendid.

4. Probably meaning "later."

Love is a growing, or full constant light;
And his first minute, after noon, is night.

1635

Sonnet. The Token[5]

Send me some token, that my hope may live,
  Or that my easeless thoughts may sleep and rest;
Send me some honey to make sweet my hive,
  That in my passions I may hope the best.
I beg no riband wrought with thine own hands,
  To knit our loves in the fantastic strain
Of new-touched youth; nor ring to shew the stands[6]
  Of our affection, that, as that's round and plain,
So should our loves meet in simplicity;
  No, nor the corals which thy wrist enfold,
Laced up together in congruity,
  To shew our thoughts should rest in the same hold;
No, nor thy picture, though most gracious,
  and most desired, because best like the best;
Nor witty lines, which are most copious
  Within the writings which thou hast addressed.[7]

  Send me nor this nor that to increase my store,
  But swear thou think'st I love thee, and no more.

1650

Self-Love[8]

He that cannot choose but love,
And strives against it still,
Never shall my fancy move,
For he loves 'gainst his will;
Nor he which is all his own,
And can at pleasure choose,—
When I am caught he can be gone,
And, when he list, refuse;
Nor he that loves none but fair,
For such by all are sought;

5. By reason of its additional four lines and its rhyme scheme, this poem is not actually a sonnet in the strict sense of the term. The poem is not characteristic of Donne, and for various reasons may only dubiously be ascribed to him.
6. Status.
7. Written.
8. This poem, which also may only dubiously be ascribed to Donne, has no title in the early editions and manuscripts. The title "Self-Love" was first given by Sir Edmund Chambers in his edition of 1896 and has since been followed by most subsequent editors, including Grierson. Theodore Redpath's suggestion, "The Rejection," is also an apt title, for the female speaker of the poem rejects various kinds of lovers.

Nor he that can for foul ones care,
For his judgment then is nought;
Nor he that hath wit, for he
Will make me his jest or slave;
Nor a fool, for when others . . . ,
He can neither . . . . ,[9]
Nor he that still his mistress pays,
For she is thralled therefore;
Nor he that pays not, for he says
Within,[1] she's worth no more.
Is there then no kind of men
Whom I may freely prove?[2]
I will vent that humor then
In mine own self-love.

1650

9. Lines 15–16 are incomplete in the early editions. One MS. completes line 16 with "want nor crave"; see R. E. Bennett, *The Complete Poems of John Donne*, pp. 51, 297.
1. To himself.
2. Approve; try.

Elegies

Elegy I. Jealousy

Fond[1] woman, which wouldst have thy husband die,
And yet complain'st of his great jealousy;
If swol'n with poison, he lay in his last bed,
His body with a sere-bark[2] covered,
Drawing his breath, as thick and short, as can
The nimblest crocheting[3] musician,
Ready with loathsome vomiting to spew
His soul out of one hell, into a new,
Made deaf with his poor kindred's howling cries,
Begging with few feigned tears, great legacies,
Thou wouldst not weep, but jolly, and frolic be,
As a slave, which tomorrow should be free;
Yet weep'st thou, when thou seest him hungrily
Swallow his own death, heart's-bane[4] jealousy.
O give him many thanks, he is courteous,
That in suspecting kindly warneth us.
We must not, as we used, flout openly,
In scoffing riddles, his deformity;
Nor at his board together being sat,
With words, nor touch, scarce looks adulterate.
Nor when he swol'n, and pampered with great fare,
Sits down, and snorts, caged in his basket chair,
Must we usurp his own bed any more,
Nor kiss and play in his house, as before.
Now I see many dangers; for it is
His realm, his castle, and his diocese.
But if, as envious men, which would revile
Their prince, or coin his gold, themselves exile
Into another country, and do it there,
We play in another house, what should we fear?
There we will scorn his household policies,
His silly plots, and pensionary spies,[5]

1. Foolish, naive.
2. Scabs caused by some poisons.
3. To crochet is to embellish music with grace notes.
4. Poisonous.
5. Spying servants.

As the inhabitants of Thames' right side
Do London's Mayor; or Germans, the Pope's pride.[6]

Elegy III. Change

Although thy hand and faith, and good works too,
Have sealed thy love, which nothing should undo,
Yea though thou fall back, that apostasy
Confirm thy love; yet much, much I fear thee.
Women are like the Arts, forced unto[7] none,
Open to all searchers, unprized, if unknown.
If I have caught a bird, and let him fly,
Another fowler using these[8] means, as I,
May catch the same bird; and, as these things be,
Women are made for men, not him, nor me.
Foxes and goats, all beasts, change when they please,
Shall women, more hot, wily, wild than these,
Be bound to one man, and did Nature then
Idly make them apter to endure than men?
They're our clogs,[9] not their own; if a man be
Chained to a galley, yet the galley's free;
Who hath a plow-land, casts all his seed corn there,
And yet allows his ground more corn should bear;
Though Danuby into the sea must flow,
The sea receives the Rhine, Volga, and Po.
By nature, which gave it, this liberty
Thou lov'st, but oh! canst thou love it and me?
Likeness glues love: and if that thou so do,
To make us like[1] and love, must I change too?
More than thy hate, I hate it; rather let me
Allow her change, than change as oft as she,
And so not teach, but force my opinion
To love not any one, nor every one.
To live in one land is captivity,
To run all countries, a wild roguery;[2]
Waters stink soon if in one place they bide,
And in the vast sea are more putrefied:[3]
But when they kiss one bank, and leaving this
Never look back, but the next bank do kiss,
Then are they purest; Change is the nursery
Of music, joy, life and eternity.

6. Southwark, a licentious area south of the Thames, disputed the City's authority; Germans like Martin Luther were at the forefront of the Protestant Reformation.
7. Compulsory for.
8. The same.
9. Impediments, encumbrances.
1. Alike.
2. Vagrancy.
3. Made salty.

Elegy IV. The Perfume

Once, and but once found in thy company,
All thy supposed escapes[4] are laid on me;
And as a thief at bar is questioned there
By all the men that have been robbed that year,
So am I (by this traitorous means surprised)
By thy hydroptic[5] father catechized.
Though he had wont to search with glazed[6] eyes,
As though he came to kill a cockatrice,[7]
Though he hath oft sworn that he would remove
Thy beauty's beauty, and food of our love,
Hope of his goods, if I with thee were seen,
Yet close and secret, as our souls, we have been.
Though thy immortal mother, which doth lie
Still buried in her bed, yet will not die,
Takes this advantage to sleep out day-light,
And watch thy entries and returns all night,
And, when she takes thy hand and would seem kind,
Doth search what rings and armlets she can find,
And kissing notes the color of thy face,
And fearing lest thou art swol'n doth thee embrace;
And to try if thou long, doth name strange meats,
And notes thy paleness, blushing, sighs, and sweats,
And politicly[8] will to thee confess
The sins of her own youth's rank lustiness,
Yet love these sorceries did remove, and move
Thee to gull thine own mother for my love.
Thy little brethren, which like faery sprites
Oft skipped into our chamber those sweet nights,
And kissed and ingled[9] on thy father's knee,
Were bribed next day to tell what they did see;
The grim eight-foot-high iron-bound serving-man,
That oft names God in oaths, and only than,[1]
He that to bar the first gate doth as wide
As the great Rhodian Colossus[2] stride,
Which, if in hell no other pains there were,
Makes me fear hell, because he must be there,
Though by thy father he were hired to this,
Could never witness any touch or kiss.
But oh, too common ill, I brought with me
That which betrayed me to my enemy:
A loud perfume, which at my entrance cried
Even at thy father's nose; so were we spied.

4. Transgressions, especially sexual ones.
5. Dropsical; also, insatiably thirsty for information and, as the next line suggests, strong drink.
6. Covered with a film (probably from drinking too much).
7. A fabulous serpent that killed by looking.
8. Craftily.
9. Fondled.
1. Then.
2. The huge statue of Apollo at Rhodes, one of the Seven Wonders.

When, like a tyrant king, that in his bed
Smelt gunpowder, the pale wretch shivered;
Had it been some bad smell, he would have thought
That his own feet, or breath, that smell had wrought.
But as we in our Isle[3] imprisoned,
Where cattle only and diverse dogs are bred,
The precious unicorns, strange monsters call,
So thought he good strange, that had none at all.
I taught my silks their whistling to forbear,
Even my oppressed shoes dumb and speechless were,
Only, thou bitter-sweet,[4] whom I had laid
Next me, me traitorously hast betrayed,
And unsuspected hast invisibly
At once fled unto him and stayed with me.
Base excrement[5] of earth, which dost confound
Sense from distinguishing the sick from sound;
By thee the silly amorous[6] sucks his death
By drawing in a leprous harlot's breath;
By thee the greatest stain to man's estate
Falls on us, to be called effeminate;
Though you be much loved in the prince's hall,
There, things that seem exceed substantial.[7]
Gods, when ye fumed on altars, were pleased well
Because you were burnt, not that they liked your smell;
You're loathsome all, being taken simply alone.
Shall we love ill things joined, and hate each one?
If you were good, your good doth soon decay;
And you are rare, that takes the good away.
All my perfumes I give most willingly
To embalm thy father's corpse. What? will he die?

Elegy V. His Picture

Here take my picture; though I bid farewell,
Thine, in my heart, where my soul dwells, shall dwell.
'Tis like me now, but I dead, 'twill be more
When we are shadows both, than 'twas before.
When weather-beaten I come back; my hand,
Perhaps with rude oars torn, or sun-beams tanned,
My face and breast of haircloth, and my head
With care's rash sudden storms being o'erspread,
My body a sack of bones, broken within,
And powder's[8] blue stains scattered on my skin;
If rival fools tax thee to have loved a man,

3. Britain.
4. Lines 53–70 address the perfume; the rest of the poem is addressed, of course, to the speaker's mistress.
5. Growth.
6. Simple lover.
7. Appearances exceed reality, substantial things.
8. Gunpowder.

So foul, and coarse, as oh, I may seem than,[9]
This shall say what I was: and thou shalt say,
Do his hurts reach me? doth my worth decay?
Or do they reach his judging mind, that he
Should now love less, what he did love to see?
That which in him was fair and delicate,
Was but the milk, which in love's childish state
Did nurse it: who now is grown strong enough
To feed on that, which to disused[1] tastes seems tough.

Elegy VII.

Nature's lay idiot,[2] I taught thee to love,
And in that sophistry,[3] oh, thou dost prove
Too subtle: Fool, thou didst not understand
The mystic language of the eye nor hand:
Nor couldst thou judge the difference of the air
Of sighs, and say, this lies, this sounds despair:
Nor by the eye's water[4] call a malady
Desperately hot, or changing feverously.
I had not taught thee then, the alphabet
Of flowers, how they devisefully[5] being set
And bound up, might with speechless secrecy
Deliver errands mutely, and mutually.
Remember since all thy words used to be
To every suitor, *Ay, if my friends agree:*
Since, household charms, thy husband's name to teach,[6]
Were all the love-tricks, that thy wit could reach;
And since, an hour's discourse could scarce have made
One answer in thee, and that ill arrayed
In broken proverbs, and torn sentences.[7]
Thou art not by so many duties his,
That from the world's common having severed thee,
Inlaid[8] thee, neither to be seen, nor see,
As mine: who have with amorous delicacies
Refined thee into a blissful paradise.
Thy graces and good words my creatures be;
I planted knowledge and life's tree in thee,
Which oh, shall strangers taste? Must I alas
Frame and enamel plate, and drink in glass?
Chafe wax for others' seals? break a colt's force
And leave him then, being made a ready horse?

9. Then.
1. Unaccustomed.
2. Ignorant by nature, simpleton.
3. Cunning craft.
4. Tears.
5. Schemingly, to convey amorous messages.
6. Games to reveal the name of one's future husband.
7. Sayings, clichés.
8. Hidden.

Elegy VIII. The Comparison

As the sweet sweat of roses in a still,[9]
As that which from chafed musk cat's pores doth trill,[1]
As the almighty balm of the early east,[2]
Such are the sweat drops of my mistress' breast.
And on her neck her skin such lustre sets,
They seem no sweat drops, but pearl carcanets.[3]
Rank sweaty froth thy mistress' brow defiles,
Like spermatic issue of ripe menstruous boils,
Or like that scum, which, by need's lawless law
Enforced, Sanserra's[4] starved men did draw
From parboiled shoes, and boots, and all the rest
Which were with any sovereign fatness blessed,
And like vile stones lying in saffroned tin,[5]
or warts, or weals, they hang upon her skin.
Round as the world's her head, on every side,
Like to the fatal ball which fell on Ide,[6]
Or that whereof God had such jealousy,
As for the ravishing thereof we die.[7]
Thy head is like a rough-hewn statue of jet,
Where marks for eyes, nose, mouth, are yet scarce set;
Like the first Chaos, or flat seeming face
Of Cynthia, when the earth's shadows her embrace.[8]
Like Proserpine's white beauty-keeping chest,[9]
Or Jove's best fortune's urn,[1] is her fair breast.
Thine's like worm-eaten trunks, clothed in seal's skin,
Or grave, that's dust without, and stink within.
And like that slender stalk, at whose end stands
The woodbine quivering, are her arms and hands.
Like rough-barked elmboughs, or the russet skin
Of men late scourged for madness, or for sin,
Like sun-parched quarters on the city gate,
Such is thy tanned skin's lamentable state.
And like a bunch of ragged carrots stand
The short swol'n fingers of thy gouty hand.
Then like the chemic's[2] masculine equal fire,
Which in the limbeck's[3] warm womb both inspire
Into the earth's worthless dirt a soul of gold,

9. Distillery to make perfume.
1. Musk deer's secretion, used in perfumes, with perhaps a pun on muscets, a wine grape.
2. The balm of Gilead, a fragrant balsam. See Jeremiah 46.11 and John Shawcross's *The Complete Poetry of John Donne*, p. 46.
3. Jeweled necklaces.
4. Catholic troops beseiged the Protestant inhabitants of Sancerre for many months in 1573.
5. Fake jewels set in tin.
6. Golden apple that Eris, the goddess of discord, dropped among the goddesses on Mount Ida to provoke a dispute. The ensuing argument led to the Trojan War.
7. The fruit from Eden's Tree of the Knowledge of Good and Evil.
8. The moon in its early phase.
9. The box containing the ointment of beauty that Psyche took from Proserpina.
1. Zeus had two urns; the other was of ill-fortune.
2. Alchemists.
3. Vessel in which base metals were heated for transformation into gold.

Such cherishing heat her best loved part doth hold.
Thine's like the dread mouth of a fired gun,
Or like hot liquid metals newly run
Into clay moulds, or like to that Etna[4]
Where round about the grass is burnt away.
Are not your kisses then as filthy, and more,
As a worm sucking an envenomed sore?
Doth not thy fearful hand in feeling quake,
As one which gathering flowers, still fears a snake?
Is not your last act[5] harsh, and violent,
As when a plough a stony ground doth rent?
So kiss good turtles,[6] so devoutly nice
Are priests in handling reverent sacrifice,
And such in searching wounds the surgeon is
As we, when we embrace, or touch, or kiss.
Leave her, and I will leave comparing thus,
She, and comparisons are odious.

Elegy IX. The Autumnal

No spring, nor summer beauty hath such grace,
As I have seen in one autumnal face.
Young beauties force our love, and that's a rape,
This doth but counsel, yet you cannot 'scape.
If 'twere a shame to love, here 'twere no shame,
Affection here takes reverence's name.
Were her first years the Golden Age?[7] That's true,
But now she's gold oft tried, and ever new.
That was her torrid and inflaming time,
This is her tolerable tropic clime.
Fair eyes, who asks more heat than comes from hence,
He in a fever wishes pestilence.
Call not these wrinkles, graves;[8] if graves they were,
They were Love's graves; for else he is no where.
Yet lies not Love dead here, but here doth sit
Vowed to this trench, like an anachorite.[9]
And here, till hers, which must be his death, come,
He doth not dig a grave, but build a tomb.
Here dwells he, though he sojourn ev'rywhere,
In progress,[1] yet his standing house is here.
Here, where still evening is; not noon, nor night;
Where no voluptuousness, yet all delight.
In all her words, unto all hearers fit,
You may at revels, you at council, sit.

4. Active volcano in Sicily.
5. The sexual act.
6. Turtledoves.
7. The first age of mankind, an age of peace, prosperity, and contentment.
8. French word for wrinkles.
9. Hermit.
1. A visiting tour by royalty; "standing house": fixed residence.

This is love's timber, youth his underwood;[2]
There he, as wine in June, enrages blood,
Which then comes seasonabliest, when our taste
And appetite to other things is past.
Xerxes' strange Lydian love, the platane tree,[3]
Was loved for age, none being so large as she,
Or else because, being young, nature did bless
Her youth with age's glory, barrenness.
If we love things long sought, age is a thing
Which we are fifty years in compassing;
If transitory things, which soon decry,
Age must be loveliest at the latest day.
But name not winter-faces, whose skin's slack,
Lank, as an unthrift's purse, but a soul's sack;
Whose eyes seek light within, for all here's shade;
Whose mouths are holes, rather worn out, than made;
Whose every tooth to a several place is gone,
To vex their souls at Resurrection;[4]
Name not these living death's-heads unto me,
For these not ancient, but antique be.
I hate extremes; yet I had rather stay
With tombs than cradles, to wear out a day.
Since such love's natural lation[5] is, may still
My love descend and journey down the hill,
Not panting after growing beauties, so,
I shall ebb on with them who homeward go.

Elegy X. The Dream[6]

Image[7] of her (whom I love, more than she,[8]
Whose fair impression in my faithful heart
Makes me her medal, and makes her love me
As Kings do coins to which their stamps impart
The value) go, and take my heart from hence,
Which now is grown too great and good for me.
Honors oppress weak spirits, and our sense
Strong objects dull; the more, the less we see.

When you are gone, and reason gone with you,
Then fantasy[9] is queen, and soul, and all;
She can present joys meaner than you do,

2. Undergrowth.
3. On his march to Greece, Xerxes honored a plane tree in Lydia, decking it with gold and appointing a guard.
4. At the Resurrection, when the body is to rejoin the soul, all of the parts of the body, even though they may be in different places, must be recovered.
5. Motion.
6. Unlike Donne's other elegies, this poem, the title of which is from the 1635 edition, is not written in rhymed couplets. Some *MSS.* include it among the Songs and Sonnets.
7. Probably a "mental picture," which the speaker speaks of as being in his heart.
8. More than she loves it (the image). (The argument for so construing this disputed line is made by E. Schwartz in *Explicator* 19:67.)
9. Imagination or fancy.

Convenient, and more proportional.
So, if I dream I have you, I have you,
For all our joys are but fantastical.[1]
And so I 'scape the pain, for pain is true;
And sleep, which locks up sense, doth lock out all.

After a such fruition I shall wake,
And, but the waking, nothing shall repent;
And shall to love more thankful sonnets make
Than if more honor, tears, and pains were spent.
But dearest heart, and dearer image, stay;
Alas, true joys at best are dream enough;
Though you stay here you pass too fast away,
For even at first life's taper is a snuff.[2]

Filled with her love, may I be rather grown
Mad with much heart than idiot with none.

Elegy XI. The Bracelet

Upon the loss of his Mistress' Chain, for which he made satisfaction

Not that in color it was like thy hair,
For armlets of that thou mayst let me wear:
Nor that thy hand it oft embraced and kissed,
For so it had that good, which oft I missed:
Nor for that silly old morality,[3]
That as these links were knit, our love should be:
Mourn I that I thy sevenfold chain have lost;
Nor for the luck sake, but the bitter cost.
Oh, shall twelve righteous angels,[4] which as yet
No leaven of vile solder did admit;
Nor yet by any fault have strayed or gone
From the first state of their creation;
Angels, which heaven commanded to provide
All things to me, and be my faithful guide,
To gain new friends, to appease great enemies,
To comfort my soul, when I lie or rise;
Shall these twelve innocents, by thy severe
Sentence (dread judge) my sin's great burden bear?
Shall they be damned, and in the furnace thrown[5]
And punished for offences not their own?
They save not me, they do not ease my pains,
When in that hell they're burnt and tied in chains.

1. Products of "fantasy" (line 10).
2. Candle end.
3. Inscription.
4. Throughout the poem, Donne plays on two meanings of "angel": (1) spirit; (2) English gold coin.
5. In order to be melted and made into a new chain.

Were they but crowns of France,[6] I cared not,
For most of these their natural country's rot
I think possesseth, they come here to us
So pale, so lame, so lean, so ruinous;
And howsoe'er French kings most Christian be,
Their crowns are circumcised most Jewishly,[7]
Or were they Spanish stamps, still travelling,[8]
That are become as Catholic as their king,
Those unlicked bear-whelps, unfiled pistolets[9]
That (more than cannon[1] shot) avails or lets;
Which negligently left unrounded, look
Like many-angled figures in the book
Of some great conjurer that would enforce
Nature, as these do justice, from her course;
Which, as the soul quickens head, feet and heart,
As streams, like veins, run through the earth's every part,
Visit all countries, and have slyly made
Gorgeous *France*, ruined, ragged, and decayed;
Scotland, which knew no state, proud in one day;
And mangled seventeen-headed *Belgia*.[2]
Or were it such gold as that wherewithal
Almighty chemics[3] from each mineral
Having by subtle fire a soul out-pulled
Are dirtily and desperately gulled:
I would not spit to quench the fire they're in,
For they are guilty of much heinous sin.
But shall my harmless angels perish? Shall
I lose my guard, my ease, my food, my all?
Much hope which they should nourish will be dead,
Much of my able youth and lustihead
Will vanish; if thou love let them alone,
For thou wilt love me less when they are gone;
And be content that some loud squeaking crier,
Well-pleased with one lean threadbare groat, for hire,
May like a devil roar through every street,
And gall the finder's conscience, if they meet.
Or let me creep to some dread conjurer,[4]
That with fantastic schemes fills full much paper;
Which hath divided heaven in tenements,[5]
And with whores, thieves, and murderers stuffed his rents,[6]
So full, that though he pass them all in sin,
He leaves himself no room to enter in.

6. French coins.
7. Lines 24–28 refer to the clipping and debasement of the coins.
8. Spanish coins, much used abroad as bribes.
9. Gold coins of irregular shape; also, small firearms. It was thought that newly born cubs were licked into shape by their mothers.
1. Also, church (canon) laws, which allow or prohibit ("avails or lets").
2. These lines describe the effect of Spanish bribery on France, Scotland, and the seventeen states of the Lowlands.
3. Alchemists.
4. Astrologer, magician.
5. Zodiac signs.
6. Fees; holes (in the heavens).

But if, when all his art and time is spent,
He say 'twill ne'er be found, yet be content;
Receive from him that doom ungrudgingly,
Because he is the mouth of destiny.
Thou say'st (alas) the gold doth still remain,
Though it be changed, and put into a chain;
So in the first fal'n angels resteth still
Wisdom and knowledge, but 'tis turned to ill:
As these should do good works and should provide
Necessities, but now must nurse thy pride.
And they are still bad angels; mine are none;
For form gives being, and their form is gone.
Pity these angels yet; their dignities
Pass Virtues, Powers, and Principalities.[7]
But thou art resolute; thy will be done!
Yet with such anguish, as her only son
The mother in the hungry grave doth lay,
Unto the fire these martyrs I betray.
Good souls (for you give life to everything)
Good angels (for good messages you bring)
Destined you might have been to such an one
As would have loved and worshipped you alone,
One that would suffer hunger, nakedness,
Yea, death, ere he would make your number less.
But I am guilty of your sad decay;
May your few fellows longer with me stay.
But oh thou wretched finder whom I hate
So, that I almost pity thy estate:
Gold being the heaviest metal amongst all,
May my most heavy curse upon thee fall:
Here fettered, manacled, and hanged in chains,
First mayst thou be; then chained to hellish pains;
Or be with foreign gold bribed to betray
Thy country, and fail both of that and thy pay.
May the next thing thou stoop'st to reach contain
Poison, whose nimble fume rot thy moist brain,
Or libels, or some interdicted thing,
Which negligently kept, thy ruin bring.
Lust-bred diseases rot thee; and dwell with thee
Itchy desire, and no ability.
May all the evils that gold ever wrought,
All mischiefs that all devils ever thought,
Want after plenty, poor and gouty age,
The plagues of travellers, love, marriage
Afflict thee, and at thy life's last moment,
May thy swol'n sins themselves to thee present.
But I forgive; repent thee honest man:

7. Angelic orders; also, ironically, what money can buy.

Gold is restorative,[8] restore it then:
But if from it thou be'st loath to depart,
Because 'tis cordial, would 'twere at thy heart.

1635

Elegy XVI. On His Mistress

By our first strange and fatal interview,
By all desires which thereof did ensue,
By our long starving hopes, by that remorse
Which my words' masculine, persuasive force
Begot in thee, and by the memory
Of hurts which spies and rivals threatened me,
I calmly beg; but by thy father's wrath,
By all pains which want and divorcement[9] hath,
I conjure thee; and all the oaths which I
And thou have sworn to seal joint constancy,
Here I unswear, and overswear them thus,
Thou shalt not love by ways so dangerous.
Temper, O fair love, love's impetuous rage,
Be my true mistress still, not my faigned[1] page;
I'll go, and, by thy kind leave, leave behind
Thee, only worthy to nurse in my mind
Thirst to come back; oh, if thou die before,
My soul from other lands to thee shall soar.
Thy (else almighty) beauty cannot move
Rage from the seas, nor thy love teach them love,
Nor tame wild Boreas'[2] harshness; thou hast read
How roughly he in pieces shivered
Fair Orithea,[3] whom he swore he loved.
Fall ill or good, 'tis madness to have proved[4]
Dangers unurged; feed on this flattery,
That absent lovers one in the other be.
Dissemble nothing, not a boy, nor change
Thy body's habit, nor mind's; be not strange
To thyself only; all will spy in thy face
A blushing, womanly, discovering grace;
Richly clothed apes are called apes; and as soon
Eclipsed as bright, we call the moon the moon.
Men of France, changeable chameleons,
Spitals[5] of diseases, shops of fashions,
Love's fuelers, and the rightest company
Of players which upon the world's stage be,

8. Gold was used as a medical remedy.
9. Complete separation.
1. Preferred, willing, eager; with a pun on "feigned." The speaker's mistress wants to disguise herself as a male page in order to accompany the speaker on his imminent journey.
2. The north wind.
3. The abducted bride of Boreas.
4. Experienced.
5. Hospitals.

Will quickly know thee, and no less, alas![6]
The indifferent Italian, as we pass
His warm land, well content to think thee page,
Will hunt thee with such lust and hideous rage
As Lot's fair guests were vexed.[7] But none of these
Nor spongy, hydroptic[8] Dutch shall thee displease
If thou stay here. O stay here; for, for thee
England is only a worthy gallery
To walk in expectation, till from thence
Our greatest King call thee to his presence.[9]
When I am gone, dream me some happiness,
Nor let thy looks our long-hid love confess,
Nor praise, nor dispraise me, nor bless, nor curse
Openly love's force, nor in bed fright thy nurse
With midnight's startings, crying out, "Oh, oh
Nurse, oh my love is slain, I saw him go
O'er the white Alps alone; I saw him, I,
Assailed, fight, taken, stabbed, bleed, fall, and die."
Augur me better chance, except dread Jove
Think it enough for me to have had thy love.

1635

Elegy XIX. To His Mistress Going to Bed

Come, madam, come, all rest my powers defy,
Until I labor, I in labor lie.
The foe oft-times having the foe in sight,
Is tired with standing though he never fight.
Off with that girdle, like heaven's zone glistering,
But a far fairer world encompassing.
Unpin that spangled breastplate which you wear,
That the eyes of busy fools may be stopped there.
Unlace yourself, for that harmonious chime
Tells me from you that now 'tis your bed time.
Off with that happy busk,[1] which I envy,
That still can be, and still can stand so nigh.
Your gown, going off, such beauteous state reveals,
As when from flowry meads the hill's shadow steals.
Off with that wiry coronet[2] and show
The hairy diadem which on you doth grow:
Now off with those shoes, and then safely tread
In this love's hallowed temple, this soft bed.
In such white robes, heaven's angels used to be

6. Donne plays on the meanings of "know" and puns on "alas": a lass.
7. Genesis 19 tells of the angels who, visiting the Hebrew patriarch Lot, were sought by the men of Sodom, city of unnatural vice.
8. Insatiably thirsty; dropsical.
9. England is the only worthy antechamber for you to live in until God calls you.
1. Corset.
2. Part of a woman's headdress.

Received by men; thou, Angel, bring'st with thee
A heaven like Mahomet's Paradise; and though
Ill spirits walk in white, we easily know
By this these angels from an evil sprite:
Those set our hairs, but these our flesh upright.
License my roving hands, and let them go
Before, behind, between, above, below.
O my America! my new-found-land,
My kingdom, safeliest when with one man manned,
My mine of precious stones, my empery,[3]
How blest am I in this discovering thee!
To enter in these bonds is to be free;
Then where my hand is set, my seal shall be.
Full nakedness! All joys are due to thee,
As souls unbodied, bodies unclothed must be
To taste whole joys. Gems which you women use
Are like Atlanta's balls,[4] cast in men's views,
That when a fool's eye lighteth on a gem,
His earthly soul may covet theirs, not them.
Like pictures, or like books' gay coverings made
For lay-men, are all women thus arrayed;
Themselves are mystic books, which only we
(Whom their imputed grace will dignify)
Must see revealed. Then, since that I may know,
As liberally as to a midwife, show
Thyself: cast all, yea, this white linen hence,
Here is no penance, much less innocence.[5]
To teach thee, I am naked first; why than,[6]
What needst thou have more covering than a man.

1669

Elegy XX. Love's War

Till I have peace with thee, war other men,
And when I have peace, can I leave thee then?
All other wars are scrupulous;[7] only thou
O fair free city, mayst thyself allow
To any one. In Flanders, who can tell
Whether the master press, or men rebel?
Only we know, that which all idiots say,
They bear most blows which come to part the fray.[8]

3. Empire.
4. The golden apples dropped by a suitor in a foot race with Atalanta, the fleetfooted huntress of Greek myth, in order to distract and delay her. Donne here adapts the myth to his own use.
5. Penance and innocence are both represented by white.
6. Then.
7. Fought by rules.
8. The English suffered numerous defeats attempting to settle disputes between the Lowland people and their Spanish conquerors.

France in her lunatic giddiness[9] did hate
Ever our men, yea and our God of late;[1]
Yet she relies upon our angels[2] well,
Which ne'er return; no more than they which fell.
Sick Ireland is with a strange war possessed[3]
Like to an ague, now raging, now at rest,
Which time will cure, yet it must do her good
If she were purged, and her head vein let blood.
And Midas' joys our Spanish journeys[4] give,
We touch all gold, but find no food to live.
And I should be in that hot parching clime,
To dust and ashes turned before my time.
To mew[5] me in a ship, is to enthral
Me in a prison, that were like to fall;
Or in a cloister, save that there men dwell
In a calm heaven, here in a swaggering hell.
Long voyages are long consumptions,
And ships are carts for executions.
Yea they are deaths; is it not all one to fly
Into another world, as 'tis to die?
Here let me war; in these arms let me lie;
Here let me parley, batter, bleed, and die.
Thine arms imprison me, and mine arms thee;
Thy heart thy ransom is; take mine for me.
Other men war that they their rest may gain,
But we will rest that we may fight again.
Those wars the ignorant, these the experienced love,
There we are always under, here above.
There engines[6] far off breed a just true fear,
Near thrusts, pikes, stabs, yea bullets hurt not here.
There lies are wrongs, here safe uprightly lie;
There men kill men, we will make one by and by.
Thou nothing; I not half so much shall do
In these wars, as they may which from us two
Shall spring. Thousands we see which travail not
To wars, but stay swords, arms, and shot
To make at home; and shall not I do then
More glorious service, staying to make men?

9. Swift changes in French policy followed the death of the Catholic Henri III, the accession of the Protestant Henri de Navarre, and Henri de Navarre's subsequent conversion to Catholicism.
1. French Catholics persecuted Huguenot Protestants.
2. Coins borrowed from Elizabeth by Henri.
3. Hugh O'Neill's ten-year rebellion against the crown.
4. English raids on Spanish treasure ships; Midas was a mythical king whose touch turned everything to gold.
5. Enclose.
6. Long-range weapons, artillery.

Epithalamion Made at Lincoln's Inn[1]

The sun beams in the east are spread,
Leave, leave, fair bride, your solitary bed,
No more shall you return to it alone,
It nurseth sadness, and your body's print,
Like to a grave, the yielding down doth dint;[2]
You and your other you meet there anon;
Put forth, put forth that warm balm-breathing thigh,
Which when next time you in these sheets will smother,
There it must meet another,
Which never was, but must be, oft, more nigh;
Come glad from thence, go gladder than you came,
Today put on perfection, and a woman's name.

Daughters of London, you which be
Our golden mines, and furnished treasury,
You which are angels, yet still bring with you
Thousands of angels[3] on your marriage days,
Help with your presence and devise[4] to praise
These rites, which also unto you grow due;
Conceitedly dress her, and be assigned,
By you, fit place for every flower and jewel,
Make her for love fit fuel
As gay as Flora, and as rich as Ind;
So may she fair, rich, glad, and in nothing lame,
Today put on perfection, and a woman's name.

And you frolic patricians,
Sons[5] of these senators, wealth's deep oceans,
Ye painted courtiers, barrels of others' wits,
Ye country men, who but your beasts love none,
Ye of those fellowships whereof he's one,
Of study and play made strange hermaphrodites,
Here shine; this bridegroom to the temple bring.
Lo, in yon path which store of strewed flowers graceth,
The sober virgin paceth;
Except my sight fails, 'tis no other thing;
Weep not nor blush, here is no grief nor shame,
Today put on perfection, and a woman's name.

1. From 1592 to 1594 or 1595, Donne was a student at Lincoln's Inn, one of the Inns of Court, London's law schools. For the argument that the poem celebrates a mock, not a real, wedding, in keeping with the long tradition of Inns of Court reveling, see D. Novarr, "Donne's 'Epithalamion Made at Lincoln's Inn': Context and Date," *Review of English Studies* 7 (1956): 250–63. The poem may have been performed ("Made") by the male law students and may more correctly be regarded as a broadly satiric entertainment rather than as a conventional epithalamion or marriage. For a different view, see Heather Dubrow Ousby, "Donne's 'Epithalamion made at Lincolnes Inne': An Alternative Interpretation," *Studies in English Literature* 16 (1976): 131–43.

2. Indent.

3. Also, English gold coins.

4. Device, i.e., fancy, invention.

5. With a pun on "suns."

Thy two-leaved gates, fair temple, unfold,
And these two in thy sacred bosom hold,
  Till, mystically joined, but one they be;
Then may thy lean and hunger-starved womb
Long time expect their bodies and their tomb,
  Long after their own parents fatten thee.
    All elder claims, and all cold barrenness,
All yielding to new loves be far for ever,
Which might these two dissever,
    All ways all the other may each one possess;
For, the best bride, best worthy of praise and fame,
Today puts on perfection, and a woman's name.

Oh winter days bring much delight,
Not for themselves, but for they soon bring night;
  Other sweets wait thee than these diverse meats,
Other disports than dancing jollities,
Other love tricks than glancing with the eyes,
  But that the sun still in our half sphere sweats;
    He flies in winter, but now he stands still,
Yet shadows turn: noon point he hath attained,
His steeds will be restrained,
    But gallop lively down the western hill;[6]
Thou shalt, when he hath run the world's half frame,
Tonight put on perfection, and a woman's name.

The amorous evening star is rose,
Why should not then our amorous star inclose
  Herself in her wished bed? Release your strings,
Musicians, and dancers, take some truce
With these your pleasing labors, for great use
  As much weariness as perfection brings;
    You, and not only you, but all toiled beasts
Rest duly; at night all their toils are dispensed;
But in their beds commenced
    Are other labors and more dainty feasts;
She goes a maid, who, lest she turn the same,
Tonight puts on perfection, and a woman's name.

Thy virgin's girdle now untie,
And in thy nuptial bed (love's altar) lie
  A pleasing sacrifice; now dispossess
Thee of these chains and robes which were put on
To adorn the day, not thee; for thou, alone,

6. "If line 57 is read with a gradually rising pitch and a momentary pause at the end before beginning line 58, the passage will clearly signify that the sun stands still at noon before the shadows turn, that is, that his horses will be restrained for a moment at the crest of the hill (noon) but will nevertheless gallop down the western slope." J. V. Hagopian, "Some Cruxes in Donne's Poetry," *Notes and Queries* 202 (1957): 501.

Like virtue and truth, art best in nakedness;
This bed is only to virginity
A grave, but to a better state, a cradle;
Till now thou wast but able
To be what now thou art; then that by thee
No more be said, *I may be*, but, *I am*,
Tonight put on perfection, and a woman's name.

Even like a faithful man content
That this life for a better should be spent,
So she a mother's rich style doth prefer,
And at the bridegroom's wished approach doth lie
Like an appointed lamb, when tenderly
The priest comes on his knees to embowel her;
Now sleep or watch with more joy; and O light
Of heaven, tomorrow rise thou hot and early;
This sun will love so dearly
Her rest, that long, long we shall want her sight;
Wonders are wrought, for she which had no maim,
Tonight puts on perfection, and a woman's name.

Satires

Satire I

Away thou fondling motley humourist,[1]
Leave me, and in this standing wooden chest,[2]
Consorted with these few books, let me lie
In prison, and here be coffined, when I die;
Here are God's conduits,[3] grave divines; and here
Nature's secretary, the Philosopher;
And jolly statesmen, which teach how to tie
The sinews of a city's mystic body;
Here gathering[4] chroniclers, and by them stand
Giddy fantastic poets of each land.
Shall I leave all this constant company,
And follow headlong, wild uncertain thee?
First swear by thy best love in earnest
(If thou which lov'st all, canst love any best)
Thou wilt not leave me in the middle street,
Though some more spruce companion thou dost meet,
Not though a captain do come in thy way
Bright parcel gilt, with forty dead men's pay,[5]
Nor though a brisk perfumed pert courtier
Deign with a nod, thy courtesy to answer.
Nor come a velvet Justice with a long
Great train of blue coats,[6] twelve, or fourteen strong,
Wilt thou grin or fawn on him, or prepare
A speech to court his beauteous son and heir.
For better or worse take me, or leave me:
To take, and leave me is adultery.
Oh monstrous, superstitious puritan,
Of refined manners, yet ceremonial man,[7]
That when thou meet'st one, with inquiring eyes
Dost search, and like a needy broker prize[8]
The silk, and gold he wears, and to that rate

1. Whether Donne addresses an aspect of himself or a foolish companion is unclear.
2. A study.
3. Channels.
4. That is, gathering information.
5. Gilt means rich in gold, with a pun on guilty; and officers often kept the names of dead men on company paylists to pad their own income.
6. Worn by liveried servants and also minor officials.
7. A purist of manners, monstrous in linking ceremony and Puritanism.
8. A pawnbroker appraises.

So high or low, dost raise thy formal hat:
That wilt consort none, until thou have known
What lands he hath in hope, or of his own,
As though all thy companions should make thee
Jointures,[9] and marry thy dear company.
Why shouldst thou (that dost not only approve,
But in rank itchy lust, desire, and love
The nakedness and barrenness to enjoy,
Of thy plump muddy whore, or prostitute boy)
Hate virtue, though she be naked, and bare?
At birth, and death, our bodies naked are;
And till our souls be unapparelled
Of bodies, they from bliss are banished.
Man's first blessed state was naked, when by sin
He lost that, yet he was clothed but in beast's skin,
And in this coarse attire, which I now wear,
With God, and with the Muses I confer.
But since thou like a contrite penitent,
Charitably warned of thy sins, dost repent
These vanities, and giddinesses, lo
I shut my chamber door, and come, let's go.
But sooner may a cheap whore, that hath been
Worn by as many several men in sin,
As are black feathers, or musk-colour hose,
Name her child's right true father, 'mongst all those:
Sooner may one guess, who shall bear away
The Infanta of London, heir to an India;[1]
And sooner may a gulling weather spy[2]
By drawing forth heaven's scheme tell certainly
What fashioned hats, or ruffs, or suits next year
Our subtle-witted antic youths will wear;
Than thou, when thou depart'st from me, canst show
Whither, why, when, or with whom thou wouldst go.
But how shall I be pardoned my offence
That thus have sinned against my conscience?
Now we are in the street; he first of all
Improvidently proud, creeps to the wall,[3]
And so imprisoned, and hemmed in by me
Sells for a little state[4] his liberty;
Yet though he cannot skip forth now to greet
Every fine silken painted fool we meet,
He them to him with amorous smiles allures,
And grins, smacks, shrugs, and such an itch endures,
As 'prentices, or school-boys which do know
Of some gay sport abroad, yet dare not go.

9. Property held jointly by husband and wife.
1. The eldest daughter of the king and queen of Spain. More generally, Donne refers to any heir of great wealth.
2. A fraudulent astrologer.
3. That is, takes the inside position on the path, as befits higher rank.
4. Status.

And as fiddlers stop lowest, at highest sound,
So to the most brave, stoops he nigh'st the ground.
But to a grave man, he doth move no more
Than the wise politic horse would heretofore,
Or thou O elephant or ape wilt do,[5]
When any names the King of Spain to you.
Now leaps he upright, jogs me, and cries, "Do you see
Yonder well-favoured youth?" "Which?" "Oh, 'tis he
That dances so divinely"; "Oh," said I,
"Stand still, must you dance here for company?"
He drooped, we went, till one (which did excel
The Indians, in drinking his tobacco well)[6]
Met us; they talked; I whispered, "Let us go,
'T may be you smell him not, truly I do."
He hears not me, but, on the other side
A many-coloured peacock having spied,
Leaves him and me; I for my lost sheep stay;
He follows, overtakes, goes on the way,
Saying, "Him whom I last left, all repute[7]
For his device, in handsoming a suit,[8]
To judge of lace, pink, panes,[9] print, cut, and pleat
Of all the Court, to have the best conceit."[1]
"Our dull comedians want him, let him go;
But Oh, God strengthen thee, why stoop'st thou so?"
"Why? he hath travelled." "Long?" "No, but to me
(Which understand none), he doth seem to be
Perfect French, and Italian"; I replied,
"So is the pox"[2] he answered not, but spied
More men of sort, of parts, and qualities;
At last his love he in a window spies,
And like light dew exhaled, he flings from me
Violently ravished to his lechery.
Many were there, he could command no more;
He quarrelled, fought, bled; and turned out of door
    Directly came to me hanging the head,
    And constantly a while must keep his bed.

Satire II

Sir: though (I thank God for it) I do hate
Perfectly[3] all this town, yet there's one state

5. In the 1590s, a performing horse called Morocco supposedly responded to questions put to it by its trainer, a Mr. Banks. An elephant and an ape were also exhibited.
6. As tobacco had recently been introduced, there was dispute about whether it should be inhaled or imbibed.
7. Esteem.
8. Ingenuity in adorning himself in fine clothes.
9. A pink is an ornamental, scalloped pattern. Panes are decorative slashes.
1. Idea.
2. Syphilis, thought to be endemic in France and Italy.
3. Thoroughly.

In all ill things so excellently best,[4]
That hate, towards them, breeds pity towards the rest.
Though poetry indeed be such a sin
As I think that brings dearth,[5] and Spaniards in,
Though like the pestilence and old fashioned love,[6]
Riddlingly it[7] catch men; and doth remove
Never, till it be starved out; yet their state
Is poor, disarmed, like papists,[8] not worth hate.
One (like a wretch, which at Bar judged as dead,[9]
Yet prompts him which stands next, and cannot read,
And saves his life) gives idiot actors means[1]
(Starving himself) to live by his laboured scenes;
As in some organ, puppets dance above
And bellows pant below, which them do move.
One would move love by rhythms; but witchcraft's charms
Bring not now their old fears, nor their old harms:[2]
Rams, and slings now are silly battery,[3]
Pistolets[4] are the best artillery.
And they who write to lords, rewards to get,
Are they not like singers at doors for meat?
And they who write, because all write, have still
That excuse for writing, and for writing ill.
But he is worst, who (beggarly) doth chaw
Others' wits' fruits, and in his ravenous maw
Rankly digested, doth those things out spew,
As his own things; and they are his own, 'tis true,
For if one eat my meat, though it be known
The meat was mine, the excrement is his own.
But these do me no harm, nor they which use
To outdo dildoes, and out-usure Jews;
To out-drink the sea, to outswear the Litany;
Who with sins of all kinds as familiar be
As confessors;[5] and for whose sinful sake,
Schoolmen[6] new tenements in hell must make:
Whose strange sins, canonists could hardly tell
In which commandment's large receipt they dwell.
  But these punish themselves; the insolence
Of Coscus only breeds my just offence,
Whom time (which rots all, and makes botches pox,[7]
And plodding on, must make a calf an ox)
Hath made a lawyer, which was alas of late

4. Perfectly evil.
5. Famine.
6. I.e., true love.
7. Poetry. The urge to write catches men.
8. Catholics, whose reduced state no longer warranted persecution.
9. Condemned to death.
1. Criminals would sometimes escape execution by giving proof of literacy; "idiot" signifies "ignorant."
2. Trying to win love by poems is as foolish as trying to work spells by witchcraft.
3. Ineffective weapons.
4. A pun—pistols and Spanish coins.
5. Priests who hear confessions.
6. Theologians who assign each sin its place in hell.
7. Reveals boils to be syphilitic.

But scarce a poet; jollier of this state,[8]
Than are new beneficed ministers, he throws
Like nets, or lime-twigs,[9] wheresoe'er he goes,
His title of barrister, on every wench,
And woos in language of the Pleas, and Bench:
"A motion, Lady"; "Speak Coscus"; "I have been
In love, ever since *tricesimo* of the Queen,[1]
Continual claims I have made, injunctions got
To stay my rival's suit, that he should not
Proceed"; "Spare me"; "In Hilary term[2] I went,
You said, if I return next 'size[3] in Lent,
I should be in remitter of[4] your grace;
In the interim my letters should take place
Of affidavits"; words, words, which would tear
The tender labyrinth of a soft maid's ear,
More, more, than ten Sclavonians scolding,[5] more
Than when winds in our ruined abbeys roar.
When sick with poetry, and possessed with Muse
Thou wast, and mad, I hoped; but men which choose
Law practice for mere gain, bold soul, repute
Worse than embrothelled strumpets prostitute.
Now like an owl-like watchman, he must walk
His hand still at a bill,[6] now he must talk
Idly, like prisoners, which whole months will swear
That only suretyship[7] hath brought them there,
And to every suitor lie in everything,
Like a king's favourite, yea like a king;
Like a wedge in a block, wring to the bar,
Bearing like asses, and more shameless far
Than carted whores,[8] lie, to the grave judge; for
Bastardy abounds not in kings' titles, nor
Simony and sodomy in churchmen's lives,
As these things do in him; by these he thrives.
Shortly (as the sea) he will compass[9] all the land;
From Scots, to Wight; from Mount, to Dover strand.[1]
And spying heirs melting with luxury,[2]
Satan will not joy at their sins, as he.
For as a thrifty wench scrapes kitchen stuff,
And barrelling the droppings, and the snuff,
Of wasting candles, which in thirty year
(Relic-like kept) perchance buys wedding gear;
Piecemeal he gets lands, and spends as much time

8. I.e., his position as lawyer.
9. Traps or snares for birds.
1. Thirtieth year of the queen's reign (1588).
2. First term of the English legal year, January 23 to February 12.
3. Next assize.
4. Retrospectively entitled to.
5. The harsh foreign sound of Slavic speech.
6. He must clutch money, also sign petitions.
7. Being in prison as guarantee for another's debt.
8. Convicted prostitutes were carried through the streets in carts to the whipping posts.
9. Encompass.
1. From Scotland in the north to the Isle of Wight in the south; from St. Michael's Mount (Cornwall) in the west to the Dover shore in the east.
2. Spying out heirs whose debauchery will lead to an early death.

Wringing each acre, as men pulling prime.[3]
In parchments then, large as his fields, he draws
Assurances, big, as glossed civil laws,[4]
So huge, that men (in our time's forwardness)[5]
Are Fathers of the Church for writing less.
These he writes not; nor for these written pays,
Therefore spares no length; as in those first days
When Luther was professed,[6] he did desire
Short *Pater nosters*, saying as a friar
Each day his beads, but having left those laws,
Adds to Christ's prayer, the power and glory clause.[7]
But when he sells or changes land, he impairs
His writings, and (unwatched) leaves out, *ses heires*,[8]
As slily as any commenter goes by
Hard words, or sense; or in Divinity
As controverters,[9] in vouched texts, leave out
Shrewd words, which might against them clear the doubt.
Where are those spread woods which clothed heretofore
Those bought lands? not built, nor burnt within door.
Where's the old landlord's troops, and alms? In great halls
Carthusian fasts, and fulsome bacchanals[1]
Equally I hate; means bless; in rich men's homes
I bid kill some beasts, but no hecatombs,[2]
None starve, none surfeit so; but oh we allow,
Good works as good, but out of fashion now,
Like old rich wardrobes; but my words none draws
Within the vast reach of the huge statute laws.

Satire III

Kind pity chokes my spleen;[3] brave scorn forbids
Those tears to issue which swell my eyelids;
I must not laugh, nor weep sins, and be wise,
Can railing then cure these worn maladies?
Is not our mistress, fair Religion,
As worthy of all our soul's devotion,
As virtue was to the first blinded age?[4]
Are not heaven's joys as valiant to assuage
Lusts, as earth's honor was to them? Alas,
As we do them in means, shall they surpass

3. Extorting, wresting, each acre, as men drawing a winning hand in the card game of primero.

4. Deeds of conveyance, as big as commentaries on civil law.

5. Our modern times.

6. Took religious vows.

7. As a young monk, Luther preferred short prayers, but later he added the phrase "For thine is the Kingdom, the Power and the Glory, now and forever" to the Lord's Prayer.

8. By omitting the phrase, "his heirs," an unscrupulous lawyer could secure an inheritance for himself.

9. Controversialists.

1. Fasts of a monastic order noted for austerity, and gross orgies.

2. Wholesale slaughter of animals for sacrifice.

3. Regarded, in Donne's time, as the seat of both melancholy and mirth.

4. Pagan antiquity.

Us in the end, and shall thy father's spirit
Meet blind philosophers[5] in heaven, whose merit
Of strict life may be imputed[6] faith, and hear
Thee, whom he taught so easy ways and near
To follow, damned? O if thou dar'st, fear this;
This fear great courage and high valor is.
Dar'st thou aid mutinous Dutch, and dar'st thou lay
Thee in ships, wooden sepulchers, a prey
To leaders' rage, to storms, to shot, to dearth?
Dar'st thou dive seas and dungeons of the earth?
Hast thou courageous fire to thaw the ice
Of frozen North discoveries? And thrice
Colder than salamanders,[7] like divine
Children in the oven,[8] fires of Spain, and the line,[9]
Whose countries limbecks[1] to our bodies be,
Canst thou for gain bear? And must every he
Which cries not "Goddess!" to thy mistress, draw,[2]
Or eat thy poisonous words? Courage of straw!
O desperate coward, wilt thou seem bold, and
To thy foes and His (Who made thee to stand
Sentinel in His world's garrison) thus yield,
And for forbidden wars, leave the appointed field?
Know thy foes: the foul Devil, whom thou
Strivest to please, for hate, not love, would allow
Thee fain his whole realm to be quit;[3] and as
The world's all parts[4] wither away and pass,
So the world's self, thy other loved foe, is
In her decrepit wane,[5] and thou, loving this,
Dost love a withered and worn strumpet; last,
Flesh (itself's death) and joys which flesh can taste,
Thou lovest; and thy fair goodly soul, which doth
Give this flesh power to taste joy, thou dost loathe.
Seek true religion. O where? Mirreus,
Thinking her unhoused here, and fled from us,
Seeks her at Rome; there, because he doth know
That she was there a thousand years ago;
He loves her rags so, as we here obey
The statecloth[6] where the Prince sat yesterday.
Crantz to such brave[7] Loves will not be enthralled,
But loves her only, who at Geneva is called
Religion, plain, simple, sullen, young,

5. Pagan philosophers.
6. Accounted as.
7. Reputed to be able to survive fire because they are cold-blooded.
8. For refusing to worship a golden idol, Shadrach, Meshach, and Abednego were cast into the fiery furnace but were miraculously unharmed (Daniel 3).
9. The Inquisition and the equator (objects of "bear," line 26).
1. Distilling retorts.
2. I.e., draw his sword.
3. To be rid of you.
4. All the parts of the world.
5. Decline.
6. We do obeisance to the cloth over the throne.
7. Splendid.

Contemptuous, yet unhandsome; as among
Lecherous humors, there is one that judges
No wenches wholesome but coarse country drudges.
Graius stays still at home here, and because
Some preachers, vile ambitious bawds, and laws,
Still new like fashions, bid him think that she
Which dwells with us is only perfect, he
Embraceth her whom his godfathers will
Tender to him, being tender, as wards still
Take such wives as their guardians offer, or
Pay values.[8] Careless Phrygius doth abhor
All, because all cannot be good, as one,
Knowing some women whores, dares marry none.
Gracchus loves all as one, and thinks that so
As women do in diverse countries go
In divers habits, yet are still one kind,
So doth, so is Religion; and this blind-
ness too much light breeds; but unmoved thou
Of force must one, and forced but one allow;
And the right; ask thy father which is she,
Let him ask his, though truth and falsehood be
Near twins, yet truth a little elder is;
Be busy to seek her, believe me this,
He's not of none, nor worst,[9] that seeks the best.
To adore, or scorn an image, or protest,
May all be bad; doubt wisely; in strange way
To stand inquiring right is not to stray;
To sleep, or run wrong is. On a huge hill,
Cragged and steep, Truth stands, and he that will
Reach her, about must, and about must go;
And what the hill's suddenness resists, win so;
Yet strive so, that before age, death's twilight,
Thy soul rest, for none can work in that night.
To will implies delay, therefore now do.
Hard deeds, the body's pains; hard knowledge too
The mind's endeavors reach,[1] and mysteries
Are like the sun, dazzling, yet plain to all eyes.
Keep the truth which thou hast found; men do not stand
In so ill case here that God hath with His hand
Signed kings blank charters to kill whom they hate,
Nor are they vicars, but hangmen to fate.
Fool and wretch, wilt thou let thy soul be tied
To man's laws, by which she shall not be tried
At the last day? Oh, wilt it then boot[2] thee
To say a Philip, or a Gregory,

8. Sums paid for refusing an arranged marriage; here compared to fines recusants paid for not attending the national church.
9. Not of no faith, nor the worst faith.
1. Difficult deeds are accomplished by the body's pains; difficult knowledge is attained by the mind's endeavors.
2. Profit.

A Harry, or a Martin[3] taught thee this?
Is not this excuse for mere contraries
Equally strong? Cannot both sides say so?
That thou mayest rightly obey power, her bounds know;
Those passed, her nature, and name is changed; to be
Then humble to her is idolatry.
As streams are, power is; those blest flowers that dwell
At the rough stream's calm head, thrive and do well,
But having left their roots, and themselves given
To the stream's tyrannous rage, alas, are driven
Through mills, and rocks, and woods, and at last, almost
Consumed in going, in the sea are lost:
So perish souls, which more choose men's unjust
Power from God claimed, than God Himself to trust.

Satire IV

Well; I may now receive,[4] and die; my sin
Indeed is great, but I have been in
A purgatory,[5] such as feared hell is
A recreation, and scant map of this.
My mind, neither with pride's itch, nor yet hath been
Poisoned with love to see, or to be seen.
I had no suit there, nor new suit to show,
Yet went to Court; but as Glaze[6] which did go
To a Mass in jest, catched, was fain to disburse
The hundred marks, which is the Statute's curse,[7]
Before he 'scaped, so it pleased my destiny
(Guilty of my sin of going), to think me
As prone to all ill, and of good as forget-
ful, as proud, as lustful, and as much in debt,
As vain, as witless, and as false as they
Which dwell at Court, for once going that way.
Therefore I suffered this; towards me did run
A thing more strange than on Nile's slime the sun
E'er bred,[8] or all which into Noah's Ark came:
A thing, which would have posed[9] Adam to name:
Stranger than seven antiquaries' studies,
Than Afric's monsters, Guiana's rarities,[1]
Stranger than strangers;[2] one, who for a Dane,

3. Philip II of Spain; Pope Gregory XIII or Gregory XIV; Henry VIII of England; Martin Luther.
4. Receive the last sacrament—Extreme Unction. Some editors suggest Holy Communion.
5. I.e., the Court.
6. A fictitious character whose name (Glare in some manuscripts) indicates superficiality.
7. Statutory fine for attending Mass.
8. According to Pliny, the sun spontaneously generated small creatures from the Nile's mud.
9. Confounded.
1. Exotic creatures—including people "whose heads appear not above their shoulders" and others with "eyes in their shoulders, and their mouths in the middle of their breasts"—as described in Sir Walter Raleigh's *The Discovery of Guiana* (1596).
2. Foreigners.

In the Danes' Massacre[3] had sure been slain,
If he had lived then; and without help dies,
When next the 'prentices 'gainst strangers rise.[4]
One, whom the watch at noon[5] lets scarce go by,
One, to whom, the examining Justice sure would cry,
"Sir, by your priesthood[6] tell me what you are."
His clothes were strange, though coarse; and black, though bare;[7]
Sleeveless his jerkin was, and it had been
Velvet, but 'twas now (so much ground was seen)
Become tufftaffaty;[8] and our children shall
See it plain rash[9] awhile, then naught at all.
This thing hath travelled, and saith, speaks all tongues
And only knoweth what to all states belongs,
Made of the accents, and best phrase of all these,
He speaks one language; if strange meats displease,
Art[1] can deceive, or hunger force my taste,
But pedant's motley tongue, soldier's bombast,
Mountebank's drugtongue,[2] nor the terms of law
Are strong enough preparatives,[3] to draw
Me to bear this, yet I must be content
With his tongue: in his tongue, called compliment:
In which he can win widows, and pay scores,
Make men speak treason, cozen[4] subtlest whores,
Out-flatter favourites, or out-lie either
Jovius, or Surius,[5] or both together.
He names me, and comes to me; I whisper, "God!
How have I sinned, that thy wrath's furious rod,
This fellow, chooseth me?" He sayeth, "Sir,
I love your judgement; whom do you prefer,
For the best linguist?" And I sillily
Said, that I thought Calepine's Dictionary;[6]
"Nay but of men, most sweet Sir". Beza[7] then,
Some Jesuits, and two reverend men
Of our two Academies, I named. There
He stopped me, and said; "Nay, your Apostles were
Good pretty linguists, and so Panurge[8] was;
Yet a poor gentleman, all these may pass
By travail."[9] Then, as if he would have sold

3. In 1012, the Danes in England were slaughtered by King Etherred the Unready.
4. In 1517, the apprentices of London rioted against foreign traders.
5. The guard in full daylight.
6. Catholic priests were liable to prosecution and execution.
7. Threadbare.
8. Taffetta or thin glossy silk with tufts.
9. Smooth fabric.
1. The culinary art.
2. The jargon of quack doctors.
3. Medical term referring to means by which a patient is prepared for treatment; also, an appetizer.
4. Cheat.
5. Paulus Jovius (1483–1552) and Laurentius Surius (1522–1578), whose Counterreformation tracts infuriated Protestants.
6. Polyglot dictionary edited by Ambrose Calepine in 1502.
7. French Calvinist Theodore de Beze, who translated the Greek New Testament into Latin.
8. Polyglot character in Rabelais's *Gargantua and Pantagruel*.
9. A pun on travel and toil.

His tongue, he praised it, and such wonders told
That I was fain to say, "If you had lived, Sir,
Time enough to have been interpreter
To Babel's bricklayers, sure the Tower had stood."[1]
He adds, "If of Court life you knew the good,
You would leave loneness." I said, "Not alone
My loneness is; but Spartan's fashion,[2]
To teach by painting drunkards, doth not last
Now; Aretine's pictures[3] have made few chaste;
No more can princes' Courts, though there be few
Better pictures of vice, teach me virtue";
He, like to a high stretched lute string squeaked, "O Sir,
'Tis sweet to talk of kings." "At Westminster,"
Said I, "the man that keeps the Abbey tombs,
And for his price doth with whoever comes,
Of all our Harrys, and our Edwards talk,
From king to king and all their kin can walk:
Your ears shall hear naught, but kings; your eyes meet
Kings only; The way to it, is King Street."[4]
He smacked, and cried, "He's base, mechanic,[5] coarse,
So are all your Englishmen in their discourse.
Are not your Frenchmen neat?" "Mine? as you see,
I have but one Frenchman, look, he follows me."
"Certes they are neatly clothed. I of this mind am,
Your only wearing is your grogaram."[6]
"Not so Sir, I have more." Under this pitch[7]
He would not fly; I chaffed[8] him; but as itch
Scratched into smart, and as blunt iron ground
Into an edge, hurts worse: so, I (fool) found,
Crossing[9] hurt me; to fit my sullenness,
He to another key his style doth address,
And asks, "What news?" I tell him of new plays.
He takes my hand, and as a still,[1] which stays
A semi-breve[2] 'twixt each drop, he niggardly,
As loth to enrich me, so tells many a lie,
More than ten Holinsheds, or Halls, or Stows,[3]
Of trivial household trash he knows; he knows
When the Queen frowned, or smiled, and he knows what
A subtle statesman may gather of that;
He knows who loves; whom; and who by poison

1. God prevented men from completing the tower of Babel by fracturing their common language into many.
2. The Spartans commonly dissuaded their young men from drinking by exhibiting drunken slaves.
3. Erotic paintings by Giulio Romano, acompanied by obscene sonnets by Pietro Aretino.
4. The street leading from Charing Cross to the King's Palace at Westminster.
5. Low.
6. Grosgrain, a coarse fabric.
7. The height to which a trained falcon flies, with possible puns on other meanings of "pitch."
8. Teased.
9. I.e., disputing him.
1. Distilling apparatus.
2. Duration of a musical "whole note."
3. Authors of anecdotal chronicles of England.

Hastes to an office's reversion;[4]
He knows who hath sold his land, and now doth beg
A licence, old iron, boots, shoes, and egg-
Shells to transport; shortly boys shall not play
At span-counter, or blow-point,[5] but they pay
Toll to some courtier; and wiser than all us,
He knows what lady is not painted; thus
He with home-meats[6] tries me; I belch, spew, spit,
Look pale, and sickly, like a patient; yet
He thrusts on more; and as if he undertook
To say *Gallo-Belgicus*[7] without book
Speaks of all states, and deeds, that have been since
The Spaniards came, to the loss of Amiens.[8]
Like a big wife, at sight of loathed meat,
Ready to travail: so I sigh, and sweat
To hear this Macaron[9] talk: in vain; for yet,
Either my humour, or his own to fit,
He like a privileged spy, whom nothing can
Discredit, libels now 'gainst each great man.
He names a price for every office paid;
He saith, our wars thrive ill, because delayed;
That offices are entailed,[1] and that there are
Perpetuities of them, lasting as far
As the last day; and that great officers,
Do with the pirates share, and Dunkirkers.[2]
Who wastes in meat, in clothes, in horse, he notes;
Who loves whores, who boys, and who goats.
I more amazed than Circe's prisoners,[3] when
They felt themselves turn beasts, felt myself then
Becoming traitor, and methought I saw
One of our giant Statues ope his jaw
To suck me in; for hearing him, I found
That as burnt venomed lechers do grow sound
By giving others their sores,[4] I might grow
Guilty, and he free: therefore I did show
All signs of loathing; but since I am in,
I must pay mine, and my forefathers' sin
To the last farthing; therefore to my power[5]
Toughly and stubbornly I bear this cross; but the hour
Of mercy now was come; he tries to bring
Me to pay a fine to 'scape his torturing,
And says, "Sir, can you spare me"; I said, "Willingly";

4. Right of succession.
5. Children's games.
6. Gossip.
7. *Mercurious Gallo-Belgius* was a compilation of European gossip and current events.
8. I.e., from 1588, the year of the Armada, to the fall of Amiens to the Spanish in 1597.
9. Fop.
1. Settled in perpetuity.
2. Dunkirk was a haven for pirates.
3. Odysseus and his men.
4. Superstitition held that venereal disease could be cured if passed on to others.
5. To the limits of my power.

"Nay, Sir, can you spare me a crown?" Thankfully I
Gave it, as ransom; but as fiddlers, still,
Though they be paid to be gone, yet needs will
Thrust one more jig upon you; so did he
With his long complimental thanks vex me.
But he is gone, thanks to his needy want,
And the prerogative of my crown: scant
His thanks were ended, when I, (which did see
All the Court filled with more strange things than he)
Ran from thence with such or more haste, than one
Who fears more actions, doth make from prison.
At home in wholesome solitariness
My precious soul began, the wretchedness
Of suitors at Court to mourn, and a trance
Like his, who dreamed he saw hell,[6] did advance
Itself on me, such men as he saw there,
I saw at Court, and worse, and more; low fear
Becomes the guilty, not the accuser; then,
Shall I, none's slave, of high-born, or raised men[7]
Fear frowns? And, my mistress Truth, betray thee
To the huffing braggart, puffed nobility?
No, no, thou which since yesterday hast been
Almost about the whole world, hast thou seen,
O sun, in all thy journey, vanity,
Such as swells the bladder of our Court? I
Think he which made your waxen garden, and
Transported it from Italy to stand
With us, at London, flouts our Presence, for
Just such gay painted things, which no sap, nor
Taste have in them, ours are; and natural
Some of the stocks are, their fruits, bastard all.
'Tis ten a-clock and past; all whom the mews,
Balloon, tennis, diet, or the stews,[8]
Had all the morning held, now the second
Time made ready, that day, in flocks, are found
In the Presence, and I, (God pardon me).
As fresh, and sweet their apparels be, as be
The fields they sold to buy them; "For a King
Those hose are," cry the flatterers; and bring
Them next week to the theatre to sell;
Wants reach all states;[9] me seems they do as well
At stage, as Court; all are players; whoe'er looks
(For themselves dare not go) o'er Cheapside books,[1]
Shall find their wardrobe's inventory. Now,

6. Dante.
7. Men who acquire, as opposed to inherit, rank.
8. Mews are stables; balloon is a game like handball; diet refers both to church councils and to aphrodisiacal foods; stews are brothels.
9. I.e., both rich and poor feel want.
1. Ledger books of Cheapside tailors, to whom these courtiers are in debt.

The ladies come; as pirates, which do know
That there came weak ships fraught with cochineal,[2]
The men board them; and praise, as they think, well,
Their beauties; they the men's wits; both are bought.
Why good wits ne'er wear scarlet gowns,[3] I thought
This cause: these men, men's wits for speeches buy,
And women buy all reds which scarlets dye.
He called her beauty lime-twigs, her hair net;[4]
She fears her drugs ill laid,[5] her hair loose set.
Would not Heraclitus laugh to see Macrine,[6]
From hat, to shoe, himself at door refine,
As if the Presence were a moschite,[7] and lift
His skirts and hose, and call his clothes to shrift,
Making them confess not only mortal
Great stains and holes in them, but venial
Feathers and dust, wherewith they fornicate;
And then by Dürer's rules[8] survey the state
Of his each limb, and with strings the odds tries
Of his neck to his leg, and waist to thighs.
So in immaculate clothes, and symmetry
Perfect as circles, with such nicety
As a young preacher at his first time goes
To preach, he enters, and a lady which owes
Him not so much as good will, he arrests,
And unto her protests protests protests[9]
So much as at Rome would serve to have thrown
Ten Cardinals into the Inquisition;
And whispered "By Jesu", so often, that a
Pursuivant[1] would have ravished him away
For saying of our Lady's psalter,[2] but 'tis fit
That they each other plague, they merit it.
But here comes Glorius[3] that will plague them both,
Who, in the other extreme, only doth
Call a rough carelessness, good fashion;
Whose cloak his spurs tear; whom he spits on
He cares not, his ill words do no harm
To him; he rusheth in, as if "Arm, arm,"
He meant to cry; and though his face be as ill
As theirs which in old hangings[4] whip Christ, still
He strives to look worse, he keeps all in awe;
Jests like a licensed fool, commands like law.

2. Coloring agent used in rouge.
3. Gowns of high rank or government office.
4. Trite compliments, both referring to ways of capturing small birds.
5. Makeup badly applied.
6. Heraclitus, known as "the weeping philosopher," here laughs at Macrine, whose name is invented (like Glaze—see p. 75, n.6).
7. As if the Queen's presence were a mosque.
8. Albrecht Dürer's *Of Human Proportion* (1528) set rules for proportions of the human body.
9. He protests love; he protests that she must not protest. He is protestant.
1. Officer who investigates charges of Popery.
2. Saying the Rosary, a Catholic act of worship.
3. Like Macrine and Glaze, fictitious.
4. Tapestries.

Tired, now I leave this place, and but pleased so
As men which from gaols to execution go,
Go through the great chamber (why is it hung
With the seven deadly sins?).[5] Being among
Those Ascaparts,[6] men big enough to throw
Charing Cross[7] for a bar, men that do know
No token of worth, but Queen's man, and fine
Living, barrels of beef, flagons of wine,
I shook like a spied spy. Preachers which are
Seas of wit and arts, you can, then dare,
Drown the sins of this place, for, for me
Which am but a scarce brook, it enough shall be
To wash the stains away; though I yet
With Maccabees' modesty,[8] the known merit
Of my work lessen: yet some wise man shall,
I hope, esteem my writs canonical.

Satire V

Thou shalt not laugh in this leaf, Muse, nor they
Whom any pity warms; he[9] which did lay
Rules to make courtiers, (he being understood
May make good courtiers, but who courtiers good?)
Frees from the sting of jests all who in extreme
Are wretched or wicked: of these two a theme
Charity and liberty[1] give me. What is he
Who officers' rage, and suitors' misery
Can write, and jest? If all things be in all,
As I think, since all, which were, are, and shall
Be, be made of the same elements:
Each thing, each thing implies or represents.
Then man is a world; in which, officers
Are the vast ravishing seas; and suitors,
Springs; now full, now shallow, now dry; which, to
That which drowns them, run: these self[2] reasons do
Prove the world a man, in which, officers
Are the devouring stomach, and suitors
The excrements, which they void; all men are dust,
How much worse are suitors, who to men's lust
Are made preys. O worse than dust, or worm's meat,
For they do eat you now, whose selves worms shall eat.
They are the mills which grind you, yet you are

5. Tapestries illustrating the seven deadly sins.
6. Ascapart was a legendary giant, thirty feet tall.
7. Huge Gothic cross erected by Edward I.
8. The Book of the Maccabees concludes "And if [this work] has been well . . . written, that is what I wanted; but if it is poor . . . , that was all I could do.
9. Castiglione, author of *The Courtier* (1528).
1. Charity toward the wretched; liberty to censure the wicked.
2. Same.

The wind which drives them; and a wasteful war
Is fought against you, and you fight it; they
Adulterate law, and you prepare their way
Like wittols;[3] the issue your own ruin is.
   Greatest and fairest Empress,[4] know you this?
Alas, no more than Thames' calm head doth know
Whose meads[5] her arms drown, or whose corn o'erflow:
You Sir,[6] whose righteousness she loves, whom I
By having leave to serve, am most richly
For service paid, authorized, now begin
To know and weed out this enormous sin.
   O age of rusty iron! Some better wit
Call it some worse name, if aught equal it;
The Iron Age that was, when justice was sold, now
Injustice is sold dearer far; allow
All demands, fees, and duties; gamesters, anon
The money which you sweat, and swear for, is gone
Into other hands: so controverted lands
'Scape, like Angelica,[7] the strivers' hands.
If law be in the judge's heart, and he
Have no heart to resist letter, or fee,[8]
Where wilt thou appeal? power of the courts below
Flow from the first main head,[9] and these can throw
Thee, if they suck thee in, to misery,
To fetters, halters; but if the injury
Steel thee to dare complain, alas, thou go'st
Against the stream, when upwards: when thou art most
Heavy and most faint; and in these labours they,
'Gainst whom thou shouldst complain, will in the way
Become great seas, o'er which, when thou shalt be
Forced to make golden bridges, thou shalt see
That all thy gold was drowned in them before;
All things follow their like, only who have may have more.
Judges are gods; he who made and said them so,
Meant not that men should be forced to them to go,
By means of angels;[1] when supplications
We send to God, to Dominations,
Powers, Cherubins, and all heaven's Courts, if we
Should pay fees as here, daily bread would be
Scarce to kings; so 'tis. Would it not anger

3. A man who acquiesces to his wife's adultery.
4. Queen Elizabeth I.
5. Meadows.
6. Sir Thomas Egerton (1540?–1617), Donne's patron and employer, who, in his position as Lord Keeper, attempted to reform the Star Chamber, a court of inquisitorial and criminal jurisdiction.
7. The sense of lines 37–42 is: due to inflated legal costs, suitors for justice are merely gambling and wind up losing in legal fees what they hope to gain in compensation; so disputed lands are lost or escape the suitors' grasp as Angelica, the heroine of Ariosto's *Orlando Furioso*, made escapes from romantic suitors.
8. Letter from a person of influence, or a bribe.
9. I.e., from the queen.
1. A pun on gold coins.

A stoic, a coward, yea a martyr,
To see a pursuivant[2] come in, and call
All his clothes, copes; books, primers;[3] and all
His plate, chalices; and mistake[4] them away,
And ask a fee for coming? Oh, ne'er may
Fair Law's white reverend name be strumpeted,
To warrant thefts: she is established
Recorder to Destiny, on earth, and she
Speaks Fate's words, and but tells us who must be
Rich, who poor, who in chairs,[5] who in gaols:
She is all fair, but yet hath foul long nails,
With which she scratcheth suitors; in bodies
Of men, so in law, nails are the extremities,
So officers stretch to more than Law can do,
As our nails reach what no else part comes to.
Why barest thou[6] to yon officer? Fool, hath he
Got those goods, for which erst men bared to thee?
Fool, twice, thrice, thou hast bought wrong, and now hungrily
Begg'st right; but that dole comes not till these[7] die.
Thou hadst much, and law's Urim and Thummim[8] try
Thou wouldst for more; and for all hast paper[9]
Enough to clothe all the Great Carrack's pepper.[1]
Sell that, and by that thou much more shalt leese,[2]
Than Haman,[3] when he sold his antiquities.
O wretch that thy fortunes should moralize
Aesop's fables, and make tales, prophecies.
Thou'rt the swimming dog whom shadows cozened,
And div'st, near drowning, for what vanished.[4]

2. Legal agents who sought evidence of Roman Catholic practices and artifacts and thereby profited by confiscation or blackmail.
3. Prayerbooks; copes are priestly vestments.
4. Take by fraud.
5. Sedan chairs, or chairs of high office.
6. Respectfully remove your hat.
7. These corrupt officials.
8. Gems permitting the wearer to speak with divine authority. The Hebrew words mean light and integrity.
9. Reams of legal documents.
1. A seven-decker Spanish ship, captured in 1592, loaded with a cargo of pepper.
2. Lose.
3. A biblical character, hanged for his attempt to pay for the slaughter of Jews.
4. In Aesop's fable, a greedy dog tries to seize the meat from the mouth of his own reflection in the water, thus losing the real meat he holds.

Verse Letters to Several Personages

The Storm

TO MR. CHRISTOPHER BROOKE[1]

Thou which art I ('tis nothing to be so),
Thou which art still thyself, by these shalt know
Part of our passage; and a hand, or eye
By *Hilliard*[2] drawn, is worth an history
By a worse painter made; and (without pride)
When by thy judgment they are dignified,
My lines are such: 'tis the pre-eminence
Of friendship only to impute excellence.
England to whom we owe what we be and have,
Sad that her sons did seek a foreign grave
(For Fate's or Fortune's drifts none can soothsay,
Honor and misery have one face and way),
From out her pregnant entrails sighed a wind
Which at the air's middle marble room did find
Such strong resistance that itself it threw
Downward again;[3] and so when it did view
How in the port our fleet dear time did leese,[4]
Withering like prisoners, which lie but for fees,[5]
Mildly it kissed our sails, and, fresh and sweet,
As to a stomach starved, whose insides meet,
Meat comes, it came, and swole[6] our sails, when we
So joyed as *Sarah* her swelling joyed to see.[7]
But 'twas but so kind as our countrymen
Which bring friends one day's way, and leave them then.
Then, like two mighty kings which, dwelling far
Asunder, meet against a third to war,
The South and West winds joined, and, as they blew,

1. This poem and "The Calm" describe incidents of the English naval expedition of 1597, the famous "Islands Expedition." "The Calm" was probably also addressed to Christopher Brooke, Donne's close friend and, later, his best man at his wedding.
2. Nicholas Hilliard (1537–1619), English painter.
3. Winds were supposed to be caused by the earth's exhalations and to be driven back upon contact with the hard or frozen middle region of the air.
4. Lose.
5. I.e., fees due to the jailer.
6. Swelled.
7. In old age, Sarah, wife of Abraham, bore him a son, Isaac (Genesis 21).

Waves like a rolling trench before them threw.
Sooner than you read this line, did the gale,
Like shot, not feared till felt, our sails assail;
And what at first was called a gust, the same
Hath now a storm's, anon a tempest's name.
Jonas,[8] I pity thee, and curse those men
Who when the storm raged most, did wake thee then;
Sleep is pain's easiest salve, and doth fulfill
All offices of death, except to kill.
But when I waked, I saw that I saw not;
Ay, and the sun, which should teach me, had forgot
East, west, day, night, and I could only say,
If the world had lasted, now it had been day.
Thousands our noises were, yet we 'mongst all
Could none by his right name, but thunder, call.
Lightning was all our light, and it rained more
Than if the sun had drunk the sea before.
Some coffined in their cabins lie, equally
Grieved that they are not dead and yet must die;
And as sin-burdened souls from graves will creep
At the last day, some forth their cabins peep
And tremblingly ask what news, and do hear so,
Like jealous husbands, what they would not know.
Some, sitting on the hatches, would seem there
With hideous gazing to fear away fear.
Then note they the ship's sicknesses, the mast
Shaked with this ague, and the hold and waist
With a salt dropsy clogged, and all our tacklings
Snapping, like too-high-stretched treble strings.
And from our tattered sails, rags drop down so,
As from one hanged in chains a year ago.
Even our ordnance, placed for our defense,
Strive to break loose and 'scape away from thence.
Pumping hath tired our men, and what's the gain?
Seas into seas thrown we suck in again;
Hearing hath deafed our sailors; and if they
Knew how to hear, there's none knows what to say.
Compared to these storms, death is but a qualm,[9]
Hell somewhat lightsome, and the Bermudas calm.
Darkness, light's elder brother,[1] his birthright
Claims o'er this world, and to heaven hath chased light.
All things are one, and that one none can be,
Since all forms, uniform deformity
Doth cover, so that we, except God say
Another *fiat*, shall have no more day.

8. Jonah, awakened during a storm and later cast into the sea (Jonah 1).
9. A feeling of faintness or sickness.
1. Darkness existed before light was created by God's command or "fiat" (see line 72 and Genesis 1).

So violent, yet long these furies be,
That though thine absence starve me, I wish not thee.

The Calm

Our storm is past, and that storm's tyrannous rage,
A stupid calm, but nothing it, doth 'suage.
The fable is inverted, and far more
A block afflicts, now, than a stork before.[2]
Storms chafe, and soon wear out themselves, or us;
In calms, Heaven laughs to see us languish thus.
As steady as I can wish that my thoughts were,
Smooth as thy mistress' glass,[3] or what shines there,
The sea is now. And, as the Isles which we
Seek when we can move, our ships rooted be.
As water did in storms, now pitch runs out
As lead when a fired church becomes one spout.[4]
And all our beauty and our trim decays,
Like courts removing, or like ended plays.
The fighting place now seamen's rags supply;
And all the tackling is a frippery.[5]
No use of lanterns; and in one place lay
Feathers and dust, today and yesterday.
Earth's hollownesses, which the world's lungs are,
Have no more wind than the upper vault of air.
We can nor lost friends nor sought foes recover,
But meteor-like, save that we move not, hover.
Only the calenture[6] together draws
Dear friends, which meet dead in great fishes' jaws.
And on the hatches as on altars lies
Each one, his own priest and own sacrifice.
Who live, that miracle do multiply
Where walkers in hot ovens do not die.[7]
If in despite of these, we swim, that hath
No more refreshing than our brimstone bath,
But from the sea into the ship we turn
Like parboiled wretches on the coals to burn.
Like *Bajazet* encaged, the shepherds' scoff,[8]
Or like slack-sinewed Samson, his hair off,
Languish our ships. Now, as a myriad

2. In medieval versions of Aesop's fable, when the frogs asked for a king they were given a log of wood, which they scorned; so they were then given a stork, which ate them.

3. Mirror.

4. Pitch was used to caulk the seams of ships; churches were often roofed with lead.

5. A secondhand-clothes shop.

6. A tropical disease that causes sailors deliriously to mistake the sea for green fields and to leap overboard.

7. Three Jews, cast into a fiery furnace, walked on unharmed (see "Satire III," line 24, and Daniel 3).

8. In Marlowe's *Tamburlaine*, the Turkish emperor Bajazeth is captured and kept in a cage by the former shepherd Tamburlaine.

Of ants durst the emperor's loved snake invade,[9]
The crawling galleys, sea-jails, finny chips,
Might brave our pinnaces,[1] now bed-rid ships.
Whether a rotten state and hope of gain,
Or to disuse me from the queasy pain
Of being beloved and loving, or the thirst
Of honor or fair death out-pushed me first,
I lose my end: for here as well as I
A desperate may live, and a coward die.
Stag, dog, and all which from, or towards flies,
Is paid with life, or prey, or doing dies.
Fate grudges us all, and doth subtly lay
A scourge, 'gainst which we all forget to pray.
He that at sea prays for more wind, as well
Under the poles may beg cold, heat in hell.
What are we then? How little more, alas,
Is man now than before he was! he was
Nothing; for us, we are for nothing fit;
Chance or ourselves still disproportion it.
We have no power, no will, no sense; I lie,
I should not then thus feel this misery.

To Sir Henry Wotton

Sir, more than kisses, letters mingle souls;
For, thus friends absent speak. This ease controls[2]
The tediousness of my life: but for these
I could ideate[3] nothing, which could please,
But I should wither in one day, and pass
To a bottle[4] of hay, that am a lock of grass.
Life is a voyage, and in our life's ways
Countries, courts, towns are rocks, or remoras;[5]
They break or stop all ships, yet our state's such,
That though than pitch they stain worse, we must touch.
If in the furnace of the even line,[6]
Or under the adverse icy poles thou pine,
Thou know'st two temperate regions girded in,
Dwell there: But Oh, what refuge canst thou win
Parched in the Court, and in the country frozen?
Shall cities, built of both extremes, be chosen?
Can dung and garlic be a perfume? or can
A scorpion and torpedo[7] cure a man?

9. Suetonius's *Life of Tiberius* tells of Tiberius's pet snake devoured by ants.
1. Because of the calm, the slow galleys, which were often rowed by prisoners (hence "sea-jails") and looked small like chips with finlike oars, might challenge the ordinarily quick-sailing pinnaces.
2. Relieves.
3. Form an idea of.
4. Bundle.
5. Impediments. The remora was a small sucking fish supposedly capable of stopping ships by attaching itself to their hulls.
6. The equator.
7. The electric ray, whose sting numbs, is opposed to the scorpion, whose sting maddens.

Cities are worst of all three; of all three
(O knotty riddle) each is worst equally.
Cities are sepulchres; they who dwell there
Are carcases, as if no such[8] there were.
And Courts are theatres, where some men play
Princes, some slaves, all to one end, and of one clay.
The country is a desert, where no good,
Gained (as habits, not born,) is understood.
There men become beasts, and prone to more evils;
In cities blocks,[9] and in a lewd Court, devils.
As in the first Chaos confusedly
Each element's qualities were in the other three;[1]
So pride, lust, covetize,[2] being several
To these three places, yet all are in all,
And mingled thus, their issue incestuous.
Falsehood is denizened.[3] Virtue is barbarous.
Let no man say there, 'Virtue's flinty wall
Shall lock vice in me, I'll do none, but know all.'
Men are sponges, which to pour out, receive,
Who know false play, rather than lose, deceive.
For in best understandings, sin began,
Angels sinned first, then devils, and then man.
Only perchance beasts sin not; wretched we
Are beasts in all, but white integrity.[4]
I think if men, which in these places live
Durst look for themselves, and themselves retrieve,
They would like strangers greet themselves, seeing then
Utopian youth, grown old Italian.[5]
Be thine own home, and in thyself dwell;
Inn anywhere, continuance[6] maketh hell.
And seeing the snail, which everywhere doth roam,
Carrying his own house still, still is at home,
Follow (for he is easy paced) this snail,
Be thine own palace, or the world's thy gaol.[7]
And in the world's sea, do not like cork sleep
Upon the water's face; nor in the deep
Sink like a lead without a line: but as
Fishes glide, leaving no print where they pass,
Nor making sound, so closely thy course go,
Let men dispute, whether thou breathe, or no.
Only in this one thing, be no Galenist:[8] to make
Courts' hot ambitions wholesome, do not take
A dram of country's dullness; do not add

8. I.e., no people.
9. Blockheads.
1. Before God created order, the four elements—air, water, fire, and earth—were mingled.
2. Desire.
3. Naturalized.
4. Innocence.
5. I.e., crafty and corrupt.
6. Remaining in one place.
7. Jail.
8. Galenists cured by applying remedies for one bodily humour to correct an excess of its opposite.

Correctives, but as chemics,[9] purge the bad.
But, Sir, I advise not you, I rather do
Say o'er those lessons, which I learned of you:
Whom, free from German schisms, and lightness
Of France, and fair Italy's faithlessness,
Having from these sucked all they had of worth,
And brought home that faith, which you carried forth,
I throughly[1] love. But if myself, I have won
To know my rules, I have, and you have

Donne.

To Mr Roland Woodward

Like one who in her third widowhood doth profess
Herself a nun, tied to retiredness,
So affects my Muse now, a chaste fallowness;

Since she to few, yet to too many hath shown
How love-song weeds, and satiric thorns are grown
Where seeds of better arts, were early sown.[2]

Though to use, and love poetry, to me,
Betrothed to no one art, be no adultery;
Omissions of good, ill, as ill deeds be.[3]

For though to us it seem, and be light and thin,
Yet in those faithful scales, where God throws in
Men's works, vanity weighs as much as sin.

If our souls have stained their first white, yet we
May clothe them with faith, and dear honesty,
Which God imputes, as native purity.

There is no virtue, but religion:
Wise, valiant, sober, just, are names, which none
Want, which want not vice-covering discretion.

Seek we then ourselves in ourselves; for as
Men force the sun with much more force to pass,
By gathering his beams with a crystal glass;[4]

9. Alchemists, who cured illness by purging its essence from the body through use of an antagonistic medicine.
1. Thoroughly.
2. Perhaps refers to Donne's previous verse: the songs and sonnets, the elegies and satires, and verse letters, though not all of the poems currently so grouped would have been written at the time of this poem.
3. Omitting to do good is as bad as committing evil.
4. Magnifying glass.

So we, if we into ourselves will turn,
Blowing our sparks of virtue, may outburn
The straw,[5] which doth about our hearts sojourn.

You know, physicians,[6] when they would infuse
Into any oil, the souls of simples, use
Places, where they may lie still warm, to choose.[7]

So works retiredness in us; to roam
Giddily, and be everywhere, but at home,
Such freedom doth a banishment become.

We are but farmers[8] of our selves, yet may,
If we can stock our selves, and thrive, uplay
Much, much dear treasure for the great rent day.[9]

Manure thy self then, to thy self be approved,
And with vain outward things be no more moved,
But to know, that I love thee and would be loved.

To Sir Henry Wotton

Here's no more news, than virtue; I may as well
Tell you *Cales'* or *Saint Michael's* tale[1] for news as tell
That vice doth here habitually dwell.

Yet, as to get stomachs[2] we walk up and down,
And toil to sweeten rest, so may God frown
If, but to loathe both, I haunt court or town.

For here no one is from the extremity
Of vice by any other reason free
But that the next to him still is worse than he.

In this world's warfare, they whom rugged Fate
(God's commissary[3]) doth so throughly hate
As in the court's squadron to marshal their state,

If they stand armed with silly[4] honesty,
With wishing prayers, and neat integrity,
Like Indians 'gainst Spanish hosts they be.

5. I.e., vanity.
6. Alchemists.
7. An alchemical process meant to infuse the essence of a simple substance into the "oil," or liquid form, of a metal, by mixing the elements in a glass container and burying it in a warm place.
8. I.e., tenant farmers.
9. The day of reckoning. Cf. "lay up for yourselves treasures in heaven" (Matthew 6.20).
1. Refers to the Cadiz and the Islands expeditions, on which Donne served in 1596 and 1597. Two MSS, date this letter July 20, 1598.
2. Appetites or relish for food.
3. Deputy; "throughly": thoroughly.
4. Simple.

Suspicious boldness to this place belongs,
And to have as many ears as all have tongues;
Tender to know, tough to acknowledge wrongs.

Believe me, sir, in my youth's giddiest days,
When to be like the court was a play's praise,
Plays were not so like courts as courts are like plays.

Then let us at these mimic antics jest,
Whose deepest projects and egregious gests[5]
Are but dull morals of a game at chests.[6]

But now 'tis incongruity to smile,
Therefore I end; and bid farewell a while,
At court, though *from court* were the better style.

To the Countess of Bedford

Madam,
Reason is our soul's left hand, faith her right,
By these we reach divinity, that's you;
Their loves, who have the blessings of your light,
Grew from their reason, mine from fair faith grew.

But as, although a squint lefthandedness
Be ungracious, yet we cannot want[7] that hand,
So would I, not to increase, but to express
My faith, as I believe, so understand.

Therefore I study you first in your saints,
Those friends whom your election glorifies,
Then in your deeds, accesses, and restraints,
And what you read, and what yourself devise.

But soon the reasons why you're loved by all
Grow infinite, and so pass reason's reach,
Then back again to implicit faith I fall,
And rest on what the catholic[8] voice doth teach:

That you are good: and not one heretic
Denies it: if he did, yet you are so.
For rocks which high-topped and deep-rooted stick
Waves wash, not undermine, nor overthrow.

5. Flagrant exploits; with possible puns on "guests" and "jests."
6. Symbolical figures of a game of chess.
7. Lack, do without.
8. Universal.

In everything there naturally grows
A *balsamum*[9] to keep it fresh and new,
If 'twere not injured by extrinsic blows;
Your birth and beauty are this balm in you.

But you of learning and religion,
And virtue, and such ingredients, have made
A mithridate,[1] whose operation
Keeps off or cures what can be done or said.

Yet this is not your physic,[2] but your food,
A diet fit for you; for you are here
The first good angel, since the world's frame stood,
That ever did in woman's shape appear.

Since you are then God's masterpiece, and so
His factor[3] for our loves, do as you do,
Make your return home gracious; and bestow
This life on that; so make one life of two.
For so God help me, I would not miss you there
For all the good which you can do me here.

To the Countess of Bedford

Madam,
You have refined me, and to worthiest things
(Virtue, art, beauty, fortune,) now I see
Rareness, or use, not nature value brings;[4]
And such, as they are circumstanced, they be.
Two ills can ne'er perplex us, sin to excuse;[5]
But of two good things, we may leave and choose.

Therefore at Court, which is not virtue's clime,
(Where a transcendent height, (as, lowness me)
Makes her not be, or not show)[6] all my rhyme
Your virtues challenge, which there rarest be;
For, as dark[7] texts need notes; there some must be
To usher virtue, and say, *This is she*.

So in the country is beauty;[8] to this place
You are the season (Madam) you the day,

9. A balm within all things which preserves life and cures wounds.
1. An immunizing medicine. (Mithridates, king of Pontus, is said to have immunized himself by taking poison in gradually increased doses.)
2. Medicine.
3. Agent.
4. An alchemical image: the countess has refined the poet's judgment so that he sees that value adheres according to rareness or usefulness, rather than any intrinsic quality.
5. God never forces us to choose between two evils, so there is no excuse for sin.
6. The countess's virtue is too high, and Donne's position too low, to be noticed at court.
7. Obscure.
8. As her virtue transcends the court, so her beauty gives value to the country.

'Tis but a grave of spices, till your face
Exhale them, and a thick close bud display.[9]
Widowed and reclused else, her sweets she enshrines
As China, when the sun at Brazil dines.

Out from your chariot, morning breaks at night,
And falsifies both computations so;[1]
Since a new world doth rise here from your light,
We your new creatures, by new reckonings go.
This shows that you from nature loathly stray,
That suffer not an artificial day.

In this you have made the Court the antipodes,[2]
And willed your delegate, the vulgar sun,[3]
To do profane autumnal offices,
Whilst here to you, we sacrificers run;
And whether priests, or organs, you we obey,
We sound your influence, and your dictates say.

Yet to that deity which dwells in you,
Your virtuous soul, I now not sacrifice;
These are petitions and not hymns; they sue
But that I may survey the edifice.[4]
In all religions as much care hath been
Of temples' frames, and beauty, as rites within.

As all which go to Rome, do not thereby
Esteem religions, and hold fast the best,
But serve discourse, and curiosity,
With that which doth religion but invest,
And shun the entangling labyrinths of schools,[5]
And make it wit, to think the wiser fools:

So in this pilgrimage I would behold
You as you're virtue's temple, not as she,
What walls of tender crystal her enfold,
What eyes, hands, bosom, her pure altars be;
And after this survey, oppose to all
Babblers of chapels, you the Escurial.[6]

Yet not as consecrate, but merely as fair,
On these I cast a lay and country eye.[7]

9. Her face, like the sun, opens the buds and causes them to exhale scent.
1. The countess's arrival in the country, even by night, brings day, falsifying both diurnal and calendrical calculations.
2. The court lacks the sun when the countess goes to Twickenham.
3. I.e., the common sun.
4. Sue for permission to visit the countess.
5. Disputatious schools of thought.
6. El Escorial, one of the largest religious centers in the world, was constructed outside Madrid by Philip II of Spain. By comparison, all other churches are mere chapels.
7. Donne also admires the countess's beauty from the perspective of an ordinary layman.

Of past and future stories, which are rare,
I find you all record, all prophecy.
Purge but the book of Fate,[8] that it admit
No sad nor guilty legends, you are it.

If good and lovely were not one, of both
You were the transcript, and original,
The elements, the parent, and the growth,
And every piece of you, is both their all:
So entire are all your deeds, and you, that you
Must do the same thing still; you cannot two.

But these[9] (as nice thin school divinity
Serves heresy to further or repress)
Taste of poetic rage, or flattery,
And need not, where all hearts one truth profess;
Oft from new proofs, and new phrase, new doubts grow,
As strange attire aliens the men we know.

Leaving then busy praise, and all appeal
To higher courts, sense's decree is true,
The mine, the magazine, the commonweal,
The story of beauty, in Twicknam is, and you.
Who hath seen one, would both; as, who had been
In Paradise, would seek the cherubin.

To Sir Edward Herbert at Juliers[1]

Man is a lump where all beasts kneaded be,
Wisdom makes him an ark where all agree;
The fool in whom these beasts do live at jar[2]
Is sport to others, and a theater;
Nor 'scapes he so, but is himself their prey;
All which was man in him is eat away,
And now his beasts on one another feed,
Yet couple in anger, and new monsters breed.
How happy is he which hath due place assigned
To his beasts and disafforested his mind!
Empaled[3] himself to keep them out, not in;
Can sow, and dares trust corn, where they have been;
Can use his horse, goat, wolf, and every beast,
And is not ass himself to all the rest.
Else, man not only is the herd of swine,
But he's those devils, too, which did incline

8. The Book of Life, in which are recorded all man's deeds.
9. I.e., the praises in this poem.
1. Lord Herbert of Cherbury, the brother of the poet George Herbert and himself a poet and philosopher, was with the English army at the seige of Juliers.
2. In discord.
3. Enclosed, fenced in.

Them to a headlong rage and made them worse:[4]
For man can add weight to heaven's heaviest curse.
As souls (they say) by our first touch take in
The poisonous tincture of Original Sin,
So to the punishments which God doth fling,
Our apprehension contributes the sting.
To us, as to His chickens, He doth cast
Hemlock, and we, as men, His hemlock taste;
We do infuse to what He meant for meat,
Corrosiveness, or intense cold or heat.[5]
For, God no such specific poison hath
As kills we know not how; His fiercest wrath
Hath no antipathy, but may be good
At least for physic, if not for our food.
Thus man, that might be his pleasure, is his rod,
And is his devil, that might be his God.
Since then our business is to rectify
Nature to what she was,[6] we're led awry
By them who man to us in little show;[7]
Greater than due, no form we can bestow
On him; for man into himself can draw
All; all his faith can swallow, or reason chaw.[8]
All that is filled, and all that which doth fill,
All the round world, to man is but a pill;
In all it works not, but it is in all
Poisonous, or purgative, or cordial,
For, knowledge kindles Calentures[9] in some,
And is to others icy *Opium*.
As brave as true is that profession than[1]
Which you do use to make: that you know man.
This makes it credible; you have dwelt upon
All worthy books, and now are such an one.
Actions are authors, and of those in you
Your friends find every day a mart[2] of new.

To Mr C. B.[3]

Thy friend, whom thy deserts to thee enchain,
Urged by this inexcusable[4] occasion,
Thee and the saint of his affection[5]

4. When Jesus cast out devils into a herd of swine, the herd ran violently down a cliff into the sea (Matthew 8).
5. What is harmless to some animals is poison to man, because of what man's own nature infuses or adds to the food.
6. Before the Fall.
7. Show or contend man to be merely a world in little, corresponding to the universe. In *Devotions upon Emergent Occasions*, Donne writes, "It is too little to call Man a little world; Except God, Man is a diminutive to nothing."
8. Chew.
9. A tropical disease, characterized by delirium; fever, burning passion.
1. Then.
2. Market, fair; specifically, the German booksellers' fair, held at Easter.
3. Probably Christopher Brooke, to whom Donne also addressed "The Storm" (see p. 84, n. 1).
4. Unavoidable.
5. The poet's beloved.

Leaving behind, doth of both wants complain;
And let the love I bear to both sustain
No blot nor maim by this division,
Strong is this love which ties our hearts in one,
And strong that love pursued with amorous pain;
But though besides thyself I leave behind
Heaven's liberal, and earth's thrice-fairer sun,[6]
Going to where stern winter aye doth won,
Yet, love's hot fires, which martyr my sad mind,
Do send forth scalding sighs, which have the art
To melt all ice, but that which walls her heart.

To E. of D. with Six Holy Sonnets[7]

See Sir, how as the sun's hot masculine flame
Begets strange creatures on Nile's dirty slime,[8]
In me, your fatherly yet lusty rhyme
(For, these songs are their fruits) have wrought the same;
But though the engendering force from whence they came
Be strong enough, and nature do admit
Seven to be born at once,[9] I send as yet
But six; they say, the seventh hath still some maim.
I choose your judgement, which the same degree
Doth with her sister, your invention, hold,
As fire these drossy rhymes to purify,
Or as elixir, to change them to gold;
You are that alchemist which always had
Wit, whose one spark could make good things of bad.

To Sir Henry Wotton, at his going Ambassador to Venice[1]

After those reverend papers,[2] whose soul is
Our good and great King's loved hand and feared name,
By which to you he derives[3] much of his,
And (how he may) makes you almost the same,

A taper of his torch, a copy writ
From his original, and a fair beam

6. Traveling north, the poet leaves behind the sun and also his lady, who is even "thrice-fairer."
7. There have been several conjectures as to the identity of E. of D. and also as to which sonnets are referred to by the title. Most likely, this poem is addressed to the earl of Dorset.
8. Refers to Pliny's theory that small creatures were generated spontaneously by the sun from the Nile's mud.
9. Pliny reported such multiple births in Egypt.
1. After being elevated to the peerage by King James I, Sir Henry Wotton sailed to Venice in July 1604 to take up his new post as British ambassador.
2. Wotton's commission.
3. Imparts, delegates.

Of the same warm, and dazzling sun, though it
  Must in another sphere his virtue stream:

After those learned papers which your hand
  Hath stored with notes of use and pleasure too,
From which rich treasury you may command
  Fit matter whether you will write or do:

After those loving papers, where friends send
  With glad grief, to your sea-ward steps, farewell,
Which thicken on you now, as prayers ascend
  To heaven in troops at a good man's passing bell:

Admit this honest paper,[4] and allow
  It such an audience as yourself would ask;
What you must say at Venice this means now,
  And hath for nature, what you have for task.

To swear much love, not to be changed before
  Honour alone will to your fortune fit;
Nor shall I then honour your fortune, more
  Than I have done your honour wanting it.

But 'tis an easier load (though both oppress)
  To want, than govern greatness, for we are
In that, our own and only business,
  In this, we must for others' vices care;

'Tis therefore well your spirits now are placed
  In their last furnace, in activity;
Which fits them (schools and Courts and wars o'erpast)
  To touch and test in any best degree.[5]

For me, (if there be such a thing as I)
  Fortune (if there be such a thing as she)
Spies that I bear so well her tyranny,
  That she thinks nothing else so fit for me;[6]

But though she part us, to hear my oft prayers
  For your increase, God is as near me here;
And to send you what I shall beg,[7] his stairs
  In length and ease are alike everywhere.

4. Receive this letter.
5. A reference to alchemical process: activity is the furnace that will refine Wotton's spirit until it becomes a touchstone capable of refining the spirits of everyone he meets.
6. Donne has grown "fit," or accustomed, to the lack of preferment caused by his injudicious marriage.
7. I.e., God's blessing.

An Anatomy of the World:[1] The First Anniversary

The entry into the work.

When that rich soul which to her heaven is gone,
Whom all they celebrate who know they have one,
(For who is sure he hath a soul, unless
It see, and judge, and follow worthiness,
And by deeds praise it? He who doth not this,
May lodge an in-mate soul, but 'tis not his);
When that queen ended here her progress[2] time,
And, as to her standing house,[3] to heaven did climb,
Where, loath to make the saints attend[4] her long,
She's now a part both of the choir and song,
This world in that great earthquake languished;
For in a common bath of tears it bled,
Which drew the strongest vital spirits[5] out:
But succored then with a perplexed doubt,
Whether the world did lose or gain in this,
(Because since now no other way there is
But goodness to see her, whom all would see,
All must endeavor to be good as she,)
This great consumption to a fever turned,
And so the world had fits; it joyed, it mourned.
And as men think that agues physic are,
And the ague being spent, give over care,
So thou, sick world, mistak'st thyself to be
Well, when, alas, thou art in a lethargy.
Her death did wound and tame thee then, and than[6]
Thou might'st have better spared the sun, or man;
That wound was deep, but 'tis more misery,
That thou hast lost thy sense and memory.
'Twas heavy[7] then to hear thy voice of moan,
But this is worse, that thou art speechless grown.
Thou hast forgot thy name, thou hadst; thou wast
Nothing but she, and her thou hast o'erpast.
For as a child kept from the font, until
A prince, expected long, come to fulfill
The ceremonies, thou unnamed had'st laid,
Had not her coming, thee her palace made:
Her name defined thee, gave thee form and frame,
And thou forget'st to celebrate thy name.

1. Following this title in the 1611 edition are the words, "Wherein, by occasion of the untimely death of Mistress Elizabeth Drury the frailty and decay of this whole world is represented." Elizabeth Drury was the younger daughter of Sir Robert Drury, patron and friend of Donne. Although she is the overt subject of this poem and of "The Progress of the Soul: The Second Anniversary," published in 1612, Donne himself told Ben Jonson "that he described the Idea of Woman and not as she was."
2. Visiting tour.
3. Permanent residence.
4. Wait for.
5. Elements in the blood that hold body and soul together.
6. Then.
7. Mournful.

Some months she hath been dead (but being dead,
Measures of times are all determined[8])
But long she hath been away, long, long, yet none
Offers to tell us who it is that's gone.
But as in states doubtful of future heirs,
When sickness without remedy impairs
The present prince, they're loath it should be said,
The prince doth languish, or the prince is dead:
So mankind feeling now a general thaw,
A strong example gone, equal to law,
The cement which did faithfully compact
And glue all virtues, now resolved, and slacked,
Thought it some blasphemy to say she was dead,
Or that our weakness was discovered
In that confession; therefore spoke no more
Than tongues, the soul being gone, the loss deplore.
But though it be too late to succor thee,
Sick world, yea, dead, yea putrefied, since she,
Thy intrinsic balm and thy preservative,
Can never be renewed, thou never live,
I (since no man can make thee live) will try
What we may gain by thy anatomy.[9]
Her death hath taught us dearly that thou art
Corrupt and mortal in thy purest part.
Let no man say, the world itself being dead,
'Tis labor lost to have discovered
The world's infirmities, since there is none
Alive to study this dissection;

What life the world hath still.

For there's a kind of world remaining still,
Though she which did inanimate and fill
The world be gone, yet in this last long night,
Her ghost doth walk; that is, a glimmering light.
A faint weak love of virtue and of good
Reflects from her on them which understood
Her worth; and though she have shut in all day,
The twilight of her memory doth stay;
Which, from the carcass of the old world, free,
Creates a new world; and new creatures be
Produced: the matter and the stuff of this,
Her virtue, and the form our practice is:
And though to be thus elemented, arm
These creatures, from home-born intrinsic harm,
(For all assumed[1] unto this dignity,
So many weedless Paradises be,
Which of themselves produce no venomous sin,
Except some foreign serpent bring it in)

8. Ended.
9. By dissecting and analyzing the dead body of the world.
1. Raised; elected.

Yet, because outward storms the strongest break,
And strength itself by confidence grows weak,
This new world may be safer, being told
The sicknesses of the world. The dangers and diseases of the old:
For with due temper men do then forgo,
Or covet things, when they their true worth know.
Impossibility of health. There is no health; physicians say that we,
At best, enjoy but a neutrality.
And can there be worse sickness than to know
That we are never well, nor can be so?
We are born ruinous:[2] poor mothers cry
That children come not right, nor orderly,
Except they headlong come and fall upon
An ominous precipitation.
How witty's ruin! how importunate
Upon mankind! It labored to frustrate
Even God's purpose; and made woman, sent
For man's relief, cause of his languishment.
They were to good ends, and they are so still,
But accessory, and principal in ill.
For that first marriage[3] was our funeral:
One woman at one blow then killed us all,
And singly, one by one, they kill us now.
We do delightfully ourselves allow
To that consumption; and profusely blind,
We kill ourselves to propagate our kind.[4]
And yet we do not that; we are not men:
There is not now that mankind which was then
When as the sun and man did seem to strive
Shortness of life. (Joint tenants of the world) who should survive;
When stag, and raven,[5] and the long-lived tree,
Compared with man, died in minority;
When, if a slow-paced star had stolen away
From the observer's marking, he might stay
Two or three hundred years to see it again,
And then make up his observation plain;
When, as the age was long, the size was great;
Man's growth confessed and recompensed the meat;[6]
So spacious and large, that every soul
Did a fair kingdom and large realm control;
And when the very stature, thus erect,
Did that soul a good way towards Heaven direct.
Where is this mankind now? who lives to age,
Fit to be made *Methusalah* his page?
Alas, we scarce live long enough to try

2. Falling into ruin.
3. Of Adam and Eve.
4. These lines play on a secondary meaning of "kill" or "die" in the seventeenth century: to consummate the sexual act; and they refer to the notion that each sexual act shortens life.
5. Thought to be exceedingly long-lived animals.
6. The food of early man was believed to have been much better than it later became.

Whether a new made clock run right, or lie.
Old grandsires talk of yesterday with sorrow,
And for our children we reserve tomorrow.
So short is life that every peasant strives,
In a torn house, or field, to have three lives.
And as in lasting, so in length is man

Smallness of stature.

Contracted to an inch, who was a span;[7]
For had a man at first in forests strayed,
Or shipwrecked in the sea, one would have laid
A wager that an elephant or whale
That met him would not hastily assail
A thing so equal to him: now, alas,
The fairies and the pigmies well may pass
As credible; mankind decays so soon,
We're scarce our fathers' shadows cast at noon.
Only death adds to our length: nor are we grown
In stature to be men, till we are none.
But this were light,[8] did our less volume hold
All the old text; or had we changed to gold
Their silver; or disposed into less glass
Spirits of virtue, which then scattered was.
But 'tis not so: we're not retired, but damped;[9]
And as our bodies, so our minds are cramped:
'Tis shrinking, not close weaving, that hath thus
In mind and body both bedwarfed us.
We seem ambitious, God's whole work to undo;
Of nothing He made us, and we strive, too,
To bring ourselves to nothing back; and we
Do what we can to do it so soon as He.
With new diseases on ourselves we war,
And with new physic,[1] a worse engine far.
Thus man, this world's vice-emperor, in whom
All faculties, all graces are at home;
And if in other creatures they appear,
They're but man's ministers, and legates there,
To work on their rebellions, and reduce
Them to civility, and to man's use.
This man, whom God did woo, and loath to attend[2]
Till man came up, did down to man decend,
This man, so great, that all that is, is his,
Oh what a trifle, and poor thing he is!
If man were anything, he's nothing now:
Help, or at least some time to waste, allow
To his other wants, yet when he did depart
With her whom we lament, he lost his heart.
She, of whom the ancients seemed to prophesy

7. Nine inches.
8. Of small consequence.
9. Not refined, but deadened.
1. Medicine.
2. Wait.

When they called virtues by the name of *she*;
She in whom virtue was so much refined
That for alloy unto so pure a mind
She took the weaker sex; she that could drive
The poisonous tincture, and the stain of *Eve*,
Out of her thoughts and deeds; and purify
All, by a true religious alchemy;
She, she is dead; she's dead: when thou knowest this,
Thou knowest how poor a trifling thing man is.
And learn'st thus much by our anatomy,
The heart being perished, no part can be free.
And that except thou feed (not banquet) on
The supernatural food, religion,
Thy better growth grows withered and scant;
Be more than man, or thou art less than an ant.
Then, as mankind, so is the world's whole frame
Quite out of joint, almost created lame:
For, before God had made up all the rest,
Corruption entered and depraved the best.
It seized the angels, and then first of all
The world did in her cradle take a fall,
And turned her brains, and took a general maim,
Wronging each joint of the universal frame.
The noblest part, man, felt it first; and than[3]
Both beasts and plants, curst in the curse of man.

Decay of nature in other parts.

So did the world from the first hour decay,
That evening was beginning of the day,
And now the springs and summers which we see,
Like sons of women after fifty be.
And new philosophy[4] calls all in doubt,
The element of fire is quite put out;[5]
The sun is lost, and the earth, and no man's wit
Can well direct him where to look for it.[6]
And freely men confess that this world's spent,
When in the planets and the firmament
They seek so many new; they see that this
Is crumbled out again to his atomies.
'Tis all in pieces, all coherence gone;
All just supply, and all relation:
Prince, subject, father, son, are things forgot,
For every man alone thinks he hath got
To be a phoenix, and that there can be
None of that kind, of which he is, but he.[7]
This is the world's condition now, and now
She that should all parts to reunion bow,

3. Then.
4. The new science, especially astronomy.
5. The new science proved false the notion that the earth was surrounded by fire.
6. The idea of a concentric universe with the earth at its center was disproved by the new astronomy. The following lines also refer to new discoveries of astronomers.
7. These lines refer to social and religious changes and a growing individualism.

She that had all magnetic force alone,
To draw, and fasten sundered parts in one;
She whom wise nature had invented then
When she observed that every sort of men
Did in their voyage in this world's sea stray,
And needed a new compass for their way;
She that was best, and first original
Of all fair copies, and the general
Steward to Fate; she whose rich eyes and breast
Gilt the West Indies, and perfumed the East;[8]
Whose having breathed in this world did bestow
Spice on those Isles, and bade them still smell so,
And that rich Indy which doth gold inter,
Is but as single money, coined from her:
She to whom this world must itself refer,
As suburbs, or the microcosm of her,
She, she is dead; she's dead: when thou know'st this,
Thou know'st how lame a cripple this world is.
And learn'st thus much by our anatomy,
That this world's general sickness doth not lie
In any humor,[9] or one certain part;
But, as thou sawest it rotten at the heart,
Thou seest a hectic fever hath got hold
Of the whole substance, not to be controlled,
And that thou hast but one way not to admit
The world's infection, to be none of it.
For the world's subtlest immaterial parts
Feel this consuming wound, and age's darts.
Disformity of parts. For the world's beauty is decayed or gone;
Beauty, that's color and proportion.
We think the heavens enjoy their spherical,
Their round proportion embracing all.
But yet their various and perplexed course,
Observed in divers ages, doth enforce
Men to find out so many eccentric parts,[1]
Such divers down-right lines, such overthwarts,[2]
As disproportion that pure form. It tears
The firmament in eight and forty shares,
And in those constellations there arise
New stars,[3] and old do vanish from our eyes:
As though heav'n suffered earthquakes, peace or war,
When new towns rise, and old demolished are.
They have impaled within a zodiac

8. The West Indies were reputed to be a source of precious metals, and the East Indies were a source of spices and perfumes.
9. There were four bodily fluids or "humors," according to medical theory of the time, which accounted for a man's temperament.
1. The eccentric circles of the old or Ptolemaic astronomy were efforts to reconcile differing and perplexing astronomical observations.
2. Vertical and horizontal lines.
3. Ptolemy had divided the stars into forty-eight constellations, which were thought to be unchanging—until the discovery of new stars in Donne's lifetime.

The free-born sun, and keep twelve signs awake
To watch his steps; the Goat and Crab control,
And fright him back, who else to either pole
(Did not these tropics fetter him) might run:
For his course is not round; nor can the sun
Perfect a circle, or maintain his way
One inch direct; but where he rose today
He comes no more, but with a cozening line,
Steals by that point, and so is serpentine:
And seeming weary with his reeling thus,
He means to sleep, being now fall'n nearer us.
So, of the stars which boast that they do run
In circle still, none ends where he begun.
All their proportion's lame, it sinks, it swells.
For of meridians and parallels,
Man hath weaved out a net and this net thrown
Upon the heavens, and now they are his own.
Loath to go up the hill, or labor thus
To go to heaven, we make heaven come to us.
We spur, we rein the stars, and in their race
They're diversely content to obey our pace.
But keeps the earth her round proportion still?[4]
Doth not a Tenerife,[5] or higher hill
Rise so high like a rock, that one might think
The floating moon would shipwreck there and sink?
Seas are so deep that whales being struck today
Perchance tomorrow, scarce at middle way
Of their wished journey's end, the bottom, die.
And men, to sound depths, so much line untie,
As one might justly think that there would rise
At end thereof, one of the antipodes:
If under all, a vault infernal be[6]
(Which sure is spacious, except that we
Invent another torment, that there must
Millions into a strait hot room be thrust),
Then solidness and roundness have no place.
Are these but warts and pock-holes in the face
Of the earth? Think so: but yet confess, in this
The world's proportion disfigured is,
Disorder in the world. That those two legs whereon it doth rely,
Reward and punishment are bent awry.
And, Oh, it can no more be questioned,
That beauty's best, proportion, is dead,
Since even grief itself, which now alone
Is left us, is without proportion.

4. Refers to the notion that the earth was created perfectly round.
5. The volcanic peak on Tenerife, the largest of the Canary Islands.
6. Medieval theologians contended that hell was located in the center of the earth.

She by whose lines proportion should be
Examined, measure of all symmetry,
Whom had that ancient seen, who thought souls made
Of harmony, he would at next[7] have said
That harmony was she, and thence infer
That souls were but resultances[8] from her,
And did from her into our bodies go,
As to our eyes, the forms from objects flow;
She, who if those great doctors truly said
That the ark[9] to man's proportions was made,
Had been a type for that, as that might be
A type of her in this, that contrary
Both elements and passions lived at peace
In her, who caused all civil war to cease;
She, after whom, what form soe'er we see,
Is discord, and rude incongruity;
She, she is dead, she's dead; when thou know'st this,
Thou know'st how ugly a monster this world is:
And learn'st thus much by our anatomy,
That here is nothing to enamor thee:
And that, not only faults in inward parts,
Corruptions in our brains, or in our hearts,
Poisoning the fountains, whence our actions spring,
Endanger us: but that if everything
Be not done fitly and in proportion,
To satisfy wise and good lookers-on
(Since most men be such as most think they be),
They're loathsome too, by this deformity.
For good, and well, must in our actions meet:
Wicked is not much worse than indiscreet.
But beauty's other second element,
Color, and luster now, is as near spent.
And had the world his just proportion,
Were it a ring still, yet the stone is gone.
As a compassionate turquoise which doth tell
By looking pale the wearer is not well,
As gold falls sick being stung with mercury,
All the world's parts of such complexion be.
When nature was most busy, the first week,
Swaddling the new-born earth, God seemed to like
That she should sport herself sometimes and play,
To mingle and vary colors every day.
And then, as though she could not make enow,[1]
Himself His various rainbow did allow.

7. Immediately.
8. Emanations.
9. Noah's ark, on which ordinarily hostile or "contrary" animals lived in peace.
1. Enough.

Sight is the noblest sense of any one,
Yet sight hath only color to feed on,
And color is decayed: summer's robe grows
Dusky, and like an oft dyed garment shows.
Our blushing red, which used in cheeks to spread,
Is inward sunk, and only our souls are red.[2]
Perchance the world might have recovered,
If she whom we lament had not been dead:
But she, in whom all white, and red, and blue
(Beauty's ingredients) voluntary grew,
As in an unvexed Paradise; from whom
Did all things verdure, and their luster come,
Whose composition was miraculous,
Being all color, all diaphanous
(For air and fire but thick gross bodies were,
And liveliest stones but drowsy and pale to her),
She, she is dead; she's dead: when thou know'st this,
Thou know'st how wan a ghost this our world is:
And learn'st thus much by our anatomy,
That it should more affright than pleasure thee.
And that, since all fair color then did sink,
'Tis now but wicked vanity to think

Weakness in the want of correspondence of heaven and earth.

To color vicious deeds with good pretence,
Or with bought colors to illude[3] men's sense.
Nor in aught more this world's decay appears,
Than that her influence the heav'n forbears,
Or that the elements do not feel this,
The father or the mother barren is.
The clouds conceive not rain, or do not pour
In the due birth time, down the balmy shower;
The air doth not motherly sit on the earth,
To hatch her seasons and give all things birth;
Springtimes were common cradles, but are tombs;
And false conceptions fill the general wombs.
The air shows such meteors[4] as none can see,
Not only what they mean, but what they be.
Earth such new worms[5] as would have troubled much
The Egyptian Mages[6] to have made more such.
What artist now dares boast that he can bring
Heaven hither, or constellate anything,
So as the influence of those stars may be
Imprisoned in an herb, or charm, or tree,
And do by touch all which those stars could do?
The art is lost, and correspondence too.
For heaven gives little, and the earth takes less,

2. The color of sin.
3. With cosmetics to mock, trick.
4. Any atmospheric phenomenon.
5. Serpents.
6. The Egyptian magicians who changed their rods into serpents (Exodus 7).

And man least knows their trade and purposes.
If this commerce 'twixt heaven and earth were not
Embarred, and all this traffic quite forgot,
She, for whose loss we have lamented thus,
Would work more fully and pow'rfully on us.
Since herbs and roots by dying lose not all,
But they, yea ashes too, are medicinal,
Death could not quench her virtue so, but that
It would be (if not followed) wondered at:
And all the world would be one dying swan,
To sing her funeral praise, and vanish than.[7]
But as some serpents' poison hurteth not,
Except it be from the live serpent shot,
So doth her virtue need her here, to fit
That unto us; she working more than it.
But she, in whom to such maturity
Virtue was grown, past growth, that it must die;
She, from whose influence all impressions came,
But, by receivers' impotencies, lame,
Who, though she could not transubstantiate
All states to gold, yet gilded every state,
So that some princes have some temperance,
Some counselers some purpose to advance
The common profit, and some people have
Some stay, no more than kings should give, to crave,
Some women have some taciturnity,
Some nunneries some grains of chastity;
She that did thus much, and much more could do,
But that our age was iron,[8] and rusty too,
She, she is dead; she's dead: when thou know'st this,
Thou know'st how dry a cinder this world is.
And learn'st thus much by our anatomy,
That 'tis in vain to dew or mollify
It with thy tears, or sweat, or blood: nothing
Is worth our travail, grief, or perishing,
But those rich joys, which did possess her heart,
Of which she's now partaker and a part.
Conclusion. But as in cutting up a man that's dead,
The body will not last out to have read
On every part, and therefore men direct
Their speech to parts that are of most effect,
So the world's carcass would not last if I
Were punctual[9] in this anatomy.
Nor smells it well to hearers, if one tell
Them their disease, who fain would think they're
well.

7. Then.
8. As contrasted with the earlier (and superior) golden and silver ages.
9. Dealing with a matter point by point; detailed.

Here therefore be the end: and, blessed maid,
Of whom is meant whatever hath been said,
Or shall be spoken well by any tongue,
Whose name refines coarse lines, and makes prose
song,
Accept this tribute, and his first year's rent,
Who till his dark short taper's end be spent,
As oft as thy feast sees this widowed earth,
Will yearly celebrate thy second birth,
That is, thy death. For though the soul of man
Be got when man is made, 'tis born but than[1]
When man doth die; our body's as the womb,
And, as a midwife, death directs it home.
And you, her creatures, whom she works upon,
And have your last and best concoction
From her example and her virtue, if you
In reverence to her, do think it due
That no one should her praises thus rehearse,
As matter fit for chronicle, not verse,
Vouchsafe to call to mind that God did make
A last, and lasting'st piece, a song.[2] He spake
To *Moses* to deliver unto all
That song, because He knew they would let fall
The Law, the Prophets, and the History,
But keep the song still in their memory.
Such an opinion (in due measure) made
Me this great office boldly to invade.
Nor could incomprehensibleness deter
Me from thus trying to emprison her,
Which when I saw that a strict grave could do,
I saw not why verse might not do so too.
Verse hath a middle nature: heaven keeps souls,
The grave keeps bodies, verse the fame enrols.

1611

1. Then.

2. The Song of Moses (Deuteronomy 32).

Divine Poems

LA CORONA[1]

1.

Deign at my hands this crown of prayer and praise,
Weaved in my low devout melancholy,
Thou which of good hast, yea, art treasury,
All changing unchanged Ancient of days;
But do not, with a vile crown of frail bays,
Reward my muse's white sincerity,
But what Thy thorny crown gained, that give me,
A crown of Glory, which doth flower always;
The ends crown our works, but Thou crown'st our ends,
For, at our end begins our endless rest;
This first last end,[2] now zealously possessed,
With a strong sober thirst, my soul attends.
'Tis time that heart and voice be lifted high,
Salvation to all that will is nigh.

2. Annunciation

Salvation to all that will is nigh;
That All, which always is All everywhere,
Which cannot sin, and yet all sins must bear,
Which cannot die, yet cannot choose but die,
Lo, faithful Virgin, yields Himself to lie
In prison, in thy womb; and though He there
Can take no sin, nor thou give, yet He'll wear,
Taken from thence, flesh, which death's force may try.
Ere by the spheres time was created, thou
Wast in His mind, who is thy Son, and Brother,
Whom thou conceiv'st, conceived; yea thou art now
Thy Maker's maker, and thy Father's mother;

1. These seven sonnets are probably the "Holy Hymns and Sonnets" that Donne sent to Mrs. Magdalen Herbert, along with an introductory sonnet addressed to her, in July 1607. "Corona" means both crown and wreath.

2. The Saviour. "I am * * * the first and the last" (Revelation 1.11).

Thou hast light in dark; and shutst in little room,
Immensity cloistered in thy dear womb.

3. Nativity

Immensity cloistered in thy dear womb,
Now leaves His well-beloved imprisonment,
There he hath made Himself to His intent
Weak enough, now into our world to come;
But oh, for thee, for Him, hath the Inn no room?
Yet lay Him in this stall, and from the Orient,
Stars, and wisemen will travel to prevent[3]
The effect of Herod's jealous general doom.[4]
Seest thou, my soul, with thy faith's eyes, how He
Which fills all place, yet none holds Him, doth lie?
Was not His pity towards thee wondrous high,
That would have need to be pitied by thee?
Kiss Him, and with Him into Egypt go,
With His kind mother, who partakes thy woe.

4. Temple

With His kind mother who partakes thy woe,
Joseph turn back; see where your child doth sit,
Blowing, yea blowing out those sparks of wit,
Which Himself on those Doctors did bestow;
The Word but lately could not speak, and lo
It suddenly speaks wonders; whence comes it,
That all which was, and all which should be writ,
A shallow seeming child should deeply know?
His Godhead was not soul to His manhood,
Nor had time mellowed Him to this ripeness,
But as for one which hath a long task, 'tis good,
With the Sun to begin his business,
He in His age's morning thus began
By miracles exceeding power of man.

5. Crucifying

By miracles exceeding power of man,
He faith in some, envy in some begat,
For, what weak spirits[5] admire, ambitious hate;
In both affections many to Him ran,

3. Precede.
4. I.e., the Massacre of the Innocents; "doom" means "judgment."
5. Cf. Matthew 5.3: "Blessed are the poor in spirit: for theirs is the kingdom of heaven."

But, oh! the worst are most, they will and can,
Alas, and do, unto the immaculate,
Whose creature Fate is, now prescribe a Fate,
Measuring self-life's infinity to a span,
Nay to an inch. Lo, where condemned He
Bears His own cross, with pain, yet by and by
When it bears Him, He must bear more and die.
Now Thou art lifted up, draw me to Thee,
And at Thy death giving such liberal dole,
Moist, with one drop of Thy blood, my dry soul.

6. Resurrection

Moist with one drop of Thy blood, my dry soul
Shall (though she now be in extreme degree
Too stony hard, and yet too fleshly) be
Freed by that drop from being starved, hard or foul,
And life, by this death abled, shall control
Death, whom Thy death slew; nor shall to me
Fear of first or last death bring misery,
If in Thy little book my name Thou enroll,
Flesh in that long sleep is not putrefied,
But made that there, of which, and for which 'twas;
Nor can by other means be glorified.
May then sin's sleep, and death's, soon from me pass,
That waked from both, I again risen may
Salute the last, and everlasting day.

7. Ascension

Salute the last and everlasting day,
Joy at the uprising of this Sun, and Son,
Ye whose just tears, or tribulation
Have purely washed, or burnt your drossy clay;
Behold the Highest, parting hence away,
Lightens the dark clouds, which He treads upon,
Nor doth He by ascending, show alone,
But first He, and He first enters the way.
O strong Ram, which hast battered heaven for me,
Mild Lamb, which with Thy blood hast marked the path;
Bright Torch, which shin'st, that I the way may see,
Oh, with Thine own blood quench Thine own just wrath,
And if Thy holy Spirit, my Muse did raise,
Deign at my hands this crown of prayer and praise.

HOLY SONNETS[1]

(1633)

1 (II)

As due by many titles I resign
Myself to Thee, O God, first I was made
By Thee, and for Thee, and when I was decayed
Thy blood bought that the which before was Thine;
I am Thy son, made with Thyself to shine,
Thy servant, whose pains thou hast still repaid,
Thy sheep, Thine Image, and, till I betrayed
Myself, a temple of Thy Spirit divine;
Why doth the devil then usurp on[2] me?
Why doth he steal, nay ravish that's Thy right?
Except Thou rise and for Thine own work fight,
Oh I shall soon despair, when I do see
That Thou lov'st mankind well, yet wilt not choose me,
And Satan hates me, yet is loath to lose me.

2 (IV)

Oh my black soul! now thou art summoned
By sickness, death's herald, and champion;
Thou art like a pilgrim, which abroad hath done
Treason, and durst not turn to whence he is fled,
Or like a thief, which till death's doom be read,
Wisheth himself delivered from prison;
But damned and haled to execution,
Wisheth that still he might be imprisoned.
Yet grace, if thou repent, thou canst not lack;
But who shall give thee that grace to begin?
Oh make thyself with holy mourning black,
And red with blushing, as thou art with sin;
Or wash thee in Christ's blood, which hath this might
That being red,[3] it dyes red souls to white.

1. The numbering (in Roman numerals) of the Holy Sonnets in the 1635 to 1669 editions and in Sir Herbert Grierson's edition has been retained in parentheses, for the critics have usually referred to the Holy Sonnets by means of these Roman numerals; but the sequence suggested by Helen Gardner in her edition of *The Divine Poems* has been adopted and her renumbering followed. If the sonnets are separate ejaculations, as Grierson thought, the order in which they are printed is not of consequence; however, if they in fact form a sequence, that fact will more readily become apparent by studying them in the proper sequence.

2. Claim unjustly; appropriate wrongfully.

3. With a pun on "read" (understood); red, as applied to man's soul, is the color of sin.

3 (VI)

This is my play's last scene, here heavens appoint
My pilgrimage's last mile; and my race,
Idly yet quickly run, hath this last pace,
My span's last inch, my minute's last point,
And gluttonous death will instantly unjoint
My body and soul, and I shall sleep a space,
But my ever-waking part shall see that face
Whose fear[4] already shakes my every joint:
Then, as my soul to heaven, her first seat, takes flight,
And earth-born body in the earth shall dwell,
So, fall my sins, that all may have their right,
To where they're bred, and would press me, to hell.
Impute me righteous, thus purged of evil,
For thus I leave the world, the flesh, the devil.

4 (VII)

At the round earth's imagined corners,[5] blow
Your trumpets, angels, and arise, arise
From death, you numberless infinities
Of souls, and to your scattered bodies go,
All whom the flood did, and fire shall o'erthrow,
All whom war, dearth, age, agues, tyrannies,
Despair, law, chance, hath slain, and you whose eyes
Shall behold God and never taste death's woe.[6]
But let them sleep, Lord, and me mourn a space,
For if above all these my sins abound,
'Tis late to ask abundance of Thy grace
When we are there; here on this lowly ground,
Teach me how to repent; for that's as good
As if Thou hadst sealed my pardon with Thy blood.

5 (IX)

If poisonous minerals, and if that tree
Whose fruit threw death on else immortal us,
If lecherous goats, if serpents envious
Cannot be damned, alas, why should I be?
Why should intent or reason, born in me,
Make sins, else equal, in me more heinous?
And mercy being easy, and glorious

4. The fear of whom.
5. "* * * I saw four angels standing on the four corners of the earth," (Revelation 7.1).
6. "* * * there be some standing here, which shall not taste of death, till they see the kingdom of God." (Luke 9.27; see also 1 Corinthians 15.51–57).

To God, in His stern wrath why threatens He?
But who am I that dare dispute with Thee?
O God, oh! of thine only worthy blood,
And my tears, make a heavenly Lethean[7] flood,
And drown in it my sin's black memory.
That Thou remember them,[8] some claim as debt,
I think it mercy, if Thou wilt forget.

6 (X)

Death be not proud, though some have called thee
Mighty and dreadful, for thou art not so;
For those whom thou think'st thou dost overthrow
Die not, poor death, nor yet canst thou kill me.
From rest and sleep, which but thy pictures be,
Much pleasure; then from thee much more must flow,
And soonest our best men with thee do go,
Rest of their bones, and soul's delivery.[9]
Thou art slave to fate, chance, kings, and desperate men,
And dost with poison, war, and sickness dwell;
And poppy or charms can make us sleep as well,
And better than thy stroke; why swell'st[1] thou then?
One short sleep past, we wake eternally,
And death shall be no more; death, thou shalt die.

7 (XI)

Spit in my face you Jews, and pierce my side,
Buffet, and scoff, scourge, and crucify me,
For I have sinned, and sinned, and only He
Who could do no iniquity hath died:
But by my death cannot be satisfied[2]
My sins, which pass the Jews' impiety:
They killed once an inglorious man, but I
Crucify him daily, being now glorified.
Oh let me then His strange love still admire:
Kings pardon, but He bore our punishment.
And Jacob came clothed in vile harsh attire
But to supplant, and with gainful intent,[3]
God clothed himself in vile man's flesh that so
He might be weak enough to suffer woe.

7. Inducing forgetfulness.
8. In order to pardon them.
9. Rescue, deliverance; also, the bringing forth or "birth" of the soul.
1. Puff up with pride.
2. Atoned for.
3. By disguising himself as his older brother, Jacob gained his father's blessing (Genesis 27).

8 (XII)

Why are we by all creatures waited on?
Why do the prodigal elements supply
Life and food to me, being more pure than I,
Simple, and further from corruption?[4]
Why brook'st thou, ignorant horse, subjection?
Why dost thou, bull and boar, so sillily
Dissemble weakness, and by one man's stroke die,
Whose whole kind you might swallow and feed upon?
Weaker I am, woe is me, and worse than you,
You have not sinned, nor need be timorous.
But wonder at a greater wonder, for to us
Created nature doth these things subdue,
But their Creator, whom sin nor nature tied,
For us, His creatures, and his foes, hath died.

9 (XIII)

What if this present were the world's last night?
Mark in my heart, O soul, where thou dost dwell,
The picture of Christ crucified, and tell
Whether that countenance can thee affright,
Tears in His eyes quench the amazing light,
Blood fills His frowns, which from His pierced head fell.
And can that tongue adjudge thee unto hell,
Which prayed forgiveness for His foes' fierce spite?
No, no; but as in my idolatry
I said to all my profane mistresses,
Beauty, of pity, foulness only is
A sign of rigor:[5] so I say to thee,
To wicked spirits are horrid shapes assigned,
This beauteous form assures a piteous mind.

10 (XIV)

Batter my heart, three-personed God; for You
As yet but knock, breathe, shine, and seek to mend;
That I may rise and stand, o'erthrow me, and bend
Your force, to break, blow, burn, and make me new.
I, like an usurped town, to another due,
Labor to admit You, but Oh, to no end!
Reason, Your viceroy in me, me should defend,

4. Being uncompounded, and thus less subject to decay.

5. Beauty is a sign of pity; ugliness is a sign of strictness, harshness.

But is captived, and proves weak or untrue.
Yet dearly I love You, and would be loved fain,
But am betrothed unto Your enemy:
Divorce me, untie or break that knot again,
Take me to You, imprison me, for I,
Except You enthrall me, never shall be free,
Nor ever chaste, except You ravish me.

11 (XV)

Wilt thou love God, as He thee? then digest,
My soul, this wholesome meditation,
How God the Spirit, by angels waited on
In heaven, doth make His Temple in thy breast.[6]
The Father, having begot a Son most blest,
And still begetting (for he ne'er begun),
Hath deigned to choose thee, by adoption,
Coheir to His glory and sabbath's endless rest;
And as a robbed man which by search doth find
His stol'n stuff sold must lose or buy it again,
The Son of glory came down, and was slain,
Us whom He had made, and Satan stol'n,[7] to unbind.
'Twas much that man was made like God before,
But that God should be made like man, much more.

12 (XVI)

Father, part of His double interest
Unto Thy kingdom, Thy Son gives to me;
His jointure in the knotty Trinity[8]
He keeps, and gives to me His death's conquest.
This Lamb, whose death with life the world hath blest,
Was from the world's beginning slain, and He
Hath made two wills,[9] which with the legacy
Of His and Thy kingdom do Thy Sons invest.
Yet such are those laws that men argue yet
Whether a man those statutes can fulfill;
None doth; but all-healing grace and Spirit
Revive again what law and letter kill.[1]
Thy law's abridgment and Thy last command
Is all but love;[2] oh let that last will stand!

6. "Know ye not that ye are the temple of God, and that the Spirit of God dwelleth in you?" (1 Corinthians 3.16).
7. And whom Satan had stolen.
8. "Jointure": "the holding of an estate by two or more persons in joint-tenancy"; "knotty": "hard to explain" as well as, perhaps, "closely or inextricably tied together."
9. I.e., the Old and New Testaments.
1. "* * * the letter killeth, but the spirit giveth life." (2 Corinthians 3.6).
2. "This is my commandment, That ye love one another, as I have loved you." (John 15.12).

HOLY SONNETS

(added in 1635)

1 (I)

Thou hast made me, and shall Thy work decay?
Repair me now, for now mine end doth haste,
I run to death, and death meets me as fast,
And all my pleasures are like yesterday;
I dare not move my dim eyes any way,
Despair behind and death before doth cast
Such terror, and my feebled flesh doth waste
By sin in it, which it towards hell doth weigh;
Only Thou art above, and when towards Thee
By Thy leave I can look, I rise again;
But our old subtle foe so tempteth me
That not one hour myself I can sustain;
Thy grace may wing me to prevent[1] his art,
And thou like adamant[2] draw mine iron heart.

1635

2 (V)

I am a little world made cunningly
Of elements and an angelic sprite,
But black sin hath betrayed to endless night
My world's both parts, and, oh, both parts must die.
You which beyond that heaven which was most high
Have found new spheres, and of new lands can write,[3]
Pour new seas in mine eyes, that so I might
Drown my world with my weeping earnestly,
Or wash it if it must be drowned no more.[4]
But oh it must be burnt![5] Alas, the fire
Of lust and envy have burnt it heretofore,
And made it fouler; let their flames retire,
And burn me, O Lord, with a fiery zeal
Of Thee and Thy house, which doth in eating heal.[6]

1635

1. Strengthen me to frustrate.
2. A magnet.
3. Donne addresses the astronomers and explorers who had made new discoveries.
4. After the Flood, God promised Noah that "neither shall there any more be a flood to destroy the earth." (Genesis 9.11).
5. By the fire that, it was believed, would end the world.
6. "For the zeal of thine house hath eaten me up;" (Psalms 69.9).

3 (III)

O might those sighs and tears return again
Into my breast and eyes, which I have spent,
That I might in this holy discontent
Mourn with some fruit, as I have mourned in vain;
In mine idolatry[7] what showers of rain
Mine eyes did waste! What griefs my heart did rent![8]
That sufferance[9] was my sin; now I repent;
'Cause I did suffer I must suffer pain.
The hydroptic[1] drunkard and night-scouting thief,
The itchy lecher and self-tickling proud[2]
Have the remembrance of past joys for relief
Of coming ills. To poor me is allowed
No ease; for long yet vehement grief hath been
The effect and cause, the punishment and sin.

1635

4 (VIII)

If faithful souls be alike glorified
As angels, then my father's soul doth see,
And adds this even to full felicity,
That valiantly I hell's wide mouth o'erstride.
But if our minds to these souls be descried
By circumstances and by signs that be
Apparent in us, not immediately,
How shall my mind's white truth by them be tried?[3]
They see idolatrous lovers weep and mourn,
And vile blasphemous conjurers to call
On Jesus' name, and pharisaical
Dissemblers feign devotion. Then turn,
O pensive soul, to God, for He knows best
Thy true grief, for He put it in my breast.

1635

7. I.e., when I worshiped a mistress.
8. Tear in pieces.
9. Suffering; also, indulgence in excessive grief.
1. Dropsical; insatiably thirsty.
2. Proud man.
3. Do the faithful souls who have departed this world know our minds by immediate intuition, as angels know, or do they know our minds by reasoning from outer circumstances and signs? If the latter, how can they distinguish between true grief and the falseness of idolatrous lovers, of conjurers (who try to effect a supernatural event by invoking a sacred name), and of pharisees (self-righteous hypocrites)?

HOLY SONNETS

(from the Westmoreland MS.)

1 (XVII)

Since she whom I loved hath paid her last debt
To nature, and to hers, and my good is dead,[1]
And her soul early into heaven ravished,
Wholly in heavenly things my mind is set.
Here the admiring her my mind did whet
To seek Thee, God; so streams do show the head;
But though I have found Thee, and Thou my thirst hast fed,
A holy thirsty dropsy melts me yet.
But why should I beg more love, when as Thou
Dost woo my soul, for hers off'ring all Thine:
And dost not only fear lest I allow
My love to saints and angels, things divine,
But in Thy tender jealousy dost doubt[2]
Lest the world, flesh, yea devil put Thee out.

W

2 (XVIII)

Show me, dear Christ, Thy spouse, so bright and clear.
What, is it she which on the other shore
Goes richly painted?[3] or which robbed and tore
Laments and mourns in Germany and here?[4]
Sleeps she a thousand, then peeps up one year?
Is she self-truth and errs? now new, now outwore?
Doth she, and did she, and shall she evermore
On one, on seven, or on no hill appear?[5]
Dwells she with us, or like adventuring knights
First travail[6] we to seek, and then make love?
Betray, kind husband, Thy spouse to our sights,
And let mine amorous soul court Thy mild Dove,
Who is most true and pleasing to Thee then
When she is embraced and open to most men.

W

1. Donne's wife, Anne More, who died on August 15, 1617, the fifth day after the birth of her twelfth child.
2. Fear.
3. The Church of Rome.
4. The Protestant church.
5. Mt. Moriah, where Solomon's temple stood; the seven hills of Rome; the Genevan church stood on no hill.
6. Labor; travel.

3 (XIX)

Oh, to vex me, contraries meet in one;
Inconstancy unnaturally hath begot
A constant habit; that when I would not
I change in vows and in devotion.
As humorous[7] is my contrition
As my profane love, and as soon forgot:
As riddlingly distempered, cold and hot;
As praying, as mute; as infinite, as none.
I durst not view heaven yesterday; and today
In prayers and flattering speeches I court God;
Tomorrow I quake with true fear of His rod.
So my devout fits come and go away
Like a fantastic ague:[8] save that here
Those are my best days when I shake with fear.

W

The Cross[1]

Since Christ embraced the Cross itself, dare I
His image, the image of his Cross deny?
Would I have profit by the sacrifice,
And dare the chosen altar to despise?
It bore all other sins, but is it fit
That it should bear the sin of scorning it?
Who from the picture would avert his eye,
How would he fly his pains, who there did die?
From me, no pulpit, nor misgrounded law,
Nor scandal taken, shall this Cross withdraw,[2]
It shall not, for it cannot; for, the loss
Of this Cross, were to me another cross;
Better were worse, for, no affliction,
No cross is so extreme, as to have none;
Who can blot out the Cross, which the instrument
Of God, dewed on me in the Sacrament?
Who can deny me power, and liberty
To stretch mine arms, and mine own cross to be?
Swim, and at every stroke, thou art thy cross,
The mast and yard[3] make one, where seas do toss.
Look down, thou spiest out crosses in small things;
Look up, thou seest birds raised on crossed wings;
All the globe's frame, and sphere's, is nothing else

7. Changeable.

8. A fever, with hot and cold spells and shaking or shivering.

1. This poem responds to the Puritan objection to the cross as a symbol of idolatry.

2. Puritans objected to and were scandalized by the cross as an icon; they sought laws against its use.

3. Yardarm.

But the meridians crossing parallels.
Material crosses then, good physic be,
And yet spiritual have chief dignity.
These for extracted chemic medicine[4] serve,
And cure much better, and as well preserve;
Then are you your own physic, or need none,
When stilled,[5] or purged by tribulation.
For when that Cross ungrudged, unto you sticks,
Then are you to yourself, a crucifix.
As perchance, carvers do not faces make,
But that away, which hid them there, do take:
Let crosses, so, take what hid Christ in thee,
And be his image, or not his, but he.
But, as oft alchemists do coiners[6] prove,
So may a self-despising, get self-love.
And then as worst surfeits, of best meats be,
So is pride, issued from humility,
For, 'tis no child, but monster; therefore cross
Your joy in crosses, else, 'tis double loss,
And cross thy senses, else, both they, and thou
Must perish soon, and to destruction bow.
For if the eye seek good objects, and will take
No cross from bad, we cannot 'scape a snake.
So with harsh, hard, sour, stinking, cross the rest,
Make them indifferent; call nothing best.
But most the eye needs crossing, that can roam,
And move; to the others[7] the objects must come home.
And cross thy heart: for that in man alone
Points downwards, and hath palpitation.
Cross those dejections, when it downward tends,
And when it to forbidden heights pretends.
And as the brain through bony walls doth vent
By sutures, which a cross's form present,
So when thy brain works, ere thou utter it,
Cross and correct concupiscence of wit.[8]
Be covetous of crosses, let none fall.
Cross no man else, but cross thyself in all.
Then doth the Cross of Christ work faithfully
Within our hearts, when we love harmlessly
That Cross's pictures much, and with more care
That Cross's children, which our crosses are.

4. According to Paracelsian medicine, the extracted essence of certain plants and minerals purged disease.
5. Distilled.
6. Forgers of coins.
7. The other four senses, which cannot choose among near and far objects.
8. Intellectual pride.

Resurrection, imperfect[9]

Sleep sleep old sun, thou canst not have repassed[1]
As yet, the wound thou took'st on Friday last;[2]
Sleep then, and rest; the world may bear thy stay,
A better sun rose before thee today,
Who, not content to enlighten all that dwell
On the earth's face, as thou, enlightened hell,
And made the dark fires languish in that vale,
As, at thy presence here, our fires grow pale.
Whose body having walked on earth, and now
Hasting to heaven, would, that he might allow
Himself unto all stations,[3] and fill all,
For these three days become a mineral;
He was all gold when he lay down, but rose
All tincture,[4] and doth not alone dispose
Leaden and iron wills to good, but is
Of power to make even sinful flesh like his.
Had one of those, whose credulous piety
Thought, that a soul one might discern and see
Go from a body, at this sepulchre been,
And, issuing from the sheet, this body seen,
He would have justly thought this body a soul,
If not of any man, yet of the whole.
Desunt caetera.[5]

Upon the Annunciation and Passion Falling upon One Day. 1608[6]

Tamely,[7] frail body, abstain today; today
My soul eats twice, Christ hither and away.
She sees Him man, so like God made in this,
That of them both a circle emblem is,
Whose first and last concur; this doubtful day
Of feast or fast, Christ came and went away;
She sees Him nothing twice at once, who's all;
She sees a Cedar[8] plant itself and fall,
Her Maker put to making, and the head
Of life at once not yet alive yet dead;
She sees at once the virgin mother stay
Reclused at home, public at Golgotha;[9]

9. The poem is incomplete.
1. Recovered from.
2. Refers to the eclipse that darkened the sky on Good Friday.
3. Every earthly state of being.
4. The essence of gold with alchemical power to transform base metals.
5. The rest is lacking.
6. In 1608, Good Friday occurred on March 25, the annual date of the feast of the Annunciation, when the Angel Gabriel announced to the Virgin Mary the Incarnation of Christ.
7. Submissively.
8. Symbol of God.
9. The place where Christ was crucified.

Sad and rejoiced she's seen at once, and seen
At almost fifty and at scarce fifteen;
At once a Son is promised her, and gone;
Gabriel gives Christ to her, He her to John;
Not fully a mother, she's in orbity,[1]
At once receiver and the legacy;
All this, and all between, this day hath shown,
The abridgment of Christ's story, which makes one
(As in plain maps, the furthest west is east)
Of the Angels' *Ave* and *Consummatum est*.[2]
How well the Church, God's court of faculties,
Deals in some times and seldom joining these!
As by the self-fixed Pole we never do
Direct our course, but the next star[3] thereto,
Which shows where the other is and which we say
(Because it strays not far) doth never stray,
So God by His Church, nearest to Him, we know
And stand firm, if we by her motion go;
His Spirit, as His fiery pillar doth
Lead, and His Church, as cloud, to one end both.
This Church, by letting these days join, hath shown
Death and conception in mankind is one:
Or 'twas in Him the same humility
That He would be a man and leave to be:
Or as creation He had made, as God,
With the last judgment but one period,
His imitating Spouse would join in one
Manhood's extremes: He shall come, He is gone:
Or as though one blood drop, which thence did fall,
Accepted, would have served, He yet shed all;
So though the least of His pains, deeds, or words,
Would busy a life, she all this day affords;
This treasure then, in gross, my soul uplay,
And in my life retail it every day.

Good Friday, 1613. Riding Westward

Let man's soul be a sphere, and then, in this,
The intelligence that moves, devotion is,[4]
And as the other spheres, by being grown
Subject to foreign motions,[5] lose their own,
And being by others hurried every day,
Scarce in a year their natural form obey,

1. Bereavement.
2. The first word of Gabriel to Mary was *Ave*, "Hail" (Luke 1.28), and Christ's last words before dying on the cross were "It is finished" (John 19.30).
3. The North Star, which guides sailors even though it is not the actual North Pole, the zenith of which is about one degree distant from the North Star.
4. Each sphere was thought to have a guiding intelligence; so devotion should be the guiding principle or form of a man's soul.
5. I.e., of other spheres.

Pleasure or business, so our souls admit
For their first mover, and are whirled by it.[6]
Hence is 't that I am carried towards the West
This day, when my soul's form bends toward the East.
There I should see a Sun, by rising, set,
And by that setting endless day beget;
But that Christ on this cross did rise and fall,
Sin had eternally benighted all.
Yet dare I almost be glad I do not see
That spectacle of too much weight for me.
Who sees God's face, that is self life, must die;[7]
What a death were it then to see God die?
It made His own lieutenant, Nature, shrink;
It made His footstool crack, and the sun wink.[8]
Could I behold those hands which span the poles,
And tune[9] all spheres at once, pierced with those holes?
Could I behold that endless height which is
Zenith to us, and our antipodes,[1]
Humbled below us? or that blood which is
The seat of all our souls, if not of His,
Make dirt of dust, or that flesh which was worn
By God, for His apparel, ragg'd and torn?
If on these things I durst not look, durst I
Upon his miserable mother cast mine eye,
Who was God's partner here, and furnished thus
Half of that sacrifice which ransomed us?
Though these things, as I ride, be from mine eye,
They're present yet unto my memory,
For that looks towards them; and Thou look'st towards me,
O Saviour, as Thou hang'st upon the tree;
I turn my back to Thee but to receive
Corrections, till Thy mercies bid Thee leave.[2]
O think me worth Thine anger, punish me,
Burn off my rusts and my deformity,
Restore Thine image so much, by Thy grace,
That Thou may'st know me, and I'll turn my face.

Upon the translation of the Psalms by Sir Philip Sidney, and the Countess of Pembroke his sister

Eternal God, (for whom who ever dare
Seek new expressions, do the circle square,[3]

6. Our souls are moved or influenced not by devotion to God but by the sphere of pleasure or business.

7. "* * * Thou canst not see my face: for there shall no man see me, and live." (Exodus 33.20).

8. The earth is God's footstool (Isaiah 56.1); an earthquake and an eclipse attended Christ's crucifixion (Matthew 27.51, 45).

9. Give motion and music to.

1. "Zenith": the point in the sky directly overhead; highest point or state. "Antipodes": those who dwell on the opposite side of the globe; exact opposite.

2. Stop.

3. To square a circle is to attempt the impossible: to enclose infinity in finite explanations.

And thrust into strait corners of poor wit
Thee, who art cornerless and infinite)
I would but bless thy name, not name thee now;
(And thy gifts are as infinite as thou:)
Fix we our praises therefore on this one,
That, as thy blessed spirit fell upon
These Psalms' first author in a cloven tongue;[4]
(For 'twas a double power by which he sung
The highest matter in the noblest form;)
So thou hast cleft that spirit, to perform
That work again, and shed it, here, upon
Two, by their bloods, and by thy spirit one;
A brother and a sister, made by thee
The organ, where thou art the harmony.
Two that make one John Baptist's holy voice,[5]
And who that psalm, *Now let the Isles rejoice*,[6]
Have both translated, and applied it too,
Both told us what, and taught us how to do.
They show us Islanders our joy, our King,
They tell us why, and teach us how to sing;
Make all this all, three choirs, heaven, earth, and spheres;
The first, heaven, hath a song, but no man hears,
The spheres have music, but they have no tongue,
Their harmony is rather danced than sung;
But our third choir, to which the first gives ear,
(For, angels learn by what the church does here)
This choir hath all. The organist is he[7]
Who hath tuned God and man, the organ we:
The songs are these, which heaven's high holy Muse
Whispered to David, David to the Jews:
And David's successors, in holy zeal,
In forms of joy and art do re-reveal
To us so sweetly and sincerely too,
That I must not rejoice as I would do
When I behold that these Psalms are become
So well attired abroad, so ill at home,[8]
So well in chambers, in thy church so ill,
As I can scarce call that reformed until
This be reformed; would a whole state present
A lesser gift than some one man hath sent?
And shall our church, unto our spouse and king,
More hoarse, more harsh than any other, sing?
For that we pray, we praise thy name for this,
Which, by this Moses and this Miriam, is

4. The psalms are attributed to David, whose tongue is "cloven" because he speaks both personally and for God, both verbally and musically.
5. John the Baptist was one "voice crying in the wilderness" preparing for the coming of Christ.
6. Psalm 97.
7. I.e., Christ.
8. The Sydneys' "well-attired" translations are "abroad" in that they are read privately, outside the church. The liturgical versions employed "at home," in the reformed church, are inferior by comparison.

Already done; and as those Psalms we call
(Though some have other authors) David's all:
So though some have, some may some psalms translate,
We thy Sydnean Psalms shall celebrate,
And, till we come the extemporal[9] song to sing,
(Learned the first hour, that we see the King,
Who hath translated these translators) may
These their sweet learned labours, all the way
Be as our tuning, that, when hence we part
We may fall in with them, and sing our part.

To Mr *Tilman* after he had taken orders

Thou, whose diviner soul hath caused thee now
To put thy hand unto the holy plough,
Making lay-scornings[1] of the Ministry,
Not an impediment, but victory;
What bringst thou home with thee? how is thy mind
Affected since the vintage?[2] Dost thou find
New thoughts and stirrings in thee? and as steel
Touched with a loadstone,[3] dost new motions feel?
Or, as a ship after much pain and care,
For iron and cloth brings home rich Indian ware,
Hast thou thus trafficked, but with far more gain
Of noble goods, and with less time and pain?
Thou art the same materials, as before,
Only the stamp is changed; but no more.
And as new crowned kings alter the face,
But not the money's substance; so hath grace
Changed only God's old image by creation,
To Christ's new stamp, at this thy coronation;
Or, as we paint angels with wings, because
They bear God's message, and proclaim his laws,
Since thou must do the like, and so must move,
Art thou new feathered with celestial love?
Dear, tell me where thy purchase[4] lies, and show
What thy advantage is above, below.[5]
But if thy gaining do surmount expression,
Why doth the foolish world scorn that profession,
Whose joys pass speech? Why do they think unfit
That gentry should join families with it?
As if their day were only to be spent
In dressing, mistressing and compliment;
Alas poor joys, but poorer men, whose trust

9. Spontaneous; also, beyond time.
1. Laymen's scorn for the clerical profession, referred to again in line 26.
2. Your maturity, and your taking religious orders.
3. A magnet.
4. Pursuit, gain (OED).
5. Show here below on earth what advantage you have gained in heaven, or what advantage you have gained above and below.

Seems richly placed in refined dust;
(For, such are clothes and beauty, which though gay,
Are, at the best but as sublimed clay.)
Let then the world thy calling disrespect,
But go thou on, and pity their neglect.
What function is so noble, as to be
Ambassador to God and destiny?
To open life, to give kingdoms to more
Than kings give dignities; to keep heaven's door?
Mary's prerogative was to bear Christ, so
'Tis preachers' to convey him, for they do
As angels out of clouds, from pulpits speak;
And bless the poor beneath, the lame, the weak.
If then the astronomers, whereas they spy
A new-found star, their optics[6] magnify,
How brave are those, who with their engines,[7] can
Bring man to heaven, and heaven again to man?
These are thy titles and pre-eminences,
In whom must meet God's graces, men's offences,
And so the heavens which beget all things here,
And the earth our mother, which these things doth bear,
Both these in thee, are in thy calling knit,
And make thee now a blessed hermaphrodite.[8]

A Hymn to Christ, at the Author's Last Going into Germany[9]

In what torn ship soever I embark,
That ship shall be my emblem of Thy ark;
What sea soever swallow me, that flood
Shall be to me an emblem of Thy blood;
Though Thou with clouds of anger do disguise
Thy face, yet through that mask I know those eyes,
Which, though they turn away sometimes,
They never will despise.

I sacrifice this island[1] unto Thee,
And all whom I loved there, and who loved me;
When I have put our seas 'twixt them and me,
Put thou Thy sea[2] betwixt my sins and Thee.
As the tree's sap doth seek the root below
In winter, in my winter now I go
Where none but Thee, the eternal root
Of true love, I may know.

6. Telescopes.
7. Devices.
8. One who combines opposites, such as those mentioned in preceding lines.
9. Donne traveled abroad in 1619–20 on a diplomatic mission.
1. England.
2. Christ's blood.

Nor Thou nor Thy religion dost control[3]
The amorousness of an harmonious soul,
But Thou would'st have that love Thyself; as Thou
Art jealous, Lord, so I am jealous now;
Thou lov'st not, till from loving more, Thou free
My soul: whoever gives, takes liberty:
O, if Thou car'st not whom I love,
Alas, Thou lov'st not me.

Seal then this bill of my divorce to all
On whom those fainter beams of love did fall;
Marry those loves which in youth scattered be
On fame, wit, hopes (false mistresses) to Thee.
Churches are best for prayer that have least light:
To see God only, I go out of sight;
And to 'scape stormy days, I choose
An everlasting night.

Hymn to God my God, in my Sickness[4]

Since I am coming to that holy room
Where, with Thy choir of saints forevermore,
I shall be made Thy Music, as I come
I tune the instrument here at the door,
And what I must do then, think now before.

Whilst my physicians by their love are grown
Cosmographers, and I their map,[5] who lie
Flat on this bed, that by them may be shown
That this is my South-west discovery
Per fretum febris, by these straits to die,[6]

I joy, that in these straits, I see my West;
For, though their current yield return to none,
What shall my West hurt me? As West and East[7]
In all flat maps (and I am one) are one,
So death doth touch the resurrection.

Is the Pacific Sea my home? Or are
The Eastern riches? Is *Jerusalem?*
Anyan,[8] and *Magellan*, and *Gibraltar*,

3. Censure.
4. Izaak Walton dated this poem eight days before Donne's death on March 31, 1631; but there is other evidence that the poem may have been written during Donne's illness in 1623.
5. It was believed that every man was a "little world."
6. As Magellan made a southwest journey through the Straits of Magellan (and later died in the Philippines), so Donne will make his last journey "through the straits of fever" (*per fretum febris*); south connotes heat, and west, where the sun sets, connotes death.
7. The east, where the sun (Son) rises, connotes life, rebirth.
8. Bering Strait.

All straits, and none but straits, are ways to them,
Whether where *Japhet* dwelt, or *Cham*, or *Shem*.[9]

We think that *Paradise* and *Calvary*,
Christ's Cross, and *Adam's* tree, stood in one place;
Look, Lord, and find both *Adams* met in me;
As the first *Adam's* sweat surrounds my face,
May the last *Adam's*[1] blood my soul embrace.

So, in His purple[2] wrapped, receive me, Lord,
By these His thorns give me His other crown;
And as to others' souls I preached Thy word,
Be this my text, my sermon to mine own,
Therefore that He may raise, the Lord throws down.

1635

A Hymn to God the Father[3]

Wilt Thou forgive that sin where I begun,
Which is my sin, though it were done before?
Wilt Thou forgive those sins through which I run,
And do them still, though still I do deplore?
When Thou hast done, Thou hast not done,
For I have more.

Wilt Thou forgive that sin by which I have won
Others to sin? and made my sin their door?
Wilt Thou forgive that sin which I did shun
A year or two, but wallowed in a score?
When Thou hast done, Thou hast not done,
For I have more.

I have a sin of fear, that when I have spun
My last thread, I shall perish on the shore;
Swear by Thyself that at my death Thy Sun
Shall shine as it shines now, and heretofore;
And, having done that, Thou hast done,
I have no more.

9. Noah's sons, whose descendants were said to inhabit, respectively, Europe, Africa, Asia.
1. Christ's.
2. Christ's blood; also, the color of royal robes and of the garments the soldiers put on Christ (Mark 15.17).
3. Donne puns on his name throughout this poem, which Walton says Donne wrote in his illness of 1623.

Textual Notes

With the following exceptions, the text of this edition is that of the 1633 edition:

> 1611 edition: *An Anatomy of the World: The First Anniversary.* (The marginal notes and the subtitle, *The First Anniversary,* are from the 1612 edition of *The Anniversaries.*)
> 1635 edition: "Farewell to Love," "A Lecture upon the Shadow," Elegies XI and XVI, Holy Sonnets I, III, V, VIII, "Upon the Translation of the Psalms . . . ," "To Mr. *Tilman* . . . ," "Hymn to God my God, in my Sickness."
> 1650 edition: "Sonnet. The Token" and "Self-Love."
> 1669 edition: Elegy XIX.
> Westmoreland manuscript: Elegy XX, Holy Sonnets XVII, XVIII, XIX.

This is to say that the text is based upon the first edition of each poem or, in the case of Elegy XX and the three Holy Sonnets not printed in the early editions, upon the Westmoreland manuscript. Some of the poems printed in 1633 did not have titles; the titles for these few poems, titles which have since become standard, are supplied by editions subsequent to 1633 and by manuscripts. In order to avoid needless clutter and to make these textual notes most useful for the student, I have excluded semi-substantive and inconsequential departures and variants and have noted only substantive departures from the authoritative text of any poem and some significant variants in other manuscripts and editions. Excepting the Westmoreland manuscript, manuscript information is obtained mainly from Sir Herbert Grierson's edition of *The Poems of John Donne,* though other editions have also been consulted. In the following notes, the editions, which almost invariably have some manuscript authority behind them, are indicated by the year of their publication; *1633–69* means all three of the editions of 1633, 1635, and 1669; *1635–69* means the editions of 1635 and 1669; *W* means the Westmoreland manuscripts; *MSS.* means "at least some manuscripts"; and *om.* means "omitted in."

An additional word about my principles for updating would seem to be in order. One of the major problems of updating the punctuation is to bring it more in accord with modern practice without losing any of the original meaning and without introducing any new, extraneous meanings. In general, this principle would make for a somewhat lighter punctuation than Donne's. There are, however, numerous complications. For example, the original 1633 punctuation of lines 2 and 3 of "The Sun Rising" permits two readings: line 3 as appositive to "thus"; and "thus" as an adverb modifying "call." Although the second reading is perhaps more likely, to select editorially only one reading over another seems, in this case and many similar ones, unwarranted and arbitrary. Wherever possible, the reader should be presented with the alternatives of the original and be allowed to choose for himself. Thus, although modern practice would call for the removal of the commas after "thus" and "windows," in this instance heavier punctuation (an additional comma after "curtains") is required rather than lighter. In the last stanza of "The Canonization," for another example, modern practice of punctuation calls for the addition of quotation marks, a parenthesis, and an exclamation point. But because such heavier punctuation is in this case interpretive, the Textual Notes indicate what the original punctuation was (as well as the variants "our love" and "your love"), so that a teacher or student may argue for another reading if he chooses. Updating spelling and capitalization is relatively easier, since the great majority of cases offers no difficulties or complications. Nothing significant is lost, for example, by dropping the extra final *e* from two words in the first line of "The Indifferent": "I can love both faire and browne." (Indeed, besides permitting some greater ease of reading, updating can prevent misreadings and save classroom time: one student, zealously looking for hidden meanings, asked, "Might Donne mean 'I can love both fairy and brownie?' ") On the other hand, in some instances, Donne's original spelling must stand: to change "thorough" to "through" would affect the meter; to correct "than" to "then" would sometimes spoil a rhyme; to alter "travail" to "travel" would obscure a pun; and so on. In such instances, I have printed the original and glossed the text where necessary. On the interesting and complicated matter of Donne's elision, these principles and practices have been followed: (1) the silent *e* has been inserted before the *d* in such worlds as "lov'd" and "wean'd." An accent over *ed* has not been inserted even when it seemed likely that the *ed* should be sounded as an extra syllable; instead, following the original text, I have left the decision to the reader. (2) Many of Donne's elisions are like modern practice; or can readily be made so: for example, "oe'r," "return'st," " 'gainst"; "she'is" becomes "she's," "I'am" becomes "I'm," and so on. (Sometimes Donne inserts the apostrophe before *st*, sometimes not: "hadst" and "had'st," for example, appear within four lines of each other.) (3) Donne often uses an apostrophe between two words (sometimes eliding a letter, sometimes not) when the first word ends with a vowel and the next begins with a vowel (or *h*). Since this is very unlike modern practice and the student may have some difficulty determining what is intended, the apostrophe has been deleted and the elided letter (if any) restored. With this note (and perhaps even left to his own devices) the student should be able to make most such elisions naturally. (4) For a very few of Donne's spellings it has been necessary to add an apostrophe, with results that are not strictly in accord with modern practice: although such words as "shouldst" and "leftst" remain as they are, "wandring" becomes "wand'ring," "swolne" becomes "swol'n," and so forth. If strict consistency has been sacrificed, it has been, I believe, for the sake of better, special purposes.

The Good-Morrow
14/ our world *MSS.*
21/ Love just alike in all, none of these loves can die. *1635–69.*

Song, "Go and catch * * *"
10/ borne *1633–35*; born *1669.*
11/ go see *1669.*

The Sun Rising
12/ Dost thou not think *1635–69.*
14/ long? *1635–69.*

Love's Usury
13/ sport *1633–35*; sport; *1669.*
15/ let not report *1635.*
20/ Thou covet most, *1633, 1669*; Thou covet most *1635*; Thou covet, most *MSS.*

The Canonization
15/ one man *1669.*
37–45/ *no quotations marks, parenthesis, exclamation point 1633–69.*
40/ extract *MSS.*; contract *1633–69.*
45/ our love, *1633–35*; your love. *1669.*

The Legacy
14/ did lie, *1633*; should lie, *1635*; should lie *1669.*

The Anniversary
3/ as these pass, *1635*; (which makes times, as they pass) *1669.*
22/ But now *1633–69*; But we *MSS.*

Twickenham Garden
15/ nor leave this garden, *1635–69*; nor yet leave loving, *1633.*
17/ groan *MSS.*; grow *1633–69.*

A Valediction: Of the Book
18/ Record. *1633, 1669*; Record, *1635.*
25/ Goths inundate us, *MSS*; the Goths invade us, *1633–35*; Goths invade us, *1669.*
53/ their nothing *1635*; there something *1633, 1669.*

Community
3/ there *1635–69*; these *1633.*

Love's Growth
9/ stuffs, paining soul, or sense, *1633*; stuffs, vexing soul, or sense, *1635*; stuffs vexing soul, or sense, *1669.*

Love's Exchange
36/ For, this *1633–69.*

Confined Love
11/ all night *1669.*
16/ with all *1635–69.*

The Dream
10/ do *MSS.*; act *1633–69.*
14/ (Thou lovest truth) but an Angel, *MSS.*

A Valediction: Of Weeping
8/ thou falls *MSS.*; thou falst *1633–69.*

Love's Alchemy
23–24/ *MSS.*; at their best, Sweetness, and wit they'are, but, *Mummy*, possessed. *1633–35*; *no punctuation* 1669.

The Curse
14–16/ Or may he for her virtue reverence
One that hates him only for impotence,
And equal Traitors be she and his sense. *1635–69.*

A Nocturnal upon St. Lucy's Day * * *
12/ every *1633*; a very *1635–69.*
16/ emptiness *1633–35*; emptiness, *1669.*

The Broken Heart
8/ flask *1633*; flash *1635–69.*

The Ecstasy
55/ forces, sense, *MSS.*; senses force *1633–69.*

Love's Diet
25/ reclaim'd *1635–69*; redeem'd *1633.*

The Will
36/ do *1635–69*; did *1633.*

The Funeral
17/ with me, *1635–69*; by me, *1633.*
24/ save *MSS.*; have *1633–69.*

The Blossom
24/ *MSS.*; need your heart? *1633–69.*

The Damp
24/ Naked *1635–69*; In that *1633.*

The Dissolution
12/ neere *1635–69*; ne'r *1633.*

The Prohibition
5/ *1635–69*; By being to me then that which thou wast; *1633*.
18/ neither's *MSS.*; ne'r their *1633–69*.
22/ Stage, *1635–69*; stay, *1633*.
23–24/ *MSS.*; Then lest thou thy * * * too. *1635*;
Lest thou thy love and hate and me undo
To let me live, oh love and hate me too. *1633*.

The Expiration
9/ Or, *1635–69*; Oh, *1633*.

The Paradox
20/ lie *MSS.*; die *1633–69*.

Farewell to Love
30/ Eager, *1635–69*.

A Lecture upon the Shadow
26/ first *MSS.*; short *1635–69*.

Sonnet. The Token
14/ desir'd because * * * best; *MSS.*; desired 'cause 'tis like thee best; *1650*; desired, 'cause 'tis like the best; *1669*.

Self-Love
6/ *MS.*; And cannot pleasure chose, *1650*, *1669*.
17/ *MSS.*; prays, *1650*, *1669*.

Elegy I
25/ that is *MSS.*
30/ We into some third place retired were *MSS.*
34/ Mayor *1669*; Major *1633–35*.

Elegy IV
7–8/ *1635–69*; *om*. *1633*.
21/ And to try *1635–69*; To try *1633*.

Elegy V
1/ picture, . . . farewell; *1633*.
6/ Perchance *MSS.*
8/ With care's rash, sudden storms, being o'erspread, *1633*; With care's rash, cruel sudden storms o'erprest, *MSS.* With care's harsh sudden hoariness o-erspread, *W*, *MSS.*
16/ like and love less, *MSS.*, *W*.
19/ nourish it: *MSS.*

Elegy VII
7/ cast *MSS.*
10/ their device in being set *MSS.*
12/ meet errands *MSS.*

Elegy VIII
5/ brow *MSS.*
6/ carcanets. *MSS.*, *W*; coronets. *1633–69*.
13/ vile lying stones *1635*, *MSS.*
14/ they hang *1635*, *MSS.*; it hangs *1633*.
34/ thy gouty hand. *1635–69*, *MSS.*, *W*; her gouty hand; *1633*.
37/ dirt *1635–69*; part *1633*.
46/ feared *MSS.*
48/ when *1635–69*; where *1633*.
51/ such *MSS.*, *W*; nice *1633*.

Elegy IX
3/ *1633*; your love *1635*.
8/ she's *1635–69*, *MSS.*; they're *1633*.
50/ ebb on *1635–69*, *MSS.*; ebb out *1633*.

Elegy XI
11/ fault *MSS.*; taint *MSS.*; way *1635–69*.
24/ *MSS.*; their Country's natural *1669*, *MSS.*
40/ *1669*; ruin'd: ragged and decay'd *1635*.
60/ schemes *MSS.*; scenes *1635–69*.

Elegy XVI
28/ mind's *MSS.*; mind *1635–69*.
37/ *1635*; Will quickly know thee, and know thee, and alas *W*.

Elegy XIX
5/ glistering *MSS.*; glittering *1669*.
10/ 'tis your *MSS.*; it is *1669*.
14/ from *MSS.*; through *1669*.
16/ on you *MSS.*; on your head *1669*.
17/ safely *MSS.*; softly *1669*.
20/ Received by *MSS.*; Revealed to *1669*.
28/ *MSS.*; My Kingdom's safest, *1669*.
30/ *MSS.*; How am I blest in thus *1669*.
38/ covet theirs, *MSS.*; court that, *1669*.
41/ *MSS.*; Themselves are only mystic books, which we, *1669*.
44/ a *MSS.*; thy *1669*.
46/ *MSS.*; There is no penance due to innocence: *1669*.

Elegy XX
7/ most *MSS.*
19/ that *MSS.*; the *W*, *MSS.*

Epithalamion Made at Lincoln's Inn
23/ *MSS.*; fair and rich, in *1633–69*.
26/ *W*; Some of these Senators wealths deep oceans, *1633*, *MSS.*; Sons of those Senators, *1635–69*, *MSS.*
46/ *W*; Always *1633–69*.
59/ run *MSS.*; come *1633*.

Satire I
1/ changeling *1635–69*, *MSS.*, *W*.
5/ conduits, . . . divines; *1650*, *MSS.*; conduits; . . . divines, *1633*.
19/ Nor *MSS.*, *W*. Not *1633–69*.
45/ best *MSS.*
58/ Infanta *MSS.*; Infant *1633*.
62/ supple-witted *MSS.*
70/ his *1635–69*, *MSS.*; high *1633*.
81–82/ *om*. *1633*.
101/ 'Why? he hath travelled.' 'Long?' 'No, but to me *MSS.*; 'Why he hath travelled long?' *1633*.
108/ lechery *MSS.*; liberty *1633*.

Satire II
Title/ Law Satire *MS.*; Against Poets and Lawyers *MS.*

6/ As I'm afraid brings *MSS.*; dearths *MSS.*
8/ It riddlingly *MSS.*
17/ rhymes *MSS.*
22/ Boys singing at doors *MSS.*
32/ dildoes *MSS.*; —; *1633.*
33/ *1633* replaces Litany with a dash.
34/ sins all Kinds *MSS.*
44/ a scarce *MSS.*, *W.*
69–70/ first printed in Chambers; omitted (noted by dashes) in *1633.*
74–75/ *MSS.*; omitted in *1633.*
77/ our land *MSS.*
79/ gluttony *MSS.*
84/ Relique-like *MSS.*; Reliquely *1633–69.*
87/ parchments *MSS.*, *W*; parchment *1633–69.*
105/ . . . alms? In great halls *MSS.*; . . . alms? great halls *1633*, *MSS.*

Satire III
33–34/ foe, the foul devil h'is, whom *1633*; foes the foul devil, he, whom *1635*; foes: The foul devil (he, whom *1669*; Know thy foes; the foul Devil whom *MSS.*
85/ do. *1635–69*; do *1633.*
90/ here *MSS.*; *om.* *1633–69.*

Satire IV
2/ but yet I *1635–69*, *MSS.*
8/ Glare *1635–69*, *MSS.*
9/ To a Mass *MSS.*; To Mass *1633–69*, *MSS.*
16/ at Court *MSS.*, *W*; in Court *1633–69.*
38/ no language *MSS.*
59/ Panurge *1635*; Panirge *1633*, *MSS.*
62/ wonders *1635–69*, *MSS.*; words *1633*, *MSS.*
67/ loneness *1635–69*, *MSS.*; lonliness *1633*, *MSS.*
83/ Mine? *1635*, *MSS.*; Fine, *1633.*
90/ dress. *1635*, *MSS.*
98/ trash he knows; he knows *MSS.*; trash; he knows; he knows *1633.*
106/ At blow-point or span-counter *MSS.*, *W*; They pay *MSS.*; shall pay *1633–69.*
117/ his *MSS.* talk: in vain; for *MSS.*; talk in vain: for *1633.*
134–36/ *om.* and represented by dashes in *1633.*
141/ my redemption *MSS.*
156/ piteous *MSS.*
164/ the huffing braggart, *1669*, *MSS.*; huffing, braggart, *1633.*
171/ our Court here *MSS.*, *W.*
216/ Topcliffe would have ravished him quite away *MSS.*
226/ still *1635–69*, *MSS.*; yet still *1633*, *MSS.*
230/ men which from *MSS.*; men from *1633–69.*
236/ Living, barrels *1669*; Living barrels *1633.*
238/ Wit *1669*; Wits *1633.*

Satire V
Title/ Satire V. *1633–69*, *MSS.*; Satire 5, Of the misery of the poor suitors at Court *MS.*
12/ implies *1635–69*; employs *1633*, *MSS.*
61/ Courts, *1635–69*, *MSS.*; Court, *1633*, *MSS.*
68/ ask *1669*, *MSS.*; lack *1633–35*, *MSS.*
72/ and but tells us who *MSS.*; and tells who *1633–69*, *MSS.*
80/ erst *om.* *1633.*

The Storm
38/ I, and the Sun, *1633–69.*

The Calm
38/ Pinnaces *1635*; venices *1633.*

To Sir Henry Wotton: "Sir, more than kisses"
11/ even *MSS.*; raging *1633.*
12/ poles *MSS.*; pole *1633.*
23/ there were *MSS.*; they were *1633.*
27/ mere *MSS.*
44/ for themselves *MSS.*; in themselves *1633–69.*
47/ Be then *MSS.*
52/ gaol *1669*, *MSS.*; goal *1633.*

To Mr Roland Woodward
Title/ A Letter of Dr Donne to one that desired some of his papers *MSS.*
3/ holiness *MSS.*
10/ to use it, *MSS.*
25/ soul *MSS.*, *W.*
31/ farmers *1635–69*, *MSS.*; termers *1633.*

To Sir Henry Wotton: "Here's no more news"
2/ Calis *1633–69.*
14/ wishing prayers, *1633*; wishes, prayers, *1635*; wishing, prayers, *1669.*

To the Countess of Bedford: "Reason is our soul's left hand"
16/ voice *1635–69*; faith *1633.*
19/ *1633*; high to sense deep-rooted stick, *1635*; high do seem, deep-rooted stick, *1669.*
36/ This *1635–69*; Thy *1633.*

To the Countess of Bedford: "You have refined me"
8/ (Where *1633*; Where *1635–69.*
9/ show *1635–69*; show: *1633.*
48/ Builders *1669.*
50/ eye; *1635–69*; eye, *1633.*
52/ all *MSS.*; and *1633.*
57/ growth, *1669*; growth *1633.*
66/ alters *1635*, *MSS.*

To Sir Edward Herbert * * *
35/ show; *1669*; show, *1633–35.*
38/ All, All * * * chaw. *1633*; All: All * * * chaw, *1635*; All; All * * * chaw, *1669.*

To Mr C. B.
2/ inexcusable *MSS.*; unexcusable *1633–69.*
9/ myself *1669.*
10/ thrice-fairer *MSS.*, *W*; thrice-fair *1633–69*, *MSS.*
11/ starved *1635–69*, *MSS.*
13/ send out *MSS.*

To Sir Henry Wotton, at his going Ambassador to Venice
Title/ *1669, MSS.*; To Sir H. W. etc. *1633*.
10/ pleasure *1635–69, MSS.*; pleasures *1633*.

An Anatomy of the World
2/ Who all do celebrate *1633*.
129/ try *1633*; try; *1611–12*.
130/ new *1611*, *1612 errata*; true *1612*, *1633*.
153/ close weaving *1633*; close-weaning *1611–12*.
217/ there *1612 errata*; then *1611*, *1612*, *1633*.
259/ there *1612 errata*; then *1611*, *1612*, *1633*.
262/ towns *1612 errata*; towers *1611*, *1612*, *1633*.
474/ fame *1612 errata*, *1633*; same *1611*, *1612*.

La Corona
3. Nativity
8/ *MSS.*, *1669*; effects *1633–35*.

6. Resurrection
8/ little *1633*; life *1635–69*.
12/ *MSS.*; death *1633–69*.

Holy Sonnets
3 (VI)
4/ last point, *MSS.*; latest point, *1633–69*.
7/ *1633*; Or presently, I know not, see that Face, *MSS.*

4 (VII)
6/ dearth *W*; death *1633–69, MSS.*

8 (XII)
1/ am I *W*.

9 (XIII)
4/ that *MSS.*; his *1633–69*.
14/ assures *MSS.*; assumes *1633–69*.

12 (XVI)
9/ those *MSS.*; these *1633–69*; thy *MSS.*
11/ None doth, but thy * * * Spirit, *1633*;
None doth; but thy * * * Spirit *1635–69*;
None doth; but all-healing * * * Spirit *MSS.*
14/ that *MSS.*; this *1633–69*; thy *MSS.*

2 (V)
6/ lands *MSS.*; land *1635–69*.
11/ have *MSS.*; *om.* *1635–69*.

3 (III)
7/ sin, now I repent; *W*; sin I now repent, *1635*.

4 (VIII)
7/ us, *W*; us *1635–69*.
14/ true *W*; *om.* *1635–69*. in *W*; into *1635–69*.

1 (XVII)
10/ Dost woe my soul for hers; *W*.

The Cross
Title/ Of the Cross *MSS.*
20/ When *MSS.*
44/ corruption *MSS.*
52/ Points *MSS.*; Pants *1633–69*, *MSS.*
53/ defections *MSS.*; detorsions *1635–69*, *MSS.*
61/ fruitfully *MSS.*
63/ That *MSS.*; The *1633–69*.

Upon the Annunciation and Passion * * *
10/ and dead; *1635–69*.
37/ had *MSS.*; hath *1633*.

Good Friday, 1613 * * *
22/ tune *1633–69*; turn *MSS.*
24/ and *1633–69*; and to' *MSS.*
27/ Make *MSS.*; Made *1633–69*.

Upon the Translation of the Psalms . . .
46/ this Moses *MSS.*; thy Moses *1635*.
53/ these *MSS.*; those *1635*.

To Mr *Tilman* After He Had Taken Orders
6/ in *MSS.*
13/ Art thou . . . more? *MSS.*
18/ coronation? *MSS.*
29/ Would they think it well if the day were spent *MSS.*
32/ refined *MSS.*; sublimed *1635*.
34/ as *MSS.*; of *1635*.
47/ engines *MSS.*; engine *1635*.

A Hymn to God the Father
2/ is *MSS.*; was *1633*.
3/ those sins *MSS.*; that sin; *1633*.
4/ do them *MSS.*; do run *1633*.
15/ Swear * * * Sun *MSS.*; But swear * * * son *1633*.
16/ it *MSS.*; he *1633*.
18/ have *MSS.*; fear *1633*.

CRITICISM

Donne and Metaphysical Poetry

BEN JONSON

[Conversations on Donne]†

That Done's Anniversarie was profane and full of blasphemies: that he told Mr. Done, if it had been written of the Virgin Marie it had been something; to which he answered that he described the Idea of a Woman, and not as she was. That Done, for not keeping of accent, deserved hanging.* * *

He esteemeth John Done the first poet in the world in some things: his verses of the Lost Chaine he heth by heart; and that passage of the Calme, *That dust and feathers doe not stirr, all was so quiet*. Affirmeth Done to have written all his best pieces ere he was 25 years old.* * *

Done's grandfather, on the mother side, was Heywood the Epigramatist. That Done himself, for not being understood, would perish.* * *

THOMAS CAREW

An Elegie upon the Death of the Deane of Pauls, Dr. John Donne††

Can we not force from widdowed Poetry,
Now thou art dead (Great DONNE) one Elegie
To crowne thy Hearse? Why yet dare we not trust
Though with unkneaded dowe-bak't[1] prose thy dust,
Such as the uncisor'd[2] Churchman from the flower
Of fading Rhetorique, short liv'd as his houre,
Dry as the sand that measures it, should lay
Upon thy Ashes, on the funerall day?
Have we no voice, no tune? Did'st thou dispense

† In 1618–19 Jonson journeyed to Scotland and stayed with William Drummond of Hawthornden, who recorded Jonson's opinions in a short book, *Ben Jonson's Conversations with Drummond of Hawthornden* (published 1833), from which these extracts were taken.

†† This elegy was first printed in *Poems* (1633).

1. Dough-baked; i.e., inadequately baked [*Editor*].
2. Unshorn, as a sign of mourning [*Editor*].

Through all our language, both the words and sense?
'Tis a sad truth; The Pulpit may her plaine,
And sober Christian precepts still retaine,
Doctrines it may, and wholesome Uses frame,
Grave Homilies, and Lectures, But the flame
Of thy brave Soule, that shot such heat and light,
As burnt our earth, and made our darknesse bright,
Committed holy Rapes upon our Will,
Did through the eye the melting heart distill;
And the deepe knowledge of darke truths so teach,
As sense might judge, what phansie could not reach;
Must be desir'd[3] for ever. So the fire,
That fills with spirit and heat the Delphique quire,[4]
Which kindled first by the Promethean[5] breath,
Glow'd here a while, lies quench't now in thy death;
The Muses garden with Pedantique weedes
O'rspred, was purg'd by thee; The lazie seeds
Of servile imitation throwne away;
And fresh invention planted, Thou didst pay
The debts of our penurious bankrupt age;
Licentious thefts, that make poëtique rage
A Mimique fury, when our soules must bee
Possest, or with Anacreons Extasie,
Or Pindars,[6] not their owne; The subtle cheat
Of slie Exchanges, and the jugling feat
Of two-edg'd words, or whatsoever wrong
By ours was done the Greeke, or Latine tongue,
Thou hast redeem'd, and open'd Us a Mine
Of rich and pregnant phansie, drawne a line
Of masculine expression, which had good
Old Orpheus[7] seene, Or all the ancient Brood
Our superstitious fooles admire, and hold
Their lead more precious, then thy burnish't Gold,
Thou hadst beene their Exchequer, and no more
They each in others dust, had rak'd for Ore.
Thou shalt yield no precedence, but of time,
And the blinde fate of language, whose tun'd chime
More charmes the outward sense; Yet thou maist claime
From so great disadvantage greater fame,
Since to the awe of thy imperious wit
Our stubborne language bends, made only fit
With her tough-thick-rib'd hoopes to gird about
Thy Giant phansie, which had prov'd too stout
For their soft melting Phrases. As in time

3. Longed for; the subject of "must be desired" is "flame" (line 14) [*Editor*].

4. The choir of Apollo, god of poetry, whose temple is located in Delphi. [*Editor*].

5. Prometheus was the Titan who took fire from heaven and gave it to man for his use [*Editor*].

6. Anacreon and Pindar were ancient Greek poets [*Editor*].

7. A Thracian singer and lyre-player, son of Apollo [*Editor*].

They had the start, so did they cull the prime
Buds of invention many a hundred yeare,
And left the rifled fields, besides the feare
To touch their Harvest, yet from those bare lands
Of what is purely thine, thy only hands
(And that thy smallest worke) have gleaned more
Then all those times, and tongues could reape before;
But thou are gone, and thy strict lawes will be
Too hard for Libertines in Poetrie.
They will repeale the goodly exil'd traine
Of gods and goddesses, which in thy just raigne
Were banish'd nobler Poems, now, with these
The silenc'd tales o'th' Metamorphoses[8]
Shall stuffe their lines, and swell the windy Page,
Till Verse refin'd by thee, in this last Age
Turne ballad rime, Or those old Idolls bee
Ador'd againe, with new apostasie;
Oh, pardon mee, that breake with untun'd verse
The reverend silence that attends thy herse,
Whose awfull solemne murmures were to thee
More then these faint lines, A loud Elegie,
That did proclaime in a dumbe eloquence
The death of all the Arts, whose influence
Growne feeble, in these panting numbers lies
Gasping short winded Accents, and so dies:
So doth the swiftly turning wheele not stand
In th'instant we withdraw the moving hand,
But some small time maintaine a faint weake course
By vertue of the first impulsive force:
And so whil'st I cast on thy funerall pile
Thy crowne of Bayes, Oh, let it crack a while,
And spit disdaine, till the devouring flashes
Suck all the moysture up, then turne to ashes.
I will not draw the envy to engrosse
All thy perfections, or weepe all our losse;
Those are too numerous for an Elegie,
And this too great, to be express'd by mee.
Though every pen should share a distinct part,
Yet art thou Theme enough to tyre all Art;
Let others carve the rest, it shall suffice
I on thy Tombe this Epitaph incise.

Here lies a King, that rul'd as hee thought fit
The universall Monarchy of wit;
Here lie two Flamens,[9] and both those, the best,
Apollo's first, at last, the true Gods Priest.

8. Tales by Ovid, ancient Roman poet [*Editor*].

9. Priests [*Editor*].

JOHN DRYDEN

[Donne "Affects the Metaphysics"] †

You [the Earl of Dorset] equal Donne in the variety, multiplicity, and choice of thoughts; you excel him in the manner and the words. I read you both with the same admiration, but not with the same delight. He affects the metaphysics, not only in his satires, but in his amorous verses, where nature only should reign; and perplexes the minds of the fair sex with nice speculations of philosophy, when he should engage their hearts, and entertain them with the softnesses of love.

* * *

Would not Donne's *Satires*, which abound with so much wit, appear more charming, if he had taken care of his words, and of his numbers? But he followed Horace so very close, that of necessity he must fall with him; and I may safely say it of this present age, that if we are not so great wits as Donne, yet certainly we are better poets.

SAMUEL JOHNSON

["The Metaphysical Poets"] ††

Cowley, like other poets who have written with narrow views, and, instead of tracing intellectual pleasures in the mind of man, paid their court to temporary prejudices, has been at one time too much praised, and too much neglected at another.

Wit, like all other things subject by their nature to the choice of man, has its changes and fashions, and at different times takes different forms. About the beginning of the seventeenth century appeared a race of writers that may be termed the *metaphysical poets*, of whom, in a criticism on the works of Cowley, it is not improper to give some account.

The metaphysical poets were men of learning, and to show their learning was their whole endeavour; but, unluckily resolving to show it in rhyme, instead of writing poetry they only wrote verses, and very often such verses as stood the trial of the finger better than of the ear; for the modulation was so imperfect, that they were only found to be verses by counting the syllables.

If the father of criticism has rightly denominated poetry *τέχνη μιμητική, an imitative art*, these writers will, without great wrong, lose

† From *A Discourse Concerning the Original and Progress of Satire* (1693).

†† From *Lives of the Poets* (1779–81), a series of short critical biographies written by Johnson to preface collections of the work of English poets. "Cowley," from which this extract is taken, was the first of the series.

their right to the name of poets, for they cannot be said to have imitated anything; they neither copied nature nor life, neither painted the forms of matter, nor represented the operations of intellect.

Those, however, who deny them to be poets, allow them to be wits. Dryden confesses of himself and his contemporaries, that they fall below Donne in wit, but maintains that they surpass him in poetry.

If wit be well described by Pope, as being "that which has been often thought, but was never before so well expressed," they certainly never attained, nor ever sought it; for they endeavoured to be singular in their thoughts, and were careless of their diction. But Pope's account of wit is undoubtedly erroneous: he depresses it below its natural dignity, and reduces it from strength of thought to happiness of language.

If by a more noble and more adequate conception that be considered as wit which is at once natural and new, that which, though not obvious, is, upon its first production, acknowledged to be just; if it be that which he that never found it wonders how he missed, to wit of this kind the metaphysical poets have seldom risen. Their thoughts are often new, but seldom natural; they are not obvious, but neither are they just; and the reader, far from wondering that he missed them, wonders more frequently by what perverseness of industry they were ever found.

But wit, abstracted from its effects upon the hearer, may be more rigorously and philosophically considered as a kind of *discordia concors*; a combination of dissimilar images, or discovery of occult resemblances in things apparently unlike. Of wit, thus defined, they have more than enough. The most heterogeneous ideas are yoked by violence together; nature and art are ransacked for illustrations, comparisons, and allusions; their learning instructs, and their subtlety surprises; but the reader commonly thinks his improvement dearly bought, and, though he sometimes admires, is seldom pleased.

From this account of their compositions it will be readily inferred that they were not successful in representing or moving the affections. As they were wholly employed on something unexpected and surprising, they had no regard to that uniformity of sentiment which enables us to conceive and to excite the pains and the pleasure of other minds: they never inquired what, on any occasion, they should have said or done, but wrote rather as beholders than partakers of human nature; as beings looking upon good and evil, impassive and at leisure; as Epicurean deities, making remarks on the actions of men, and the vicissitudes of life, without interest and without emotion. Their courtship was void of fondness, and their lamentation of sorrow. Their wish was only to say what they hoped had been never said before.

Nor was the sublime more within their reach than the pathetic; for they never attempted that comprehension and expanse of thought which at once fills the whole mind, and of which the first effect is sudden astonishment, and the second rational admiration. Sublimity is produced by aggregation, and littleness by dispersion. Great thoughts are always general, and consist in positions not limited by exceptions, and in descriptions not descending to minuteness. It is with great propriety that subtlety, which in its original import means exility of particles, is taken in its metaphorical meaning for nicety of distinction. Those writers who lay on the watch for novelty could have little hope of greatness; for great things cannot have escaped former observation. Their attempts were always analytic; they broke every image into fragments; and could no more represent, by their slender conceits and laboured particularities, the prospects of nature, or the scenes of life, than he who dissects a sunbeam with a prism can exhibit the wide effulgence of a summer noon.

What they wanted however of the sublime, they endeavoured to supply by hyperbole; their amplification had no limits; they left not only reason but fancy behind them; and produced combinations of confused magnificence, that not only could not be credited, but could not be imagined.

Yet great labour, directed by great abilities, is never wholly lost: if they frequently threw away their wit upon false conceits, they likewise sometimes struck out unexpected truth; if their conceits were far-fetched, they were often worth the carriage. To write on their plan, it was at least necessary to read and think. No man could be born a metaphysical poet, nor assume the dignity of a writer, by descriptions copied from descriptions, by imitations borrowed from imitations, by traditional imagery, and hereditary similes, by readiness of rhyme, and volubility of syllables.

In perusing the works of this race of authors, the mind is exercised either by recollection or inquiry; either something already learned is to be retrieved, or something new is to be examined. If their greatness seldom elevates, their acuteness often surprises; if the imagination is not always gratified, at least the powers of reflection and comparison are employed; and in the mass of materials which ingenious absurdity has thrown together, genuine wit and useful knowledge may be sometimes found buried perhaps in grossness of expression, but useful to those who know their value; and such as, when they are expanded to perspicuity, and polished to elegance, may give lustre to works which have more propriety though less copiousness of sentiment.

This kind of writing, which was, I believe, borrowed from Marino and his followers, had been recommended by the example of Donne, a man of a very extensive and various knowledge; and by Jonson, whose manner resembled that of Donne more in the ruggedness of his lines than in the cast of his sentiments.

When their reputation was high, they had undoubtedly more imitators than time has left behind. Their immediate successors, of whom any remembrance can be said to remain, were Suckling, Waller, Denham, Cowley, Cleveland, and Milton. Denham and Waller sought another way to fame, by improving the harmony of our numbers. Milton tried the metaphysic style only in his lines upon Hobson the Carrier. Cowley adopted it, and excelled his predecessors, having as much sentiment and more music. Suckling neither improved versification, nor abounded in conceits. The fashionable style remained chiefly with Cowley; Suckling could not reach it, and Milton disdained it.

SAMUEL TAYLOR COLERIDGE

[Notes on Donne] †

Versification of Donne

To read Dryden, Pope, &c., you need only count syllables; but to read Donne you must measure *Time*, and discover the *Time* of each word by the sense of Passion. I would ask no surer test of a Scotchman's *substratum* (for the turf-cover of pretension they all have) than to make him read Donne's satires aloud. If he made manly metre of them and yet strict metre, then,—why, then he wasn't a Scotchman, or his soul was geographically slandered by his body's first appearing there.

Doubtless, all the copies I have ever seen of Donne's Poems are grievously misprinted. Wonderful that they are not more so, considering that not one in a thousand of his readers have any notion how his lines are to be read—to the many, five out of six appear antimetrical. How greatly this aided the compositor's negligence or ignorance, and prevented the corrector's remedy, any man may ascertain by examining the earliest editions of blank verse plays, Massinger, Beaumont and Fletcher, &c. Now, Donne's rhythm was as inexplicable to the many as blank verse, spite of his rhymes—*ergo*, as blank verse, misprinted. I am convinced that where no mode of rational declamation by pause, hurrying of voice, or apt and sometimes double emphasis, can at once make the verse metrical and bring out the sense of passion more prominently, that there we are entitled to alter the text, when it can be done by simple omission or addition of *that*, *which*, *and*, and such 'small deer;' or by mere new placing of the same words—I would venture nothing beyond.

> And by delighting many, frees again
> Grief which Verse did restrain.
> *The Triple Fool*, v. 15.

A good instance how Donne read his own verses. We should write 'The Grief, verse did restrain;' but Donne roughly emphasized the two main words, Grief and Verse, and, therefore, made each the first syllable of a trochee or dactyl:—

> Grief, which | verse did re | strain.

> And we join tō't our strength,
> And we teach it art and length.
> *Song*.

† From "Coleridgiana II," *Literary World*, 12 (April 30, 1853): 349–50, and *The Literary Remains of Samuel Taylor Coleridge*, ed. H. N. Coleridge, 1 (London, 1836) 148–49.

The anapest judiciously used, in the eagerness and haste to confirm and aggravate. This beautiful and perfect poem proves, by its title "Song," that *all* Donne's Poems are equally *metrical* (misprints allowed for) though smoothness (i.e., the metre necessitating the proper reading) be deemed appropriate to *songs;* but in poems where the writer *thinks*, and expects the reader to do so, the sense must be understood in order to ascertain the metre.

Satire III

If you would teach a scholar in the highest form how to *read*, take Donne, and of Donne this satire. When he has learnt to read Donne, with all the force and meaning which are involved in the words, then send him to Milton, and he will stalk on like a master, *enjoying* his walk.

Notes on "Songs and Sonnets"
On Donne's First Poem [*The Flea*]

Be proud as Spaniards. Leap for pride, ye Fleas!
In Nature's *minim* realm ye're now grandees.
Skip-jacks no more, nor civiller skip-johns;
Thrice-honored Fleas! I greet you all as *Dons*.
In Phoebus's archieves registered are ye,
And this your patent of nobility.

What ever dies is not mixt equally;
If our two loves be one, both thou and I
Love just alike in all; none of these loves can die.
The Good Morrow.

Too good for mere wit. It contains a deep practical truth, this triplet.

To Woman's Constancy

After all, there is but one Donne! and now tell me yet, wherein, in *his own kind*, he differs from the similar power in Shakspeare? Shakspeare was all men, potentially, except Milton; and they differ from him by negation, or privation, or both. This power of dissolving orient pearls, worth a kingdom, in a health to a whore!—this absolute right of dominion over all thoughts, that dukes are bid to clean his shoes, and are yet honored by it! But, I say, in this lordliness of opulence, in which *the* positive of Donne agrees with a positive of Shakspeare, what is it that makes them *homo*iousian, indeed: yet not homoousian?

To Canonization

One of my favorite poems. As late as ten years ago, I used to seek and find out grand lines and fine stanzas; but my delight has been far greater since it has consisted more in tracing the leading thought thro'out the whole. The former is too much like coveting your neighbor's goods; in the latter you merge yourself in the author, you *become* He.

To a Valediction Forbidding Mourning

An admirable poem which none but Donne could have written. Nothing was ever more admirably made out than the figure of the Compass.

To The Extacy

I should never find fault with metaphysical poems, were they all like this, or but half as excellent.

To The Primrose

I am tired of expressing my admiration; else I could not have passed by the Will, the Blossom, and the Primrose, with the Relique.

* * *

With Donne, whose muse on dromedary trots,
Wreathe iron pokers into true-love knots;
Rhyme's sturdy cripple, fancy's maze and clue,
Wit's forge and fire-blast, meaning's press and screw.

The wit of Donne, the wit of Butler, the wit of Pope, the wit of Congreve, the wit of Sheridan—how many disparate things are here expressed by one and the same word. Wit!—Wonder-exciting vigour, intenseness and peculiarity of thought, using at will the almost boundless stores of a capacious memory, and exercised on subjects, where we have no right to expect it—this is the wit of Donne! The four others I am just in the mood to describe and inter-distinguish;—what a pity that the marginal space will not let me!

SIR HERBERT GRIERSON

[Donne and Metaphysical Poetry] †

Metaphysical Poetry, in the full sense of the term, is a poetry which, like that of the *Divina Commedia*, the *De Natura Rerum*, perhaps Goethe's *Faust*, has been inspired by a philosophical conception of the universe and the rôle assigned to the human spirit in the great drama of

† From Sir Herbert Grierson, *Metaphysical Lyrics and Poems of the Seventeenth Century*, Copyright 1921, 1959. Pp. xiii–xxviii. Reprinted by permission of the publishers, The Clarendon Press, Oxford.

existence. These poems were written because a definite interpretation of the riddle, the atoms of Epicurus rushing through infinite empty space, the theology of the schoolmen as elaborated in the catechetical disquisitions of St. Thomas, Spinoza's vision of life *sub specie aeternitatis*, beyond good and evil, laid hold on the mind and the imagination of a great poet, unified and illumined his comprehension of life, intensified and heightened his personal consciousness of joy and sorrow, of hope and fear, by broadening their significance, revealing to him in the history of his own soul a brief abstract of the drama of human destiny. 'Poetry is the first and last of all knowledge—it is as immortal as the heart of man.' Its themes are the simplest experiences of the surface of life, sorrow and joy, love and battle, the peace of the country, the bustle and stir of towns, but equally the boldest conceptions, the profoundest intuitions, the subtlest and most complex classifications and 'discourse of reason', if into these too the poet can 'carry sensation', make of them passionate experiences communicable in vivid and moving imagery, in rich and varied harmonies.

It is no such great metaphysical poetry as that of Lucretius and Dante that the present essay deals with, which this volume seeks to illustrate. Of the poets from whom it culls, Donne is familiar with the definitions and distinctions of Mediaeval Scholasticism; Cowley's bright and alert, if not profound mind, is attracted by the achievements of science and the systematic materialism of Hobbes. Donne, moreover, is metaphysical not only in virtue of his scholasticism, but by his deep reflective interest in the experiences of which his poetry is the expression, the new psychological curiosity with which he writes of love and religion. The divine poets who follow Donne have each the inherited metaphysic, if one may so call it, of the Church to which he is attached, Catholic or Anglican. But none of the poets has for his main theme a metaphysic like that of Epicurus or St. Thomas passionately apprehended and imaginatively expounded. Donne, the most thoughtful and imaginative of them all, is more aware of disintegration than of comprehensive harmony, of the clash between the older physics and metaphysics on the one hand and the new science of Copernicus and Galileo and Vesalius and Bacon on the other:

The new philosophy calls all in doubt,
The element of fire is quite put out;
The sun is lost and the earth, and no man's wit
Can well direct him where to look for it.
And freely men confess that this world's spent,
When in the planets and the firmament
They seek so many new; they see that this
Is crumbled out again to his atomies.

Have not all souls thought
For many ages that our body is wrought

Of air and fire and other elements?
And now they think of new ingredients;
And one soul thinks one, and another way
Another thinks, and 'tis an even lay.

The greatest English poet, indeed, of the century was, or believed himself to be, a philosophical or theological poet of the same order as Dante. *Paradise Lost* was written to be a justification of 'the ways of God to men', resting on a theological system as definite and almost as carefully articulated in the *De Doctrina Christiana* as that which Dante had accepted from the *Summa* of Aquinas. And the poet embodied his argument in a dramatic poem as vividly and intensely conceived, as magnificently and harmoniously set forth, as the *Divina Commedia*. But in truth Milton was no philosopher. The subtleties of theological definition and inference eluded his rationalistic, practical, though idealistic, mind. He proved nothing. The definitely stated argument of the poem is an obvious begging of the question. What he did was to create, or give a new definiteness and sensible power to, a great myth which, through his poem, continued for a century or more to dominate the mind and imagination of pious protestants without many of them suspecting the heresies which lurked beneath the imposing and dazzling poem in which was retold the Bible story of the fall and redemption of man.

Metaphysical in this large way, Donne and his followers to Cowley are not, yet the word describes better what is the peculiar quality of their poetry than any other, e.g. fantastic, for poetry may be fantastic in so many different ways, witness Skelton and the Elizabethans, and Hood and Browning. It lays stress on the right things—the survival, one might say the reaccentuation, of the metaphysical strain, the *concetti metafisici ed ideali* as Testi calls them in contrast to the simpler imagery of classical poetry, of mediaeval Italian poetry; the more intellectual, less verbal, character of their wit compared with the conceits of the Elizabethans; the finer psychology of which their conceits are often the expression; their learned imagery; the argumentative, subtle evolution of their lyrics; above all the peculiar blend of passion and thought, feeling and ratiocination which is their greatest achievement. Passionate thinking is always apt to become metaphysical, probing and investigating the experience from which it takes its rise. All these qualities are in the poetry of Donne, and Donne is the great master of English poetry in the seventeenth century.

The Italian influence which Wyatt and Surrey brought into English poetry at the Renaissance gave it a more serious, a more thoughtful colour. They caught, especially Wyatt in some of the finest of his sonnets and songs, that spirit of 'high seriousness' which Chaucer with all his admiration of Italian poetry had failed to apprehend. English mediaeval poetry is often gravely pious, haunted by the fear of death and the judgement, melancholy over the 'Falls of Princes'; it is never serious and thoughtful in the introspective, reflective, dignified manner which it became in Wyatt and Sackville, and our 'sage and serious' Spenser, and in the songs of the first group of Elizabethan courtly poets, Sidney and Raleigh and Dyer. One has but to recall 'My lute, awake! perform the last', 'Forget not yet the tried intent', 'My mind to me a kingdom is', and to contrast them in mind with the songs which Henry VIII and Cornish were still composing and singing when Wyatt began to write, in order to realize what Italy and the Renaissance did to deepen the strain of English lyric poetry as that had flowed under French influence from the thirteenth to the sixteenth centuries. But French influence, the influences of Ronsard and his fellows, renewed itself in the seventies, and the great body of Elizabethan song is as gay and careless and impersonal as the earlier lyric had been, though richer in colour and more varied in rhythm. Then came Donne and Jonson (the schoolman and the classical scholar, one might say, emphasizing for the moment single aspects of their work), and new qualities of spirit and form were given to lyrical poetry, and not to lyrical poetry alone.

In dealing with poets who lived and wrote before the eighteenth century we are always confronted with the difficulty of recovering the personal, the biographical element, which, if sometimes disturbing and disconcerting, is yet essential to a complete understanding of their work. Men were not different from what they are now, and if there be hardly a lyric of Goethe's or Shelley's that does not owe something to the accidents of their lives, one may feel sure it was in varying degrees the same with poets three hundred years ago. Poems are not written by influences or movements or sources, but come from the living hearts of men. Fortunately, in the case of Donne, one of the most individual of poets, it is possible to some extent to reproduce the circumstances, the inner experiences from which his intensely personal poetry flowed.,

He was in the first place a Catholic. Our history text-books make so little of the English Catholics that one is apt to forget they existed and were, for themselves at any rate, not a political problem, but real and suffering individuals. 'I had my first breeding and conversation', says Donne, 'with men of a suppressed and afflicted religion, accustomed to the despite of death and hungry of an imagined martyrdom.' In these circumstances, we gather, he was carefully and religiously educated, and after some years at Oxford and Cambridge was taken or sent abroad, perhaps with a view to entering foreign service, more probably with a view to the priesthood, and visited Italy and Spain. And then, one conjectures, a reaction took place, the rebellion of a full-blooded, highly intellectual temperament against a superimposed bent. He entered the Inns of Court in 1592, at the age of nineteen, and flung himself into the life of a student and the life of a young man about town, Jack Donne, 'not dissolute but very neat, a great visitor of ladies, a great frequenter of plays, a great writer of conceited verses'. 'Neither was it possible that a vulgar soul should dwell in such promising features.' He joined the band of reckless and raffish young men who sailed with Essex to Cadiz and the Islands. He was taken into the service of Sir Thomas Egerton. Ambition began to vie with the love of pleasure, when a hasty marriage closed a promising career, and left him bound in shallows and in miseries, to spend years in the suitorship of the great, and to find at last, not altogether willingly, a haven in the Anglican priesthood, and reveal himself as the first great orator that Church produced.

The record of these early years is contained in Donne's satires—harsh, witty, lucid, full of a young man's scorn of fools and low callings, and a young thinker's consciousness of the problems of religion in an age of divided faiths, and of justice in a corrupt world—and in his Love Songs and Sonnets and Elegies. The satires were more generally known; the love poems the more influential in courtly and literary circles.

Donne's genius, temperament, and learning gave to his love poems certain qualities which immediately arrested attention and have given them ever since a power at once fascinating and disconcerting despite the faults of phrasing and harmony which, for a century after Dryden, obscured, and to some still outweigh, their poetic worth. The first of these is a depth and range of feeling unknown to the majority of Elizabethan sonneteers and song-writers. Over all the Elizabethan sonnets, in greater or less measure, hangs the suggestion of translation or imitation. Watson, Sidney, Daniel, Spenser, Drayton, Lodge, all of them, with rarer or more frequent touches of individuality, are pipers of Petrarch's woes, sighing in the strain of Ronsard or more often of Desportes. Shakespeare, indeed, in his great sequence, and Drayton in at any rate one sonnet, sounded a deeper note, revealed a fuller sense of the complexities and contradictions of passionate devotion. But Donne's treatment of love is entirely unconventional except when he chooses to dally half ironically with the convention of Petrarchian adoration. His songs are the expression in unconventional, witty language of all the moods of a lover that experience and imagination have taught him to understand—sensuality aerated by a brilliant wit; fascination and scornful anger inextricably blended:

> When by the scorn, O murdress, I am dead
> And that thou think'st thee free
> From all solicitations from me,
> Then shall my ghost come to thy bed;

the passionate joy of mutual and contented love:

> All other things to their destruction draw,
>   Only our love hath no decay;
> This no to-morrow hath nor yesterday,
>   Running it never runs from us away,
> But truly keeps his first, last, everlasting day;

the sorrow of parting which is the shadow of such joy; the gentler pathos of temporary separation in married life:

Let not thy divining heart
  Forethink me any ill,
Destiny may take thy part,
  And may thy fears fulfil;
    But think that we
Are but turn'd aside to sleep;
They who one another keep
  Alive ne'er parted be;

the mystical heights and the mystical depths of love:

Study me then you who shall lovers be
At the next world, that is, at the next Spring:
For I am every dead thing
In whom love wrought new Alchemy.

If Donne had expressed this wide range of intense feeling as perfectly as he has done at times poignantly and startling; if he had given to his poems the same impression of entire artistic sincerity that Shakespeare conveys in the greater of his sonnets and Drayton once achieved; if to his many other gifts had been added a deeper and more controlling sense of beauty, he would have been, as he nearly is, the greatest of love poets. But there is a second quality of his poetry which made it the fashion of an age, but has been inimical to its general acceptance ever since, and that is its metaphysical wit. 'He affects the metaphysics', says Dryden, 'not only in his satires but in his amorous verses where nature only should reign; and perplexes the minds of the fair sex with nice speculations of philosophy when he should engage their hearts and entertain them with the softnesses of love.' 'Amorous verses', 'the fair sex', and 'the softnesses of love' are the vulgarities of a less poetic and passionate age than Donne's, but metaphysics he does affect. But a metaphysical strand, *concetti metafisici ed ideali*, had run through the mediaeval love-poetry of which the Elizabethan sonnets are a descendant. It had attained its fullest development in the poems of Dante and his school, had been subordinated to rhetoric and subtleties of expression rather than thought in Petrarch, and had lost itself in the pseudo-metaphysical extravagances of Tebaldeo, Cariteo, and Serafino. Donne was no conscious reviver of the metaphysics of Dante, but to the game of elaborating fantastic conceits and hyperboles which was the fashion throughout Europe, he brought not only a full-blooded temperament and acute mind, but a vast and growing store of the same scholastic learning, the same Catholic theology, as controlled Dante's thought, jostling already with the new learning of Copernicus and Paracelsus. The result is startling and disconcerting,—the comparison of parted lovers to the legs of a pair of compasses, the deification of his mistress by the discovery that she is only to be defined by negatives or that she can read the thoughts of his heart, a thing 'beyond an angel's art'; and a thousand other subtleties of quintessences and nothingness, the mixture of souls and the significance of numbers, to say nothing of the aerial bodies of angels, the phoenix and the mandrake's *root*, Alchemy and Astrology, legal contracts and *non obstantes*, 'late schoolboys and sour prentices', 'the king's real and his stamped face'. But the effect aimed at and secured is not entirely fantastic and erudite. The motive inspiring Donne's images is in part the same as that which led Shakespeare from the picturesque, natural and mythological, images of *A Midsummer-Night's Dream* and *The Merchant of Venice* to the homely but startling phrases and metaphors of *Hamlet* and *Macbeth*, the 'blanket of the dark', the

fat weed
That rots itself in ease on Lethe wharf,

'the rank sweat of an enseamed bed'. It is the same desire for vivid and dramatic expression. The great master at a later period of dramatic as well as erudite pulpit oratory coins in his poems many a startling, jarring, arresting phrase:

For God's sake hold your tongue and let me love:

Who ever comes to shroud me do not harm
  Nor question much
That subtle wreath of hair, which crowns my arm:

I taught my silks their rustling to forbear,
Even my oppress shoes dumb and silent were.

I long to talk with some old lover's ghost
Who died before the God of love was born;

Twice or thrice had I loved thee
Before I knew thy face or name,
So in a voice, so in a shapeless flame,
Angels affect us oft and worshipped be;

And whilst our souls negotiate there
  We like sepulchral statues lay;
All day the same our postures were
  And we said nothing all the day

My face and brest of haircloth, and my head
With care's harsh, sudden hoariness o'erspread.

These vivid, simple, realistic touches are too quickly merged in learned and fantastic elaborations, and the final effect of every poem of Donne's is a bizarre and blended one; but if the greatest poetry rises clear of the bizarre, the fantastic, yet very great poetry may be bizarre if it be the expression of a strangely blended temperament, an intense emotion, a vivid imagination.

What is true of Donne's imagery is true of the other disconcerting element in his poetry, its harsh and rugged verse. It is an outcome of the same double motive, the desire to startle and the desire to approximate poetic to direct, unconventional, colloquial speech. Poetry is always a balance, sometimes a compromise, between what has to be said and the prescribed pattern to which the saying of it is adjusted. In poetry such as Spenser's, the musical flow, the melody and harmony of line and stanza, is dominant, and the meaning is adjusted to it at the not infrequent cost of diffuseness—if a delightful diffuseness—and even some weakness of phrasing logically and rhetorically considered. In Shakespeare's tragedies the thought and feeling tend to break through the prescribed pattern till blank verse becomes almost rhythmical, the rapid overflow of the lines admitting hardly the semblance of pause. This is the kind of effect Donne is always aiming at, alike in his satires and lyrics, bending and cracking the metrical pattern to the rhetoric of direct and vehement utterance. The result is often, and to eighteenth-century ears attuned to the clear and defined, if limited, harmony of Waller and Dryden and Pope was, rugged and harsh. But here again, to those who have ears that care to hear, the effect is not finally inharmonious. Donne's verse has a powerful and haunting harmony of its own. For Donne is not simply, no poet could be, willing to force his accent, to strain and crack a prescribed pattern; he is striving to find a rhythm that will express the passionate fullness of his mind, the fluxes and refluxes of his moods; and the felicities of verse are as frequent and startling as those of phrasing. He is one of the first masters, perhaps *the* first, of the elaborate stanza or paragraph in which the discords of individual lines or phrases are resolved in complex and rhetorically effective harmony of the whole group of lines:

If yet I have not all thy love,
Deare, I shall never have it all,
I cannot breathe one other sigh, to move,
Nor can entreat one other tear to fall,
And all my treasure, which should purchase thee,
Sighs, tears, and oaths, and letters I have spent.
Yet no more can be due to me,
Than at the bargain made was meant,
If then thy gift of love was partial,
That some to me, some should to others fall,
   Deare, I shall never have thee all.

But I am none; nor will my sunne renew.
You lovers for whose sake the lesser sunne
   At this time to the Goat is run
   To fetch new lust and give it you,
      Enjoy your summer all;
Since she enjoys her long night's festival,

Let me prepare towards her, and let me call
This hour her Vigil and her Eve, since this

Both the years | and the days | deep mid|night is.

The wrenching of accent which Jonson complained of is not entirely due to carelessness or indifference. It has often both a rhetorical and a harmonious justification. Donne plays with rhythmical effects as with conceits and words and often in much the same way. Mr. Fletcher Melton's interesting analysis of his verse has not, I think, established his main thesis, which like so many 'research' scholars he over-emphasizes, that the whole mystery of Donne's art lies in his use of the same sound now in *arsis*, now in *thesis*; but his examples show that this is one of many devices by which Donne secures two effects, the troubling of the regular fall of the verse stresses by the intrusion of rhetorical stress on syllables which the metrical pattern leaves unstressed, and, secondly, an echoing and re-echoing of similar sounds parallel to his fondness for resemblances in thoughts and things apparently the most remote from one another. There is, that is to say, in his verse the same blend as in his diction of the colloquial and the bizarre. He writes as one who *will* say what he has to say without regard to conventions of poetic diction or smooth verse, but what he has to say is subtle and surprising, and so are the metrical effects with which it is presented. There is nothing of unconscious or merely careless harshness in such an effect as this:

Poor soul, in this thy flesh what dost thou know?
Thou know'st thyself so little that thou knowst not
How thou didst die, nor how thou was begot.
Thou neither know'st how thou at first camest in,
Nor how thou took'st the poison of man's sin;
Nor dost thou though thou know'st that thou art so
By what way thou art made immortal know.

In Donne's pronunciation, as in southern English to-day, 'thou', 'how', 'soul', 'know', 'though', and 'so' were not far removed from each other in sound and the reiterated notes ring through the lines like a tolling bell. Mr. Melton has collected, and any careful reader may discover for himself, many similar subtleties of poetical rhetoric; for Donne is perhaps our first great master of poetic rhetoric, of poetry, used, as Dryden and Pope were to use it, for effects of oratory rather than of song, and the advance which Dryden achieved was secured by subordinating to oratory the more passionate and imaginative qualities which troubled the balance and movement of Donne's packed but imaginative rhetoric.

It was not indeed in lyrical verse that Dryden followed and developed Donne, but in his eulogistic, elegiac, satirical, and epistolary verse. The progress of Dryden's eulogistic style is traceable from his earliest metaphysical extravagances through lines such as those addressed to the

Duchess of York, where Waller is his model, to the verses on the death of Oldham in which a more natural and classical strain has entirely superseded his earlier extravagances and elegancies. In truth Donne's metaphysical eulogies and elegies and epistles are a hard nut to crack for his most sympathetic admirers. And yet they have undeniable qualities. The metaphysics are developed in a more serious, a less paradoxical, strain than in some of the songs and elegies. In his letters he is an excellent, if far from a perfect, talker in verse; and the personality which they reveal is a singularly charming one, grave, loyal, melancholy, witty. If some of the elegiac pieces are packed with tasteless and extravagant hyperboles, the *Anniversaries* (especially the second) remains, despite all its faults, one of the greatest poems on death in the language, the fullest record in our literature of the disintegrating collision in a sensitive mind of the old tradition and the new learning. Some of the invocational passages in *Of the Progresse of the Soule* are among the finest examples of his subtle and passionate thinking as well as of his most elaborate verse rhetoric.

But the most intense and personal of Donne's poems, after the love songs and elegies, are his later religious sonnets and songs; and their influence on subsequent poetry was even more obvious and potent. They are as personal and as tormented as his earlier 'love-song weeds', for his spiritual Aeneid was a troubled one. To date his conversion to Anglicanism is not easy. In his satires there is a veiled Roman tone. By 1602 he disclaims to Egerton 'all love of a corrupt religion', but in the autumn of the previous year he had been meditating a satire on Queen Elizabeth as one of the world's great heretics. His was not a conversion but a reconciliation, an acquiescence in the faith of his country, the established religion of his legal sovereign, and the act cost him some pangs. 'A convert from Popery to Protestantism,' said Dr. Johnson, 'gives up so much of what he has held as sacred as anything that he retains, there is so much laceration of mind in such a conversion, that it can hardly be sincere and lasting.' Something of that laceration of mind is discernible in Donne's religious verse:

> Show me dear Christ that spouse so bright and clear.

But the conflict between the old and the reformed faiths was not the only, nor perhaps the principal trouble for Donne's enlightened mind ready to recognize in all the Churches 'virtual beams of one sun', 'connatural pieces of one circle'. A harder fight was that between the secular, the 'man of the world' temper of his mind and the claims of a pious and ascetic calling. It was not the errors of his youth, as the good Walton supposed, which constituted the great stumbling block, though he never ignores these:

> O might those sighs and tears return again
> Into my breast and eyes, which I have spent,

That I might in this holy discontent
Mourn with some fruit, as I have mourned in vain.

It was rather the temperament of one who, at a time when a public career was more open to unassisted talent, might have proved an active and useful, if ambitious, civil servant, or professional man, at war with the claims of a religious life which his upbringing had taught him was incompatible with worldly ambition. George Herbert, a much more contented Anglican than Donne ever became, knew something of the same struggle before he bent his neck to the collar.

The two notes then of Donne's religious poems are the Catholic and the personal. He is the first of our Anglo-Catholic poets, and he is our first intensely personal religious poet, expressing always not the mind simply of the Christian as such, but the conflicts and longings of one troubled soul, one subtle and fantastic mind. For Donne's technique—his phrasing and conceits, the metaphysics of mediaeval Christianity, his packed verse with its bold, irregular fingering and echoing vowel sounds—remains what it had been from the outset. The echoing sounds in lines such as these cannot be quite casual:

O might those *sighs* and tears return again
Into my breast and *eyes*, which *I* have spent,
That *I* might in this holy discontent
Mourn with some fruit, as *I* have mourned in vain;
In mind *Idolat'ry* what showers of rain
Mine eyes did waste? What griefs *my* heart did rent?
That sufferance was *my* sin; now *I* repent
Cause *I* did suffer *I* must suffer pain.

In the remaining six lines the same sound never recurs.

A metaphysical, a philosophical poet, to the degree to which even his contemporary Fulke Greville might be called such, Donne was not. The thought in his poetry is not his primary concern but the feeling. No scheme of thought, no interpretation of life became for him a complete and illuminating experience. The central theme of his poetry is ever his own intense personal moods, as a lover, a friend, an analyst of his own experiences worldly and religious. His philosophy cannot unify these experiences. It represents the reaction of his restless and acute mind on the intense experience of the moment, a reading of it in the light now of one, now of another philosophical or theological dogma or thesis caught from his multifarious reading, developed with audacious paradox or more serious intention, as an expression, an illumination of that mood to himself and to his reader. Whether one choose to call him a metaphysical or a fantastic poet, the stress must be laid on the word 'poet'. Whether verse or prose be his medium, Donne is always a poet, a creature of feeling and imagination, seeking expression in vivid phrase and complex harmonies, whose acute and subtle intellect was the servant, if sometimes the unruly servant, of passion and imagination.

T. S. ELIOT

The Metaphysical Poets †

By collecting these poems[1] from the work of a generation more often named than read, and more often read than profitably studied, Professor Grierson has rendered a service of some importance. Certainly the reader will meet with many poems already preserved in other anthologies, at the same time that he discovers poems such as those of Aurelian Townshend or Lord Herbert of Cherbury here included. But the function of such an anthology as this is neither that of Professor Saintsbury's admirable edition of Caroline poets nor that of the *Oxford Book of English Verse*. Mr. Grierson's book is in itself a piece of criticism, and a provocation of criticism; and we think that he was right in including so many poems of Donne, elsewhere (though not in many editions) accessible, as documents in the case of 'metaphysical poetry'. The phrase has long done duty as a term of abuse, or as the label of a quaint and pleasant taste. The question is to what extent the so-called metaphysicals formed a school (in our own time we should say a 'movement'), and how far this so-called school or movement is a digression from the main current.

Not only is it extremely difficult to define metaphysical poetry, but difficult to decide what poets practice it and in which of their verses. The poetry of Donne (to whom Marvell and Bishop King are sometimes nearer than any of the other authors) is late Elizabethan, its feeling often very close to that of Chapman. The 'courtly' poetry is derivative from Jonson, who borrowed liberally from the Latin; it expires in the next century with the sentiment and witticism of Prior. There is finally the devotional verse of Herbert, Vaughan, and Crashaw (echoed long after by Christina Rossetti and Francis Thompson); Crashaw, sometimes more profound and less sectarian than the others, has a quality which returns through the Elizabethan period to the early Italians. It is difficult to find any precise use of metaphor, simile, or other conceit, which is common to all the poets and at the same time important enough as an element of style to isolate these poets as a group. Donne, and often Cowley, employ a device which is sometimes considered characteristically 'metaphysical'; the elaboration (contrasted with the condensation) of a figure of speech to the furthest stage to which ingenuity can carry it. Thus Cowley develops the commonplace comparison of the world to a chess-board through long stanzas *(To Destiny)*, and Donne, with more grace, in A *Valediction*, the comparison of two lovers to a pair of compasses. But elsewhere we find, instead of the mere explication of the content of a comparison,

† From *Selected Essays*, New Edition, by T. S. Eliot,

1. *Metaphysical Lyrics and Poems of the Seventeenth Century*: Donne to Butler. Selected and edited, with an Essay, by Herbert J. C. Grierson (Oxford: Clarendon Press. London: Milford).

a development by rapid association of thought which requires considerable agility on the part of the reader.

> On a round ball
> A workeman that hath copies by, can lay
> An Europe, Afrique, and an Asia,
> And quickly make that, which was nothing, *All*,
> So doth each teare,
> Which thee doth weare,
> A globe, yea world by that impression grow,
> Till thy tears mixt with mine doe overflow
> This world, by waters sent from thee, my heaven dissolved so.

Here we find at least two connexions which are not implicit in the first figure, but are forced upon it by the poet: from the geographer's globe to the tear, and the tear to the deluge. On the other hand, some of Donne's most successful and characteristic effects are secured by brief words and sudden contrasts:

> A bracelet of bright hair about the bone,

where the most powerful effect is produced by the sudden contrast of associations of 'bright hair' and of 'bone'. This telescoping of images and multiplied associations is characteristic of the phrase of some of the dramatists of the period which Donne knew; not to mention Shakespeare, it is frequent in Middleton, Webster, and Tourneur, and is one of the sources of the vitality of their language.

Johnson, who employed the term 'metaphysical poets', apparently having Donne, Cleveland, and Cowley chiefly in mind, remarks of them that 'the most heterogeneous ideas are yoked by violence together'. The force of this impeachment lies in the failure of the conjunction, the fact that often the ideas are yoked but not united; and if we are to judge of styles of poetry by their abuse, enough examples may be found in Cleveland to justify Johnson's condemnation. But a degree of heterogeneity of material compelled into unity by the operation of the poet's mind is omnipresent in poetry. We need not select for illustration such a line as:

> Notre âme est un trois-mâts chercant son Icarie;

we may find it in some of the best line of Johnson himself (*The Vanity of Human Wishes*):

> His fate was destined to a barren strand,
> A petty fortress, and a dubious hand;
> He left a name at which the world grew pale,
> To point a moral, or adorn a tale.

where the effect is due to a contrast of ideas, different in degree but the same in principle, as that which Johnson mildly reprehended. And in one of the finest poems of the age (a poem which could not have been written in any other age), the *Exequy* of Bishop King, the extended comparison is used with perfect success: the idea and the simile become one, in the passage in which the Bishop illustrates his impatience to see his dead wife, under the figure of a journey:

> Stay for me there; I will not faile
> To meet thee in that hollow Vale.
> And think not much of my delay;
> I am already on the way,
> And follow thee with all the speed
> Desire can make, or sorrows breed.
> Each minute is a short degree,
> And ev'ry houre a step towards thee.
> At night when I betake to rest,
> Next morn I rise nearer my West
> Of life, almost by eight houres sail,
> Than when sleep breath'd his drowsy gale. . . .
> But heark! My Pulse, like a soft Drum
> Beats my approach, tells *Thee* I come;
> And slow howere my marches be,
> I shall at last sit down by *Thee*.

(In the last few lines there is that effect of terror which is several times attained by one of Bishop King's admirers, Edgar Poe.) Again, we may justly take these quatrains from Lord Herbert's Ode, stanzas which would, we think, be immediately pronounced to be of the metaphysical school:

> So when from hence we shall be gone,
>   And be no more, nor you, nor I,
>   As one another's mystery,
> Each shall be both, yet both but one.
>
> This said, in her up-lifted face,
>   Her eyes, which did that beauty crown,
>   Were like two starrs, that having faln down,
> Look up again to find their place:
>
> While such a moveless silent peace
>   Did seize on their becalmed sense,
>   One would have thought some influence
> Their ravished spirits did possess.

There is nothing in these lines (with the possible exception of the stars, a simile not at once grasped, but lovely and justified) which fits Johnson's general observations on the metaphysical poets in his essay on Cowley. A good deal resides in the richness of association which is at the same time borrowed from and given to the word 'becalmed'; but the meaning is clear, the language simple and elegant. It is to be observed that the language of these poets is as a rule simple and pure; in the verse of George Herbert this simplicity is carried as far as it can go—a simplicity emulated without success by numerous modern poets. The *structure* of the sentences, on the other hand, is sometimes far from simple, but this is not a vice; it is fidelity to thought and feeling. The effect, at its best, is far less artificial than that of an ode by Gray. And as this fidelity induces variety of thought and feeling, so it induces variety of music. We doubt whether, in the eighteenth century, could be found two poems in nominally the same metre, so dissimilar as Marvell's *Coy Mistress* and Crashaw's *Saint Teresa*; the one producing an effect of great speed by the use of short syllables, and the other an ecclesiastical solemnity by the use of long ones:

> Love, thou art absolute sole lord
> Of life and death.

If so shrewd and sensitive (though so limited) a critic as Johnson failed to define metaphysical poetry by its faults, it is worth while to inquire whether we may not have more success by adopting the opposite method: by assuming that the poets of the seventeenth century (up to the Revolution) were the direct and normal development of the precedent age; and, without prejudicing their case by the adjective 'metaphysical', consider whether their virtue was not something permanently valuable, which subsequently disappeared, but ought not to have disappeared. Johnson has hit, perhaps by accident, on one of their peculiarities, when he observes that 'their attempts were always analytic'; he would not agree that, after the dissociation, they put the material together again in a new unity.

It is certain that the dramatic verse of the later Elizabethan and early Jacobean poets expresses a degree of development of sensibility which is not found in any of the prose, good as it often is. If we except Marlowe, a man of prodigious intelligence, these dramatists were directly or indirectly (it is at least a tenable theory) affected by Montaigne. Even if we except also Jonson and Chapman, these two were notably erudite, and were notably men who incorporated their erudition into their sensibility: their mode of feeling was directly and freshly altered by their reading and thought. In Chapman especially there is a direct sensuous apprehension of thought, or a recreation of thought into feeling, which is exactly what we find in Donne:

> in this one thing, all the discipline
> Of manners and of manhood is contained;
> A man to join himself with th' Universe
> In his main sway, and make in all things fit
> One with that All, and go on, round as it;
> Not plucking from the whole his wretched part,
> And into straits, or into nought revert,
> Wishing the complete Universe might be
> Subject to such a rag of it as he;
> But to consider great Necessity.

We compare this with some modern passage:

No, when the fight begins within himself,
A man's worth something. God stoops o'er his head,
Satan looks up between his feet—both tug—
He's left, himself, i' the middle; the soul wakes
And grows. Prolong that battle through his life!

It is perhaps somewhat less fair, though very tempting (as both poets are concerned with the perpetuation of love by offspring), to compare with the stanzas already quoted from Lord Herbert's Ode the following from Tennyson:

One walked between his wife and child,
With measured footfall firm and mild,
And now and then he gravely smiled.
  The prudent partner of his blood
  Leaned on him, faithful, gentle, good,
  Wearing the rose of womanhood.
And in their double love secure,
The little maiden walked demure,
Pacing with downward eyelids pure.
  These three made unity so sweet,
  My frozen heart began to beat,
  Remembering its ancient heat.

The difference is not a simple difference of degree between poets. It is something which had happened to the mind of England between the time of Donne or Lord Herbert of Cherbury and the time of Tennyson and Browning; it is the difference between the intellectual poet and the reflective poet. Tennyson and Browning are poets, and they think; but they do not feel their thought as immediately as the odour of a rose. A thought to Donne was an experience; it modified his sensibility. When a poet's mind is perfectly equipped for its work, it is constantly amalgamating disparate experience; the ordinary man's experience is chaotic, irregular, fragmentary. The latter falls in love, or reads Spinoza, and these two experiences have nothing to do with each other, or with the noise of the typewriter or the smell of cooking; in the mind of the poet these experiences are always forming new wholes.

We may express the difference by the following theory: The poets of the seventeenth century, the successors of the dramatists of the sixteenth, possessed a mechanism of sensibility which could devour any kind of experience. They are simple, artificial, difficult, or fantastic, as their predecessors were; no less nor more than Dante, Guido Cavalcanti, Guinicelli, or Cino. In the seventeenth century a dissociation of sensibility set in, from which we have never recovered; and this dissociation, as is natural, was aggravated by the influence of the two most powerful poets of the century, Milton and Dryden. Each of these men performed certain poetic functions so magnificently well that the magnitude of the effect concealed the absence of others. The language went on and in some respects improved; the best verse of Collins, Gray, Johnson, and even Goldsmith satisfies some of our fastidious demands better than that of Donne or Marvell or King. But while the language became more refined, the feeling became more crude. The feeling, the sensibility, expressed in the *Country Churchyard* (to say nothing of Tennyson and Browning) is cruder than that in the *Coy Mistress*.

The second effect of the influence of Milton and Dryden followed from the first, and was therefore slow in manifestation. The sentimental age began early in the eighteenth century, and continued. The poets revolted against the ratiocinative, the descriptive; they thought and felt by fits, unbalanced; they reflected. In one or two passages of Shelley's *Triumph of Life*, in the second *Hyperion*, there are traces of a struggle toward unification of sensibility. But Keats and Shelley died, and Tennyson and Browning ruminated.

After this brief exposition of a theory—too brief, perhaps, to carry conviction—we may ask, what would have been the fate of the 'metaphysical' had the current of poetry descended in a direct line from them, as it descended in a direct line to them? They would not, certainly, be classified as metaphysical. The possible interests of a poet are unlimited; the more intelligent he is the better; the more intelligent he is the more likely that he will have interests: our only condition is that he turn them into poetry, and not merely meditate on them poetically. A philosophical theory which has entered into poetry is established, for its truth or falsity in one sense ceases to matter, and its truth in another sense is proved. The poets in question have, like other poets, various faults. But they were, at best, engaged in the task of trying to find the verbal equivalent for states of mind and feeling. And this means both that they are more mature, and that they wear better, than later poets of certainly not less literary ability.

It is not a permanent necessity that poets should be interested in philosophy, or in any other subject. We can only say that it appears likely that poets in our civilization, as it exists at present, must be *difficult*. Our civilization comprehends great variety and complexity, and this variety and complexity, playing upon a refined sensibility, must produce various and complex results. The poet must become more and more comprehensive, more allusive, more indirect, in order to force, to dislocate if necessary, language into his meaning. (A brilliant and extreme statement of this view, with which it is not requisite to associate oneself, is that of M. Jean Epstein, *La Poésie d'aujourdhui*.) Hence we get something which looks very much like the conceit—we get, in fact, a method curiously similar to that of the 'metaphysical poets', similar also in its use of obscure words and of simple phrasing.

> O géraniums diaphanes, guerroyeurs sortilèges,
> Sacrilèges monomanes!
> Emballages, dévergondages, douches! O pressoirs

Des vendanges des grands soirs!
Layettes aux abois,
Thyrses au fond des bois!
Transfusions, représailles,
Relevailles, compresses et l'éternal potion,
Angélus! n'en pouvior plus
De débâcles nuptiales! de débâcles nuptiales![2]

The same poet could write also simply:

Elle est bien loin, elle pleure,
Le grand vent se lamente aussi . . .[3]

Jules Laforgue, and Tristan Corbière in many of his poems, are nearer to the 'school of Donne' than any modern English poet. But poets more classical than they have the same essential quality of transmuting ideas into sensations, of transforming an observation into a state of mind.

Pour l'enfant, amoureux de cartes et d'estampes,
L'univers est égal à son vaste appétit.
Ah, que le monde est grand à la clarté des lampes!
Aux yeux du souvenir que le monde est petit![4]

In French literature the great master of the seventeenth century—Racine—and the great master of the nineteenth—Baudelaire—are in some ways more like each other than they are like anyone else. The greatest two masters of diction are also the greatest two psychologists, the most curious explorers of the soul. It is interesting to speculate whether it is not a misfortune that two of the greatest masters of diction in our language, Milton and Dryden, triumph with a dazzling disregard of the soul. If we continued to produce Miltons and Drydens it might not so much matter, but as things are it is a pity that English poetry has remained so incomplete. Those who object to the 'artificiality' of Milton or Dryden sometimes tell us to 'look into our hearts and write'. But that is not looking deep enough; Racine or Donne looked into a good deal more than the heart. One must look into the cerebral cortex, the nervous system, and the digestive tracts.

May we not conclude, then, that Donne, Crashaw, Vaughan, Herbert and Lord Herbert, Marvell, King, Cowley at his best, are in the direct current of English poetry, and that their faults should be reprimanded by this standard rather than coddled by antiquarian affection? They have been enough praised in terms which are implicit limitations

2. "O transparent geraniums, warrior incantations, / Monomaniac sacrileges! / Packing materials, shamelessnesses, shower baths! O wine presses / Of great evening vintages! / Hard-pressed baby linen, / Thyrsis in the depths of the woods! / Transfusions, reprisals, / Churchings, compresses, and the eternal potion, / Angelus! no longer to be borne (are) / Catastrophic marriages!" This passage is from *Derniers vers X* ("Last Poems," 1890), by Jules Laforgue (1860–87) [*Editor*].

3. "She is far away, she weeps, / The great wind mourns also." From *Derniers vers XI, Sur une déjunte* ("On a Dead Woman") [*Editor*].

4. From Baudelaire's *Le Voyage*: "For the child, in love with maps and prints, / The universe matches his vast appetite. / Ah, how big the world is by lamplight! How small the world is to the eyes of memory!" [*Editor*].

because they are 'metaphysical' or 'witty', 'quaint' or 'obscure', though at their best they have not these attributes more than other serious poets. On the other hand, we must not reject the criticism of Johnson (a dangerous person to disagree with) without having mastered it, without having assimilated the Johnsonian canons of taste. In reading the celebrated passage in his essay on Cowley we must remember that by wit he clearly means something more serious than we usually mean to-day; in his criticism of their versification we must remember in what a narrow discipline he was trained, but also how well trained; we must remember that Johnson tortures chiefly the chief offenders, Cowley and Cleveland. It would be a fruitful work, and one requiring a substantial book, to break up the classification of Johnson (for there has been none since) and exhibit these poets in all their difference of kind and of degree, from the massive music of Donne to the faint, pleasing tinkle of Aurelian Townshend—whose *Dialogue between a Pilgrim and Time* is one of the few regrettable omissions from the excellent anthology of Professor Grierson.

J. B. LEISHMAN

["Dissociation of Sensibility"] †

> In the seventeenth century a dissociation of sensibility set in, from which we have never recovered; and this dissociation, as is natural, was aggravated by the influence of the two most powerful poets of the century, Milton and Dryden. Each of these men performed certain poetic functions so magnificently well that the magnitude of the effect concealed the absence of others. The language went on and in some respects improved; the best verse of Collins, Gray, Johnson, and even Goldsmith satisfies some of our fastidious demands better than that of Donne or Marvell or King. But while the language became more refined, the feeling became more crude. The feeling, the sensibility, expressed in the *Country Churchyard* (to say nothing of Tennyson and Browning) is cruder than that in the *Coy Mistress.*[1]

This famous *pronunciamento* occurs in the essay on *The Metaphysical Poets*; in his essay on Marvell Mr. Eliot returns to this picture and fills in some of the detail: Dryden, he there declares, isolated the element of wit and exaggerated it into something like pure fun, while Milton dispensed with it altogether and contented himself (if I understand Mr. Eliot aright) with mere magniloquence. The phrase 'dissociation of sensibility', which Mr. Eliot coined to describe the process he deplored,

† From J. B. Leishman, *The Monarch of Wit*, copyright 1951, 1959. Pp. 91–94. Reprinted by permission of the publishers, Hutchinson Publishing Group Ltd.

1. *Selected Essays*, 274.

and to which he accused Milton and Dryden of contributing, soon led to the coinage (not, I think, by Mr. Eliot himself) of the phrase 'unified sensibility' to describe that 'mechanism of sensibility' which the earlier seventeenth-century poets possessed, or were supposed to have possessed; and it is perhaps not going too far to say that these two phrases alone have enabled several later writers to set up in business and drive quite a prosperous trade as literary and historical critics.

In these views, these very influential views, on seventeenth-century poetry, which I have tried to expound and explain as clearly and fairly as I could, there is, as I said at the outset, much that is true and illuminating together with much that is either very limitedly true or almost wholly untrue. The question, though, which I chiefly want to raise is this: *how much* of the work of our so-called metaphysical poets, and, in particular, to how much of Donne's poetry, does Mr. Eliot's definition of seventeenth-century wit and his praise of undissociated, or pre-dissociated, seventeenth-century sensibility really apply? Does it, for example, apply to any or all of Donne's Elegies, those poems which we have been reviewing and analysing so carefully? 'Fidelity to thought and feeling', 'a direct sensuous apprehension of thought, or a recreation of thought into feeling', 'a recognition, implicit in the expression of every experience, of other kinds of experience which are possible': such phrases might well find a place in a description of the ideal modern poet, the kind of poet Mr. Eliot believes (or once believed) that a modern poet should be—uncommitted, unanchored, unaccommodated, with, ultimately, only one subject, his own direct experience of a very puzzling world; an essentially exploring poet, dealing in hints and guesses rather than in statements; not expounding, illustrating, or building upon some inherited world-picture, philosophy, religion or point of view common to himself and to his readers, but suggesting, glimpsing, various kinds of unity and relationship in a world which both to himself and to his readers is infinitely complex, puzzling, and questionable. They are indeed the kind of phrases I myself should be inclined to apply to the later work of Rilke. But Donne's Elegies, not only *The Anagram*, *The Comparison* and the rest, but even the splendidly dramatic ones—for them, with their fundamental unseriousness, is not this rather high language rather out of place? Although it is perhaps not out of place for some of the *Songs and Sonets*, some of the *Divine Poems*, some of Marvell's poems—in a word, for some of the very best seventeenth-century poetry. Is it, though, quite fair, or even quite sensible, to generalize about our so-called metaphysical poetry on the basis of a few anthology pieces, and then to condemn other poets and other poetry for not normally displaying the same virtues? And are even the best pieces, the anthology pieces, quite what Mr. Eliot in these two essays implies? Is he not, to some considerable extent, describing an ideal of poetry which the best work of these poets has suggested to him, and does there not still remain some gap between his praise and even their finest achievements? It is true that he praises them for taking no subject either too lightly or too seriously, but, in his continual insistence on experience and exploration, is he not, perhaps, taking even their more serious poems too seriously, and neglecting, or under-emphasizing, even their very considerable element of play? For although, in comparison with Milton, Donne and Marvell are explorers rather than expounders, they were not explorers in the sense in which Rilke was an explorer: they were never so disinherited, so dependent on their own resources, so naked, so without all hope of receiving any answer from outside themselves as was the poet who exclaimed:

> Who, if I cried, from among the angelic orders
> would hear me?

Beneath all their disinterested curiosity and play of mind there is a fundamental assurance about ultimate things, and even in their most apparently serious explorations there is nearly always something of light-heartedness, something of play.

But I do not propose to use the example of Rilke in order to depreciate the achievements of Donne and Marvell, as Mr. Eliot used the examples of Donne and Marvell to depreciate the achievement of Milton: all I want to do is to examine the achievement of our so-called metaphysical poets, especially of Donne, rather more disinterestedly, and, in particular, to examine Mr. Eliot's theory and to decide how much of Donne's characteristic wit may be regarded as the expression of what has been called a unified sensibility.

This theory of a dissociation of sensibility which set in during the seventeenth-century is still widely accepted as a proven fact, as a firm foundation upon which to build, but to what extent Mr. Eliot himself still believes in it I do not know; neither, if he does still believe in it, do I know which seventeenth-century poets he still regards as possessing, in contrast to Milton and Dryden, a sensibility that was as yet undissociated. For between 1921 and 1931 Mr. Eliot seems to have lost some of his earlier enthusiasm for Donne. In 1931, in an essay on *Donne in our Time* which he contributed to a volume entitled *A Garland for John Donne,* he declared, as proof that Donne's mind was essentially unmedieval, that, while the encyclopaedic knowledge of the Schoolmen was always directed towards unification, 'in Donne there is a manifest fissure between thought and sensibility'—words which, whatever else they may mean, seem to mean the opposite of that 'direct sensuous apprehension of thought, or recreation of thought into feeling' which in 1921 Mr. Eliot found in Chapman and which, he added, 'is exactly what we find in Donne'.[2] 'One reason,' continues Mr. Eliot, in his 1931 essay,

> one reason why Donne has appealed so powerfully to the recent time is that there is in his poetry hardly any attempt at organization;

2. *Selected Essays*, 272.

> rather a puzzled and humorous shuffling of the pieces; and we are inclined to read our own more conscious awareness of the apparent irrelevance and unrelatedness of things into the mind of Donne.[3]

I think I am probably right in supposing that this passage contains a kind of oblique confession, or recantation, and that when Mr. Eliot speaks of Donne's having 'appealed so powerfully to the recent time' he means, partly at least, 'appealed so powerfully to me ten years ago and to many of my readers'; also that, as the result of deepened in·ight, he has found the 'apparent irrelevance and unrelatedness of things' more merely apparent and less real, and is therefore less inclined to read a conscious awareness of such irrelevance and unrelatedness into the mind of Donne. As I say, I do not know whether Mr. Eliot still believes that a dissociation of sensibility set in during the seventeenth-century; neither do I know which, if any, of our seventeenth-century poets he would still regard as exempt from that infection. At any rate, by 1931 he had discovered in Donne 'a manifest fissure between thought and sensibility', which would seem to mean, in the terminology of 1921, that Donne's sensibility was dissociated. * * *

JOSEPH ANTHONY MAZZEO

A Critique of Some Modern Theories of Metaphysical Poetry †

Numerous theories of "metaphysical" poetry have been advanced ever since the appearance of Sir Herbert Grierson's great edition of Donne's poems in 1912 initiated the modern revaluation of the "metaphysical" poets. However, few of these theories seem to have approached the problem from the perspectives offered by sixteenth- and seventeenth-century literary critics themselves. One of the reasons for this oversight is the curious fact that there is no body of critical literature in English on the metaphysical movement written when that movement, under various names, such as "Concettismo," "Marinismo," and "Gongorismo," was flourishing throughout Europe. Another reason is that we seem to have forgotten that the word "conceit," "concetto," or "concepto" also meant metaphor as well as "conceit" in the sense in which Dr. Johnson used the word. This is especially surprising when we consider that many modern critics find the most striking characteristic of the metaphysical poet to be his desire to extend the range and variety of metaphorical expression.

3. *op. cit.*, 8.

† From *Modern Philology*, L (November, 1952), pp. 88–96. Reprinted by permission of the publishers, The University of Chicago Press, and Joseph A. Mazzeo.

Giordano Bruno, the first critic to attempt a conceptual formulation of "concettismo," as the "metaphysical" style was known in Italy, began his argument to *De gli eroici furori* with an attack on the Petrarchan theory of poetic inspiration. For the older notion of "amore" directed toward personal beauty, Bruno attempted to substitute the idea of "heroic love" directed toward the universe. This second kind of love he interprets as the gift which both the philosopher and the poet have for perceiving the unity of dissimilars or, in other terms, for making heterogeneous analogies. Thus, for Bruno, "metaphysical" poetry was essentially concerned with perceiving and expressing the universal correspondences in his universe.

This conception of the poet as one who discovers and expresses the universal analogies binding the universe together was later developed by the theorists of the conceit in the seventeenth century, the most familiar of whom are Baltasar Gracián in Spain and Emmanuele Tesauro in Italy, and was made the basis for a poetic of "concettismo" or, as I have called it elsewhere, "a poetic of correspondences."[1]

One of the cardinal tenets of the critics of the conceit is that the conceit itself is the expression of a correspondence which actually obtains between objects and that, since the universe is a network of universal correspondences or analogies which unite all the apparently heterogeneous elements of experience, the most heterogeneous metaphors are justifiable. Thus the theorists of the conceit justify the predilection of the "school of wit" for recondite and apparently strained analogies by maintaining that even the more violent couplings of dissimilars were simply expressions of the underlying unity of all things.

It is, of course, true that analogical thought is a fundamental property of the human mind in any age and that the notion of universal analogy has a long history which reaches back to Plato. The important point is that Bruno and the theorists of the conceit employed the principle as the basis of a poetic for the first time. The fact that they did so does not "explain" metaphysical poetry any more than Aristotle's *Poetics* "explains" Sophocles. This is not the function of a poetic or a theory of poetry. Rather, it formulates conceptually a concrete body of literature already in existence. As Hegel put it in his preface to *The Philosophy of Right*, "When philosophy paints its gray in gray, a shape of life has grown old . . . it cannot be rejuvenated but only understood. The owl of Minerva spreads its wings at twilight."

What a poetic can do, however, is make explicit the cultural presuppositions which may underlie a particular body of literature, a style, or a genre. That Bruno and the theorists of the conceit should have based their poetic on the principle of universal analogy meant that they wished

1. Giordano Bruno, *Opere italiane*, ed. Giovanni Gentile, Vol. II (Barir, 1927). I refer the reader to two articles of mine which are in process of publication. One, "A Seventeenth-Century Theory of Metaphysical Poetry," has appeared in *RR* (December, 1951). The other, "Metaphysical Poetry and the Poetic of Correspondences," will appear in *JHI*.

to justify and formulate philosophically the actual practice of metaphysical poets in making recondite and heterogeneous analogies and in using mundane and "learned" images.

The principle of universal analogy as a poetic, or the poetic of correspondences, offers, in my opinion, a theory of metaphysical poetry which is simpler, in greater harmony with the evidence, and freer from internal contradictions than the major modern theories that have yet been formulated. It is in the light of this theory, contemporary to the metaphysical movement, that I propose to review the various modern theories.

One popular modern theory derives "metaphysical" poetry from the Petrarchan and troubadour traditions and describes it as a decadent and exaggerated version of these earlier traditions.[2] If this is so, we can hardly understand the deliberately "irregular" versification of many of the greatest "metaphysical" poets, such as Donne; the colloquial tone and the homely and technical imagery characteristic of "concettismo"; the fact that Bruno, a "concettista" himself and the probable founder of Neapolitan "concettismo," began his *De gli eroici furori* with an attack on the Petrarchan and troubadour conventions and offered a clear and determined substitute theory. He, at least, was certain that he was doing something else, and the poetic creations of the "metaphysicals" is sufficient evidence that he was. We can avoid this conclusion only if we insist on regarding the conceit as merely an odd or unusual image, in which case we can find it everywhere (and therefore nowhere) and even take its origin back to Martial. But it is clear that literary history cannot be made from superficial similarities and that the historian of taste must seek and determine the different cultural presuppositions that underlie the creations of minds as diverse as Bruno and Arnaut Daniel, without, at the same time, swallowing up the individual uniqueness and greatness of every great artist and work of art in the general historical categories we construct for them.

Another theory would attribute the "metaphysical" style to the influence of Ramistic logic, but it seems to me that this view raises more questions than it answers. Norman E. Nelson has made an acute criticism of the confusion between poetry, rhetoric, and logic that the defenders of the Ramistic theory are involved in.[3] It is at least questionable whether any system of inference or any empirical construction like rhetoric can have the kind of effect on a culture that Miss Tuve, the originator of this theory, describes. If her almost deterministic view of the influence of logic and rhetoric were true, she would still have to explain away the fact that Milton, who wrote a Ramist logic and defended Ramist theories, was surely no "metaphysical" poet. The connection between "concettismo" and Ramism, if one can be established, is not a causal

2. Helmut Hatzfeld, "A Clarification of the Baroque Problem in the Romance Literatures," *Comparative Literature*, I (1949), 115–16.

3. This theory is advanced primarily by Rosemond Tuve, *Elizabethan and Metaphysical Imagery* (Chicago, 1946). Nelson's article on *Peter Ramus and the Confusion of Logic, Rhetoric and Poetry* is in the series "University of Michigan Contributions in Modern Philology," No. 2 (April 1947).

relationship. Rather, they are both expressive, in different ways, of what we might call the "rhetoricizing" tendency of Renaissance humanism, the belief shared with Ramus by Valla and others that literature or rhetoric, rather than the old scholastic logic, revealed the true path which the mind must take in its quest for truth.[4] It would seem that the confusion of logic and poetry characteristic of our modern "Ramists" is a result of the current use of the term "logical image" to refer to the kind of expanded metaphor characteristic of much "metaphysical" poetry. It is, of course, clear that the "logic" of development of an expanded metaphor has often very little to do with the logic of a syllogism or system of inference and is, indeed, directed toward a different end.

Another group of scholars relates the "metaphysical" style to the baroque, but variously, sometimes completely identifying it with the baroque and sometimes distinguishing the two. Croce, for example, calls "concettismo" a baroque phenomenon but considers anything baroque a negative aspect of Renaissance history whose only excuse for existence was to purge Western civilization from medievalism. It is otherwise with Hatzfeld, who, distinguishing "concettismo" and baroque, gives the honors to the latter, of which the conceit and its uses are, at most, a degenerate parody.[5] It is difficult to discuss the views of this group, since the term "baroque" itself is, like "Renaissance" and "Romantic," so variable in reference. However, the notion has been applied with greatest success to the study of the visual arts, where it is at least referable to specific techniques. I do not propose to complicate further this already complex problem, but it would seem desirable to keep the characteristics of baroque painting, sculpture, and architecture firmly in mind when we extend this term to other cultural spheres and not allow ourselves to be misled by chronological simultaneity alone. The original fruitful use of the concept of the baroque with reference to the plastic arts suggests that Cassirer's category of "form" and the principle of universal analogy might well be kept separated and that true "concettismo" belongs to the latter, while the baroque, as Croce suggested, is best understood as the transformation of the Renaissance interest in "form" into a preoccupation with "ornament" and in a weakening of the distinctions between the arts.

Perhaps the most widespread theory of the "metaphysical" style is the emblem theory. This view, establishing a causal connection between the emblem movement or "emblem habit" and the conceit which is purportedly its result, is usually expressed in terms of a baroque theory of the "metaphysical" style. Mario Praz, the foremost representative of this

4. This view was characteristic of many humanists who were also nominalists and who therefore banished all previous metaphysical assumptions from logic. The new rhetoric-logic was to teach men how to follow in their voluntary thinking the same "natural" laws that were followed in involuntary thinking. Hence the numerous literary examples to be found in Ramist logics. However, although Ramus abandoned the old metaphysical assumptions, he reintroduced the old categories, arranging them by dichotomies in a purely arbitrary and empirical order.

5. See René Wellek, "The Concept of Baroque in Literary Scholarship," *Journal of Aesthetics*, V (1946), 77–109, for a discussion of the concept of baroque and for a bibliography on the subject.***

group, bases his analysis on Croce's, without assuming the latter's negative attitude toward either the baroque or the "metaphysical" styles. However, his study of the actual creations of this literary movement leads him to a view of the conceit and the emblem which might be called the "game" theory, a position he assumes when he says of the conceit and emblem that they are of the nature of the charade or riddle—the by-products of an amusing, lighthearted (perhaps perverse?) verbal and pictorial game.[6] This is surely an astonishing description of a style in which some of the greatest religious poetry of all time was written, and it is, in effect, denied by the sensitivity of Praz's concrete criticism of John Donne and Richard Crashaw.

I believe that this conclusion is a consequence of Praz's insistence on the intimate relationship between emblem and conceit and between the mass of different styles, some of them quite perverse, which went under the name of "Marinismo," "Gongorismo," "Seicentismo," "Euphuism," etc. However, not only are the resemblances between Donne and Lyly superficial at best, but the easy application of some notion of strangeness or eccentricity in style will find resemblances where none exists and lead to false or useless descriptions of cultural phenomena. Praz seems closer to a working definition of the conceit when he says that it is to poetry what the illusory perspective is to art, although, in the light of both the theory and the practice of the "metaphysical" style, this insight is of somewhat limited utility and best describes a style like Crashaw's.

Praz makes much of the fact that the emblem was usually accompanied by an epigram, and, since he seems to hold that emblem and "metaphysical" poem are related to each other as cause and effect, he concludes that the epigram is the genre most characteristic of "concettismo." This conclusion, in turn, leads to his placing great emphasis on the diffusion of the *Greek Anthology* during the Renaissance as one of the important influences on the growth of the "metaphysical" movement.[7] However, while the *Greek Anthology* stimulated many imitators, it seems to have had little effect on the best of the poets of wit. The long and "conceited" works of Marino, Gongora, Donne, and others preclude accepting this view, at least in the form in which it is stated. Praz's stress on the epigram also leads him to emphasize brevity as the most desirable quality of a good conceit, a quality which presumably helped make it "sharp" or "pointed." Brevity in the conceit was commended by the theorists of the conceit themselves, but they also recognized what we would today call the "expanded metaphor," and they often seem to mean

6. Praz, *John Donne*, p. 7. Other works in support of the emblem theory are Rosemary Freeman, *English Emblem Books* (London, 1948); Austin Warren, *Richard Crashaw: A Study in Baroque Sensibility* (University, La., 1939); Ruth Wallerstein, *Studies in Seventeenth-Century Poetic* (Madison, 1950). Miss Wallerstein also agrees with Miss Tuve on the influence of Ramist logic.

7. Praz, *Richard Crashaw*, pp. 144 ff. This desire to force "influences" leads Praz to find it strange that metaphysical poetry should have flourished in England, although the emblem did not have a very wide vogue there (cf. *Studi dul concettismo*, p. 202).

by "brevity" a quality opposed to the Ciceronian notion of *copia*. There is, of course, no reason why an epigram should not have conceits, but there is also no apparent reason to establish a determined relationship between "concettismo" and epigram and, via the epigram, between "concettismo" and the emblem. I shall take up the more fundamental inadequacies of the emblem theory in detail when I discuss the views of Austin Warren below, since he presents this theory in purer form than does Praz. In the latter's version the emblem plays an important role, but mediately, through the epigram, which had to be brief, playful, and puzzling and was analogous to illusory perspective in the arts. However, while this analysis is true of certain individual works, especially of some productions of the school of Marino, it is inadequate to the movement as a whole and gives no real clue to the *forma mentis* of a "concettista."

Indeed, this theory of the conceit was implicitly rejected by the seventeenth-century theorists of the conceit in whose works the emblem and *impresa*, as well as the epigram or "arte lapidaria," are treated as incidental topics involved in the analysis of conceit or metaphor. They were fully aware that any theory of the conceit had to be a theory of metaphor or analogy, not a theory of genres. Emmanuele Tesauro, for example, analyzed all genres, literary and artistic, as forms of "acutezze" or types of metaphorical expression by extending the categories of rhetoric to include all literary and figurative creations.[8] Thus Tesauro himself realized that the roots of "concettismo" lay deeper than any classification of genres and were rooted in the nature of expression itself. Not only the epigram but all genres, including the lyric itself, had become "metaphysical."

Austin Warren, as I observed above, shares some of Praz's conceptions about the emblem to an even greater degree. He says:

> The connection of the emblem with poetry was, from the start, close: indeed the term often transferred itself from the picture to the epigram which ordinarily accompanied it. . . . Thus the arts reinforced one another. The influence on poetry was not only to encourage the metaphorical habit but to import to the metaphors a hardness, a palpability which, merely conceived, they were unlikely to possess. And yet the metaphors ordinarily analogized impalpabilities—states of the soul, concepts, abstractions. . . . Many emblems owe their undeniable grotesqueness to the visualization of metaphors, often scriptural, which were not intended to be visualized.[9]

In this particular passage, I take it that Warren means by "hardness" a kind of precision and by "palpability" a strong visual or sensuous element in the image. In any case the "metaphysical" image purportedly

8. Emmanuele Tesauro, *Il Cannochiale Aristotelico* (2d ed., 1663), chaps. xiv, xv. In these two chapters Tesauro sketched the outline of his generalized theory of wit. Cf. Croce, *Problemi di estetica*, pp. 313 ff.

9. Warren, pp. 73–74.

acquired these properties from the "emblem habit," which helped to develop metaphorical habits of mind and, presumably, habits for making recondite metaphors instead of commonplace ones.

However, as I have already explained, the theorists of the conceit either do not deal with the emblem at all or treat it merely as one aspect of the general theory of wit, making no direct connection between emblem and conceit. Taking our cue from them once more, we might observe that the qualities of precision and the strong sensuous element to be found in much "metaphysical" poetry can be accounted for, to the degree that any poetic "accounts for" a living and creative poetic tradition, by their theory of wit *(ingegno, ingenio, esprit)* as the faculty which, like Bruno's *genio*, finds and expresses the universal analogies latent in the data of experience. The desire to draw correspondences between heterogeneous things and thereby reveal the unity of what appears fragmentary and the desire to develop these correspondences are bound to give to the resultant imagery some of those qualities Warren discerns in the poets of wit.

From a more general critical point of view, the "palpability" or "hardness" of an image is, after all, a function of what the poet wishes to say and can say. In its own way Dante's imagery is as "hard" and "palpable" as one could wish. What the poet can say and the way he can say it are in part given by his culture, in so far as the culture makes him a man of a particular place, time, and environment, and in large part by his imaginative power, which enables him to "inform" and universalize his cultural and personal experience. No poetic has yet explained the secret of his power, although a poetic which is true to the concrete works of art it attempts to describe theoretically can give us insight into the nature of the imagination by telling us what it did with what it worked with. Universal analogy and its later formulation as a poetic can thus tell us something about the Renaissance imagination and throw light on Donne, Marino, Crashaw, and others, in spite of their differences. In this light, it would seem to be an error to attribute a movement such as "concettismo" to some secondary cultural phenomenon such as the "emblem habit" or Ramist logic and try, by so doing, to obliterate the differences between poets by swallowing them up in an influence.

Warren's version of the emblem theory of "metaphysical" poetry is based on a general theory of imagery involving the nature of the analogues in a metaphor:

> All imagery is double in its reference, a composite of perception and conception. Of the ingredients, the proportions may vary. The metaphorist can collate image with image, or image with concept, or concept with image, or concept with concept.[1]

After discussing the series of combinations according to which the "ingredients" of an image may be arranged, he continues:

1. *Ibid.*, p. 177.

> Then too, the metaphorists differ widely in the degree of visualization for which they project their images. The epic simile of Homer and of Spenser is fully pictorial; the intent, relative to the poet's architecture, is decorative. On the other hand, the "sunken" and "radical" types of imagery—the conceits of Donne and the "symbols" of Hart Crane—expect scant visualization by the senses.[2]

This passage is especially important because the author is here distinguishing between those poets called "metaphysical" (he also seems to include the modern "neo-metaphysicals") and all others. However, in this passage Warren is not analyzing the school of wit and its imagery in terms of "palpability" or "hardness" purportedly derived from the emblem; indeed, he seems to be saying that the Donnean conceit is capable of "scant visualization." It would therefore lack the properties which the emblem supposedly gave to the conceit. In the passage previously cited, Warren closely connected the emblem to the conceit, while in this passage the conceit is completely severed from those properties which it was supposed to have derived from the emblem.

It is clear that we are involved in a contradiction. Unintentionally, Warren is pointing out one important thing about "metaphysical" poetry and about poetic imagery in general. The qualities of the "metaphysical" image seem to have nothing to do with whether or not it can be visualized or with the sensory content of the image itself, although it may be prominent. The qualities of the "metaphysical" image are a function of the *manner* in which the analogues are related, and it is this very point that the theorists of the conceit make when they insist that the wit is in the "form" of the conceit and not in the "matter."

A further reason for the inevitable inadequacy of the emblem theory is the historical fact that the emblem movement, initiated by the introduction of the *Hieroglyphica* of Horapollo to Renaissance Europe, is a cultural phenomenon distinct from the poetry of wit and has other cultural presuppositions. Although emblem and conceit were later found together, they are found together at a relatively late date and usually in minor authors like Quarles, who gave emblems already in existence a verse commentary.[3] Granted that a poet might find an emblem suggestive of some image or another, the vast bulk of the creations of the school of wit do not seem to be related to the emblem literature in any intrinsic way. The very grotesqueness of many of the emblems is testimony to the fact that the conceit preceded—and was therefore independent of—its graphic expression. If anything, it was the conceit which made the emblem grotesque rather than the emblem making the conceit "harder" and more "palpable." Emblems drawn to many of the conceits of Donne or Crashaw or to much of the so-called "decorative imagery" of Homer would all be equally grotesque.

Perhaps the basic unexamined assumption in this whole theory is that

2. *Ibid.*
3. Cf. *The Hieroglyphics of Horapollo,* trans. George Boas (New York, 1950). Mr. Boas' introduction is quite valuable.***

there is a radical distinction in kinds of imagery. The sharp cleavage between what are called "decorative" imagery and "functional" imagery needs to be closely examined. We might begin by asking in what sense the imagery of Homer can be said to be decorative. It is clear even from a cursory reading of the *Iliad* that many of Homer's analogues for the events of battle are drawn from the world of peaceful endeavor. One of the obvious functions of these analogues is to heighten the pitch of the battle scenes and to bring the "great" world of peace into relationship with the "little" world of war. In this sense the *Iliad* is as much about peace as about war; metaphor is the link between these two worlds, revealing the nature of war through analogy with the events and experiences of peace. It follows that the poet's "choice" of analogues depends upon what he wants to say, upon what elements in the world of men he wishes to bring into the world of his poem. This is at least one sense in which the microcosm-macrocosm analogy is still profoundly vital.

When Homer compares an attacking army to a huge wave breaking on a beach, he would, in the opinion of some, be making a fully pictorial metaphor. However, all the reader has to do is to try to think of the various ways in which an emblem might be constructed to represent this metaphor to see how grotesque the results could be. Two *separate* pictures could be drawn, and they could be quite photographic. But this would not result in the creation of an emblem, for the emblem would have to embody the whole metaphor at once in one representation. We must bear in mind that the metaphor is part identity and part difference. What Homer wants us to see is the way in which a wave under certain conditions is like an army under certain other conditions. By joining these two particular analogues, he selects those qualities of waves which can be transferred to armies. The pictorial quality is not in the whole metaphor or in the identity but in each analogue separately as a kind of sensuous residue remaining after the identity has been established, and as such it is part of the total effect of the image. Thus the pictorial quality remains precisely that aspect of the image which cannot be transferred from one analogue to the other.

It follows from this analysis that, when we speak of "pictorial imagery," we cannot mean that the metaphor can necessarily be absorbed into a pictorial representation or that, conversely, it was necessarily created by a graphic representation. Both historical evidence and theoretical necessity, therefore, require abandoning the emblem theory of "metaphysical" poetry. The emblem movement is more closely related to the tendency in the baroque plastic arts toward breaking down the barriers between the arts in the effort to create a universal art which would somehow combine all of them. Its great vogue was largely the work of the Jesuits, who found the emblem a useful pedagogic device for propagating the faith.

The failure to see the way in which the emblem is related and the extent to which it is not related to the conceit can lead to some further misinterpretations. Praz, for example, derives the limbeck image as used in the writings of the spiritual alchemists from the emblem tradition and believes that this image is a mere "conceit" or witticism.[4] But it was part of the religious and symbolic vocabulary derived from the symbols of empirical alchemy by application of the principle of universal analogy whereby they were extended to apply to all levels of existence. The limbeck was thus no mere suggestive and fanciful image but the symbol of a process that was recapitulated in every order of a universe seen *sub specie alchemiae*. The failure to realize the nature of this image leads Praz to misunderstand the significance of the work of Michael Maier, the alchemist who published an alchemical work containing both emblems and music to be sung to the various stages of the alchemical process, as a very strange example of baroque sensibility or "concettismo."[5] However, what Maier did was to use the emblems for their pedagogic value, much as a chemistry textbook might have illustrations and equations. Music as a necessary part of the alchemical process was a characteristic result of the conviction that all things are universally related and affect each other through correspondences.

Although, as Warren maintains, "both the emblem and the conceit proceed from wit," they do not proceed from the same kind of wit, or in the same way.[6] The relationship is not, above all, filial but, at most, cousinly. Our own time is less "witty" than the time of Donne, and universal analogy has passed out of existence as a common habit of thought; the difficulty we have in penetrating this view of the world from within and somehow understanding it as "natural" and not "perverse" is, perhaps, the most important reason of all for the confusion about the nature of the poetry of wit. Many students of the movement have been aware that what may impress us as perverse, shocking, or recondite need not have had the same effect on contemporaries. This has sometimes been attributed to habitual usage and "taste." However, the "metaphysical" poets and their contemporaries possessed a view of the world founded on universal analogy and derived habits of thought which prepared them for finding and easily accepting the most heterogeneous analogies.[7]

4. Praz, *Studi sul concettismo*, pp. 49–50 n., 199–200.

5. Michael Maier, *Atalanta fugiens* (Oppenheim, 1618). Also John Read, *Prelude to Chemistry* (New York, 1937), chap. vi, which is on Maier. Some samples of his music in modern notation are appended to the work. For spiritual alchemy see H. Bremond, *Histoire littéraire du sentiment religieux en France* (Paris, 1925), Vol. VII, Part II, chap. v; and Evelyn Underhill, *Mysticism* (16th ed.; New York, 1948), pp. 140 ff.

6. Warren, p. 75.

7. *Ibid.*, p. 173.

Donne's Love Poetry

JOAN BENNETT

The Love Poetry of John Donne†

A Reply to Mr. C. S. Lewis

In that brilliant and learned book *The Allegory of Love* Mr. Lewis writes, 'cynicism and idealism about women are twin fruits on the same branch—are the positive and negative poles of a single thing'. Few poets provide a better illustration of this than John Donne. These *Songs and Sonets* and *Elegies* which, Mr. Lewis would have us believe, never explain 'why people write poems about love at all', are the work of one who has tasted every fruit in love's orchard, from that which pleased only while he ate it—

> And when hee hath the kernell eate
> Who doth not fling away the shell?—

to that which raised a thirst for even fuller spiritual satisfaction, so that he wrote:

> Here the admyring her my mind did whett
> To seeke thee God.

How is it that distinguished critics wonder what it is all about; that Dryden declares 'Donne perplexes the minds of the fair sex with nice speculations of philosophy, when he should engage their hearts and entertain them with the softness of love'; and that Mr. Lewis wonders 'what any sensible woman can make of such love-making'? A part of the trouble is, I believe, that they are accustomed to, or that they prefer, another kind of love poetry, in which the poet endeavours to paint the charms of his mistress:

> Some asked me where Rubies grew
> And nothing I did say:
> But with my finger pointed to
> The lips of Julia.

† From *Seventeenth-Century Studies Presented to Sir Herbert Grierson*, copyright 1938. Pp. 85–104. Reprinted by permission of the publishers, The Clarendon Press, Oxford.

Some asked how Pearls did grow and where?
Then spoke I to my Girle,
To part her lips and show them there
the Quarelets of Pearl.

Donne tells us very little about that beauty of 'colour and skin' which he describes in *The Undertaking* as 'but their oldest clothes'. He writes almost exclusively about the emotion, and not about its cause; he describes and analyses the experience of being in love, if I may use that word for the moment to cover his many kinds of experience which range from the mere sensual delight presupposed in *Elegy XIX* to the 'marriage of true minds' celebrated in *The Good-morrow*, or in *The Valediction: forbidding mourning*. In *Elegy XIX*, for instance, Donne is writing of the same kind of experience as that of which Carew writes in *The Rapture*. But Carew expends his poetic gifts in description of the exquisite body of the woman, so that the reader can vicariously share his joys. Donne, on the other hand, gives two lines to description, and even so they are not really about what he sees; he is content to suggest by analogy the delight of the eye when the woman undresses:

Your gown going off, such beauteous state reveals,
As when from flowry meads th' hills shadow steales.

The poem is not about her exquisite body, but about what he feels like when he stands there waiting for her to undress. Now it may be that 'any sensible woman' would rather be told of

Thy bared snow and thy unbraided gold,

but I am not sure. She can see that in her looking-glass, or she may believe she sees these things reflected in the work of some painter, for the painter's art can show such things better than any words. It may interest her more to know what it feels like to be a man in love. In any case, it is of that that Donne chooses to write. He is not incapable of describing physical charms; his description of a blush in *The Second Anniversary*:

her pure, and eloquent blood
Spoke in her cheekes, and so distinctly wrought,
That one might almost say, her body thought;

is better, in my judgement, than Spenser's

And troubled bloud through his pale face was seene
To come and goe with tydings from the hart.[1]

Or again, Mr. Lewis speaks of the radiance of Lovelace's line,

But shake your head and scatter day,

which was anticipated, and perhaps suggested, by Donne's

1. *The Faerie Queene*, I. ix, 51.

Ev'ry thy haire for love to worke upon
Is much too much, some fitter must be sought;
For, nor in nothing, nor in things
Extreme, and scatt'ring bright, can love inhere.

But the fact remains that such touches of description are very rare in Donne's poetry. His interest lay elsewhere, namely in dramatizing, and analysing, and illustrating by a wealth of analogy the state, or rather states, of being in love.

But what does he mean by love? We have the whole mass of Donne's poems before us, thrown together higgledy-piggledy with no external evidence as to when or to whom any one of them was written. And in some of them love is 'imposture all', or 'a winter-seeming summers night'; in others physical union is all in all so that two lovers in bed are a whole world; and elsewhere we are told that

Difference of sex no more wee knew
Than our Guardian Angells doe.

And elsewhere again:

Our bodies why doe wee forbeare?
They are ours, though they are not wee, Wee are
The intelligences, they the spheare.
We owe them thankes because they thus
Did us, to us, at first convay,
Yeelded their forces, sense, to us,
Nor are drosse to us, but allay.

The temptation to assign each poem to a particular period and to associate each with a particular woman is very strong. It has been yielded to again and again, not only in Sir Edmund Gosse's biography, but much more recently. Yet it must be resisted for two reasons: first because we have no evidence as to when any one of the *Songs and Sonets* was written, and secondly because we cannot know how far the experience of which any one of them treats was real or imaginary. Mr. Lewis is very well aware of these things. But it is no less misleading to go to the other extreme and read them as though they were all written at one time, or all with equal seriousness and sincerity. We have some important facts to guide us. Between the years 1597 and 1601 Donne fell in love with Anne More. He married her in 1601, as Walton puts it, 'without the allowance of those friends whose approbation always was, and ever will be necessary, to make even a virtuous love become lawful'. He had nine children by her, and watched over them with her when they were sick, and suffered with her when some of them died. He had been married seven years when he wrote a letter headed 'From mine hospital at Mitcham', in which he says:

> I write from the fire-side in my parlour, and in the noise of three gamesome children, and by the side of her whom, because I have

> transplanted to such a wretched fortune, I must labour to disguise that from her by all such honest devices, as giving her my company and discourse.

Three years later, in 1611, Donne is reluctant to leave home and travel with his patron Sir Robert Drury, because his wife, who was then with child, 'professed an unwillingness to allow him any absence from her saying her divining soul boded her some ill in his absence'. The wording of that sentence, quoted by Walton, is heard again in one of Donne's loveliest songs, but the sense is reversed. Experience tells us that when we are afraid to let a loved one go it is not, as a rule, because *we* may come to harm in his absence. It is much more probable that Anne Donne was afraid for her husband on those dangerous seas to which his poetry so often refers, and that he then wrote the lyric for her, which pleads:

> Let not thy divining heart
> Forethinke me any ill,
> Destiny may take thy part,
> And may thy feares fulfill;
> But thinke that wee
> Are but turn'd aside to sleepe;
> They who one another keepe
> Alive n'er parted bee.

This is of course conjecture, and I claim no more than a strong probability. It was on this journey with Sir Robert, which Donne finally and reluctantly undertook, that he saw that 'vision of his wife a dead child in her arms' that Walton so convincingly describes. I am not concerned with the authenticity or otherwise of the vision, but with the direction of Donne's thoughts. In 1614, thirteen years after his marriage, we have further evidence of the constancy and of the quality of Donne's love for his wife. In a letter to Sir Robert More, on 10 August of that year, he again explains why he cannot and will not leave Anne in solitude:

> When I begin to apprehend that, even to myself, who can relieve myself upon books, solitariness was a little burdensome, I believe it would be much more so to my wife if she were left alone. So much company therefore, as I am, she shall not want; and we had not one another at so cheap a rate as that we should ever be weary of one another.

Such words need no comment. But if any more evidence is required as to the nature and endurance of Donne's love for his wife, we have *Holy Sonnet XVII*, written after her death in 1617:

> Since she whom I lov'd hath payd her last debt
> To Nature, and to hers, and my good is dead,
> And her Soule early into heaven ravished,
> Wholly on heavenly things my mind is sett.

Here the admyring her my mind did whett
To seeke thee God; so streames do shew their head.

Without claiming any knowledge as to the dates of particular poems, we are bound to recognize that seventeen years of married love will have taught Donne something he did not know when he wrote, for instance, *Elegy VII*. And we do, in fact, find that the poems express views of love which could scarcely all have been held at the same time.

Mr. Lewis, of course, recognizes that Donne's love poetry is 'not all of a piece'. 'There are poems', he admits, 'in which Donne attempts to sing of a love perfectly in harmony with the moral law, but they are not very numerous and I do not think they are usually among his best pieces'. That judgement seems to me very odd, but it is impossible to discuss it without first deciding of what 'moral law' we are thinking. The moral law governing sexual relations has been very differently conceived of in different periods of the world's history. No one has expounded the medieval view more clearly than Mr. Lewis himself in *The Allegory of Love* where he explains[2] that, for the medieval Church,

> love itself was wicked and did not cease to be wicked if the object of it were your own wife. . . . The views of the medieval churchman on the sexual act within marriage are limited by two complementary agreements. On the one hand nobody ever asserted that the act was intrinsically sinful. On the other hand all were agreed that some evil element was present in every concrete instance of it since the Fall.

Mr. Lewis believes that Donne never for long freed himself from this 'medieval sense of the sinfulness of sexuality'. Born a Roman Catholic, and deeply read in the Fathers of the Church, he must of course have considered it. But does his poetry support the belief that he continued to accept it? The value of Donne's love poetry largely depends upon the answer. 'The great central movement of love poetry in Donne's time', Mr. Lewis reminds us, was a variance with the medieval view. It was now believed that marriage sanctified sexual love; and for Spenser, once the marriage ceremony is over, the sexual act is its proper consummation and the chaste moon bears witness to it in the *Epithalamion*:

Who is the same, which at my window peepes?
Or whose is that faire face that shines so bright?
Is it not Cinthia, she that never sleepes,
But walkes about high heaven al the night?
O fayrest goddesse, do thou not envy
My love with me to spy:
For thou likewise didst love, though now unthought,
And for a fleece of wooll, which privily
The Latmian shepherd once unto thee brought,

2. On page 14 [of *The Allegory of Love* (Oxford, 1936)—*Editor*].

His pleasure with thee wrought.
Therefore to us be favorable now;
And sith of womens labours thou hast charge,
And generation goodly dost enlarge,
Encline thy will t'effect our wishful vow,
And the chaste wombe informe with timely seed,
That may our comfort breed:
Till which we cease our hopeful hap to sing,
Ne let the woods us answere, nor our Eccho ring.

On the other hand, in Chapman's *Hero and Leander*, to which Mr. Lewis especially invites our attention, we have the reverse aspect of this view of the morality of love. The sexual act before marriage, albeit the expression of true love, is not in harmony with the moral law:

By this the Sovereign of Heavens golden fires,
And young *Leander*, Lord of his desires,
Together from their lovers armes arose:
Leander into Hellespontus throwes
His Hero-handled bodie, whose delight
Made him disdaine each other Epithete,
And as amidst the enamoured waves he swims,
The God of gold of purpose guilt his lims,
That this word guilt, including double sence,
The double guilt of his *Incontinence*,
Might be exprest, that had no stay t'employ
The treasure which the Love-God let him joy
In his deare Hero, with such sacred thrift,
As had beseemed so sanctified a gift:
But like a greedie vulgar Prodigall
Would on the stock dispend, and rudely fall
Before his time, to that unblessed blessing,
Which for lusts plague doth perish with possessing.

Where does Donne stand in relation either to this belief that marriage, and marriage alone, sanctifies the sexual act, or to the medieval view that it is alike sinful within or without the marriage bond? If I read the poetry aright, he accepts neither view, or rather he totally rejects the second and does not consider the first. The purity or otherwise of the act depends for him on the quality of the relation between the lovers. We have in *The Sunne Rising* a celebration of the same event as in the stanza quoted from *Epithalamion*; but the difference in treatment is noteworthy. Donne is joyously impudent to the sun, whereas Spenser is ceremoniously respectful to the moon, and (which is the point here relevant), in Donne's poem we neither know nor care whether the marriage ceremony has taken place. For Donne, if delight in one another is mutual, physical union is its proper consummation; but, if the lovers are not 'inter-assuréd of the mind', then 'the sport' is 'but a winter-seeming summers night', and

at their best
Sweetnesse and wit they are but *mummy* possest.

There are a number of poems in which Donne is writing about love which has not reached physical consummation, but there is only one, *The Undertaking*, in which he writes as though this state of affairs were satisfactory. Elsewhere he makes it plain that he has merely acquiesced, not without protest, in the human laws that forbade what he holds to be the natural expression of human loves. This reluctant obedience to the rules is most clearly stated in *The Relique*, where he explains precisely how he and the woman behaved, and makes known in a parenthesis what he thinks of the law that inhibited them:

Comming and going, wee
Perchance might kisse, but not between those meales
Our hands ne'er toucht the seales,
Which nature, injur'd by late law, sets free.

Donne's poetry is not about the difference between marriage and adultery, but about the difference between love and lust. He does not establish the contrast between them in any one poem, but we arrive at his views by submitting ourselves to the cumulative evidence of all his poetry and, in so far as they are relevant, of his prose and his life as well. The most important part of this evidence is the violent contrast between his cynical poems and those in which he celebrates

our waking souls
Which watch not one another out of feare.

In order to establish that contrast I must, unfortunately, refer to the vexed question of Donne's rhythm. Mr. Lewis assures us that 'most modern readers do not know how to scan'. However that may be, unless they can hear the difference between quick and slow movements, or between smooth and staccato, and unless they can submit to the rhythm sufficiently to throw the emphasis precisely where Donne has arranged for it to fall, they cannot understand his poetry. If they can hear these things they will be aware of the difference between the bored, flippant tone of

Will no other vice content you?
Will it not serve your turn to do, as did your mothers?
Or have you all old vices spent, and now would finde out others?
Or doth a feare, that men are true, torment you?
Oh we are not, be not you so,
Let mee, and doe you, twenty know;

and the tone of angry scorn in

Must I alas
Frame and enamell Plate, and drinke in Glasse?
Chase waxe for others seales? breake a colts force
And leave them then, beeing made a ready horse;

and, so utterly remote from either, the controlled emotion in

I scarce believe my love to be so pure
  As I had thought it was,
  Because it doth endure
Vicissitude, and season, as the grasse;
Methinks I lyed all winter when I swore,
My love was infinite, if spring make' it more.

The greatness of Donne's love poetry is largely due to the fact that his experience of the passion ranged from its lowest depths to its highest reaches. No one, not even Shakespeare, knew better than he that

The expense of spirit in a waste of shame
Is lust in action; and till action, lust
Is perjured, murderous, bloody, full of blame,
Savage, extreme, rude, cruel, not to trust;
Enjoy'd no sooner but despised straight;
Past reason hunted; and no sooner had,
Past reason hated.

Many of the *Songs and Sonets* and the *Elegies* dramatize the experience which Shakespeare here describes. But Donne came to know also the 'marriage of true minds', and many of his poems are about that experience. Nor does he repent of this love poetry in the *Holy Sonnets*; on the contrary, he expressly states that love for his wife led directly to the love of God. He does not even overlook his grosser experiences, but it prepared to use 'prophane love' to illustrate his faith in Christ's pity:

No, no, but as in my idolatrie
I said to all my profane mistresses
Beauty, of pitty, foulnesse only is
A signe of rigour: so I say to thee,
To wicked spirits are horrid shapes assign'd
This beauteous forme assures a piteous minde.

There is no note of shame here, neither wallowing self-abasement nor a hiding or forgetting of the past. He is simply using, characteristically, just what is relevant for his present purpose. Physical beauty, which his poetry so seldom describes, he nevertheless accepts as a type of the soul's beauty:

For though mind be the heaven where love doth sit
Beauty a convenient type may be to figure it.

Donne never despised the flesh. Even in a Lenten sermon he asks his hearers 'what Christian is denied a care of his health and a good habitude of body, or the use of those things which may give a cheerfulness to his heart and a cheerfulness to his countenance', and in his *Litany* he prays

From thinking us all soule, neglecting thus
Our mutuall duties, Lord deliver us.

Mr. Lewis's objections to *The Extasie* depend upon Donne's treatment of the relation between soul and body, and it is therefore important to discover what in fact Donne thought about this. 'Love does not', writes Mr. Lewis, 'prove itself pure by talking about purity. It does not keep on drawing distinctions between spirit and flesh to the detriment of the latter and then explaining that the flesh is after all to be used.' I must admit that I find this rather perplexing. Perhaps nothing can be proved by talking about it, neither the purity of love nor the purity of Donne's poetry. But language is the poet's only means of communication, and if Chapman is allowed to express his conception of the immorality of premarital relations by talking about it, why may not Donne, by the same means, express his belief that

> As our blood labours to beget
> Spirits as like soules as it can,
> Because such fingers need to knit
> That subtile knot that makes us man:
> So must pure lovers soules descend
> T'affections, and to faculties,
> Which sense may reach and apprehend,
> Else a great Prince in prison lies.

On what grounds does Mr. Lewis object to Donne 'drawing distinctions between spirit and flesh to the detriment of the latter'? What else could he do? Could a man of his time and of his religion have thought of the flesh either as equal to or as indistinguishable from the spirit? Donne, like any man of his time, and, I suppose, any Christian of any time, thinks of the body as inferior to the soul, although it can be the 'temple of the Holy Ghost'. He is not singular in supposing that, in this life, the soul can and must express itself through the body. Milton goes so far as to assert that even the Angels need some equivalent for this means of expression:

> Whatever pure thou in the body enjoy'st
> (And pure thou wert created,) we enjoy
> In eminence; and obstacle find none
> Of membrane, joint, or limb, exclusive bars;
> Easier than air with air, if Spirits embrace,
> Total they mix, union of pure with pure
> Desiring, nor restrain'd conveyance need,
> As flesh to mix with flesh, or soul with soul.[3]

Donne, in *The Extasie*, is attempting (by his usual means of employing a series of analogies) to explain that the union of spirit with spirit expresses itself in the flesh, just as the soul lives in the body and, in this world, cannot exist without it. The passage quoted above includes one of these analogies, an obscure one for modern readers because it depends on

3. *Paradise Lost*, Bk. viii, 622–9.

contemporary physiology. Sir Herbert Grierson supplies a quotation from Burton's *Anatomy of Melancholy* which gives the explanation:

> The spirits in a man which are the thin and active part of the blood, and so are of a kind of middle nature, between soul and body, those spirits are able to doe, and they doe the office, to unite and apply the faculties of the soul to the organs of the body, and so there is a man.

Sir Herbert also refers us to Donne's twenty-sixth sermon which throws yet more light on the notion to which the poem refers:

> As the body is not the man [writes Donne], nor the soul is not the man, but the union of the soul and the body, by those spirits through which the soul exercises her faculties in the organs of the body, makes up the man; so the union of the Father and the Son to one another, and of both to us, by the Holy Ghost, makes up the body of the Christian religion.

There are, I suppose, three possible views of the relation between soul and body: the Manichaean view that the body is the work of the Devil; the materialist view that 'explains all psychical processes by physical and chemical changes in the nervous system', and so makes the soul non-existent; and the orthodox Christian view that the body and the soul are both from God and therefore both good. We seem to have wandered far from Donne's *Extasie,* and if Mr. Lewis is right in thinking it a 'nasty' poem, these philosophical considerations are irrelevant, and these theological considerations even worse. But is he right? The point Donne wishes to make in *The Extasie,* as in so many of his serious love poems, is that a man and a woman united by love may approach perfection more nearly than either could do alone:

> A single violet transplant
> The strength, the colour, and the size,
> (All which before was poore, and scant,)
> Redoubles still, and multiplies.
> When love, with one another so
> Interinanimates two soules,
> That abler soule, which thence doth flow,
> Defects of loneliness controules.

I have tried to show that Donne was very far from retaining 'the medieval view of the sinfulness of sex'; but Mr. Lewis has yet another accusation to bring, equally incompatible with my own belief that Donne is one of the greatest love poets in the English language. Contempt for women seems to him to permeate the poetry. Once again I shall be forced to assume that readers are more sensitive to rhythm than Mr. Lewis supposes, for I am going to quarrel with Mr. Lewis's interpretation of *Elegy XVI* largely by appealing to the reader's ear. He admits that he 'may be deceived' when he finds here 'a sickened male contempt for the whole female world of nurses and "midnight startings" ' Most certainly he is deceived, and the varied rhythms of that poem are an important index of the extent of that deception. One of the most remarkable things about the poem is the contrast between the solemn, tender music of the verse whenever Donne addresses the woman, and the boisterous staccato in which he describes the foreign lands to whose dangers she will be exposed if she insists upon following him abroad. I must beg leave to quote the poem at sufficient length to illustrate the nature and extent of this difference.

By our first strange and fatall interview,
By all desires which thereof did ensue,
By our long starving hopes, by that remorse
Which my words masculine perswasive force
Begot in thee, and by the memory
Of hurts, which spies and rivals threatned me,
I calmly beg: But by thy fathers wrath,
By all paines, which want and divorcement hath
I conjure thee, and all the oathes which I
And thou have sworne to seale joynt constancy,
Here I unsweare, and overswear them thus,
Thou shalt not love by wayes so dangerous.
Temper, O faire love, loves impetuous rage,
Be my true Mistris still, not my faign'd Page.

It is tempting to quote even more of his melodious pleading, but this is enough to illustrate the liturgical music of his address to this beloved of whom Mr. Lewis can think Donne is contemptuous. When, in the same poem, he wants to express contempt, his music is very different:

Men of France, changeable Camelions,
Spittles of diseases, shops of fashions,
Loves fuellers, and the rightest company
Of Players, which upon the worlds stage be,
Will quickly know thee, and no lesse, alas!
Th'indifferent Italian, as we passe
His warme land, well content to thinke thee Page,
Will hunt thee with such lust, and hideous rage,
As *Lots* faire guests were vext.

And now, in case the point is not yet proven, let us hear how he speaks of her 'midnight startings', and how the rhythm changes once again as she comes back into the picture:

When I am gone, dreame me some hapinesse,
Nor let thy lookes our long hid love confesse,
Nor praise, nor dispraise me, nor blesse, nor curse
Openly loves force, nor in bed fright thy Nurse
With midnight startings, crying out oh, oh
Nurse, O my love is slaine, I saw him goe
O'r the white Alpes alone; I saw him I,

Assail'd, fight, taken, stabb'd, bleed, fall, and die.
Augure me better chance, except dread *Jove*
Thinke it enough for me to'have had thy love.

I said I would argue my case 'almost' solely on the grounds of rhythm, but in case Mr. Lewis is right in thinking modern readers are for the most part impervious to the music of verse, they will, I trust, be convinced that the mere prose sense of the last line is incompatible with contempt for the woman.

No one will deny that at one period of his life Donne wrote of women with contempt. At this time he despised them equally for yielding to his lust or for denying themselves to him. There is nothing to choose between his contempt for the woman whom he addresses as 'Nature's lay Idiot' in *Elegy VII* and his contempt for the woman who has refused him, and to whom he addresses that brilliant piece of vituperation *The Apparition*. (Whether either situation had its exact counterpart in real life is beside the point, the contempt in the poems is real enough.) At this time he treats with equal scorn the whore, both

Her whom abundance melts and her whom want betraies,

and the 'fain'd vestall', and the woman who

will be
False e'er I come, to two or three.

But the measure of his contempt for easy virtue, coyness, and faithlessness is the measure of his admiration when he finds a woman to whom he can say

So thy love may be my love's sphere.

But to Mr. Lewis that, too, sounds contemptuous; and as *Aire and Angels* has been variously understood, it is worth while to pause and examine the sentence in its context. The poem is an account of Donne's search for, and final discovery of, the true object of love. It begins with much the same idea as he expresses in the first stanza of *The Good-morrow:*

If ever any beauty I did see,
Which I desired, and got, 'twas but a dream of thee.

In *Aire and Angels:*

Twice or thrice had I loved thee,
Before I knew thy face or name;
So in a voice, so in a shapelesse flame,
Angells affect us oft, and worship'd bee;
Still when, to where thou wert, I came
Some lovely glorious nothing I did see.

And here, as so often elsewhere in the *Songs and Sonets*, Donne asserts his belief that 'pure lovers soules' must 'descend t'affections, and to faculties':

But since my soule, whose child love is,
Takes limmes of flesh, and else could nothing doe,
More subtile than the parent is,
Love must not be, but take a body too.

And at first he imagines that the physical beauty of the loved woman is the object of his search:

And therefore what thou wert, and who,
I bid love aske, and now
That it assume thy body, I allow,
And fix it selfe in thy lip, eye, and brow.

So far the progress is one to which we are accustomed, both in the literature of love and in experience; from a general reaching out after beauty to a particular worship of one person who sums up and overreaches all that had seemed fair in others. So Romeo catches sight of Juliet and forgets Rosalind:

Did my heart love till now? forswear it, sight!
For I ne'er saw true beauty till this night.

But Donne is not satisfied. There is no rest for his love in the bewildering beauty of his mistress:

Whilst thus to ballast love, I thought,
And so more steddily to have gone,
With wares that would sinke admiration,
I saw, I had loves pinnace overfraught,
Ev'ry thy haire for love to worke upon
Is much too much, some fitter must be sought;
For, nor in nothing, nor in things
Extreme, and scatt'ring bright, can love inhere.

The search is not yet over. But it is to end in a discovery surely more pleasing to any woman in love than would be the mere worship of her beauty. Beauty is transient, but love can last if it be for something which, though expressed in the body, is yet not the body:

Then as an Angell, face and wings
Of aire, not pure as it, yet pure doth weare,
So thy love may be my loves spheare.

The doctrine of St. Thomas Aquinas, about the Angels assuming a body of air, provided Donne with the analogy he wanted:

> Et sic Angeli assumunt corpora ex aere, condensando ipsum virtute divina, quantam necesse est ad corporis assumendi formationem.

So much is necessary; the point of the image for Donne is that the air-body of the Angels is neither nothing, nor too much, but just sufficient to confine a spirit on earth. So the woman's love for him is a resting-place for his spirit. It is, of course, the final couplet of the poem that has led to mis-understanding. Dr. Leavis, in *Revaluations*,[4] speaks of 'the blandly insolent matter-of-factness of the close' of *Aire and Angels*; and, isolated from its context, that is how it sounds:

> Just such disparitie
> As is twixt Aire and Angells puritie,
> 'Twixt womens love, and mens will ever bee.

There are two possible ways of reading this. The way which I am combating supposes that Donne, reversing the sentiment of the rest of the poem, throws out a contemptuous generalization about the impurity of woman's love in comparison with man's. My own view is that Donne, satisfied with the logical aptness of his image, is, characteristically, indifferent to the associations of the word 'purity', whose meaning is, to his mind, made sufficiently clear by the context. The air-body is only less pure than the angel in so far as it can exist on earth and so enable a spirit to appear to men. A woman's love is only less pure than a man's in so far as it is focused upon a single object and does not continually reach out towards 'some lovely glorious nothing'. I would support this view by referring the reader to other instances in which Donne shows a similar indifference to the irrelevant associations his words may suggest. The use of the word 'pure' in *Loves Growth* is similarly circumscribed by its context:

> I scarce believe my love to be so pure
> As I had thought it was,
> Because it doth endure
> Vicissitude, and season as the grasse.

The sense in which it is not so pure is explained in the next stanza:

> Love's not so pure, and abstract, as they use
> To say, which have no Mistresse but their Muse,
> But as all else, being elemented too,
> Love sometimes would contemplate, sometimes do.

Donne is not saying that love is unclean, or less clean than he had supposed; we have already seen that he does not think of the flesh as impure in that sense, but that, like everything else on earth, it is composed of diverse elements. He is arguing that the quickening of love in the springtime is not an increase, since his love was complete before,

> And yet no greater, but more eminent
> Love by the spring is growne;
> As, in the firmament,
> Starres by the sunne are not inlarg'd, but showne;

and, to make his meaning clear, Donne adds three more images or illustrations:

4. p. 12.

> Gentle love deeds, as blossomes on a bough,
> From loves awakened root do bud out now.
> If, as in water stir'd more circles bee
> Produc'd by one, love such additions take,
> Those like so many spheares, but one heaven make,
> For, they are all concentrique unto thee.

And finally, the 'blandly matter-of-fact' image:

> As princes doe in times of action get
> New taxes, but remit them not in peace.

Here, however, the last line of the poem,

> No winter shall abate this spring's increase,

prevents the reader from supposing that the prosaic image implies a reversal of the emotional tone of the poem. The point relevant to my argument about *Aire and Angels* is that Donne always trusts the reader to ignore irrelevant associations. The political image here is logically apt, and that is a sufficient reason for him to use it. In a sermon on *The Nativity* he develops at some length an image in which the Saviour is likened to a good coin with which man's debt to God is paid:

> First he must pay it in such money as was lent; in the nature and flesh of man; for man had sinned and man must pay. And then it was lent in such money as was coined even with the image of God; man was made according to his image: that image being defaced, in a new mint, in the womb of the blessed Virgin, there was new money coined; the image of the invisible God, the second person in the Trinity, was imprinted into the human nature. And then, that there might be all fulness, as God, for the payment of this debt, sent down in bullion, and the stamp, that is, God to be conceived in man, and as he provided the mint, the womb of the blessed Virgin, so hath he provided an exchequer, where this money is issued; that is his church, where his merits should be applied to the discharge of particular consciences.

No one, I suppose, will imagine that because Donne uses this mundane imagery he is speaking irreverently of God, of the Virgin Mary, of Christ, and of the Church. He chooses the image, here as elsewhere, because it provides him with an apt analogy.

I hope I may have persuaded some readers that Donne did not think sex sinful, and that contempt for women is not a general characteristic of his love poetry. But Mr. Lewis brings yet one more accusation against him: 'He is perpetually excited and therefore perpetually cut off from the deeper and more permanent springs of his own excitement'. Now one way of answering this would be to say that love is an exciting experience, and that great love poetry is therefore bound to communicate excitement. But with this I am not quite content. Love is exciting, but it is also restful. Unreciprocated love is a torment of the spirit, but reciprocated love is peace and happiness. In the astonishment and uncertainty of the early stages of love there is excitement and there is also fear, but there comes a time when there is confidence and a sense of profound security. Donne is a great love poet because his poetry records and communicates these diverse experiences. He would be less great if it were true that he is 'perpetually excited'. The truth is that, just as his early contempt for women is the measure of his later reverence for one woman, so his vivid experience of the torment of insecure love has made him the more keenly relish the peace of a love

inter-assured of the mind.

He tells in *The Good-morrow* of lovers who

Watch not one another out of feare;

and in *The Anniversarie* the final glory of a well-spent year is the sense of safety with which it has endowed the lovers:

Who is so safe as wee? Where none can doe
Treason to us except one of us two.

In *The Canonization* he tells us that future lovers will address him and his mistress as

You to whom love was peace, that now is rage.

And in *The Dissolution* we read of a love so secure that the 'elements' of love, 'fire of Passion, sighs of ayre, water of teares and earthly sad despaire' were ne'ere worne out by loves securitie'. There are two alternative readings of this line; it may be 'ne'ere worne out' (never) or 'neere worne out' (nearly). The former seems to me the more probable reading, since Donne is arguing that he is now overburdened with elements, which he is more likely to be if they had not been spent. Moreover, in 'loves securitie', 'fire of Passion, sighs of ayre, water of teares and earthly sad despaire' are not 'worne out' (such love does not call for the expense of spirit); 'never' fits the sense better than 'nearly', but, for my present argument, it is not of vital importance which reading we choose, the significant word is 'securitie'. Nor does Donne merely tell us of the fearlessness, safety, peace, and security that love may give; the serenity of which he speaks is reflected in the movement of his verse, the quiet speaking voice is heard in the rhythm of *The Good-morrow*, and in *A Valediction: forbidding mourning*, and quiet pleading in the last stanza of *A Valediction: of weeping*:

O more then Moone,
Draw not up seas to drowne me in thy spheare,
Weepe me not dead, in thine armes but forbeare
To teach the sea, what it may do too soone;
Let not the winde
Example finde,
To doe me more harme, than it purposeth;

> Since thou and I sigh one another's breath,
> Who e'r sighs most, is cruellest, and hasts the others death;

and in that gracious lyric, 'Sweetest love I do not goe'.

Since writing the above I have read Professor Crofts's article on John Donne in *Essays and Studies*, vol. xxii, in which he presents much the same case against the love poetry as Mr. Lewis. Their hostility to Donne springs from the same causes. Both are unable to believe that a poet so brilliantly cynical is to be taken seriously when he is reverent or tender. Yet this very diversity of experience and feeling is among Donne's singular merits. Professor Crofts complains (p. 131) that for Donne 'Love when it comes is not an experience which . . . wipes away the trivial, fond records of youthful apostasy'. And that is true; the memory of trivial and bitter moments was clear enough for him to draw upon them for analogies even in the *Holy Sonnets*; whether this is regrettable or no is a matter of taste. There is no doubt, however, that Donne's habit of drawing upon all and any of his past experience bewilders some readers; it is not customary. Equally unusual is the absence of description which vexes both Mr. Lewis and Professor Crofts. 'He cannot see her—does not apparently want to see her; for it is not of her that he writes but of his relation to her'. That also is perfectly true; the only question is whether good love poetry need be descriptive.

But, in addition to these matters of taste and opinion, Professor Crofts adduces two matters of fact in opposition to the view that Donne's conception of love was altered by his relations with Anne More. The first is Ben Jonson's remark in the *Conversations with Drummond* that 'all his best pieces were written ere he was twenty five years of age'. But we neither know which poems Jonson had read when he made his remark, nor which he thought were the best. The second fact is that the *Metempsychosis* was dated by Donne himself Aug. 1601, four months before his marriage, and it contains cynical generalizations about women. As it is a fragment of a bitter satire against Queen Elizabeth, prompted by the sacrifice of Essex, that is not surprising. Moreover, it is so strange to be contemptuous of many, or even of most women and to love and reverence a few? The love and friendships which Donne enjoyed did not expunge his former experiences, but they enlarged his understanding so that the body of his poetry has a completeness which it could not otherwise have had. He had felt almost everything a man can feel about a woman, scorn, self-contempt, anguish, sensual delight, and the peace and security of mutual love. And he shapes such poems out of all this that we are, as Professor Crofts says, 'aware of the man speaking in a manner and to a degree hardly to be paralleled in our reading of lyric poetry. Every word is resonant with his voice, every line seems to bear the stamp of his peculiar personality'. Is this not enough to set him among the great love poets?

CLEANTH BROOKS

The Language of Paradox †

Few of us are prepared to accept the statement that the language of poetry is the language of paradox. Paradox is the language of sophistry, hard, bright, witty; it is hardly the language of the soul. We are willing to allow that paradox is a permissible weapon which a Chesterton may on occasion exploit. We may permit it in epigram, a special subvariety of poetry; and in satire, which though useful, we are hardly willing to allow to be poetry at all. Our prejudices force us to regard paradox as intellectual rather than emotional, clever rather than profound, rational rather than divinely irrational.

Yet there is a sense in which paradox is the language appropriate and inevitable to poetry. It is the scientist whose truth requires a language purged of every trace of paradox; apparently the truth which the poet utters can be approached only in terms of paradox. I overstate the case, to be sure; it is possible that the title of this chapter is itself to be treated as merely a paradox. But there are reasons for thinking that the overstatement which I propose may light up some elements in the nature of poetry which tend to be overlooked.

* * *

T. S. Eliot has commented upon "that perpetual slight alteration of language, words perpetually juxtaposed in new and sudden combinations," which occurs in poetry. It *is* perpetual; it cannot be kept out of the poem; it can only be directed and controlled. The tendency of science is necessarily to stabilize terms, to freeze them into strict denotations; the poet's tendency is by contrast disruptive. The terms are continually modifying each other, and thus violating their dictionary meanings. To take a very simple example, consider the adjectives in the first lines of Wordsworth's evening sonnet: *beauteous*, *calm*, *free*, *holy*, *quiet*, *breathless*. The juxtapositions are hardly startling; and yet notice this: the evening is like a nun breathless with adoration. The adjective "breathless" suggests tremendous excitement; and yet the evening is not only quiet but *calm*. There is no final contradiction, to be sure: it is *that* kind of calm and *that* kind of excitement, and the two states may well occur together. But the poet has no one term. Even if he had a polysyllabic technical term, the term would not provide the solution for his problem. He must work by contradiction and qualification.

We may approach the problem in this way: the poet has to work by analogies. All of the subtler states of emotion, as I. A. Richards has pointed out, necessarily demand metaphor for their expression. The poet

† Abridged from "The Language of Paradox" in *The Well-Wrought Urn*, copyright 1942, 1947, by Cleanth Brooks. Pp. 3, 9–21. Reprinted by permission of Harcourt, Brace & World, Inc., and Dennis Dobson, Ltd.

must work by analogies, but the metaphors do not lie in the same plane or fit neatly edge to edge. There is a continual tilting of the planes; necessary overlappings, discrepancies, contradictions. Even the most direct and simple poet is forced into paradoxes far more often than we think, if we are sufficiently alive to what he is doing.

But in dilating on the difficulties of the poet's task, I do not want to leave the impression that it is a task which necessarily defeats him, or even that with his method he may not win to a fine precision. To use Shakespeare's figure, he can

> with assays of bias
> By indirections find directions out.

Shakespeare had in mind the game of lawnbowls in which the bowl is distorted, a distortion which allows the skillful player to bowl a curve. To elaborate the figure, science makes use of the perfect sphere and its attack can be direct. The method of art can, I believe, never be direct—is always indirect. But that does not mean that the master of the game cannot place the bowl where he wants it. The serious difficulties will only occur when he confuses his game with that of science and mistakes the nature of his appropriate instrument. Mr. Stuart Chase a few years ago, with a touching naïveté, urged us to take the distortion out of the bowl—to treat language like notation.

I have said that even the apparently simple and straightforward poet is forced into paradoxes by the nature of his instrument. Seeing this, we should not be surprised to find poets who consciously employ it to gain a compression and precision otherwise unobtainable. Such a method, like any other, carries with it its own perils. But the dangers are not overpowering; the poem is not predetermined to a shallow and glittering sophistry. The method is an extension of the normal language of poetry, not a perversion of it.

I should like to refer the reader to a concrete case. Donne's "Canonization" ought to provide a sufficiently extreme instance. The basic metaphor which underlies the poem (and which is reflected in the title) involves a sort of paradox. For the poet daringly treats profane love as if it were divine love. The canonization is not that of a pair of holy anchorites who have renounced the world and the flesh. The hermitage of each is the other's body; but they do renounce the world, and so their title to sainthood is cunningly argued. The poem then is a parody of Christian sainthood; but it is an intensely serious parody of a sort that modern man, habituated as he is to an easy yes or no, can hardly understand. He refuses to accept the paradox as a serious rhetorical device; and since he is able to accept it only as a cheap trick, he is forced into this dilemma. Either: Donne does not take love seriously; here he is merely sharpening his wit as a sort of mechanical exercise. Or: Donne does not take sainthood seriously; here he is merely indulging in a cynical and bawdy parody.

Neither account is true; a reading of the poem will show that Donne takes both love and religion seriously; it will show, further, that the paradox is here his inevitable instrument. But to see this plainly will require a closer reading than most of us give to poetry.

The poem opens dramatically on a note of exasperation. The "you" whom the speaker addresses is not identified. We can imagine that it is a person, perhaps a friend, who is objecting to the speaker's love affair. At any rate, the person represents the practical world which regards love as a silly affectation. To use the metaphor on which the poem is built, the friend represents the secular world which the lovers have renounced.

Donne begins to suggest this metaphor in the first stanza by the contemptuous alternatives which he suggests to the friend:

. . . chide my palsie, or my gout,
My five gray haires, or ruin'd fortune flout. . . .

The implications are: (1) All right, consider my love as an infirmity, as a disease, if you will, but confine yourself to my other infirmities, my palsy, my approaching old age, my ruined fortune. You stand a better chance of curing those; in chiding me for this one, you are simply wasting your time as well as mine. (2) Why don't you pay attention to your own welfare—go on and get wealth and honor for yourself. What should you care if I do give these up in pursuing my love.

The two main categories of secular success are neatly, and contemptuously epitomized in the line

Or the Kings reall, or his stamped face . . .

Cultivate the court and gaze at the king's face there, or, if you prefer, get into business and look at his face stamped on coins. But let me alone.

This conflict between the "real" world and the lover absorbed in the world of love runs through the poem; it dominates the second stanza in which the torments of love, so vivid to the lover, affect the real world not at all—

What merchants ships have my sighs drown'd?

It is touched on in the fourth stanza in the contrast between the word "Chronicle" which suggests secular history with its pomp and magnificence, the history of kings and princes, and the word "sonnets" with its suggestions of trivial and precious intricacy. The conflict appears again in the last stanza, only to be resolved when the unworldly lovers, love's saints who have given up the world, paradoxically achieve a more intense world. But here the paradox is still contained in, and supported by, the dominant metaphor: so does the holy anchorite win a better world by giving up this one.

But before going on to discuss this development of the theme, it is important to see what else the second stanza does. For it is in this second stanza and the third, that the poet shifts the tone of the poem, modulating from the note of irritation with which the poem opens into the quite different tone with which it closes.

Donne accomplishes the modulation of tone by what may be called an analysis of love-metaphor. Here, as in many of his poems, he shows that he is thoroughly self-conscious about what he is doing. This second stanza, he fills with the conventionalized figures of the Petrarchan tradition: the wind of lovers' sighs, the floods of lovers' tears, etc.—extravagant figures with which the contemptuous secular friend might be expected to tease the lover. The implication is that the poet himself recognizes the absurdity of the Petrarchan love metaphors. But what of it? The very absurdity of the jargon which lovers are expected to talk makes for his argument: their love, however absurd it may appear to the world, does no harm to the world. The practical friend need have no fears: there will still be wars to fight and lawsuits to argue.

The opening of the third stanza suggests that this vein of irony is to be maintained. The poet points out to his friend the infinite fund of such absurdities which can be applied to lovers:

> Call her one, mee another flye,
> We are Tapers too, and at our owne cost die. . . .

For that matter, the lovers can conjure up for themselves plenty of such fantastic comparisons: *they* know what the world thinks of them. But these figures of the third stanza are no longer the threadbare Petrarchan conventionalities; they have sharpness and bite. The last one, the likening of the lovers to the phoenix, is fully serious, and with it, the tone has shifted from ironic banter into a defiant but controlled tenderness.

The effect of the poet's implied awareness of the lovers' apparent madness is to cleanse and revivify metaphor; to indicate the sense in which the poet accepts it, and thus to prepare us for accepting seriously the fine and seriously intended metaphors which dominate the last two stanzas of the poem.

The opening line of the fourth stanza,

> Wee can dye by it, if not live by love,

achieves an effect of tenderness and deliberate resolution. The lovers are ready to die to the world; they are committed; they are not callow but confident. (The basic metaphor of the saint, one notices, is being carried on; the lovers in their renunciation of the world, have something of the confident resolution of the saint. By the bye, the word "legend"—

> . . . if unfit for tombes and hearse
> Our legend bee—

in Donne's time meant "the life of a saint.") The lovers are willing to forego the ponderous and stately chronicle and to accept the trifling and insubstantial "sonnet" instead; but then if the urn be well wrought, it provides a finer memorial for one's ashes than does the pompous and grotesque monument. With the finely contemptuous, yet quiet phrase, "halfe-acre tombes," the world which the lovers reject expands into something gross and vulgar. But the figure works further; the pretty sonnets will not merely hold their ashes as a decent earthly memorial. Their legend, their story, will gain them canonization; and approved as love's saint, other lovers will invoke them.

In this last stanza, the theme receives a final complication. The lovers in rejecting life actually win to the most intense life. This paradox has been hinted at earlier in the phoenix metaphor. Here it receives a powerful dramatization. The lovers in becoming hermits, find that they have not lost the world, but have gained the world in each other, now a more intense, more meaningful world. Donne is not content to treat the lovers' discovery as something which comes to them passively, but rather as something which they actively achieve. They are like the saint, God's athlete:

> Who did the whole worlds soule *contract*, and *drove*
> Into the glasses of your eyes. . . .

The image is that of a violent squeezing as of a powerful hand. And what do the lovers "drive" into each other's eyes? The "Countries, Townes," and "Courtes," which they renounced in the first stanza of the poem. The unworldly lovers thus become the most "worldly" of all.

The tone with which the poem closes is one of triumphant achievement, but the tone is a development contributed to by various earlier elements. One of the more important elements which works toward our acceptance of the final paradox is the figure of the phoenix, which will bear a little further analysis.

The comparison of the lovers to the phoenix is very skillfully related to the two earlier comparisons, that in which the lovers are like burning tapers, and that in which they are like the eagle and the dove. The phoenix comparison gathers up both: the phoenix is a bird, and like the tapers, it burns. We have a selected series of items: the phoenix figure seems to come in a natural stream of association. "Call us what you will," the lover says, and rattles off in his desperation the first comparisons that occur to him. The comparison to the phoenix seems thus merely another outlandish one, the most outrageous of all. But it is this most fantastic one, stumbled over apparently in his haste, that the poet goes on to develop. It really describes the lovers best and justifies their renunciation. For the phoenix is not two but one, "we two being one, are it"; and it burns, not like the taper at its own cost, but to live again. Its death is life: "Wee dye and rise the same . . ." The poet literally justifies the fantastic assertion. In the sixteenth and seventeenth centuries to "die" means to experience the consummation of the act of love. The lovers after the act are the same. Their love is not exhausted in mere lust. This is their title to canonization. Their love is like the phoenix.

I hope that I do not seem to juggle the meaning of *die*. The meaning that I have cited can be abundantly justified in the literature of the period; Shakespeare uses "die" in this sense; so does Dryden. Moreover, I do not think that I give it undue emphasis. The word is in a crucial position. On it is pivoted the transition to the next stanza,

> Wee can dye by it, if not live by love,
> And if unfit for tombes . . .

Most important of all, the sexual submeaning of "die" does not contradict the other meanings: the poet is saying: "Our death is really a more intense life"; "We can afford to trade life (the world) for death (love), for that death is the consummation of life"; "After all, one does not expect to live *by* love, one expects, and wants, to die *by* it." But in the total passage he is also saying: "Because our love is not mundane, we can give up the world"; "Because our love is not merely lust, we can give up the other lusts, the lust for wealth and power"; "because," and this is said with an inflection of irony as by one who knows the world too well, "because our love can outlast its consummation, we are a minor miracle, we are love's saints." This passage with its ironical tenderness and its realism feeds and supports the brilliant paradox with which the poem closes.

There is one more factor in developing and sustaining the final effect. The poem is an instance of the doctrine which it asserts; it is both the assertion and the realization of the assertion. The poet has actually before our eyes built within the song the "pretty room" with which he says the lovers can be content. The poem itself is the well-wrought urn which can hold the lovers' ashes and which will not suffer in comparison with the prince's "halfe-acre tomb."

And how necessary are the paradoxes? Donne might have said directly, "Love in a cottage is enough." "The Canonization" contains this admirable thesis, but it contains a great deal more. He might have been as forthright as a later lyricist who wrote, "We'll build a sweet little nest,/ Somewhere out in the West,/And let the rest of the world go by." He might even have imitated that more metaphysical lyric, which maintains, "You're the cream in my coffee." "The Canonization" touches on all these observations, but it goes beyond them, not merely in dignity, but in precision.

I submit that the only way by which the poet could say what "The Canonization" says is by paradox. More direct methods may be tempting, but all of them enfeeble and distort what is to be said. This statement may seem the less surprising when we reflect on how many of the important things which the poet has to say have to be said by means of paradox: most of the language of lovers is such—"The Canonization" is a good example; so is most of the language of religion—"He who would save his life, must lose it"; "The last shall be first." Indeed, almost any insight important enough to warrant a great poem apparently has to be stated in such terms. Deprived of the character of paradox with its twin concomitants of irony and wonder, the matter of Donne's poem unravels into "facts," biological, sociological, and economic. What happens to Donne's lovers if we consider them "scientifically," without benefit of the supernaturalism which the poet confers upon them? Well, what happens to Shakespeare's lovers, for Shakespeare uses the basic metaphor of "The Canonization" in his *Romeo and Juliet?* In their first conversation, the lovers play with the analogy between the lover and the pilgrim to the Holy Land. Juliet says:

> For saints have hands that pilgrims' hands do touch
> And palm to palm is holy palmers' kiss.

Considered scientifically, the lovers become Mr. Aldous Huxley's animals, "quietly sweating, palm to palm."

For us today, Donne's imagination seems obsessed with the problem of unity; the sense in which the lovers become one—the sense in which the soul is united with God. Frequently, as we have seen, one type of union becomes a metaphor for the other. It may not be too far-fetched to see both as instances of, and metaphors for, the union which the creative imagination itself effects. For that fusion is not logical; it apparently violates science and common sense; it welds together the discordant and the contradictory. Coleridge has of course given us the classic description of its nature and power. It "reveals itself in the balance or reconcilement of opposite or discordant qualities: of sameness, with difference; of the general, with the concrete; the idea, with the image; the individual, with the representative; the sense of novelty and freshness, with old and familiar objects; a more than usual state of emotion, with more than usual order. . . ." It is a great and illuminating statement, but is a series of paradoxes. Apparently Coleridge could describe the effect of the imagination in no other way.

Shakespeare, in one of his poems, has given a description that oddly parallels that of Coleridge.

> Reason in it selfe confounded,
> Saw Division grow together,
> To themselves yet either neither,
> Simple were so well compounded.

I do not know what his "The Phoenix and the Turtle" celebrates. Perhaps it *was* written to honor the marriage of Sir John Salisbury and Ursula Stanley; or perhaps the Phoenix is Lucy, Countess of Bedford; or perhaps the poem is merely an essay on Platonic love. But the scholars themselves are so uncertain, that I think we will do little violence to established habits of thinking, if we boldly pre-empt the poem for our own purposes. Certainly the poem is an instance of that magic power which Coleridge sought to describe. I propose that we take it for a moment as a poem about that power;

> So they loved as love in twaine,
> Had the essence but in one,
> Two distincts, Division none,
> Number there in love was slaine.

Hearts remote, yet not asunder,
Distance and no space was seene
Twixt this *Turtle* and his Queene;
But in them it were a wonder. . . .

Propertie was thus appalled,
That the selfe was not the same;
Single Natures double name,
Neither two nor one was called.

Precisely! The nature is single, one, unified. But the name is double, and today with our multiplication of sciences, it is multiple. If the poet is to be true to his poetry, he must call it neither two nor one: the paradox is his only solution. The difficulty has intensified since Shakespeare's day: the timid poet, when confronted with the problem of "Single Natures double name," has too often funked it. A history of poetry from Dryden's time to our own might bear as its subtitle "The Half-Hearted Phoenix."

In Shakespeare's poem, Reason is "in it selfe confounded" at the union of the Phoenix and the Turtle; but it recovers to admit its own bankruptcy:

Love hath Reason, Reason none,
If what parts, can so remaine. . . .

and it is Reason which goes on to utter the beautiful threnos with which the poem concludes:

Beautie, Truth, and Raritie,
Grace in all simplicitie,
Here enclosed, in cinders lie.

Death is now the *Phoenix* nest,
And the *Turtles* loyall brest,
To eternitie doth rest. . . .

Truth may seeme, but cannot be,
Beautie bragge, but tis not she,
Truth and Beautie buried be.

To this urne let those repaire,
That are either true or faire,
For these dead Birds, sigh a prayer.

Having pre-empted the poem for our own purposes, it may not be too outrageous to go on to make one further observation. The urn to which we are summoned, the urn which holds the ashes of the phoenix, is like the well-wrought urn of Donne's "Canonization" which holds the phoenix-lovers' ashes: it is the poem itself. One is reminded of still another urn, Keats's Grecian urn, which contained for Keats, Truth and Beauty, as Shakespeare's urn encloses "Beautie, Truth, and Raritie." But there is a sense in which all such well-wrought urns contain the ashes of a Phoenix. The urns are not meant for memorial purposes only, though that often seems to be their chief significance to the professors of literature. The phoenix rises from its ashes; or ought to rise; but it will not arise for all our mere sifting and measuring the ashes, or testing them for their chemical content. We must be prepared to accept the paradox of the imagination itself; else "Beautie, Truth, and Raritie" remain enclosed in their cinders and we shall end with essential cinders, for all our pains.

CLAY HUNT

Elegy 19: "To His Mistress Going to Bed" †

The nineteenth Elegy is the most astonishing performance of Donne's early phase as a brilliant young practitioner in the verse of wit and impudence. It is an easy poem to enjoy and to understand in general, and much of it needs no explanation to anyone past the age of twelve. But after a loosely written and relatively conventional beginning, the poem suddenly rises to verse of passion and power, and it concludes with a closely contrived passage of perverse philosophic ingenuity which is one of Donne's most intricate and exciting pieces of intellectual virtuosity. It is this latter half of the poem, especially the concluding section, which is worth our attention. These are the passages which make the Elegy something more than a piece of mere clever indecency.

The Elegy belongs almost certainly to the early or middle 1590's, to the period when Donne was writing poems like "The Indifferent," and it was clearly written against the particular social and literary background which I have described in discussing that poem. Donne expects his reader to be familiar with some of the stock imagery of Petrarchan love poetry and to be struck by the novelty in his treatment of the standard poetic propositions that a love affair is a war and the mistress the "loved foe," that the mistress is an angel, that love is religious devotion, and that the mistress's beauties are the treasures of the Indies. He is writing also against the background of the general Debate between the Body and the Soul which was the dominant intellectual issue in the literary treatment of love in the 1590's. The two most sharply opposed points of view in this debate can be roughly identified, in their literary manifestations, with the Ovidian and the Platonic traditions in Elizabethan love poetry. Those theorists on love who espoused the doctrines of Renaissance Platonism looked on the body as inessential temporal clothing for the eternal reality

† From *Donne's Poetry: Essays in Literary Analysis*, by Clay Hunt, copyright 1954 by Yale University Press. Pp. 18–31, 207–14. Reprinted by permission of Yale University Press.

of soul; and they believed, if they carried their doctrine to its ultimate conclusion, that the rational lover not only should aspire to rise above sensuality but might hope to advance beyond even a purely spiritual union with the soul of a woman, progressing up the steps of the Stair of Love until his love was finally consummated by the union of his soul with God in the Mystic Experience. Standing against the Platonists was a group of philosophic opponents who thought this conception of the essential nature of love absurd. To this school, who found their chief literary ancestor in Ovid, love was bodily passion unhampered by reason—where both deliberated, the love was slight.[1] True love, in their view, was the irrational and satisfying experience of mere lust.

An Elizabethan reader would have had some hint of what to expect of Elegy 19 from the verse form itself. As a poem about love, written in heroic couplets and entitled an "elegy," it is cast in the currently fashionable literary form derived from Ovid's *Amores*. It was to be expected that a poem in this form would adhere to the Ovidian tradition, that the author would align himself with the proponents of the Body and celebrate the techniques of seduction from the sophisticated point of view of a man about town, and that his literary style would display his ingenuity and wit in elaborate conceits. Donne does not disappoint these expectations.

The Elegy seems to present an actual dramatic situation. The poem is apparently spoken by a lover who is lying in bed waiting for his mistress to join him. It is cast in the form of an argument urging her to undress and get into bed, and it maintains a certain argumentative character throughout. But the latter part of the poem evolves into what is less a direct address to the mistress than a transcript of the private workings of the lover's excited imagination as he anticipates the successive stages of his love-making. At the end of the poem the mistress is still undressing and her lover is still waiting for her. When we have finished the poem, the dramatic situation which it presents appears to be less an actuality than a vividly imagined fiction. The Elegy is a dramatized love letter, an ovidian verse epistle to an only moderately coy mistress.

Donne starts the poem powerfully, with one of the explosive, theatrical openings which are among the distinctive effects of his love poetry. The first four lines derive from one of the most common of the Petrarchan conventions, the comparison of love to warfare, but Donne freshens this stale conceit by exploiting its latent dramatic possibilities. He makes the beginning of the poem a call to battle, a vigorous challenge delivered in a tone of swagger and arrogance. And the sexual puns which he scatters through these lines produce a tough, anti-romantic quality that accentuates the brusque tone suggested by the call-to-battle image.

After this promising beginning, the rest of the opening section (lines

1. I am using terms like "school" and "opponents" purposely. Donne himself sometimes dramatized the contemporary analysis of love as a theological dispute between rival philosophic factions. In a letter to Sir Henry Wotton he wrote: "You (I think) and I am much of one sect in the philosophy of love; which, though it be directed upon the mind, doth inhere in the body, and find piety entertainment there." (*The Works of John Donne*, ed. Alford [London, 1839], 6, 352.)

5–24) offers little more than an exercise in the mannerisms of the genre. This passage is jaunty and conventionally indelicate, but it has very little dramatic continuity and no central artistic structure. It presents merely a string of disconnected, flashy, and far-fetched conceits, enlivened by sexual innuendoes.[2] Donne is straining to be novel and clever, but what he writes in these lines is simply a routine performance in the conventional manner of Ovidian erotic verse.

But the poem comes to life again, after the slackness of these lines, in the dramatic power of the following section. The exuberant exploration conceit of this passage has become a *locus classicus* to illustrate the passion and imaginative excitement which the Elizabethans found in geographic exploration and in the discovery of the New World, but the emotional power of Donne's image is the counterpart of a lively intellectual elaboration which explores the analogy in precise detail. The basic metaphor—a comparison of the physical beauties of the mistress to be material riches which the Indies offered to the Renaissance voyagers—is one of the commonplaces of Elizabethan love poetry,[3] but Donne's dramatizing imagination works this routine material to sharp concreteness in the treatment of both the metaphor itself and the sexual experience that it describes, which is presented with an almost anatomical precision. The lover addresses the mistress in the specific role of an explorer who is requesting a royal patent ("license") which will permit him to discover a new land, explore its unknown riches, conquer it, and, having established himself as its autocratic monarch, bring it under the firm mastery of his civil authority. The political implications of the conceit are sharpened by allusions to some of the commonplaces of Renaissance political thought, to the view that an autocratic monarchy is the most stable form of government (line 28), and to the doctrine that the ruler's freedom in exercising his power is offset by the responsibilities ("bonds") which that power entails (line 31).[4] This development of the

2. The following words in the opening section either are sexual puns or carry sexual ambiguities: "powers" (1) "labour" (2), "standing," "fight" (4), "world" (6), "stand" (12), "tread" (17), "received" (20). Donne gets some minor shock effects by playing these suggestions against the theological ambiguities of certain words in these lines. "Safely" in line 17 carries the ambiguity of "in a state of salvation," and "receive" (line 20) is a technical theological term for a mortal's apprehension of supernatural influences or revelations. (Cf. Donne's use of this word in "The First Anniversary," 416. For its sexual meaning, see Webster, *The White Devil*, III, ii, 102.)

3. Cf. Sidney, *Astrophel and Stella*, Sonnet 32; Spenser, *Amoretti*, Sonnet 15; and Romeo's speech in the balcony scene (II, ii, 82):

> wert thou as far
> As that vast shore wash'd with the farthest sea,
> I would adventure for such merchandise.

The image recurs throughout Donne's poetry, usually in the form of the conventional antithesis between the two Indies—the "India of Spice" (the East Indies) and the "India of Mine" (the West Indies). The phrase "Mine of precious stones" in line 29 stands as a concrete, factual detail of the general image of America, since Donne normally thinks of the New World as the land which offers the voyager gold and precious stones. Cf. Sermon 14: "This sets up upon the two hemispheres of the world; the western hemisphere, the land of gold, and treasure, and the eastern hemisphere, the land of spices and perfumes." (*Works*, ed. Alford, *1*, 281–2.)

4. The detail of the general conceit which equates the woman's body with a "kingdom" also reflects the political cast of Donne's imagination in these lines. It derives from a conventional associative pattern in the Renaissance in which was a part of the system of "correspondences" in the ordered Universe—the analogy between the human body and the Body Politic, which the Renaissance mind usually thought of as naturally and properly a kingdom, an autocratic monarchy.

conceit comes to a lover's assumption of full command over his mistress in terms of the authoritative conclusion to a legal document or proclamation: "To this I have set my hand and seal." The pun on "seal" in this line, like the other sexual ambiguities throughout the passage, parallels the particularity of the metaphor with an equally concrete realism in presenting the experience to which the metaphor refers.[5]

These lines present, then, a splurge of virtuoso wit in Donne's elaboration of a detailed parallel between the lover's sexual advances and the discovery and political subjugation of a new land. The exploration image dramatizes vividly not only the lover's passionate excitement but also his exultant sense of power in his sexual mastery of his mistress. And the cadences of the verse—the slow, powerful surge of rhythms through "Before, behind, between, above, below" to the outburst of "O my America! my new-found-land"—underscore the metaphoric suggestion of rapt physical passion. The effect of the emotional climax of the passage in line 32, like that of the opening of the poem, is one of bold, swaggering theatricality.

This effect of cumulative intensity carries over into the exclamatory opening of the following section and is sustained throughout the passage as the lover excitedly imagines the "whole joys" of sexual consummation. And the intellectual ingenuity which has been operating in the preceding section drives to a climax of virtuosity in lines 33–45 as Donne launches into an intricate and detailed analogy between the ecstatic physical consummation of this *affairé de corps* and the consummation of a purely spiritual love in the religious ecstasy of the Beatific Vision. The link which relates this piece of breezy blasphemy to the general subject of the mistress's undressing is the conventional clothing metaphor suggested in lines 34–5, an image which Donne often used in his later serious treatments of spiritual love and of the Mystic Experience.[6] Since those who regarded love as essentially an impulse of the soul thought of the body as mere evanescent "clothing" for the eternal reality of spirit, the Mystic Ecstasy might be thought of as an experience in which the soul divested itself of its temporal clothes and went naked to immediate contact with God.[7] The basic intellectual maneuver which Donne per-

5. For Donne's use of "seal" as a sexual pun see Elegy 7, line 29, and "The Relic," 29. "License" (25) and "free" (31) both carry ambiguities of licentiousness in Renaissance usage. (Cf. *As You Like It*, II, vii, 68, where Shakespeare plays on the sexual suggestion of both of these words.) And I think Donne intends also a sexual reference in the word "mine" in line 29. (See the discussion below of the opening lines of "Love's Alchemy.") In "A Rapture," which is based in part on this Elegy, Carew makes a similar use of "mine" as a sexual metaphor (lines 33–4). The pun on "discovering" (= undressing) is, of course, the logical basis for the entire conceit, since it analogizes the situation which the poem deals with to geographical exploration.

6. This metaphor evidently made a particular appeal to Donne's imagination. He uses it as the basic image for a love directed toward the soul in his most explicitly Platonic love poem, "The Undertaking," 13–20. See also the parallel use of the image in the verse letters "To Mrs. M. H." ("Mad paper stay"), 29–32, and "To the Countess of Bedford" (Honour is so sublime perfection"), 26; and in "A Funeral Elegy," 61. In "Obsequies to the Lord Harrington," 12–13, Donne refers to an "ecstasy" as an "unapparelling" of the mind. The image appears in a sexual context in the "Epithalamion" for the Earl of Somerset, 208–11, and it recurs throughout his other poetry in connection with treatments of the doctrines of philosophic idealism.

7. Cf. Satire 1, lines 43–4:

And till our souls be unapparelled
Of bodies, they from bliss are
banishèd.

forms at this point in the poem is simply to turn this stock metaphor upside down. The fanciful argument which this section of the poem develops reduces, then, to the following logical proposition, which is implied in lines 34–5: since the Beatific Vision is like taking off your clothes to experience full joy, then taking off your clothes to experience full joy is like the Beatific Vision. This argument is expanded in the passage as a pseudo-theological validation for nakedness and lust.

Before examining the details with which Donne develops the conceit, we might pause to reflect on how a Renaissance reader would react to this analogy. It is certainly the most startling of all Donne's paradoxes. The basic conceit not only equates the sinful pleasures of the flesh with the pure bliss of heaven, but in effect it also equates the soul with the body, since it identifies the full intellectual "joys" of the naked soul with the full sensual joys of the naked body. Donne thus obliterates, by a single stroke of wit, that sharp dichotomy between Sense and Reason, body and soul, temporal matter and eternal spirit, "things visible" and "things invisible," which was not only the central organizing concept in his own thought but also one of the fundamental conceptual antitheses in the thought of the whole Renaissance. The bright young man who set himself up, at the start of his literary career, as a special practitioner in the shock effect of witty paradox never devised a more shocking paradox than this.

But the perverse wit of this passage would have had a further and more specific point for the Elizabethan reader. When one reads the poem in the context of the love debate which runs through Elizabethan love poetry, it seems certain that Donne's irreverent allusions to spiritual love and to the Beatific Vision in the climactic section of a poem celebrating the pleasures of purely physical sex could be intended only as ridicule of the school of Platonic Love. The clothing metaphor on which the conceit is based was a conventional analogy not only in Christian mysticism but also in Renaissance Platonism. Though the details of Donne's phrasing and some of the analogies which he uses suggest that his actual source for the doctrines on which the conceit is based was Christian mystical literature rather than the writings of the Renaissance Platonists, the logical progression which is suggested by the analogies in these lines is nevertheless that of the Platonic progression up the Stair of Love. In fact, the details of the conceit in this passage take on logical continuity only when one supplies the theory of Platonic Love as an implied philosophic context. The poetic proposition of this section of the Elegy asserts, in effect, that loving a woman's naked body is philosophically equivalent to loving her soul, and that consummation in sexual intercourse and consummation in the Mystic Experience add up to pretty much the same thing. And that, one might think, would dispose of the Platonists once and for all.

But this passage of the poem needs closer scrutiny, because the powerful shock of Donne's conceit derives chiefly from the rich philosophic and theological implications of the precise details with which he elaborates the basic analogy.[8] The technique of the passage is extremely compressed: Donne throws out, in quick succession, a series of literary or philosophic commonplaces which are intended to call up to the reader's mind a whole systematic body of thought. In order to make clear the logical pattern which gives continuity to the suggestions of each of these details, I will confine my commentary at this point purely to the imaginative implications of the passage, without pausing to point out what each of the details of Donne's conceit actually refers to, in terms of the facts of the situation which the poem presents. It may be useful, therefore, to set out at the start the basic imaginative equations on which Donne builds the entire structure of metaphor in these lines:

(a) As the fundamental equations:
  the body = clothes.
  the soul (or spiritual essence) = the naked body.
(b) Therefore:
  ordinary, sensual lovers = lovers who are content with women who keep their clothes on.
  enlightened, Platonic lovers = enlightened lovers like the speaker, who want women naked.
(c) Finally (lines 42–5):
  God = the mistress's naked body.
  The Beatific Vision = the sexual orgasm.

The pseudo-logical premise for this fanciful argument is laid down at the start in lines 34–5:

> As souls unbodied, bodies unclothed must be,
> To taste whole joys.

These lines refer to the intellectual joys which the soul can experience fully only by direct contact with God in heaven. The joys of mortal life, by contrast, are partial, since the soul, while it is imprisoned in the earthly body, can know God only mediately, through the distorting veil of sense experience. The soul's yearning for the "whole joys" of immediate, intellectual apprehension of God's Essence can therefore be satisfied only when it strips off the fleshly clothing of the body, when the soul is "unbodied." For most men the soul can be unbodied only after death, but a few chosen spirits are privileged to know this bliss at certain moments during mortal life, when their souls are temporarily withdrawn from their bodies in the Mystic Experience—or, to use Donne's normal terminology, in an "ecstasy."

These are the full doctrinal implications of the first two lines of the conceit. My rather specific expansion of their philosophic suggestion is based on Donne's development of these ideas in the lines which follow, and particularly on the implicit reference to the soul's apprehension of

8. Compare the different effect which Donne gets from the same analogy in stanza 6 of the "Epithalamion" for the marriage of the Princess Elizabeth. His gingerly treatment of the comparison there makes it a casual conceit, a piece of mere cleverness with little shock value.

God's Essence in lines 43–5, but the doctrines are so much a commonplace in the formal thought of the Renaissance that an alert and philosophically sophisticated contemporary reader might have guessed what Donne was doing from these lines alone.[9]

In the following lines the imagery defines more fully the implications of lines 34–5 and outlines the process by which a mortal may attain "whole joys." If one responds only to the suggestions of Donne's structure of metaphor and neglects the factual reference of these lines, the following ordered philosophic argument plays above this section of the poem like a continuous, discordant obbligato, clashing violently at every note with what Donne is actually saying. The process of attaining "whole joys" will start (lines 35–8) with the love of earthly women. But this love must not be sensual. Women's bodies ("gems" in line 35 = clothes[1]) appeal, to be sure, to men's physical senses ("views" = the sense of sight), but this sexual appeal is superficial and will attract only the unenlightened lovers ("fools"). These lovers misdirect their love into sensuality because that is all which their minds can comprehend: they have "earthly souls," which give them the faculties of physical sensation, but they lack the higher faculty of reason, which should distinguish man from the beasts.[2] Therefore their love is distracted (the Atalanta analogy[3]) from its proper object: it is spent in physical desire for the inessential temporal bodies of women ("theirs") instead of being rationally directed toward women's metaphysical essences, their eternal souls ("them").[4] But (lines 39–40) these sensual lovers misunderstand God's purpose in creating physical beauty if they believe that beautiful women are intended

9. These doctrines recur throughout Donne's work. (Cf., e.g., the distinction between mediate and immediate knowledge in "The Second Anniversary," 290–314, and the contrast between the "accidental" joys of earthly life and the "essential" joys of heaven in the conclusion to that poem, lines 471 ff.) The casual, glancing reference which Milton makes to these ideas in a passage in *Areopagitica* suggests how widely current they were in the Renaissance: "but he who thinks we . . . have attained the utmost prospect of reformation that the mortal glass wherein we contemplate can show us till we come to beatific vision . . ." (*Works* [Columbia edition], 4, 337).

1. Donne substitutes "gems" for "clothes" to permit the Atalanta conceit. He is thinking of the elaborately bejewelled dress of an Elizabethan lady.

2. The phrase "earthly soul" alludes to the scholastic doctrine of the tripartite soul. According to this doctrine, man's soul was divided into three parts: a soul of growth, which he shared with the plants; a soul of sense, which he shared with the animals; and a soul of reason, which was man's distinctive possession and which was the only part of his soul that was immortal. Or Donne may be thinking of a variant of this doctrine Renaissance Platonic literature which divided man's soul into two parts, a soul of appetite and a soul of reason. See the passage on Platonic Love in Castiglione's *Book of the Courtier* [Everyman edition], pp. 282–3.) The phrase "earthly soul" refers, then, to the soul of appetite, or the soul of sense. Compare "A Valediction: Forbidding Mourning," 13–20, where Donne draws a distinction between rational lovers, whose love is based on the soul, and common lovers, whose love is mere animal sensuality: "Dull sublunary lovers'/(Whose soul is sense) . . ."

3. The inaccuracy of Donne's reference to the Atalanta myth is interesting as an indication of the casualness of his interest in classical mythology. He evidently thinks that the golden apples were thrown by Atalanta herself to distract the lovers who were pursuing her. Donne's references to mythology are infrequent and occur mostly in the "Elegies"—probably because he had read Ovid before he wrote some of them, or because mythological allusions were part of the machinery of the genre of the love elegy.

4. Donne frequently uses this distinction between the genitive case and the other cases of personal pronouns to suggest the metaphysical difference between the body and the soul. This grammatical trick reflects the philosophic distinction between a man's "substance," his metaphysical identity (the soul—"he," "him") and the "accidents" of his substance (the body—"his"). Cf. Elegy 18, line 26; "The Ecstasy," 51; "The Cross," 36.

to serve no further end than physical satisfaction. God created the beautiful bodies of women for a purpose analogous to the church's use of religious "pictures" to instill faith in the layman. The church does not intend these pictures to be enjoyed simply in themselves and to provide mere pleasure for the senses. They are intended, rather, to give to ordinary men, who acquire knowledge solely through their senses, a visual experience of beauty which should lead them to the higher, suprasensory understanding which comes from reason and faith.[5] And, on the same grounds, those men who are intellectually incapable of a direct, rational response to the content of a sacred book may be drawn indirectly to the knowledge which it offers through their sensory responses to its beautiful binding.[6] For the same reason, God has "arrayed" a woman's soul, her essence, in a physically beautiful body. He has done this in order that ordinary men ("laymen"), after responding to the initial sensory attraction, may be led beyond this physical experience to a rational response to the beauty of her soul and thus to an awareness of the eternal reality of spirit, of which the beautiful body is merely a transitory physical manifestation.

The superior lovers ("we"), on the other hand, neither desire nor need this intermediate sensory step to attain the intellectual enlightenment which is the proper end of love. Having renounced sensuality, they feel only a rational attraction to the intellectual beauty of women's souls ("themselves," "them," as distinguished from "theirs").[7] They desire to apprehend their souls directly by seeing the souls divested of their fleshly clothing ("themselves . . . we . . . must see revealed").

At this point in the poem (lines 42–3) Donne's language takes on a specifically theological reference. This shift in the connotative suggestions of his diction produces a quick imaginative transition. It suggests that, in the metaphoric structure of his conceit, Donne is no longer thinking merely of women's souls as an example of the kind of metaphysical essence which may be apprehended by the enlightened lover, but has turned his thoughts instead to the Essence of God. What actually happens here, as Donne elaborates the logic of his conceit, is that his imagination suddenly takes a quick skip up several steps of the Platonic Stair. According to the doctrine of the Platonists, the lover who has learned to love the beauty of his mistress's soul and to rise above the attraction of her bodily beauty has reached only the first step in the Stair of Love. As he progresses up the logical steps of the stair he proceeds,

5. Donne is referring here to a traditional justification for religious iconography. Cf. Sermon 27: "They had wont to call pictures in the church, the layman's book, because in them, he that could not read at all might read much." (*Works, 1,* 542.) Donne cites Calvin as his source for this analogy in Sermon 122, where he presents an expanded discussion of the idea and distinguishes between the "right use" and the "abuse" of religious pictures (*Works*, 5, 177.)

6. The contrast between the binding and the book as an image for the distinction between the body and the soul is a common metaphor in Elizabethan literature. Cf. *Romeo and Juliet*, III, ii, 83–4 ("Was ever book containing such vile matter/ So fairly bound?"), and Lady Capulet's extended development of the conceit in I, iii, 81ff.

7. For Donne's use of "self" to mean "soul" see Satire 3, line 37, and Sermon 38: "Remember that thy soul is thyself" (*Works*, 2, 80). This usage seems to have been common in the Renaissance. Cf. Sidney, *Astrophel and Stella*, Sonnet 52, line 13.

next, to a love of the beauty of all women; then to the formulation of a universal concept of beauty "that is generally spread over all the nature of man"; and finally to an awareness of God as "the fountain of the sovereign and right beauty." He sees then that the consummation which his amorous soul desires is that of being "haled from the body" and "coupled" with God in the Mystic Experience.[8]

Donne's imagination jumps to this final stage of the Platonic progression in lines 42–3 as he elaborates the hint contained in the word "mystic." "See revealed" carries strong theological overtones. It suggests a desire for a supernatural "revelation" of God rather than for a mere apprehension of a woman's soul.[9] That this transition has been accomplished—that, in the imaginative structure of the conceit, the concept of the spiritual essence of a woman ("themselves") has shaded over into the logically analogous concept of the Essence of God, and that the Platonic lover is now desiring to see God "revealed" in the Beatific Vision—is made clear by line 42, which implies that the revelation will come through the lover's receiving "imputed grace." Donne here uses a technical term from theology[1] to imply a specific theological doctrine—a doctrine which would not need to be introduced into the poem if the erotic experience to which the conceit alludes at this point were nothing beyond the Platonic lover's rational apprehension of the intellectual beauty of a woman's soul. For this kind of intellectual apprehension, the imputation of Grace would not be required. But God's Grace would have to be imputed before a mortal could enjoy the Mystic Ecstasy. The Mystic Experience was not regarded by Christian theologians as in any way an automatic reward for the Platonic lover, or for the Christian mystic, who mortified the flesh and followed a prescribed regimen of devotion. It was a privilege granted to few men in this life, and they did not receive it by virtue of any inherent right or any righteousness to which they could attain as mortals. Moreover, from the standpoint of Christian theology, the apprehension of God's Essence which resulted from the experience did not come through any natural powers that their souls possessed. The Beatific Vision was granted to the soul, and the soul was enabled to

8. I am quoting here from Hoby's translation of Peter Bembo's speech in *The Book of the Courtier* (pp. 317–22). Bembo sums up this progression in his charge to true lovers: "Let us climb up the stairs which at the lowermost step have the shadow of sensual beauty, to the high mansion place where the heavenly, amiable, and right beauty dwelleth, which lieth hid in the innermost secrets of God, lest unhallowed eyes should come to the sight of it; and there shall we find a most happy end for our desires." (Pp. 320–1.) I am citing this passage not as Donne's direct source but rather as one of the chief sources for the doctrines of Platonic Love in Elizabethan England. As I have suggested, not only this section of the Elegy but also those of Donne's other poems in which he treats Platonic Love seriously indicate that Donne was influenced only in general by the literature of Renaissance Platonism: the details of his poetic treatments of Platonic Love are usually drawn from its collateral relative, Christian mysticism, and from scholastic theology. The theological reference of a number of the details in this passage of the Elegy (lines 39–40, 42, 43–5) suggests that Donne's primary sources here are sacred rather than secular. And it is worth noting that the use of sexual imagery in treating the Mystic Experience is frequent in Christian mystical literature. The central conceit in lines 33–45 of this poem derives from a simple inversion of this kind of imagery.

9. "Revelation" is one of the terms which Donne applies specifically to the Mystic Experience. Cf. "A Letter to the Lady Carey and Mrs. Essex Riche," 53–4: "This my Ecstasy and revelation of you both." Line 42 plays, of course, with an ambiguity on "revealed" = undressed.

1. See *N.E.D.*: "impute," 2; and Holy Sonnet 6, line 13: "impute me righteous."

experience it, only through God's special "imputation" of Grace to a being who was inherently neither worthy nor capable of the experience.[2] Donne's reference to this doctrine, then, in lines 42–3, in conjunction with the word "mystic" in the preceding line, implies that the lover seeks this special dispensation which will enable him to pass beyond a union of soul with an earthly woman to the consummation of his love through the union of his naked soul with God.[3]

The following lines (43–5) climax Donne's development of the basic conceit and finally define specifically the philosophic implications of the reference to the "whole joys" of "souls unbodied" at the beginning of the passage. If one responds merely to their imaginative implication and neglects their factual reference, these lines suggest the lover's prayer to God to impute to him the Grace which will permit him to experience the Mystic Ecstasy.[4] They are a plea to God to manifest His Essence so fully ("liberally . . . show thy self") that the desires of the lover's soul may be completely satisfied.[5] This satisfaction is the experiencing of the "whole joys" referred to in line 35: it will consist in "knowing" (line 43)—and at this point Donne alludes to one of the key biblical texts which provide authority for the concept of the Beatific Vision in Christian theology.[6] The soul's joy in the Mystic Ecstasy will consist in the

2. Cf. Aquinas, *Summa Theologica*, Q. 12, Art. 4: "It follows, therefore, that to know self-subsistent being . . . is beyond the natural power of any created intellect. . . . Therefore a created intellect cannot see the essence of God unless God by His grace unites Himself to the created intellect." This line of the poem plays on the phrase "imputed grace" to suggest also a woman's gracious granting of sexual favors to a lover who is all unworthy—the conventional Petrarchan love situation.

3. The connotations of "mystic" (= pertaining to the direct communion of the soul with God) in line 41 help accomplish the imaginative transition from the subject of the spiritual love of woman to that of the Mystic Experience. But the primary function of "mystic books" is to complete the layman image of lines 39–40. The phrase develops the implied contrast between the ordinary, sensual lover (the layman who must be attracted to sacred books by their bindings) and the enlightened lover (the clergyman who is permitted to read the book and who thus learns religious mysteries directly). But it is clear from "*see* revealed," and from the rest of lines 43 and 44, which certainly refer to the Beatific Vision, that Donne discards at this point the analogy to the clergyman's understanding of a sacred book. The "revelation" of a woman's body is analogized, not just to an understanding of the religious mysteries which are "revealed" to men in a "mystic book," but rather to a kind of revelation which is seen, to the Sight of God in the Beatific Vision. The woman's body is thus equated, at this point, with God's Essence as "known" directly by the soul of the mystic, and not merely with the kind of knowledge of God which the clergyman gains through a sacred book. The ultimate reference of the book analogy to the undressing situation which the poem deals with indicates also that Donne is punning on "mystic" in its Renaissance sense of "hidden" (= dressed).

4. Compare the prayer which concludes Bembo's exposition of Platonic Love in Book 4 of *The Book of the Courtier*.

5. "Self" is used here, as in line 41, to refer to soul, or metaphysical essence. The questions of whether all souls who experienced the Beatific Vision received an equally full comprehension of God, and whether God granted, through this experience, a partial or a complete manifestation of His Essence—and thus a partial or full knowledge of Himself—had been subjects of scholastic controversy. (See *Summa Theologica*, Q. 12, Arts. 6 and 8.) Cf. Sermon 21, where Donne describes the Beatific Vision and reviews some of the controversy:

> And then [in heaven] our way to see him is *patefaction sui*, God's laying himself open, his manifestation, his revelation, his evisceration, and embowelling of himself to us there. Doth God never afford this patefaction, this manifestation of himself in his essence, to any in this life? We cannot answer yea, nor no, without offending a great part in the School, so many affirm, so many deny that God hath been seen in his essence in this life. (*Works, I*, 423.)

6. The source for Donne's phrasing in "since that I may know" is 1 Corinthians. xiii. 12: "For now we see through a glass darkly; but then face to face: now I know in part; but then shall I know even as also I am known." This biblical allusion operates to enforce the suggestion of the Beautific Vision in the other details of these lines. The same text lies behind the image of the "mortal glass" in Milton's

satisfaction of its thirst for knowledge through a complete comprehension of metaphysical reality, which, since the soul is "unbodied," will be revealed without the distortions of the veil of sense and can thus be apprehended by the soul directly and intellectually.

It may be necessary at this point to issue a reminder that this elaborate structure of philosophic idealism, in the specialized forms of the doctrines of Platonic Love and Christian mysticism, exists in the poem merely as an imaginative analogue to the factual implications of Donne's conceit in these lines. Considered in terms of its denotation, the passage is actually a pseudo-logical presentation of the metaphysic of lust, and Donne's real subject is the sheer physical pleasure of sexual intercourse. Donne brings his reader down to earth, and drives home the shock of his general conceit, by sprinkling the prayer in lines 43–5 with sexual puns. He puns, first, on the sexual meaning of "know," then on "liberally," which carries its Renaissance ambiguity of "lewdly,"[7] and on "show," which is an indecent Renaissance colloquialism for sexual exposure.[8] These ambiguities give the lines a tonal quality which is far from delicate, but Donne's final thrust is reserved for the word "self" in line 45. In line 41 "selves" refers—on the poem's factual level—to a woman's naked body; but the ambiguity on "show" and the precise anatomical suggestions of the phrase "as liberally, as to a midwife" limit the reference of the word in line 45 and make clear that "self" in that line refers not to the woman's body as a whole but rather to her genitals. This twist in the reference of the word is enforced also by the suggestion of the imagery of these lines: this imagery equates the mystic's passionate desire to see the innermost depths of God's Essence with the lustful lover's desire to see the sexually essential part of the mistress' naked body.[9] The modern, secularized reader might pause, at this point, to consider the effect of these lines for the reader of a theologically religious age:

---

reference to the Beatific Vision in the passage cited above in n. 9. And compare Donne's Sermon 154:

> *Erimus sicut angeli*, says Christ, "There we shall be as angels." The knowledge which I have by nature shall have no clouds; here it hath. That which I have by grace shall have no reluctation, no resistance; here it hath. That which I have by revelation shall have no suspicion, no jealousy; here it hath. . . . There our curiosity shall have this noble satisfaction, we shall know how the angels know by knowing as they know. (*Works*, 6, 184.)

7. Donne makes the same pun in "An Epithalamion . . . on the Lady Elizabeth and Count Palatine," 96. Cf. *Hamlet*, IV, vii, 171: "That liberal shepherds give a grosser name."

8. Cf. *Hamlet*, III, ii, 155–9:

> Hamlet: Ay, or any show that you'll show him: be not you ashamed to show, he'll not shame to tell you what it means.
> Ophelia: You are naught, you are naught.

9. I think one can trace the steps of Donne's imagination here quite closely. He seems to visualize an essence, or "form," spatially, as something located in the center of a body. See his reference, in the passage cited in note 5, to God's manifestation of His Essence as "his evisceration, and embowelling of himself." Donne's use of the word "centric" to mean "essential" carries a spatial ambiguity in "Love's Alchemy," 2, and in Elegy 18, line 36. Both of these passages show a process of imaginative association similar to that in lines 41–5 of Elegy 19. The various ambiguities which they imply for "centric" to mean "essential" carries a spatial ambiguity in "Love's Alchemy," 2, and in Elegy 18, line 36. Both of these passages show a process of imaginative association similar to that in lines 41–5 of Elegy 19. The various ambiguities which they imply for "centric" set up the following analogical progression: spiritual essence = a woman's soul = a geometric center of a body = a woman's genitals.

they do nothing less than identify a woman's genitals with the Essence of God.

The lover's imagination has now returned from metaphysical acrobatics to concrete fact, and he thinks of the moment when the mistress, in the sequence of events that he anticipates, will have removed all her clothes except her shift. The theological preoccupation of the preceding lines carries over into his final command to her, as he ironically compares her white linen to the ecclesiastical garb of virgins and religious penitents:

> Cast all, yea, this white linen hence,
> Here is no penance, much less innocence.[1]

And the poem's argument for the desirability of undressing concludes, in a summary point of wit, as the lover puns on the sexual meaning of "covering."

The Elegy shows Donne as a brilliant apprentice who is still short of technical mastery. It is an uneven performance, ordinary in some passages and dazzling in others. Though it shows more sense of form than most of Donne's Elegies, the poem as a whole lacks the clear imaginative organization and precise formal definition of his mature work. And the closing section (lines 33 ff.) certainly makes extraordinary demands on the reader. Donne's conception in these lines is brilliant, but it is only partly realized in the execution. In this passage he certainly pays heavily in loss of clarity for what he gains through compression, and I wonder how many of his contemporaries could have followed the skittering of his speculative imagination through these lines. In fact, I wonder how many of them would have noticed at all the high-powered intellectual activity which goes on, at this point, beneath the bright, slick surface of the poem.[2] On the other hand, in its dramatic power, in

1. I think this was the original form of the line. Bennett used this version in his edition of Donne's poems, but Grierson and Hayward prefer the variant reading: "There is no penance due to innocence." Each version has the support of several manuscripts. Probably both are by Donne, and one is a later revision of his original text. The version I use seems to me almost certainly what Donne originally wrote. Its tough, man-of-the-world tone is perfectly consistent with the tone of the whole poem and with the kind of love affair which the poem deals with. Also, it gives the conclusion of this section a dramatic punch which is similar to the effect that Donne builds to at the end of each of the preceding sections of the poem. The other reading of the line makes the poem go startlingly pure and sweet at this point, and for no intrinsic reason that I can see. Grierson agrees that the version which I give was probably the original form of the line and suggests a plausible explanation for Donne's having softened it up later: a marginal note in one of the manuscripts (which gives the sweeter version of the line) indicates that Donne may have revised the poem to use it as an epithalamion, possibly as his own. (*The Poems of John Donne* [Oxford, 1912], 2, 90.)

2. The marginal comment on a manuscript referred to in n. 1 suggests that a good deal of the poem went over the head of at least one of Donne's contemporary admirers. It reads: "Why may not a man write his own epithalamium if he can do it so modestly?" "Modestly" here may refer primarily to the poet's modesty about his sexual prowess, but even in this sense the word is hardly accurate for the sexual braggadocio of the speaker in the poem. And the word certainly carries connotations of a social attitude as well. When one makes every allowance for the wide difference between modern and seventeenth-century standards of sexual propriety—a difference which is suggested by the writer's feeling that this poem was perfectly proper for use as both a marriage gift to one's wife and a public document about the marriage—"modestly" is still pretty astonishing. I can conclude only that

the adventurousness ot its imaginative conjunctions, and in the vividness of its shock effects, the Elegy belongs with Donne's finest work.

The final tone of the poem, and the precise state of mind behind it, are a little hard to define. In many ways the Elegy seems simply a poem of juice and high spirits. It is verse of flash and glitter, the display of a young virtuoso who is showing what he can do with the themes of Ovidian poetry by playing them on his own instrument. But, though I think this was probably Donne's initial intention in the poem, there is a good deal left over when one tries to define the temper of the poem in this way. For one thing, the formal rhetoric of the Elegy gives it qualities of weight and dignity which are lacking in most of the Renaissance erotic verse in the Ovidian tradition.[3] And certain parts of the poem carry a voltage which is far beyond the potential of the conventional Ovidian verse of witty and sophisticated indecency. The evocative power of the exploration metaphor in lines 25–32, and the climactic effect in lines 33–45, as Donne drives the logical implications of his conceit with utter ruthlessness to a culminating intellectual shock, are of the order of intensity of serious poetry. This final section of the poem seems, in the last analysis, much more than a piece of outrageous intellectual impudence on Donne's part. When one turns back to this poem after having read "The Ecstasy," "The Canonization," "A Valediction: Forbidding Mourning," and "The Good-Morrow," the concluding section takes on a different character. One of the peculiar characteristics of those later love poems is Donne's use of extravagant intellectual ingenuity as a mode of expression for strong feeling. In these poems the florid virtuosity of wit is not, as the eighteenth century and Romantic critics thought, a force in artistic conflict with emotion—it is simply Donne's poetic vehicle for emotion. When read in the context of Donne's later work, these lines in Elegy 19 appear as some of his most passionate love poetry; and the tonal pattern of the last half of the poem seems not that of an impassioned climax in lines 25–32, followed by a passage of virtuoso cleverness, but rather that of a continuous crescendo of emotion to a point of incandescent intensity.

Moreover, when one looks back at the Elegy with an awareness of Donne's lifelong effort to find a philosophic reconciliation for the conflicting claims of the soul and of the body in his personal experience, this section has the effect of suddenly adding a new dimension to Donne's treatment of sexual experience in the poem, a dimension which is entirely lacking in Donne's assumption of the poetic role of sexual libertine in

the unknown admirer who wrote this comment missed a good deal of what goes on in lines 33–45 of the poem.

3. The distinctive quality in Donne's handling of the materials of Ovidian love poetry can be seen if one compares this poem with Carew's "A Rapture." Carew's poem shows not only the general influence of the tradition of Ovidian verse but also the particular influence of Donne's work. The central theological conceit which the title suggests is a variation of the central conceit of "The Ecstasy," and the poem shows both general and specific debts to Donne's eighteenth and nineteenth Elegies. But the sustained lightness of tone and the effect of prettily decorated indecency in "A Rapture" place it in the main stream of the Ovidian tradition and give a tonal quality quite different from that of Elegy 19.

"The Indifferent." Up to this point the Elegy has presented unreflecting passion unreflectingly. The play of Donne's intellect over this material has been directed into elaborating conceits which have little or no philosophic import. But the sustained philosophic overtones of the concluding section finally place the sexual act in a metaphysical context. Here Donne's mind seems suddenly to pierce through the flesh to see what this act means. The shock of these lines is the intellectual shock of what he sees. In effect, they present the wholehearted acceptance of sensual satisfaction as an act which entails taking up a philosophic option, which forces one to embrace a philosophic materialism and to reject completely the doctrines of philosophic idealism—to reject, in fact, the fundamental doctrines of Christianity. In these lines Donne's celebration of lust becomes literally and substantially metaphysical.

Furthermore, the rough treatment which Donne gives to the Mystic Experience in this passage shows a remarkable conceptual accuracy and reflects an interest in the subject which is clearly more than casual. And this poem's identification of sexual experience with religious mysticism echoes throughout the serious love poetry and religious poetry of Donne's maturity, as well as in some of the great prose passages in his sermons. It reappears most strikingly in "The Ecstasy," where the same comparison is presented in a different key—this time with essential seriousness, as an analogy which has a genuine psychological and metaphysical validity.

I think it would be forcing a point to insist that these portentous emotional and intellectual implications are of primary importance in the effect of the last section of this Elegy. They are present in the passage only as over- and undertones. But they give to the lines a fullness of resonance which is not the tonal quality of verse that is just wittily indecent. What seems to have happened in the writing of Elegy 19 is like what evidently happened in "The Apparition," that piece of mordant realism which takes off from one of the most artificial conventions of Petrarchan *vers de société*. I think when Donne started to write the Elegy he probably planned to write a piece of clever erotic verse in the Ovidian manner. But some of what came out, after this material was processed by a powerful literary imagination, was, for all its high-spirited gaiety, not light verse at all.

I think, then, that the artistic paradox of the Elegy—its mixture of bumptious, perverse wit with excited philosophic speculation and strong emotion—is never fully resolved in the poem. Probably the poem as a whole was never brought to complete definition in Donne's mind; it grew on him as he wrote. And I think that, for all its brilliance, the poem never quite assumes shape as an artistic whole. But for the student of Donne's poetry the Elegy provides one of the earliest glimpses of the major poet latent in the bright young man who was "a great visitor of ladies, a great frequenter of plays, a great writer of conceited verses." And the poem reveals also the identity of mind and temperament which lies beneath the surface contrast between Donne's secular verse in the

"Elegies" and the "Songs and Sonnets," and his religious verse in the "Divine Poems." In his later years, when he was Dean of St. Paul's and the most powerful and sensational preacher of his day, Donne sometimes dramatized his assumption of a new role in life by thinking of his career as divided between two lives: "Jack Donne," who had written the witty and paradoxical work of his early career, and "Doctor Donne," who was writing the sermons. But that sharp dichotomy was a theatricality of Donne's imagination. It is not surprising that in trying to elucidate the difficulties of Jack Donne's poem I have found some of the most helpful commentary in Doctor Donne's sermons.

THEODORE REDPATH

[The *Songs and Sonnets*]†

Donne's *Songs and Sonets* are among the three or four finest collections of love-lyrics in the English language. Such a high valuation still requires emphasis, despite the fact that these poems are read and appreciated far more than they were, say, fifty years ago. Too many readers of poetry, even in England, would still omit Donne's name from a list of the supreme love-lyrists of England, while readily including the names of Herrick, Shelley, Tennyson, Browning, and Swinburne. This is probably partly because the *Songs and Sonets* still remain comparatively little known:[1] but there are other reasons. One reason is the lingering prejudice that love-lyrics should be expressions of feeling unalloyed with any marked degree of cerebration. Donne's love-lyrics spring partly from a strong and ingenious head. They are therefore liable to give the impression of being merely brain-spun. In fact, that is very seldom the case, since they also come from a passionate heart. Another reason is that many people are put off by the sheer difficulty of the sense of many passages. Ben Jonson prophesied that the poetry of Donne would perish for lack of being understood. It has not yet perished, but though it is read now perhaps much more than at any time since the seventeenth century, it offers much difficulty, and it is doubtful how far even the bare sense of some of the poems is really understood. In the case of the *Songs and Sonets*, however, trouble taken in trying to understand the sense is almost always amply rewarded. A further obstacle to the just evaluation of the poems is the fairly widespread conception of Donne as a merely flippant, cyni-

† From Theodore Redpath, *The Songs and Sonnets of John Donne*, copyright 1956. Pp. xv-xvi and xxvii-xxxix. Reprinted by permission of Methuen & Co., Ltd., and Barnes & Noble.

1. In a widely circulated anthology *(The Oxford Book of English Verse)* only 7 pages are allotted to Donne (as compared with 21 to Herrick, 19 to Shelley, 23 to Tennyson, 20 to Browning, and 12 to Swinburne). Moreover, of the seven poems ascribed to Donne, one is probably not by him at all; and only four of the *Songs and Sonets* are given. Again, in the last edition of Palgrave's *Golden Treasury* (1941, reprinted 1954), not a single poem by Donne is included.

cal love poet. Among the causes of the spread of this idea are probably the choice of cynical poems for anthologies, e.g. the *Song*, 'Go and catch a falling star'; the cumulative impression of the *Songs and Sonets* and the mostly cynical *Elegies*, when taken together; and the influence of certain outstanding critical studies. In actual fact, the *Songs and Sonets* cover a very wide range of feeling from flippant cynicism to the most tender and even idealistic love. Finally, many people fail to find in Donne's love-lyrics the music which they demand from such poems. That is a pity, for there is really great variety and subtlety of music in the *Songs and Sonets*, and once it is properly sensed, it can be felt to have attractions at least equal to and sometimes transcending those of music of a more obvious character.

The *Songs and Sonets* are, in fact, superior as a body of love-lyrics to any equivalent number of poems by Herrick, Shelley, Tennyson, Browning, or Swinburne. Indeed, if we survey English poetry from end to end I doubt if we shall find any serious rivals to the *Songs and Sonets*, except the sonnets of Sidney and Shakespeare, and the love-lyrics of Yeats, and, possibly, of Hardy.

* * *

One of the most striking features of the *Songs and Sonets* is undoubtedly the way in which the most diverse thoughts, images and allusions are pressed into the service of love poetry. References are made to such varied fields as astronomy, law, religion, war and military affairs, medicine, eating and drinking, the human body, time, marriage and divorce, the weather, scholastic philosophy, politics, alchemy, death, fire and heat, astrology, business, learning, and everyday life. Very often there is an astonishing difference between the field to which reference is made and the context in which the reference appears in the poem. A celebrated instance is Donne's comparison of himself and his wife to a pair of compasses. Another particularly striking instance occurs in *A Fever*, a poem which deals with the illness of some woman to whom the poet seems greatly attached. The Stoics had disputed among themselves as to what sort of fire would consume the world at the end of each cycle of existence; and a similar controversy about the origin and nature of a world-consuming fire had occurred in the theology of the Early Christian era. Donne deliberately makes a preposterous use of that old dispute:

O wrangling schools, that search what fire
  Shall burn this world, had none the wit
Unto this knowledge to aspire,
  That this her fever might be it?
(*A Fever*, ll. 13–16)

The turn of wit adds a special strengthening savour to the poignancy of the poem. Even the most far-fetched references generally seem compellingly apt within their context in the poems. The combination of surprise and aptness is certainly one of the chief merits of the imagery and allusion in the *Songs and Sonets*.

It was possibly more especially Donne's references to scholastic philosophy that led Dryden to censure him for affecting metaphysics even 'in his amorous verses, where nature only should reign'. It was probably this censure that brought into currency the application of the term 'metaphysical' to the poetry of Donne and his followers. But the term 'metaphysical' soon acquired a more general sense than Dryden probably intended, and came to connote the employment of learning as the stuff of poetry. Later still, the term, owing to its traditional association with the work of particular poets such as Donne, Crashaw and Cowley, acquired a still broader connotation, namely the body of characteristics common and peculiar to the work of those English poets whom tradition has called 'metaphysical'. Thus the term 'metaphysical imagery', for instance, would now be quite commonly understood to refer to imagery which was *inter alia* both far-fetched and apt, like much of that of such poets as Donne, Crashaw and Cowley.

The effect of the diversity of reference in the *Songs and Sonets* is often described by the rapidity with which reference to one field succeeds reference to another sometimes very different field. Noteworthy examples occur in the last stanzas of *The Relic* and *The Broken Heart*.

Equally characteristic of the *Songs and Sonets* is the marked absence of mythological and pastoral imagery and allusion. This was early recognized as a general characteristic of Donne's poetry. It was, no doubt, partly to this feature that Carew was referring in the following lines from his admirable Elegy on Donne's death:

> The Muses' garden with pedantic weeds
> O'erspread, was purg'd by thee; the lazy seeds
> Of servile imitation thrown away,
> And fresh invention planted.
> (Carew's *Elegy* on Donne's death, ll. 25–8)

This absence of mythological and pastoral allusion entails the absence of conventional remoteness and gallantry from the *Songs and Sonets*. In their place a firm and even a stern realism is often imparted to the poems by the references to war and military affairs, death, law, politics, medicine, fire and heat, business, the human body, and many of the features of home life; while, on the other hand, a certain lofty, *recherché* strain is often provided by the references to Scholastic doctrine, astronomy, religion, and learning: and a less lofty strangeness is injected by the references to alchemy, astrology and superstition.

The *Songs and Sonets* are also remarkable for the strength and range of the feelings they express. There is the incandescent but controlled fury of *The Apparition*; there is the violent allergy to love expressed in

Love's Usury; there is the uprush of poignant longing in the opening lines of *A Fever*; there is the turbulent sadness of parting in *A Valediction: of weeping*; there is the protective tenderness of the *Song*, 'Sweetest love, I do not go'; there is the firm confidence in mutual love which pervades *A Valediction: forbidding mourning*; there is the desolate grief of *A Nocturnal upon St Lucy's Day*.

Besides the overall variety of the feeling expressed in the *Songs and Sonets* as a whole, there is also often (though not always) considerable variety of feelings within individual poems. One especially interesting type of case is where negative feelings like petulance, bitterness, cynicism, irritation or contempt arise in the course of poems which are predominantly positive. *The Sun Rising* is a happy poem of consummated love: but it is strewn with insults and scornful references. *The Canonization* is a vigorous glorification of love, but it begins with a voluminous outpouring of exasperation and contempt. Even in *Lovers' Infiniteness*, where the wooing is conducted on the whole in a tone of gentle reasonableness, there are overtones of petulance in places, e.g. in the use of such words as 'bargain' (l. 8), 'stocks' (l. 16) and 'outbid' (l. 17), which introduce the bitter suggestion of a love-market. If the matter is looked into it will be found that there is scarcely a single positive poem into which some such feelings as cynicism, bitterness or contempt does not to some degree intrude. This strengthens the poems: for just as when a hard man weeps it is impressive, so it is when a sceptical or cynical man loves.

It should be added that the feeling in the *Songs and Sonets* as a whole gives a strong impression of masculinity. Lovers may die in these poems, but they do not faint, as they do in Keats and Shelley. The language is generally manly and vigorous, and sometimes sudden, or even harsh. The detailed reference to such masculine activities as war and politics also contributes to the total impression of masculine feeling.

On the other hand, contrary to a fairly widespread idea about them, the *Songs and Sonets*, though they often express or imply the view that physical passion is a good thing, yet (in contrast with the *Elegies*) rather seldom express actual feelings of physical lust. This is one of the ways in which the *Songs and Sonets* are distinguishable from much of the work of those other great love poets, Ovid, Propertius and Ronsard.

Another leading feature of the *Songs and Sonets* is their rather peculiar sensory atmosphere. They contain very little colour: though there are, from time to time, remarkably sharp, colourless visual impressions. Even these, however, are exceptional, and the focus of attention is very rarely the visual aspect of experience. The rarity of auditory sensations is even more marked. There is nothing in the whole of the *Songs and Sonets* like Wordsworth's 'casual shout that broke the silent air', or Vigny's

> J'aime le son du cor, le soir, au fond des bois.

There is, indeed, scarcely any reference to sounds at all. Again, sense impressions of smell as distinct from taste do not seem to occur in the *Songs and Sonets*. There are, on the other hand, a few references to sensations of taste, and a fair number to the motor sensations involved in sucking, feeding, drinking, and swallowing. This strain of often rather coarse physicality gives its definite tang to the poems in which it occurs, and sometimes contrasts strangely with the intellectual and spiritual interests which lie beside it. Other motor sensations are frequently referred to, e.g. the sensations involved in running, walking, snatching, winking, leaning. So also are organic sensations, such as the sense of inflammation of the veins which love may cause, or the sensation of 'sorrowing dulness' after sexuality. In point of fact, in the *Songs and Sonets* motor and organic sensations definitely predominate over sensations of sight, sound, smell, taste, and even touch, and that is so even if we include in 'touch' cutaneous sensations of temperature as well as those of pressure. This probably helps to account for a feeling of *inwardness* that one quite frequently senses in the poems, despite all their references to the outside world.

With regard to what psychologists would call the 'feeling-tone' of the poems, painful sense-impressions are quite often stimulated in the course of poems which are predominantly pleasurable. This is a parallel feature to that already noted in the case of feelings.

The use of language in the *Songs and Sonets* has also some special features. The diction (as contrasted with the thought) is generally simple: though Donne often combines the simple words in unexpected ways, forming strange compounds or odd phrases or sentences:

And makes one little room, an *everywhere*.
(*The Good-morrow*, l. 11)

Thou are so *truth*, . . .
(*The Dream*, l. 7)

A *she-sigh* from my mistress' heart, . . .
(*Love's Diet*, l. 10)

And if some lover, such as we,
Have heard this *dialogue of one*, . . .
(*The Ecstasy*, ll. 73–4)

No *tear-floods*, nor *sigh-tempests* move; . . .
(*A Valediction: forbidding mourning*, 1.6)

But since this god produc'd a destiny,
And that *vice-nature*, custom, lets it be; . . .
(*Love's Deity*, ll. 5–6)

Sometimes he puns, though punning does not appear to be frequent. Sometimes he repeats words or types of phrase, throwing them up like a juggler. He is particularly fond of playing with pronouns and demonstrative adjectives:

> Coming and staying show'd thee, thee,
> But rising makes me doubt, that now
> Thou art not thou.
> (*The Dream*, ll. 21–3)

> To me thou, falsely, thine,
> And I to thee mine actions shall disguise.
> (A *Lecture upon the Shadows*, ll. 20–1)

This sort of passage gives a combined impression of virtuosity and intimacy.

From time to time, though rather seldom, Donne deviates from the normal simplicity of the diction, by employing learned language: and on such occasions the work takes on a certain sophistication. On the other hand, he more frequently interpolates coarse diction, which imparts to the poetry a rasping force. On other occasions special effects are obtained by the use of words with associations that are homely rather than coarse:

> Because such fingers need to *knit*
> That subtle *knot*, which makes us man: . . .
> (*The Ecstasy*, ll. 63–4)

> If he wrung from me a tear, I *brin'd* it so
> With scorn or shame, that him it nourish'd not; . . .
> (*Love's Diet*, ll. 13–14)

Donne occasionally achieves a peculiar effect of some subtlety by veiling the full meaning of a word or phrase which is really charged with intense implications. One example occurs in the first stanza of *Love's Usury*. Donne is there bargaining with Love, and begging Love not to ensnare him till middle-age, but meanwhile to allow him to give full rope to the caprices of lust:

> Till then, Love, let my body reign, and let
> Me travel, sojourn, snatch, plot, have, forget,
> Resume my last year's relict: think that yet
> We'd never met. (ll. 5–8)

The true import of the intensely contemptuous word 'relict', viz. cast-off-mistress, is veiled under its apparent generality. Other instances are the phrase 'think Thou call'st for more' (meaning more sexual play) in ll. 8–9 of *The Apparition*, and the word 'mistake' (meaning mistake and sleep with) in l. 11 of *Love's Usury*: both of which have an uncanny pregnancy. It is also possible that there is a very bold instance of this technique in stanza 2 of *The Relic*: for it is not out of the question that the vague phrase 'a something else thereby' (l. 18) may really mean a bone of Christ's.

The general tone of the language of the *Songs and Sonets* is colloquial. The poems have the flexibility and liveliness of spoken language. The openings are often particularly colloquial in tone. This has the effect of making the poems seem to grow naturally out of definite situations in individual lives. Sentences, on the other hand, are generally somewhat longer than one would expect to find in ordinary speech. Yet Donne manages to keep the vital and passionate phrases he writes, in continuity with one another, so as to form wholes which have both firmness and shape.

Donne is acutely alive to the sound-values of words: and the sound is sometimes almost magically interwoven with the sense. Particularly striking instances of this are to be found in *The Expiration*, *The Apparition*, *Twickenham Garden*, *Mummy* or *Love's Alchemy*, and *A Nocturnal upon St Lucy's Day*.

Everywhere in the poems are to be found instances of rapid and ingenious thinking. The Protean changes of imagery and allusion have already been mentioned. There is also a strange tendency to the violence of paradox, and to the sort of convolution of thought examplified in the following lines from *Love's Exchange*:

> Love, let me never know that this
> Is love, or, that love childish is;
> Let me not know that others know
> That she knows my pains, lest that so
> A tender shame make me mine own new woe.
> (ll. 17–21)

Typical, too, is the kind of intellectual juggling we find in the clever play on personal identity in stanza 2 of *The Legacy*:

> I heard me say: 'Tell her anon,
> That my self' (that is, you, not I)
> 'Did kill me'; and when I felt me die,
> I bid me send my heart, when I was gone;
> But I alas could there find none,
> When I had ripp'd me, and search'd where hearts did lie; . . .
> (ll. 9–14)

What is remarkable is that such intellectual acrobatics seldom detract from the overall strength of the poems in which they occur. Indeed they often add to it, and sometimes even (as e.g. in *The Primrose*) form a central part of the total effect.

The intellectual agility and ingenuity of the poems are special manifestations of an intellectual strength also shown in other ways, and especially in the relevance and tight concatenation of the thought throughout almost all the poems. Each poem has its specific conception, its focal centre, and there is very rarely any drifting away from the point, however diverse the objects which are referred to, or the images and ideas which occur. This is true both in the simplest sort of case, such as *The Apparition*, where the whole poem of seventeen lines consists of one sentence of concentrated ironic loathing; and in the most complex sort of case, such as that of *A Nocturnal upon St Lucy's Day*, where allusions of considerable diversity and subtlety are strewn thickly through the poem, affording intellectual satisfaction in themselves, but no less certainly contributing to the emotional and intellectual totality of the poem. Where there is apparent irrelevance it is almost certain to serve some deliberate purpose, as in the brilliant effect of the last two lines of *The Curse*. As to the concatenation of the thought within the poems, this is almost everywhere controlled and sure. It has sometimes even been said that the texture of the *Songs and Sonets* is argumentative. This is too sweeping a generalization. The thought arises at the start form the situation out of which the poem itself grows, and it then develops, sometimes indeed by way of argument, but at other times by way of narrative, or analogy, or extended metaphor, or through the play of fancy, or at the prompting of some fresh feeling which has come into play, or in some other way; though almost always so that the connections of the thought are close, whether this is obvious or appears only after scrutiny.

With regard to the attitudes towards love expressed or implied in the poems, their variety has already been indicated. It is, however, worth noticing certain other important features of these attitudes. For one thing, there runs through the *Songs and Sonets*, taken as a whole, the belief that physical passion is a good thing. Sometimes, especially in the apparently earlier poems, it is seen as good in itself, even, at times, as preferable to the perils of love. Sometimes it is seen as a necessary and valuable element in a full and satisfying mutual attachment. For another thing, love is generally considered in these poems either as a danger or as a wonder. It is not thought of coolly as something that can be handled or trifled with, and seldom thought of simply as one of the pleasures of life. We are most often in the realm of *amour passion*, comparatively rarely in the realm of *amour physique*, and never in that of *amour goût*, to make use of Stendhal's illuminating distinctions.[2] Passionate feeling is paramount; even *passionate* sensuality is secondary; mere elegant gallantry (so frequent in Restoration love-lyrics) is completely absent.

Again, there are one or two special thoughts about love, which recur in a number of the poems. One is that love is a mystery in which Donne and his lady are adepts. The most extensive expression of this thought occurs in *The Ecstasy*. Clearly linked with it is Donne's practice of crediting his beloved with religious significance, as in *The Relic*, *A Nocturnal upon St Lucy's Day* and *Air and Angels*. In *The Dream* he even goes so

2. See Stendhal, *De l'Amour*, where the distinctions are fully discussed.

far as to maintain that his lady has some of the divine attributes. This practice seems to associate some of the poems with the tradition of the *amour courtois*. Another typical thought is that two lovers are self-sufficient. Donne sometimes hyperbolically extends this idea, and asserts that together they are the whole world. In this way some of the poems become more than love poems: they become glorifications of love. On the other hand, Donne tends to be temperate in his forecast of the future of a love already in existence. We do not find him saying that it will last for ever, or even for a long time. He does express hope that a love will continue, but when he expresses a faith that it will, the faith is only a hypothetical one. 'If you and I love equally, and take care, our love will continue.' This is what Donne says in several places. Statements of this sort are indeed almost tautologous: but these near-tautologies seem much more satisfyingly near the truth than rash categorical faith in eternal constancy. Another, rather subtle, way in which Donne's thought about love distinguishes itself from more commonplace views, is in his uncertainty as to how far lovers are really united by their love (see *A Valediction: forbidding mourning*, *The Ecstasy* (ll. 41–56) and *The Good-morrow* (ll. 20–1). This uncertainty should, I believe, be regarded as the sign of an honest attempt not to exaggerate about the relationship of love, while at the same time recognizing its unifying force.

Finally, something must be said as to the forms and metres of the poems. The forms are almost all stanzaic. They are exceedingly various, and many of them are very complex. There is only one stanza form that Donne uses more than once: the simple octosyllabic quatrain with alternate rhymes, which he uses in three poems. It seem that over forty of the stanza forms were probably invented by him. The vast majority of the poems are in stanzas of from six to eleven lines. Eight- and nine-line stanzas occur most frequently. Occasionally two or three poems have the same rhyme scheme; but where that is so, they differ in line-length. It is as if Donne proudly scorned to repeat the same stanza form.

Donne is fond of reiterated rhymes. Eighteen of the poems, for instance, end in triplets or quadruplets. This gives an effect of insistence. Again, over twenty of the poems begin with a couplet; and the opening rhyme-scheme *aabb* is very common. The use of reiterated rhymes, whether in the openings or endings or in the body of the poems, acts as a counter-force to the strong tendency in many of the poems for the metric form to be distorted by the speech-rhythms which cut across it. The verse might so easily break into utter disorder. Reiterated rhymes help to prevent this. The triplets in ll. 5–7 of each stanza of *A Nocturnal upon St Lucy's Day* afford an instance of their steadying effect.

Some of the stanza forms are very attractive in themselves. Much play is made with variations of line length. Stanzas of more than six lines seem to give Donne the scope he so often needs to develop the complex interplay of thought and feeling which is so typical of him. With exceptions, the poems in shorter stanzas tend to be thin or slight.

In some cases the stanza forms seem especially appropriate to their respective poems. This is so, for instance, with the *Song*, 'Go and catch a falling star', where the piquant slightness of the short lines prepares by contrast the elongated sting in the tail of each stanza. A similar effect is achieved in *The Blossom*, where there short sixth line of each stanza sets off the epigrammatic couplet which follows. Again, the sharp changes of line length in *A Valediction: of weeping* accord magnificently with the turbulent passion underlying the poem: while the steady fixity of the lines of *A Valediction: forbidding mourning* is at one with the firm and substantial love in which the poem shows such settled confidence. The stanza forms do not always seem so peculiarly appropriate as in these cases: but they frequently delight by their intricacy; and the fact that the rich texture of passion, thought and imagery, and the odd quirks and ironies, could be made to take on shapes of such fairly strict complexity, is often a subject for wonder.

The overall forms of the poems are sometimes very clearly patterned, as in the ternary forms of *The Message*, the *Song*, 'Go and catch a falling star', *Lover's Infiniteness* and *The Prohibition*. At other times there is no apparent relation between the number of stanzas and the substance of the poem. In most cases, however, the poems give one a definite impression of firm shape. Sometimes, as in the device of the 'dialogue of one' in *The Ecstasy*, and the wonderful thematic modification of the opening line of *A Nocturnal* at the close of the poem, we come across especially satisfying examples of formal beauty.

The metres are normally iambic: but the actual rhythms which play over the basic metrical structure are very various. Drummond tells us that Ben Jonson said that 'for not keeping of accent' Donne 'deserved hanging'. In saying this, however, Jonson only revealed one of his own limitations. Remarkable literary man though Jonson was, the validity of Donne's use of true speaking language springing straight from passion and vigorous and subtle thinking, and not to be strait-laced by the demands of external metres, was beyond him. In point of fact, Donne's verse is generally more regular than Jonson's statement would suggest: provided we construe regularity more liberally than Jonson did. Let us consider, for instance, the fine bitter opening of *Twickenham Garden*. Syllabically, the first two lines are quite regular. The first has ten syllables: the second eight. Pedally, on the other hand, they are admittedly far from being examples of the basic lines, the iambic pentameter and the iambic tetrameter.

Blásted with síghs, | and surr, | óunded with téars,

is best scanned as shown, i.e. as two choriambic feet separated by a pyrrhic.[3]

3. This was apparently in part pointed out by a contemporary of Donne's, Giles Oldisworth, in his notes on Donne. (See John Sampson, 'Contemporary Light upon John Donne' [Essays and Studies of the English Association, vii, 87]).

Hither I cóme | to séek | the spring.

is best scanned as a choriambus followed by two iambic feet. Only cramping pedantry, however, could find these lines anything but excellent. If the whole poem had been written in lines of the same types as these (which would have been one way of 'regularizing' them!), then it would have been hopelessly monotonous; and the pedal character of these particular lines, which is in complete keeping with their meaning and feeling, would have lost its point. In actual fact, the lines, though pedally irregular, are made to seem regular enough: partly because, syllabically, they *are* regular; partly because the fist line has a regularity of its own, since it is perfectly symmetrical, and the second line repeats the choriambic rhythm which has been set up; and partly because the lines merge at once into the general iambic pattern, since the last two feet of the second line are both iambic, and the third line is a a regular iambic line. What is more, they satisfy us, in any case, by their force and naturalness, so that we are not inclined to think cantankerously about rules. This is a particularly striking example of Donne's regular irregularity; but it would be possible to cite countless instances from the poems. The *Songs and Sonets* are little short of miraculous in their blend of the freedom and vitality of the spoken language with the reasonable exigencies of metrical form.

* * *

R. A. DURR

Donne's "The Primrose" †

"The Primrose", though seldom noticed by students of Donne, seems to me to delineate, in ordered sequence, a fundamental action of the *Songs and Sonets* as a whole. This is the action that originates in the desire to find a true—a fixed and perfect—love and the security and rest inherent in it, that in its passage through Donne's astute and honest intellect, tutored by corrosive experience, passes into a cynical disintegration of the hope of realizing that ideal, and concludes in "gay" abandonment to the sensual flux of casual delights. "The Primrose," once recognized as microcosmic of this pattern, may thus afford a point of reference for the reading of Donne's secular verse.

The first stanza breathes the air of faith and innocence, as the poet walks upon a lovely primrose hill seeking to find a true love.[1] We under-

† From *Journal of English and Germanic Philology*, LIX (April, 1960), 218–22. Reprinted by permission of The University of Illinois Press and R. A. Durr.

1. It has been suggested to me that "true Love" might be an allusion to the Herb Paris, or Herb True-love, whose four leaves and berry form a true-love knot, according to the herbals. The allusion would be highly appropriate to Donne's theme and consonant with its imagery: in a field of primroses,

stand the ideality involved. For to Donne a true love meant the perfect union of harmonious souls, a union wherein, as in "The Extasie," their oneness seems a substance externally real between them, a third element, an "abler soule," transcending all the tensions inevitable to sex. In "The Canonization," for example, this "one neutrall thing" to which "both sexes fit" is likened to the Phoenix, an androgynous creature.[2] True love had power, moreover, to translate the lovers from the incoherent sphere of mutability into a region, a condition, free of all mundane dimension. Space, the world—expanding disconcertingly before Elizabethan eyes—contracts into the closed and numinous circle of love's involvement:

> For love, all love of other sights controules,
> And makes one little roome, an every where.
> ("The good-morrow")[3]

> She'is all States, and all Princes, I,
> Nothing else is.
> ("The Sunne Rising")

Even time cannot disturb this union:

> What ever dyes, was not mixt equally;
> If our two loves be one, or, thou and I
> Love so alike, that none doe slacken, none can die.
> ("The good-morrow")

> Love, all alike, no season knowes, nor clyme,
> Nor houres, dayes, moneths, which are the rags of time.
> ("The Sunne Rising")

> All other things, to their destruction draw,
> Only our love hath no decay . . .
> ("The Anniversarie")

The disparate and decaying world, the All, becomes distilled in love's crucible into the One of the lovers' interfused souls, and this One, in

---

in a world of ordinary—i.e., false—woman, he seeks Herb True-love, a constant woman. Yet the possibility of Donne's having used the association, except as a passing connotation, is not supported by the rest of the poem. For Herb Paris has four leaves, which is the number assigned that creature who is *less* than "mere woman," not the ideal of woman. The four, five, and six refer to different primroses—typical woman (five) and two aberrations; the choice is among these, not between Herb Paris and primrose.

2. Donne might have had in mind the alchemical use of the phoenix, along with the eagle, or the Rebis (two-headed hermaphrodite), for example, as a symbol of the *Coniunctio oppositorum*, the union of opposites, in the *hieros gamos*, or "chymical marriage," wherein, according to C. G. Jung, "the supreme opposites, male and female . . . , are melted into a unity purified of all opposition and therefore incorruptible" (*Psychology and Alchemy*, trans. R. F. C. Hull [London, 1953], p. 37). There is perhaps a left-handed allusion in stanza one of "The Primrose" to the alchemical process of distillation (*per descensum*, in this case)—the shower is no ordinary one—for what is distilled in achemy is the Elixir, the water of life, that can transmute base to perfect metal, imperfect to perfect—true—love.

3. Quotations are from *The Poems of John Donne*, ed. H. J. Grierson, 2 vols (London, 1912).

turn, becomes the All, but now transformed by love's alchemy from base to perfect metal:

> so wee shall
> Be one, and one another's All.
> ("Lovers infinitenesse")

But it is not necessary to go to Donne's other poems, except for confirmation, to realize what true love meant to him, for the imagery of the first stanza of "The Primrose" contains its own definition of that ideal. The primrose, being of the primula family and somewhat resembling a star, was sometimes called the "star-primula" in the herbals; and such star-flowers were commonly used as emblems and water marks in association with the various symbols of Eden, or the Orchard of the Rose, or the Garden of Grace—all conventionally situated upon a mountain or hill. The field of primroses is not a casual patch of simple flowers; it is a "terrestriall Galaxie," a circular swathe of star flowers (since the Milky Way was circular to seventeenth-century eyes), a symbol of heaven, perfection, on earth. These flowers thus, watered by heaven as they are nourished by earth, "grow Manna": true love is both spiritual and physical, and it is man's sustenance in his wanderings through the waste lands of a faithless and disjointed world. This primrose hill is only superficially related to Montgomery Castle. It is essentially a landmark in the country of the soul.

If stanza one, in its imagery suggestive of a fusion of earth and heaven, Flesh and spirit, defines the ideal of a true love, the second stanza dialectically destroys belief in the possibility of its attainment. We witness Donne converting "Manna to gall" ("Twicknam garden") by the action of his sceptical mind. In reality, the images of perfection of the first stanza had contained the germs of their own dissolution, not only in the hesitancy of the subjunctive mood but also in the circumstance that, while the primrose in a context of stars and circles may legitimately be associated with the connotations of the star-flower and the Garden, it was most commonly the emblem of fugacity. The "prim-rose" is the first rose and the best, the time of youth's freshness and love's first flushed exuberance, which every poet knows fast decays but which Donne would bid stay. Moreover, as with Shakespeare's primrose path of dalliance and Milton's yellow-skirted fayes who wore primroses, the flower conveyed the additional odor of wantonness; and this is prognostic of the poem's conclusion.

Reason has made it obvious that a true love, a constant woman, must be different from, either less or more than, average woman, and the poet thus finds himself faced with a disconcerting choice: either a lump of animated clay, "scarce any thing," if less than woman, or a Petrarchan abstraction, if more than woman, who would transfer relations from the properly sexual to the pallidly Platonic level of intercourse. "Both these were monsters." His decision is unavoidable; he must accept the normal woman, who is false by nature, because either alternative leads only to another and worse kind of falsity: the "four" and the "six" are monstrous, unnatural. He could better endure to deal with ordinary woman, who, in being false, is at least true to her nature—since she "can have no way but falsehood to be true" ("Womans constancy"); she at least is natural and not monstrous. By now the poet is a long way from where he started, and the progress has been all down hill; the glow of the flowery Galaxie of stanza one has been quite put out.

Ratiocination having brought him from faith in the possibility of finding a true love to the reverse conviction that "no where/lives a woman true, and faire" ("Song: Goe, and catche a falling starre"), Donne will not bemoan his loss; he will acknowledge the truth, and more than that he will cynically pursue the truth to its farthest implications. He will in the destructive element immerse and assure himself and us that the water is fine. Woman's "mysterious number" is five, which is half of ten, the "farthest number," since it includes the elements of all possible numbers and therefore, in the Pythagorean and medieval systems which the numerology assumes,[4] of all things. Hence each woman is entitled to half of all men, a generous allowance. But Donne will not pause there; if there can be no *One*, there shall be no in-between either. The resignation of a Jack Donne understands no middle way; it is defiantly and desperately abandoned. Thus he reasons, since five contains the first even and the first odd number,[5] and since all numbers are either even or odd, woman is entitled not just to half but to *all* men; she is entitled by nature, by her innate falseness, to unqualified promiscuity.

But it would be to misrepresent the final shape and course of this action in Donne's work simply to conclude where "The Primrose" concludes. His scepticism and abandonment, which appear decisive and abiding in the *Songs and Sonets*, are in reality defensive and transitional. He laid claim to wantonness, insisted upon it, because he despaired of constancy; he assumed the posture of the easy cynic because he could determine upon no way that led to Truth. His going around and around is not the motion of a mind in simple engagement with itself but the action of a soul climbing the winding stair of the watchtower of Truth, that it might find rest.

What Jack Donne wanted all along was what we would like to believe Dean Donne found—at least in that measure commensurate with a fallen world and a sinful, passionate man: the repose and fixity of a constant

4. Grierson runs into difficulties, it seems to me, in trying to interpret the last stanza outside this orientation. Charles Monroe Coffin (*John Donne and the New Philosophy* [New York, 1937], pp. 157–58) incorporates and elaborates Grierson's reading. But see E. D. Cleveland, *The Explicator*, VIII (October, 1949), 4.

5. In *Essays in Divinity* (ed. E. M. Simpson [Oxford, 1952], p. 10), Donne writes: "The Author of these first five books is *Moses*. In which number, compos'd of the first even, and first odd . . ." Miss Simpson in her note refers to "The Primrose"; but the symbolical value of the number five she cites from M. P. Ramsay—who quotes Chaignet's summary of Nicomachus of Gerasa's conception of the number—is only partially relevant to the poem, for while five may function in "The Primrose" as "le plus naturel des nombres," it does not, except perhaps by ironic inversion, function as "le plus parfait."

love. He had known something of it in this world through his wife, perhaps, but here nothing finally endures. "In this world we enjoy nothing; enjoying presumes perpetuity; and here, all things are fluid, transitory: There I shall enjoy, and possess for ever, God himself" (*L Sermons*, 48). It is God alone, he came to understand, Who is "th'Eternall root/ of true Love" ("A Hymne to Christ, at the Authors last going into Germany"); for, as the contemplatives always knew, in the words of Thomas à Kempis, "love is born of God, and cannot rest but in God, above all created things" (*The Imitation of Christ*, 111, 5). The author of the famous *Quia amore langueo* has expressed this Christian fundamental in terms peculiarly like those of Donne:

> In a valey of this restles minde
>   I soughte in mounteine and in mede,
> Trustinge a trewe love for to finde.
>   Upon an hill than I took hede . . .

He finds Christ, Who tells him, "I am true love that fals was nevere."[6]

In Holy Sonnet XVII she whom Donne had truly loved is dead, but the experience of that earthly joy has served to point him toward its sublime analogue:

> Here the admyring her my mind did whett
> To seeke thee God; so streames do shew their head . . .

We are reminded perhaps of Dante and Petrarch, or yet of Augustine, passionate lovers, and consider the voice to have spoken truth that inspired Yeats to record in *A Vision* that "the love the Saint brings to God at his twenty-seventh phase was found in some past life upon a woman's breast."

ARTHUR L. CLEMENTS

[Eros in the *Songs and Sonnets*] †

Whatever one decides about the nature of the plea in "The Exstasie," there is no question that "The Canonization" concerns sexual love, and not only because of the Renaissance pun on "die," slang for sexual consummation. Just as the lovers in "The Exstasie" are to become more fully Christlike by turning to their bodies, their ecstatic souls becoming incarnate and then their bodies becoming ecstatically united too, so the lovers in "The Canonization" are Christlike (continuing to understand Christ or the last Adam in the mythic sense of "essential self") by giving

6. *Early English Lyrics*, ed. E. K. Chambers and F. Sidgwick (London, 1926) p. 151.

† From Arthur L. Clements, *Poetry of Contemplation: John Donne, George Herbert, Henry Vaughan, and the Modern Period*, copyright © 1990. Pp. 45–57, 257–58. Reprinted by permission of the State University of New York and Arthur L. Clements. Notes have been added or abridged for this Norton Critical Edition.

up the sorry-go-round world of getting and spending, and by dying for love. There are actually two worlds, corresponding to the two selves, and thereby the seeming contradiction of condemning and enjoying the world is resolved. The two worlds are the perfect, natural world, including creatures and objects, and eternally created by the Second Person of God and by the Second Person in the redeemed individual—indeed, in Traherne's words, the "visible World is the Body of God" (*Centuries*, II, 21)—a glorious world for which, in Hebraic-Christian tradition, one renders joyful praise; and the fallen world fabricated by man's conceptualizing ego—an artificial, prideful, and ultimately illusory world, of which one should be contemptuous (the familiar but often misinterpreted theme of *contemptus mundi*). It is the first, perfect and glorious world, or a part of it, that is appreciated in the Vision of Eros or the Vision of Dame Kind. In his secular poetry, Donne concerns himself only with the former and not the latter. * * * And whereas Gerard Manley Hopkins, influenced by Duns Scotus, discovered the "individually-distinctive beauty" or "inscape" of the natural world in both the non-human and human, in Visions of Dame Kind and of Philia, Donne's discovery seems limited to the human beloved only in Visions of Eros.[1] So while Hopkins would say that "the just man" particularly (and each person potentially), Donne might only say that the beloved

> Acts in God's eye what in God's eye he [or she] is—
> Christ—for Christ plays in ten thousand places,
> Lovely in limbs and lovely in eyes not his
> To the Father through the features of . . . faces.
> ("As kingfishers catch fire," ll. 11–14)

The idea that "the just man" or essential self "is Christ" and the idea embodied in the line "Christ plays in ten thousand places" are wholly consistent, as the priests Hopkins and Donne may be expected to have known, with biblical and patristic views. Wisdom, as it were, playing before the throne of God. Justin and Clement of Alexandria, for example, develop the Johannine theme that the indwelling Logos is the source of all spiritual and intellectual enlightenment. Donne's frequent microcosm-macrocosm distinction and comparison should be understood in these terms. The psyche's larger fallen world may well be given up for pneuma's perception and realization of the beloved's Christlikeness.

* * *

1. "Vision" is used not in the sense of any abnormal psychic phenomenon but in the sense of a profound, usually transforming experience of divine reality, either immanent and sensuously perceived (as in the Visions of Eros, Philia or brotherly love, and Dame Kind or Mother Nature) or transcendant and non-sensuously apprehended (Vision of God). These terms are defined by W. H. Auden in his "Introduction" to *The Protestant Mystics*, ed. Anne Fremantle (London, 1964). "Like the Vision of Dame Kind, the Vision of Eros is a revelation of creaturely glory, but whereas in the former it is the glory of a multiplicity of non-human creatures which is revealed, in the latter it is the glory of a single human being," the human beloved (p. 19). The biblical terms "psyche" and "pneuma," subsequently used, mean respectively the false self or closed ego and the true or essential self.

In celebrating the theme that the world, the fallen world, is well lost for love, "The Canonization," after the false-lead opening of the first two stanzas, effects a radical transformation of self that paradoxically is both merely witty and playful and yet wholly serious. It may very well be that the combination of witty levity and seriousness was, if not the only, one of the very few ways Donne could in his day express his views on human love as both erotic and divine. The first two stanzas basically are catalogs, that poetic form which Renaissance books of rhetoric advised novice poets to practice, though of course the catalog device would continue to be of use to the mature poet. Form here follows content: both stanzas are skillfully accomplished but elementary compared to the third stanza. The speaker brilliantly but simply lists, in the first stanza, alternative castigatings or courses that his audience (presumably, a well-meaning friend) might practice rather than prevent the speaker's loving. The second stanza is mainly an imagistically anti-Petrarchan series of rhetorical questions designed to establish the lovers' innocence and innocuousness: the world continues its routine, businesslike, often quarrelsome and militant way even "Though she and I do love." Stylistically, but not thematically, these two stanzas are like the poems of Group One; such poems as "Womans Constancy" and "The Indifferent" consist wholly or in large part of catalogs and anti-Petrarchan images. Thematically, and to some extent tonally, these two stanzas are like the poems of Group Three, seemingly Platonic in the insisted innocuousness and innocence of the lovers.[2]

While the reader of the poem is initially led falsely to believe that the lovers' love is without significant consequences for the world, the central, fulcrum third stanza begins to turn that misbelief all around, as it begins to present its transformation of the lovers' selves. The rhetorical tactic of the false-lead opening of the first two stanzas has been that of concession. Stylistically, symbolically, and semantically much more complex than the first two stanzas, the third stanza begins in the same mode of concession and listing; the speaker-lover in the first two lines of this stanza, lines 19–20, enjoins his audience-friend to call the lovers what he will, and even provides the disparaging labels or epithets—provides the ammunition, so to speak. Lines 19–20, like stanza one, are in the imperative mood; stanza two, except for its last three lines, is in the interrogative mood, but with the instructive declarative mood of the rest of stanza three, lines 21–27, and of all of stanza four, Donne turns the false-lead opening completely around to a thorough exaltation of the lovers. This achievement and the wit of the marvelous third stanza obtain

2. The grouping of Donne's Songs and Sonnets is based on groupings by Herbert Grierson and Helen Gardner, and is characterized as follows on p. 241 of *Poetry of Contemplation*:

Group One: poems of inconstant, false, or incomplete love; anti-Petrarchan. Usually, the focus is on physical love.

Group Two: poems of faithful or true love, usually both physical and spiritual.

Group Three: poems of Platonic love (using "Platonic" in the popular sense, "without sexual love"); with qualification, also called Petrarchan. Usual focus is on spiritual love.

not only in the abruptness yet consistency of a rich, compressed imagery and symbolism, but also in the rapid traversing (by means of this same imagery) of the Renaissance chain of being, a metaphor which expresses the plenitude, order, and unity of God's creation. This chain, as E. M. W. Tillyard points out (though his views are now contested), in the Elizabethan world view stretches from the base of God's throne to the lowest of inanimate objects and includes every entity and aspect of creation as a link in the chain (23). Donne's poem moves from the lowest link to nearly the highest in the chain of being, from the inanimate taper to the glorified saints, sitting below the angels next to God. Using imagery derived from Petrarch, the third stanza enjoins the friend to call the lovers flies, general symbols of the ephemeral and lustful as well as a Christian symbol of sin,[3] * * * frequently associated with the devil; and, as if to be even more outrageous, this stanza then declares the lovers are also tapers, which are even lower than flies and are self-consuming, "at our owne cost die." At this point it becomes certain because of the pun on *die* that the protestations of innocence in the second stanza do not include sexual innocence. The lovers die at their own cost because, according to Renaissance medical belief, sexual activity reduced one's life span.

In anticipation of the symbolism of the rest of the stanza, lines 20–21 indirectly refer to a moth or taper-fly which burns itself to death by approaching a flame and which was considered "hermaphroditic and resurrectable" (A. B. Chambers, "The Fly in Donne's 'Canonization'," 255). Continuing the imagery of flight and fire, Donne moves quickly to "Eagle" and "Dove" and "Phoenix," which, as well as being advancing steps in the alchemical process ("flying eagle" and "Diana's doves") leading to the philosopher's stone ("phoenix"), are complex Christian symbols of higher realities, especially associated with Christ and the Resurrection. On a secondary level, the dove appropriately also functions "as the bird of Venus and as a symbol of conjugal love" (Chambers, 253).

Associated with biblical stories of purification (Luke 2:22,24) and the Flood (Genesis 8), the dove in Christian art represents purity and peace (see line 39), but it is most significantly representative of the Holy Spirit, this symbolism first appearing in the story of Christ's baptism (John 1:32). The highest order of bird in the chain of being, the eagle, which similarly also signalizes new life begun at baptism, usually symbolizes the Resurrection and Christ both because of the belief that the eagle periodically renewed its plumage and youth by flying toward the sun and then plunging into water and because of the belief that it could gaze into the dazzling noon sun. A particular symbol of St. John the Evangelist, the eagle also stands more generally for those who are just and for the virtue of contemplation (Ferguson, 15–17). As Gardner points out, the dove

3. George Ferguson, *Signs and Symbols in Christian Art* (Oxford, 1966), p. 18. When not given in footnotes, full bibliographical references for the works cited in this article may be found in the "Selected Bibliography" of this Norton Critical Edition.

and eagle together are emblematic "of strength and gentleness. Joined, they symbolize the perfection of masculine and feminine qualities; compare Crashaw's address to St. Teresa, 'By all the Eagle in thee, all the Dove' " (*The Elegies And The Songs and Sonnets*, 204). The phoenix, the unique mythological bird that is consumed by its own funeral fire yet rises reborn from the ashes, is also, like the eagle, symbolic of the Resurrection of Christ.

So the lovers, made one by love, are consumed in their fire of passion but revive, undergo a death and resurrection. With Donne playing upon the slang meaning of "die" as consummating the sexual act, the lovers imitate Christ: they "dye and rise the same." By this mystery and miracle, by giving up the materialistic fallen world, by dying for love (as, in another sense, saints and martyrs do), the lovers are "*Canoniz'd* for Love." Dante says of Beatrice that she went straight to heaven after her death without spending any time in purgatory, the prerogative of a saint. Through the greater consciousness bestowed upon him through his love, Dante performed, as it were, his own act of canonization. So Donne performs the same for his lovers, who die and are resurrected in this life, the mark of contemplatives. Though some might possibly hear the tones and themes of Group One in the background, "The Canonization" is not merely a clever rationalization and justification of the speaker's love (or lust, his friend might say) that cynically uses mystical terminology. Rather, it is a poem about the extraordinary power of love to transmute the least into the greatest, to exalt the lowest on the chain of being into the highest, to transfigure tapers, flies, and sinners mysteriously into saints seated next to the throne of God. It is indeed for God's sake that the friend should hold his tongue and let the lovers love.

As the last stanza in the imperative mood shows, these lover-saints ("to whome love was peace" and blessedness, among other mystical characteristics) can then be invoked by the faithful, in the Roman Catholic fashion, to intercede with God on behalf of the faithful. The lovers give up the macrocosm, which is actually the lesser world of the commonwealth, the world of wealth, power, and earthly glory, and by that loss they paradoxically gain the greater world of the microcosm, the perfect and truly glorious world of their essential, Christlike selves. The humbled lovers of the first half of the poem (lines 1–21) are in the second half exalted as highly as human beings may possibly be exalted. But why?

In his brilliant and detailed study of "The Canonization," to which all subsequent discussions of the poem have been indebted, Cleanth Brooks observed that Donne "daringly treats profane love as if it is divine love," and he further remarked that "the poem then is a parody of Christian sainthood; but it is an intensely serious parody of a sort that modern man, habituated as he is to an easy yes or no, can hardly understand." Whereas, according to Brooks, modern man thinks that Donne either does not take love seriously or does not take sainthood seriously, and so thinks the poet is either simply sharpening his wit as an exercise or "merely indulging in a cynical and bawdy parody, . . . a reading of the poem will show that Donne takes both love and religion seriously" (in Clements, ed., *John Donne's Poetry*, 196–97). Brooks' reading of the poem admirably succeeds in demonstrating this thesis.[4]

I have tried to go a step further than Brooks in order to show not only that Donne takes both love and religion seriously but also that he daringly treats "profane" love as if it were divine love because it is: that is why the lovers are glorified as highly as possible. More precisely, Group One poems (sexuality without Eros) treat profane love as profane love; Group Two poems treat seemingly profane love as divine love. There are various characteristics (or the absence of such) by which we can distinguish between the two groups, the primary one being the presence or absence of the unitary consciousness or unifying vision by which the two lovers are or are seen as one. In "The Canonization," the primary characteristic finds expression in the central lines:

The Phoenix ridle hath more wit
By us, we two being one, are it,
So, to one neutrall thing both sexes fit.
Wee dye and rise the same, and prove
Mysterious by this love.

The appropriate biblical text for these lines is Galatians 3:28: "There is neither Jew nor Greek, there is neither bond nor free, there is neither male nor female: for ye are all one in Christ Jesus." The Gospel of Thomas, which Donne probably did not directly know, reads "Jesus said to them, 'When you make the two into one, when you make the inner like the outer and the outer like the inner, and the upper like the lower, when you make male and female into a single one, so that the male will not be male and the female will not be female . . . then you will enter the kingdom."[5] * * * Gregory of Nyssa understands St. Paul to mean in I Corinthians 15 that "the resurrection is nothing other than the

4. Cf. William J. Rooney, " 'The Canonization'—The Language of Paradox Reconsiderd," *ELH*, 23 (1956), 36–47, reprinted in *Essential Articles for the Study of John Donne's Poetry*, ed. John R. Roberts, pp. 271–278. Rooney asserts that the use of paradox "in the instance of 'The Canonization' is a distinctly poetical one, and from such use nothing can be concluded about whether 'Donne takes both love and religion seriously.' In apprehending this poem, the reader, modern or otherwise, is not faced with the philosophical dilemma, 'Either: Donne does not take love seriously . . . Or: Donne does not take sainthood seriously,' as Brooks asserts" (278). Nevertheless, not only modern readers but modern critics as well do respond in philosophical and moral terms. In *John Donne's Poetry*, Wilbur Sanders objects that the "canonization conceit" "entails an inflation of sentiment just as grandiose as the Petrarchan hyperboles Donne has already puntured. . . . Donne appears to argue the quasi-divine status of the lovers on the preposterous grounds that they re-enact the resurrection of Christ. . . . He is thus impertinently confounding mere carnality with a prime mystery of religion . . . this blasphemous witticism . . ." (22). Ably responding "to show how Donne's blend of wit and seriousness in hyperbole has provoked" Sanders, Brian Vickers points out in "The 'Songs and Sonnets' and the Rhetoric of Hyperbole" (*Essays in Celebration*, ed. A. J. Smith) that Sanders falls "back on a kind of puritanical thundering, a moral denunciation in which grace and humor are absent. . . . What he has quite failed to see (and he is evidently not alone) can be summed up in the paradoxical language of Traherne: hyperbole, like love, is 'infinitely Great in all Extremes . . . Excess is its true Moderation: Activity its Rest: and burning Fervency its only Refreshment' " (173–174).

5. Marvin W. Meyer, trans., *The Secret Teachings of Jesus: Four Gnostic Gospels* (New York, 1984), p. 24.

reconstitution of our nature to its pristine state."[6] * * * By their death and resurrection, imitating Christ, the two lovers overcome the effects of the Fall and become one again, become an androgynous or hermaphroditic being, "one neutrall thing" (not sexless, but containing "both sexes"), not only like the phoenix (which symbolizes the last Adam) but also like the unfallen first Adam before Eve was created out of his rib. For, as Augustine suggests, the significance of the story of Eve's creation is that the unfallen Adam contained both sexes so that the whole human race might be derived from a single unified being (*The City of God*, XII, 21). Thus the real meaning of the mystery of sexual intercourse is that it is a prefiguring realization as well as a symbolic representation of that mystical body of which we are all members, according to Paul's Epistle to the Ephesians 5:28–32:

> So ought men to love their wives as their own bodies. He that loveth his wife loveth himself.
>
> For no man ever yet hated his own flesh; but nourisheth and cherisheth it, even as the Lord the church.
>
> For we are members of his body, of his flesh, and of his bones.
>
> For this cause shall a man leave his father and mother, and shall be joined unto his wife, and they two shall be one flesh.
>
> This is a great mystery: but I speak concerning Christ and the church.

We may further distinguish between Group One and Group Two poems by observing that sexual love in the former is partial, genital, and therefore fallen (divided, 2 = 2), whereas in the latter it is polymorphously erotic and thereby redeemed (united, 2 = 1). A text from Donne's great later contemporary, John Milton, will help to explain. In *Paradise Lost*, Adam, observing the angel Raphael eat with relish, wonders in his healthy curiosity whether and how angels also make love, "for Love thou say'st / leads up to Heav'n, is both the way and guide." As if in a cherubic blush, Raphael answers affirmatively "with a smile that glow'd / Celestial rosy red":

> Let it suffice thee that thou know'st
> Us happy, and without Love no happiness.
> Whatever pure thou in the body enjoy'st
> (And pure thou wert created) we enjoy
> In eminence, and obstacle find none
> Of membrance, joint, or limb, exclusive bars:
> Easier than Air with Air, if Spirits embrace,
> Total they mix, Union of Pure with Pure
> Desiring; nor restrain'd conveyance need
> As Flesh to mix with Flesh, or Soul with Soul.
> (VIII, 611f.)

6. Henry Bettenson, ed. and trans., *The Later Christian Fathers: A Selection from the Writings of the Fathers from St. Cyril of Jerusalem to St. Leo the Great* (Oxford, 1970), p. 164.

This total mixing or union, which is a perfect hermaphroditic image for polymorphous eroticism, presumably will become Adam's and Eve's mode of loving when they ascend to Heaven, just as their reason (as Raphael tells them in Book V) in time may like angelic reason become more intuitive and less discursive. In any case, this image may serve to render more plain, vivid, and meaningful Donne's various expressions in the Group Two poems of the paradox of two-in-one. This paradox may at least in part grow out of feelings, actual physical sensations, of flowing together, of being bodily united during sexual intercourse in all parts and pores of the lovers' bodies as, conceivably, only angels could be. "So, to one neutrall thing both sexes fit." All the feelings and profound significance of the unitive polymorphously erotic love of the Vision of Eros may be symbolically suggested by the angelic love described by Raphael. In such love and Vision, the lovers mix totally "nor restrain'd conveyance need / As Flesh to mix with Flesh, or Soul with Soul" because, as Donne repeatedly makes efforts to explain, in some deeply meaningful (and actually felt and sensed) way their flesh and souls mysteriously but truly are One.

What has been said about "The Exstasie" and "The Canonization" is generally true of Group Two poems. Without belaboring it, we may illustrate the point that these poems display many of the distinctive characteristics of contemplative experience as a Vision of Eros. Some additional instances of the unitary consciousness and unifying vision, or of the typical Donnean paradox of two-in-one, follow:

> Here you see me, and I am you.
> "A Valediction: of my Name in the Window"

> Our two soules therefore, which are one.
> "A Valediction: forbidding Mourning"

> But wee will have a way more liberal,
> Then changing hearts, to joyne them, so we shall
> Be one, and one anothers All.
> "Loves Infiniteness"

> What ever dyes, was not mixt equally;
> If Our two loves be one, or, thou and I
> Love so alike, that none doe slacken, none can die.
> "The Good-morrow"

The true lovers realize their essential nature, pneuma, by becoming one, and this unitive transformation, transcending (at least in the eternal now-moment) time, decay, and death, helps to make the microcosm that is the lovers greater than the temporal, multiple or disunified, and mortal macrocosm, especially as this macrocosm is understood as the fallen world of the psyche. In the Vision of Dame Kind, which does not figure in Donne's work, the natural macrocosm as apprehended by redeemed senses is at one with or at least inextricably connected to the enlightened perceiver. Critics have shown the importance of "correspondence" in Metaphysical poetry.[7] For Donne, the "identity" of the lovers overrides the significance of the microcosm-macrocosm correspondence. In Donne's Vision of Eros the lovers, having realized their true self, are in that sense greater and more real than the outer world:

> She'is all States, and all Princes, I,
> Nothing else is.
> Princes doe but play us; compar'd to this,
> All honor's mimique; All wealth alchimie.
> Thou sunne art halfe as happy'as wee,
> In that the world's contracted thus;
> Thine age askes ease, and since thy duties bee
> To warme the world, that's done in warming us.
> Shine here to us, and thou art every where;
> This bed thy center is, these walls, thy spheare.
> "The Sunne Rising"

Commenting on these lines, Brian Vickers makes the important point that "the hyperbole 'asserts the incredible in order to arrive at the credible': it is as Sir Thomas Browne might have said, 'not only figuratively, but literally true' that—and by decoding the message I risk a banality which Donne transcended—the universe *does* revolve around them; their bed *is* the centre; nothing else *is*; love *is* 'infinitely delightful . . . infinitely high . . . infinitely great in all extremes' " ("The 'Songs and Sonnets' and the Rhetoric of Hyperbole," in Smith, ed., *Essays in Celebration*, 155). Such a "message," though different, than say, Herbert's "Thy word is all, if we could spell," also precisely describes the contemplative experience that God—or, in Donne's Group Two poems, the realized Christlike natures of the lovers—is all that truly is.

"The Sunne Rising" gives voice to the non-spatial characteristic of some contemplative experiences. At the least, it tends to despatialize the world, reduce the macrocosm to the microcosm, the redeemed latter being in any event of greater value and significance than the fallen macrocosm. This poem and others express, too, the contemplative characteristic of timelessness and, hence, of eternity:

> Love, all alike, no season knowes, nor clyme,
> Nor houres, dayes, months, which are the rags of time.
> "The Sunne Rising"

7. See, e.g., Joseph Anthony Mazzeo, "A Critique of Some Modern Theories of Metaphysical Poetry," *Modern Philology*, 50 (1952), 88–96, reprinted in my *John Donne's Poetry*, (this volume, pp. 168–77), and see also his other articles referred to there on p. 169, n. 1. In *A Lecture in Love's Philosophy: Donne's Vision of the World of Human Love in the Songs and Sonnets*, Dennis McKevlin argues that the thematically and structurally unified poems of the Songs and Sonnets may be interpreted as an attempt to establish unity within the individual, the cosmos, and the deity, based on Donne's application of the system of universal correspondences.

All other things, to their destruction draw,
Only our love hath no decay;
This, no tomorrow hath, nor yesterday,
Running it never runs from us away,
But truly keepes his first, last, everlasting day.
"The Anniversarie"

Group Two poems exhibit the sense of objectivity or reality associated with both extrovertive and introvertive mystical experiences:

'Twas so; But this, all pleasures fancies bee.
If ever any beauty I did see,
Which I desir'd, and got, 'twas but a dreame of thee.

And now good morrow to our waking soules.
"The Good-morrow"

The mystical characteristics of joy, peace, blessedness, love, etc., abound in Group Two, as various Valedictions, for example, exemplify.

Contrariwise, the common and distinctive characteristics of contemplative experience are absent from Group One poems. In general, these poems are devoid of "spiritual" qualities. As "Loves Usury" reads, "let my body raigne." There is only a partial and temporary "loving," at best, and giving of the self, versus the total genuine loving and self-giving of Group Two. Additionally, instead of the fidelity, tenderness, and blessed, joyous union of the latter, Group One exhibits inconstancy, anger, bitterness, spite, scorn, contempt, revenge, loathing, jealousy, hostility, and a desperate or agitated pleasure. Such a listing does not of course do justice to the quality of these poems as poetry nor to readers' responses to them. A. J. Smith's insightful remarks restore some balance to the mere cataloging of mostly "negative" emotions: "One responds to [the world represented in Group One] for the positive qualities it has: the life, the gusto, the sense of Rabelaisian relish for experience which expresses itself in this spirit of comic extravagance and hyperbole. This is a zest, indeed, which is so far from coarseness that it manifests itself in conduct in a marked elegance of style—a bland and jaunty insouciance, a gay self-reliance. Moreover, we are in the real world, even if it is a partial picture of it that we get" (*John Donne: The Songs and Sonnets*, 48).

This partialness deserves emphasis. Women are not regarded in their totality or fullness of real being. As Smith rightly observes, "this is a young man's world, in which women are mere objects, to be tried, enjoyed, and lightheartedly discarded" (47). We are much aware of a pose, a mask, an attitude, often misogynous. It is apparently a persona, not the poet, who in "Song: 'Goe and catche a falling starre' " believes that "No where / Lives a woman true, and faire." At the end of the witty "The Curse," which heaps up anathemas upon "Who ever guesses, thinks, or dreams he knowes / Who is my mistris," there appears the gratuitous joke or punch-line "For if it be a shee / Nature before hand hath outcursed mee." Similarly, the concluding couplet of "Loves Alchymie" suggests in a bitter punch-line manner, among other meanings, that even the sweetest and wittiest women are merely dead flesh possessed or animated by an evil demon; or are, when a man possesses them, merely bodies without minds:

> Hope not for minde in women; at their best
> Sweetnesse and wit, they'are but *Mummy*, possest.

These are poems of a divided and anxious psyche in a fallen world, driven (with great wit to be sure, but ultimately out of fear of one's own death) to seize the day and seek a desperate pleasure before fragile flesh decays. These separative poems present a failure of realized vision, not seeing the beloved at her best, as she truly is, but content to take her and discard her, only as soma. By contrast, Group Two, with the awareness that it is the relation between subject and object that is ultimately real and that therefore the two lovers are one and blessedly unafraid and peaceful in the eternal now-moment, presents unitive poems of the resurrected self, reconciling and exalting the lovers' bodies and souls through the unifying Vision of Eros, seeing the beloved for all that he or she is, divine, Christlike, one's very own essential being.

The possibility that by far most of Group One poems were written before 1599 and that by far most of Group Two poems were written during or after 1599 would suggest that Donne may indeed have gone through the equivalent of a "conversion" experience, a radical transformative realization of the true self by means of the Vision of Eros. The evidence of the poems points to the likelihood, if not the certainty, of such a realization. The date must remain uncertain, though probability would suggest sometime shortly before, during, or shortly after 1600. We know that Donne and Anne More throughout 1599 were at York House, Sir Thomas Egerton's official residence, that Sir George More removed his daughter from there sometime in 1600 with much haste, as Walton says, "to his own house" (27), and that the lovers met again in the Fall 1601 and were married in either December 1601 or January 1602.[8] A profound, life-changing experience such as a Vision of Eros might help to explain why Donne committed so seemingly rash an act as to marry Ann More. Whatever practical reasons there may have been for marrying, including the possibility that Ann was pregnant,[9] a Vision of Eros would be compelling reason enough for lovers to wish to be together for all time. About the love between John and Ann Donne, Edward Le Comte concludes, "I do not doubt it was mutual and true and lasting unto the grave and beyond. Ann, as well as God, was to be thanked for delivering Jack 'from the Egypt of lust, by confining my affections' . . . he continued to find her, or they each other, irresistible, even when he was 45 [in 1617, the year Ann died], which in those days

8. For these and other details concerning Donne, Ann More, their marriage, and the dating, see R. C. Bald's *John Donne: A Life* and Edward Le Comte's *Grace to a Witty Sinner: A Life of Donne.*

9. See Le Comte's account of the dating of the marriage and the sequence of events leading to it, "Jack Donne: From Rake To Husband" in *Just So Much Honor*, ed. Peter Amadeus Fiore.

was the threshold of old age" ("Jack Donne: From Rake to Husband" In *Just So Much Honor*, 22–23).[1]

It seems reasonable to suppose that Donne's relation with Ann More may account for the fact that, roughly speaking, at approximately sometime during and after 1600 he started to write poems of true love. Yet regardless of the biographical construction one may put or not put upon the poems, the single major difference between Groups One and Three on the one hand and Group Two on the other is the absence from the former and the presence in the latter of the Vision of Eros and all that that entails. The Poems of true love are precisely those which have received the most critical attention, and rightly so, since, as many would agree, they are Donne's best. At some particular time, Donne—a brilliant poet in any case as the early Elegies and Group One poems attest—found form, style, and expression for the extraordinary contemplative Vision of Eros and thereby produced the great love lyrics of Group Two. Even if no biographical or chronological significance is attached to them, they remain the best poetic expression of the Vision of Eros in the English language.

1. Another biographer, Derek Parker, writes that "the marriage of John and Ann Donne is on the evidence we have one of the most ideal and complete in the history of the institution; never was a couple more truly one flesh—that was an ideal Donne had always had, in his attitude to love, and it is revealed in the poems written before and after his marriage" (*John Donne And His World*, 39).

• • •

Satires, Verse Letters, and the Anniversaries

JOHN R. LAURITSEN

Donne's *Satyres:* The Drama of Self-Discovery †

While the poems of John Donne have never met with universal admiration, few of them have inspired as much silence as his *Satyres*. But if they have generally been treated with what we might call "benign neglect," they have also occasionally been assailed in ways which are neither especially benign nor especially neglectful. James Sutherland, for example, has charged that, "In Donne's satires the reader goes staggering from one couplet to another, coming upon unexpected objects in the half-darkness and never really sure where the poet is taking him."[1] Sutherland's brief indictment, however, is a pallid thing indeed beside the energetic prosecution of C. S. Lewis:

> Donne . . . writes under the influence of the old blunder which connected *satira* with *satyros* and concluded that the one should be as shaggy and 'salvage' as the other. Everything that might make his lines come smoothly off the tongue is deliberately avoided. Accents are violently misplaced . . . extra syllables are thrust in . . . and some lines defy scansion altogether. . . . The thought develops in unexpected and even tormented fashion. There is a complete absence of that cheerful normality which . . . relieves the monotony of vituperation. In Donne if any simile or allusion leads us away from the main theme, it leads us only to other objects of contempt and disgust. . . . Instead of a norm against which the object of satire stands out, we have vistas opening on corruption in every direction. . . . The formal satire invites this kind of thing because it demands, in Elizabethan eyes, a more or less continuous display of virtuous indignation. This, even when sincere, can become

† From *Studies in English Literature* 16 (1976): 117–30. Reprinted by permission of *Studies in English Literature*.

1. *English Satire: The Clark Lectures, 1956* (Cambridge, 1958), p. 33.

very tedious, and it provides the inferior writer with an excuse for dabbling in saleable dirt without loss of self-approval.[2]

If Lewis seems here to generate about as much heat as light, it remains to be said that few modern critics or editors have done as much either for or to Donne's *Satyres*. Most have been content simply to let them wither away, unnoticed and unremarked, in the relative obscurity of scholarly editions, and the amount of sustained critical treatment (as opposed to cursory and incidental notice) they have received is, to borrow George S. Kaufman's word, distinctly underwhelming. Even those who are disposed, unlike Lewis, simply to forgive and forget Donne's tendency in the *Satyres* "to pile detail upon detail, and to present us with just one damned thing after another"[3] generally attribute the existence of the *Satyres* to no more profound inspiration than a short-lived vogue in the 1590's for imitations of the formal satires of Horace, Persius, and Juvenal.[4] In the end, however, the result of this kind of charity is the consignment of a considerable chunk of Donne's most significant and provocative poetry to a wholly undeserved oblivion. If it is true that the *Satyres* do not generally "play much part in anybody's thinking about Donne,"[5] as Frank Kermode has suggested, perhaps they should.[6] If that is so, then it is better by far that the *Satyres* receive even such attention as Lewis has accorded them than that they be allowed to vanish altogether.

It is, of course, perfectly true that Donne's *Satyres* will never win any awards for that kind of copybook metrical perfection which Lewis seems greatly to prize. But this is precisely because of—not in spite of or in addition to—the fact that Donne's thought—or, more precisely, the thought of his speaker[7]—in the *Satyres* develops "in unexpected and even tormented fashion." The tortured verse of the *Satyres* mirrors exactly the torment not only of a mind which perceives a fallen world, a world in which, by definition, normality cannot be "cheerful," a world in which "vistas opening on corruption in every direction" are all that meet the believing eye, but also of a mind which is deeply uncertain of its relationship to the evils of that world, of a mind which, in short, is profoundly riddled with anxiety.[8] The tortured lines of Donne's *Satyres*,

2. *English Literature in the Sixteenth Century Excluding Drama*, (Oxford, 1954), 469–470.

3. J. B. Leishman, *The Monarch of Wit: An Analytical and Comparative Study of the Poetry of John Donne* (1951; rpt. London, 1967), p. 121.

4. For fuller treatments of the development of formal verse satire in English as well as of Donne's practice of it see the following: John Peter, *Complaint and Satire in Early English Literature* (Oxford, 1956), pp. 104–156. See especially pp. 132–136 in which Peter argues, among other things, that "Donne [as satirist] is much more than a product of his general situation" (p. 133). Alvin Kernan, *The Cankered Muse: Satire of the English Renaissance* (New Haven, 1959), p. 64 and pp. 117–118. Kernan's chapter, "The English Satyr, 'The Tamberlaine of Vice,' " pp. 81–140, is an especially full discussion of the Elizabethan satyr-satire confusion noted by C. S. Lewis. John Donne, *The Satires, Epigrams and Verse Letters*, ed. W. Milgate (Oxford, 1967), pp. xvii–xviii.

5. *John Donne* (London, 1957), p. 25.

6. This view is also held by Milgate who observes that "They [the satires and verse letters] are not merely the by-products or aberrations of a metaphysical lyrist" (p. xvii).

7. Milgate's caution, expressed in a slightly different context, is appropriate here: "we must be careful in attaching a precise autobiographical significance to what Donne says in his *persona* of the satirist" (p. 139).

8. Hence, the recurring note of "unsettlement" which Milgate has heard "in the usually confident voice" of the speaker (p. xxiv).

then, are ultimately inseparable from their meaning and an accurate reflection of the sensibility of the speaker, "an ardently willing soul"[9] who wishes to be better than he is or *can be*. That agonized and ambivalent soul is the norm for which Lewis looks in vain.

There is, as Pierre Legouis was among the first to note, an extraordinary resemblance between much of Donne's love poetry and the dramatic monologues of Robert Browning.[1] The similarity, however, is equally striking with regard to Donne's *Satyres*, for just as Browning's dramatic monologues tell us more about the speaker than his subject, so Donne's *Satyres* tell us more about the satirist than the thing satirized.[2] To put the matter another way, the full effect and meaning of satires I through IV depend upon dramatic irony, upon our perception of the speaker's unconscious or preconscious relationship to his subject. With "Satyre V," however, the speaker is finally able to tell us that "man is a world" (l. 13), and "the world a man" (l. 17).[3] The sins of the fallen world, the speaker comes finally to realize, are the sins of the fallen self, and, by way of corollary, the satirist who satirizes man's fallen condition is ultimately satirizing himself. Such is the final irony of Donne's *Satyres*.[4]

The progress, then, of the *Satyres* as a whole is the progress of self-discovery. From the faintest subliminal glimmerings of self-awareness in "Satyre I," the speaker achieves full self-knowledge toward the end of "Satyre IV" and with it a new recognition of his own relationship to the world about him, a recognition which is manifested in the radically different satire of "Satyre V." Put another way, the progress of the *Satyres* is from detachment to engagement, from that detachment which is born of a desperate need to believe that one is morally superior to the world of ordinary mortals to that moral engagement and commitment which can only come when one realizes that one is not only *in* the fallen world, but *of* it.[5]

9. The expression is George Eliot's.

1. See, for example *Donne the Craftsman: An Essay Upon the Structure of the Songs and Sonnets* (1928; rpt. New York, 1962), pp. 77–79. See also Alvin Kernan who refers to the dramatic monologue as "the mode of formal satire" (p. 142) and Gilbert Highet, *The Anatomy of Satire* (Princeton, 1962), p. 47.

2. This is not wholly to concur with John Peter's contention that Donne has no "flattering illusions" (p. 133) regarding the ability of satire to reform or correct or that "His [Donne's] own interest is not in the mere documentation of abuses but rather in the presentation of *his own* words" (pp. 133–134, emphasis added). It is, however, to insist that we, along with Alvin Kernan, distinguish between the author and the speaker, between, in the case of the *Satyres*, John Donne, the poet and the author of the *Satyres*, and the satirist (speaker, voice, persona) and, equally, that we view satire as a conscious art rather than as splenetic and often tedious reportage. (See Kernan, pp. 2–5, 14–30, 244–245, 247, and 250.) Curiously, Kernan seems least to adhere to his own *dicta* when he argues that in Donne's *Satyres* "there are no open revelations of a twisted, complex character venting its own disappointment and mental sickness in satire" (p. 117) and that "Donne concentrates on cudgeling the fools for their ostentation, their pursuit of meaningless goals, their bad manners, their persistent, boring attempts to talk to that humble and retiring scholar, John Donne" (pp. 117–118).

3. These and all subsequent references to and quotations from the *Satyres* are based upon Professor Milgate's edition.

4. Considering satire generically, John Peter has observed that "the potentiality for profundity is there, and to imagine a satire which, besides being satiric, would also be a subtle and evocative representation of a state of mind (or series of states of mind) in the satirist himself is not, perhaps, to summon up a self-contradiction or impossibility. Such a poem could be written: indeed has been, once or twice. Donne's third satire is a case in point" (p. 54). So, I would argue for the same reasons, are Donne's first, second, fourth, and fifth satires, viewed as a whole with "Satyre III," "*a* case in point."

5. Kernan makes much the same distinction regarding the satirist-revenger of Elizabethan and

In his edition of Donne's poetry, John T. Shawcross states that "Satyre I" is a "debate" between the body and the soul.[6] The use of the term "debate" may itself be debatable, but the observation itself is more right than wrong and generally applicable not only to "Satyre I," but to the *Satyres* as a group and to much of Donne's love poetry as well. In general, body and soul and the imagery associated with them define the moral polarities which operate within the sensibility of the speaker of the *Satyres*. This is to say simply that the speaker consistently associates himself with the pure and virtuous qualities of the soul and the objects of his scorn with the attributes of the body—with, that is, the grossest carnality. The satiric distance, in short, of the *Satyres* is the distance between the soul and body, spiritual endeavor and physical appetite. This same distance is also figured forth in the *Satyres* by the opposition of the speaker's solitude (as in I, III, and IV) or at least his satiric aloofness (as in II) and his subjects' engagement with society. The point which the *Satyres* then demonstrate with general consistency and to the increasing dismay of the speaker is that he is *both* body and soul, both a social being and a fallen man. And that, to state the matter baldly, is the lesson he must finally learn.

While "Satyre I" can be read, at least in part, as a more or less conventional dramatic monologue, as, that is, a vigorous discussion, debate, argument, or heated exchange between two separate and distinct individuals, only one of whom actually speaks in the poem, the central and irreducible fact remains that the speaker succumbs to temptation without the visible or audible presence of a tempter and, further, that he does so for reasons which not only lack any objective correlative whatever, but which are diametrically opposed to his own vigorously upheld best inclinations. From the unsettling first line of the poem ("AWAY thou fondling motley humorist") to line fifty-two, when the speaker suddenly and inexplicably decides to leave his chamber—that temple of the mind and spirit with which he identifies himself so exclusively as to render it, in effect, his self-image or ego—for the rowdy and randy low-life of the streets, his ostensible antagonist is neither seen or heard, and the speaker's reasons for succumbing after he has marshalled a virtual torrent of arguments and insults with which to defend his wonted virtue are, in consequence, such non-sequiturs as to seem almost surrealistic:

> But since thou like a contrite penitent,
> Charitably warn'd of thy sinnes, dost repent
> These vanities, and giddinesses, loe
> I shut my chamber doore, and 'Come, lets goe.'
> (I, 49–52)

Jacobean drama (p. 232). If (to make another point here) Donne's *Satyres* are viewed as the utterances of a speaker who changes markedly with the uttering, then they transcend what, according to Kernan, is the most distinctive quality of formal verse satire: "the absence of plot" (p. 30). That is to say that, in contradistinction to other examples of the genre, by the end of "Satyre IV" we are no longer "looking at the same world, and the same fools, and the same satirist we met at the opening of the work" (p. 30).

6. *The Complete Poetry of John Donne* (Garden City, N.Y., 1967), p. 397, n. 1. See also, p. 15, n. 1.

In the first half of the poem, then, the speaker has simply been steeling himself against his own baser impulses and, failing in that, rationalizing his failure.

That, however, is not the way the speaker, intent above all upon keeping his virtuous identity intact, would have us estimate his condition or judge his actions, and, consequently, when he and his companion leave his domain to enter the street, the realm of his companion, he insists even more anxiously upon maintaining separate identities, upon a strict I-thou relationship.[7] Room and street, soul and body, speaker and companion are nonetheless aspects of the same thing—of the speaker himself. His conscious loathing of his companion on the one hand and his magnetic and irresistible attraction to him on the other hand are, I think, inexplicable in any other way. A strident and self-proclaimed rationalist, he nevertheless submits, against all reason and even against his very reason for being, to unreason incarnate. The reason is, of course, that in the fallen state the soul is ultimately inseparable from the body, as Donne's lovers, for example, are continually learning to their everlasting anguish.

In "Satyre I," the private chamber with which the speaker identifies himself is conspicuously the domain of the soul:

> Here are Gods conduits, grave Divines; and here
> Natures Secretary, the Philosopher;
> And jolly Statesmen, which teach how to tie
> The sinewes of a cities mistique bodie;
> Here gathering Chroniclers, and by them stand
> Giddie fantastique Poëts of each land.
>
> (I, 5–10)

Just as conspicuously, the street is the domain of the body, as evidenced by the distinctly non-intellectual and non-spiritual pleasures which the speaker's companion seeks there as well as by the distinctly corporeal circumstances in which he receives his comeuppance. Speaker and companion, in turn, embody the qualities associated with their respective domains. The speaker himself is all restraint, caution, and prudence; his companion all glands and nerve-endings. The speaker behaves rationally; his companion mechanically and bestially. The speaker is articulate; his companion all grunts and grins, smacks and shrugs. Yet their profound differences notwithstanding, the speaker finds himself careering madly through the street, as if tethered by some invisible tie to his repugnant "lost sheep."

Significantly enough, the speaker perceives the irrevocable and inescapable nature of his bond to his companion just before he succumbs (see ll. 49–52 quoted above) to his outwardly invisible and inaudible entreaties and plunges with him into the inferno of the street:

7. Given the nature of the genre, this is of course a moral, artistic, and, perhaps most important, a psychological necessity. For a fuller discussion of the customary posture and effect of the satirist see Kernan, pp. 16, 21–22, 25, and 26. For a very different view from mine of Donne's speaker, see Milgate, pp. xxi–xxii.

> Mans first blest state was naked, when by sinne
> Hee lost that, yet hee'was cloath'd but in beasts skin,
> And in this course attire, which I now weare,
> With God, and with the Muses I conferre.
>
> (I, 45–48)

The bond, then, which links the speaker with his companion, soul with body, is the bond of original sin. Devout though his soul may be, the speaker is, like the rest of us, clothed in the body of an animal. He, however, cannot admit this to full conscious awareness since doing so would, he feels, plunge him forever into the street, into the community of fallen men, into the devil's own preserve. The irony, of course, is that this is precisely what happens anyway. The higher one raises himself, the farther he inevitably falls, and when the speaker returns, bloodied and bruised, to his chamber he is as close as he can come to the recovery of Eden.

Since, then, there is finally next to no actual distance between the speaker and the object of his contempt, the suggestion that the subject of "Satyre I" is "the opportunism and lechery of a young rake"[8] is not wholly adequate, if only because the speaker is, for all practical purposes, fully as rakish as the rake. The object of the speaker's contempt and the subject of "Satyre I" is ultimately his own fallen state and, by extension the fallen state of man. This, if the reader will pardon the repetition, is in fact the real—if not readily apparent—subject of the *Satyres* as a whole, or at least of satires I through IV. Thus, even though there are marked apparent differences between the subjects of the *Satyres*, the observation that each of them "attempts to convey one basic idea . . . or to characterize one specific type of person . . . or specific experiences,"[9] is finally true only to the extent that each of these things ultimately represents the same thing.

For this reason, if for no other, the subject of "Satyre" II is not merely "corrupt lawyers" nor is it simply "fraud."[1] It is instead the rather broader matter of the perversion of the word, whether this be in law, theology, or poetry. The speaker begins, however, by telling us at great length (ll. 5–39) what his subject is not, and, says the speaker (who is himself a poet), it is not poets. Instead, the object of his contempt—indeed of his "hate" (l. 1)—is, insists the poet, Coscus, a poet-turned-lawyer. But, like the mindless rake of "Satyre I," Coscus is finally only a kind of psychic strawman.[2] In "Satyre I" the speaker attempted to disguise the real object of his satiric scorn—more for his own sake than for ours—by personifying and giving objective existence to (projecting, in the jargon of psychology) warring aspects or impulses of his own divided self. In

8. N. J. C. Andreasen, "Theme and Structure in Donne's *Satyres*," *SEL*, 3 (1963), 64.
9. Sherry Zively, "Imagery in John Donne's *Satyres*," *SEL*, 6 (1966), 90.
1. Andreasen, 67.
2. This is not, however, to agree with Milgate's view that the creation of Coscus merely "enables Donne to give some appearance of unity to his satire of the abuse of poetry, and, more important, of the abuse of law" (p. 128).

"Satyre II," on the other hand, he takes the additional and still more deceptive step of excluding himself from the action of the poem altogether. Ostensibly, he is simply stating his case against Coscus to a third person, the anonymous "Sir" of line one, and sputtering with, to use C. S. Lewis' phrase, "virtuous indignation" over Coscus' soulless lechery and greed in order, as much as anything, to assure that we understand precisely how far removed he is from Coscus' immoral offenses. On the whole, the performance is, as most criticism of the poem attests, a convincing one.

To make it convincing, the speaker builds his case against Coscus very carefully until we come finally to realize that what Coscus represents is that total perversion of the word against the Word. At first, though, Coscus is only a poetic wooer, the master of a legalese verse which the speaker as poet and critic finds highly offensive—at least as much for its style as for its intent:

> . . . words, words, which would teare
> The tender labyrinth of a soft maids eare,
> More, more, then ten Sclavonians scolding, more
> Then when winds in our ruin'd Abbeyes rore.
> When sicke with Poëtrie, 'and possest with muse
> Thou wast, and mad, I hop'd; but men which chuse
> Law practise for meere gaine, bold soule, repute
> Worse than imbrothel'd strumpets prostitute.
> (II, 57–64)

Because poetry is, in the speaker's view, an essentially religious profession ("With God, and with the Muses I conferre," I, 48), the real gravity of Coscus's offense is not finally that he employs his Muse against proprieties of style or the precepts of poetic decorum, but that he employs it against God, against the Word,

> As slily'as any Commenter goes by
> Hard words, or sense; or in Divinity
> As controverters, in vouch'd Texts, leave out
> Shrewd words, which might against them cleare the doubt.
> (II, 99–102)

The threat posed by Coscus' transgressions as poet-lawyer does not, however, cease simply with his perversion of the Word, but, as the speaker makes plain in "Satyre V," it portends nothing less than the subversion of Providence itself. The Law, as we learn in "Satyre V," is

> Recorder to Destiny, on earth, and shee
> Speakes Fates words, and but tells us who must bee
> Rich, who poore, who in chaires, who in jayles. . . .
> (V, 71–73)

Given these premises, the fear that Coscus "will compasse all our land;/ From Scots, to Wight; from Mount, to Dover strand" (II, 77–78) is not wholly without foundation. Like Satan, Coscus subverts the Word to his own ends. But, wonders the speaker, does the poet, a fallen and fallible man, do this too? Lake Satan, Coscus battens on the sins of others. But so, in his way, does the satirist:

> Bastardy'abounds not in Kings titles, nor
> Symonie'and Sodomy in Churchmens lives,
> As these things do in him; by these he thrives.
>
> . . . .
>
> And spying heires melting with luxurie,
> Satan will not joy at their sinnes, as hee.
>
> (II, 74–80)

With that kind of conviction which suddenly throws all in doubt, the speaker ends "Satyre II" by answering a question that no one else has asked. Lacking an accuser, the satirist nonetheless attempts to exculpate himself from a charge that no one has made, thereby drawing attention to his own uneasy conscience. Assuring no one so much as himself that he, after all, is one person and Coscus quite another, that his dread of Coscus is not in fact a mirror image of his own guilt, that his fear of Coscus is not ultimately a fear of his own misuse of poetry, of his own perversion of the word, he ends "Satyre II" protesting lamely that "my words none drawes/ Within the vast reach of th'huge statute lawes" (II. 111–112). Is that, wonders the speaker, really the only significant difference between himself and Coscus?

In contrast to "Satyre II," "Satyre III" seems at first glance to be a positive statement about man's quest for true religion. And so, for many, it is.

Arnold Stein, for example, has called it "a remarkable doctrine in the history of religious tolerance."[3] Given the perspective of the speaker, however, given his rigid expectations of himself and the world and his inflexible conception of himself as not only apart from the world but morally superior to it, "Satyre III" becomes at once the least satirical and, for the satirist, the darkest of the *Satyres*. Thus it is that in "Satyre III" the speaker's world view and, with it, his self-esteem begin seriously to break down.

While we generally, and quite rightly, read and esteem "Satyre III" as a plea for religious tolerance, we, as opposed to Donne's speaker have accepted our fallen condition, our lostness, the disappearance of the one true way. He, however, has not and cannot. He still aspires to reach the mountain-top—in this life and in this world. And he invites us to scale the peak with him:

> Is not our Mistresse faire Religion,
> As worthy'of all our Soules devotion,
> As vertue was to the first blinded age?
>
> (III, 5–7)

3. "Donne and the Satiric Spirit," *ELH*, 11 (1944), 268.

At line forty-three, the speaker again enjoins us to "Seeke true religion." When, however, one of the faithful asks, "O where?" the speaker, carried away by his smugly satiric spirit, proceeds systematically to eliminate all available possibilities (ll. 43ff.). Instead of the Mistresses Truth and Faire Religion who are supposed to reside at the summit of that "huge hill," what the satirist discovers and presents for our delectation and consideration is a group of distinctly worldly wenches, varying in appeal from the threadbare and shop-worn beauties of Rome to the "course country drudges" of Geneva.

The selection, then, is not only unappetizing, but impossible. There is nothing to choose between them. Nevertheless, says the imperturbable speaker, "unmoved thou/ Of force must one, and forc'd but one allow;/ And the right . . ." (III, 69–71). Inevitably, however, the speaker must come to realize, as the lines following indicate, that the quest itself, rather than the end of the quest, has become, in this fallen world, the only attainable objective:

> Be busie to seeke her, beleeve me this,
> Hee's not of none, nor worst, that seekes the best.
>
> . . . .
>
> . . . doubt wisely; in strange way
> To stand inquiring right, is not to stray;
> To sleepe, or runne wrong, is. . . .
>
> (III, 74–79)

Convinced at first that he could, with every expectation of final success, seek the realm of pure spirit, the splended isolation of the hilltop, the speaker instead discovers—to his great unease, we may be sure—that he must be always seeking, climbing, and never reaching. This realization, needless perhaps to say, is far indeed from his customary posture of certitude, from his comfortable contempt for the error-ridden ways of others. If railing cannot (to paraphrase line four) cure the "worne maladies" of the world, it can lead the perceptive individual to discoveries which make them a good deal more painful. And pain, of course, has its uses.

In view of the speaker's dawning awareness of his own diminished possibilities in a fallen world, it is fitting that the beginning of "Satyre IV" should find him cast down from the hilltop into the hellish depths of the Court, the nadir of the moral world, and nagged by a sense of sinful complicity in the evil which surrounds him:

> WELL; I may now receive, and die; My sinne
> Indeed is great, but I have beene in
> A Purgatorie, such as fear'd hell is
> A recreation to,'and scarce map of this.
> My minde, neither with prides itch, nor yet hath been
> Poyson'd with love to see, or to bee seene,
> I had no suit there, nor new suite to shew,
> Yet went to Court. . . .
>
> (IV, 1–8)

Puzzled and deeply troubled by the irrationality and apparent purposelessness of his own behavior, the speaker retreats hastily from the crucial issue by sloughing off the burden of personal responsibility and by seeking quickly to displace his unwanted and unaccustomed guilt onto something he calls his "destinie":

> So'it pleas'd my destinie
> (Guilty'of my sin of going,) to thinke me
> As prone to'all ill, and of good as forget-
> full, as proud, as lustfull, and as much in debt,
> As vaine, as witlesse, and as false as they
> Which dwell at Court, for once going that way.
> (IV, 11–16)

With such spurious and desperate any-port-in-a-storm logic, then, the speaker salvages some semblance of his brittle dignity, forestalls the inevitable and impending crisis, and beats back the subversive, if still largely subliminal, suggestion that he might indeed be "as vaine, as witlesse, and as false as they." Having thus, for the time being at least, reachieved the precarious moral elevation over his subject that his kind of satiric practice necessitates, the speaker frees himself for his ridicule of the fallen and faded fop. Significantly, perhaps, the fop's conduct in the fleshly world of the Court resembles that of the mindless man-of-the-street in "Satyre I," while his interest in linguistics (ll. 52ff.) and the Babylonian confusion of tongues in which he speaks are not essentially different from Coscus'.

In any event, however instructive the speaker's satire on the Court may be, it does not tell us what, except perhaps occupational duty or sheer masochism, has drawn him to the hellish world of the Court. He did not, of course, tell us what actually drew him to the street in "Satyre I" either, but here he has himself raised the question and then, as in "Satyre I," diverted our attention from the real issue by means of his satire. Just before he leaves the Court which he supposedly contemns, however, a faint answer begins once again to glimmer across the speaker's threshold of consciousness. The satirist's identity begins to merge with that of his subject:

> . . . . hearing him, I found
> That as burnt venom'd Leachers doe grow sound
> By giving others their soares, I might growe
> Guilty, and he free. . . .
> (IV, 133–136)

Having fled the court and this harrowing double vision, the speaker reaches, in a manner reminiscent of "Satyre I," the "wholesome solitarinesse" of his home and, like Dante, there lapses into a trance:

> My precious soule began, the wretchednesse
> Of suiters at court to mourne, and a trance

> Like his, who dreamt he saw hell, did advance
> It selfe on mee, Such men as he saw there,
> I saw at court, and worse, and more. . . .
> (IV, 156–160)

Out of his conscious contempt for fallen man and the fallen world, then, the speaker's unconscious has derived something like the beginnings of compassion for the wretchedness of the human lot.

As he begins to emerge from his nightmare vision of that Inferno which is the Court, the speaker sees a face like those "which in old hangings whip Christ" (l. 226), and as he passes through the great chamber and out of the world of his dream, "As men which from gaoles to'execution goe" (l. 230), he casts an anxious glance at a tapestry depicting the seven deadly sins (ll. 231–232). What, he wonders, does it mean? And immediately upon his awakening the answer shudders throughout his entire frame: "I shooke like a spyed Spie" (IV, 237).

What the speaker has spied in his vision of the Court is, of course, himself. And it is that instant of self-discovery, the discovery that the satiric spy is also the spied, which the *Satyres* have steadily been moving toward. The sin of the Fall is the sin of all; the sins of the world are the sins of the self.

The growing awareness of self as co-partner in the corrupt world which glimmers through Donne's *Satyres* and which rises to the level of conscious recognition and explicit statement in "Satyre IV" is the vision which informs "Satyre V" and which makes it at once a summary of its predecessors and an anomaly. While the first four satires deal, ostensibly at least, with abstractions, with, that is, generalized aspects of the condition of fallen humanity—with lust, perversion of the Word, false religion, the vanity and vacuity of courtiers, with, in short, sin—"Satyre V" alone treats of a specific and at least potentially remediable evil: the bribing of the judiciary as too frequently practiced in England in the 1590's. Given the nature of a fallen world and the persistence and universality of original sin, "Satyre V" alone can aspire to be what satire is generally supposed to be: a corrective.

Far from expressing that scorn for "a world bankrupt of virtue" which C. M. Coffin perceived,[4] "Satyre V" is unique among Donne's *Satyres* in being the only one in which the speaker does not begin with a conscious and generally explicit presupposition of his moral superiority to the rest of mankind. It alone is predicated upon and pleads for pity and compassion:

> THOU shalt not laugh in this leafe, Muse, nor they
> Whom any pitty warmes; He which did lay
> Rules to make Courtiers (hee being understood
> May make good Courtiers, but who Courtiers good?)

4. Charles Monroe Coffin, *John Donne and the new Philosophy* (1937; rpt. New York, 1958), p. 58.

> Frees from the sting of jests all who'in extreme
> Are wrech'd or wicked: of these two a theame
> Charity and liberty give me.
>
> (V, 1–7)

This essentially anti-satiric sentiment issues from a speaker who has discovered that the inherent wretchedness and wickedness of mankind are not fit objects for satiric sport, if only because no one, himself especially included, is exempt from that wretchedness and wickedness.[5] And without genuine moral elevation over mankind, satire of the kind he has been accustomed to practice is neither possible nor permissible. Satire of that kind is a sport only for gods. In discovering the dimensions of his own fallen humanity, then, the speaker has discovered humanity itself.

This new awareness is bodied forth in "Satyre V" by the speaker's repeated insistence upon the interdependence and essential oneness of humanity, especially of a fallen humanity:

> If all things be in all,
> As I thinke, since all, which were, are, and shall
> Bee, be made of the same elements:
> Each thing, each thing implyes or represents.
> Then man is a world; in which, Officers
> Are the vast ravishing seas; and Suiters,
> Springs; now full, now shallow, now drye; which, to
> That which drownes them, run: These self reasons do
> Prove the world a man. . . .
>
> (V, 9–17)

Officers and suitors, victims and victimizers are the same. We are bound together in this fallen world, and if we can rise at all, we can only rise together.

Finally, then, the moral paradox implicit in Donne's *Satyres* is that it is only by recognizing and accepting one's fallen state that one can begin to rise above it.[6] The speaker's presumption of moral superiority in the earlier satires precludes that self-knowledge which is essential for the perception and correction of whatever evils are remediable in man's fallen state. Only by recognizing one's essential identity with other men can one summon the compassion and care—even the compassion and care of true satire—necessary to alleviate the wretchedness of the human condition. Only by recognizing the oneness of the human lot can one be truly human.

5. Thus the lack in "Satyre V" of the "old verve and forthrightness" noted by Milgate (p. xxiv). See also p. 165.

6. By this juncture in the *Satyres*, Donne's speaker has achieved what, in all essentials, amounts to the crucial act of perception which, according to Kernan, distinguishes tragedy from satire: "the knowledge that evil is part of the fabric of the world, not merely depravity or bad manners; and with this recognition he [the tragic hero] is forced to see his own involvement in the mixed world and accept the extraordinarily heavy price he must pay to achieve an end which is only dimly perceived" (p. 32).

DAVID AERS and GUNTHER KRESS

'Darke Texts Needs Notes': Versions of Self in Donne's Verse Epistles†

Donne's verse epistles have not received much notice from the awesome critical industry centred on his work. Any explanation of this surprising fact might make reference to an assumed lack of poetic richness in these poems, the assumption that patronage poetry is too conventional to merit serious critical attention, and perhaps even some embarrassment at a deification of living patronesses.[1] But we believe that the most significant factor is unrecognised: namely the lack of a descriptive and theoretical framework within which the real interest of these poems can be perceived and analysed. In this chapter we attempt to establish such a framework and carry out an analysis which will locate, describe, and account for versions of the self emerging within these verse letters. In the course of our critical inquiry we shall build on John Danby's hints about the explicitly social basis of so much that seems, on first sight, to be purely metaphysical speculation.[2] We hope to develop an approach which, through its very attention to the minute movements of a particular text, reveals how these become intelligible only when inserted in a wider context which includes the writer's precise social situation. In 1608 Donne wrote a poem beginning, 'You have refin'd mee', a verse epistle to his new patroness Lucy, Countess of Bedford, in what seems to have been the most personally testing period of his life.[3] Although Donne himself includes the comment that 'darke texts need notes', his editors and critics do not seem to have found this a particularly interesting poem. However, we think it both demands and rewards scrutiny. These are the first two stanzas:

> MADAME,
> You have refin'd mee, and to worthyest things
> (Vertue, Art, Beauty, Fortune,) now I see
> Rarenesse, or use, not nature value brings;
> And such, as they are circumstanc'd, they bee.
> Two ills can ne're perplexe us, sinne to' excuse;
> But of two good things, we may leave and chuse.

† From *Literature, Language and Society in England, 1580–1680*, by David Aers, Bob Hodge, and Gunther Kress; copyright © 1981. Pp. 23–34, 40–48, 200–2. Reprinted by permission of Gill and Macmillan Publishers.

1. J. F. Danby, *Elizabethan and Jacobean Poets*, London: Faber 1964 (originally published as *Poets on Fortune's Hill*, 1962) chapter 1.

2. 'Donne's assumption is the relationship of a poet to patron as of nothing to everything, and out of this he spins his conceits direct. He makes metaphysics out of the poet and patron relations, and a poet-patron relation out of metaphysics', *Elizabethan and Jacobean Poets*, 39.

3. See R. C. Bald on this period in *John Donne: A Life*, Oxford UP 1970, chapter 8; see too Donne himself in his letters: *Life and Letters of John Donne*, ed. E. Gosse, 2 vols., 1899, reprint London: Smith 1959, especially vol. I, 114–15, 166, 181, 185–7, 191.

Therefore at Court, which is not vertues clime,
(Where a transcendent height, (as, lownesse mee)
Makes her not be, or not show) all my rime
Your vertues challenge, which there rarest bee;
For, as darke texts need notes: there some must bee
To usher vertue, and say, *This is shee.*[4]

Editorial glosses on these stanzas treat them as fairly unproblematic. Grierson finds Donne's introduction of himself in 'as, lownesse mee' (stanza two), 'quite irrelevant' (and is more unsettled than Milgate), yet he assumes that he has solved any minor enigmas, and the lines seem not to need extended commentary.[5] However, there are important and unresolved tensions in these lines. The countess is alchemist, a near creator (as lines 21–22 of the poem make explicit) through whose agency the poet can now perceive things as they *really* are. This sets up a dichotomy between things as he perceives them now and things as he perceived them before. *Now* he sees that value is the product of contingent social relationships. Already there may be hints, which are clarified later in the poem, that value, being generated by rareness or use, is an aspect of market transactions. Even seemingly transcendent, platonic forms, Vertue, Art, Beauty, 'worthyest things' indeed, get their worth in this way and so have to be placed in the same category as the thoroughly contingent sub-lunar abstraction. Fortune. But before his 'refinement' the poet had assumed, in good idealist (platonic or stoic) fashion, that value transcended the contingent placings of social practice; he had assumed that value was a reflection of the object or person's intrinsic nature—that, in his own words, 'nature value brings'.

Such relativising attitudes, which are of course quite appropriate to a 'market-society', may not surprise readers today. But when we recall that the poem is addressed to Lucy, and that Donne is overtly talking about her, the worthiest thing whom he is both worshipping and elegantly asking for patronage, it is, at the very least, a strange and rather risky compliment. After all, the poem implies that she is not inherently valuable, that her worthiness is a product of contingent social circumstances, and that her refining has given him perceptions of this kind. (The second stanza is connected to the first by the logical connector 'Therefore', thus removing any lingering doubts that the first stanza is also about Lucy.) The countess's value as one of the 'worthyest things' paradoxically *depends* on her being 'circumstanc'd' in a social situation where her attributes (virtues, it so happens) are most valuable precisely because they are rare, the court rather conspicuously not being the 'clime' of virtue.

This does have a rationale and can be resolved once we see the structure of Donne's argument. He is actually working with a model which

4. All quotations are from *Donne's Poetical Works*, 2 vols., ed. H.J.C. Grierson, Oxford UP 1912, reprint Oxford UP 1966, referred to hereafter as Grierson. This quotation is from vol. I. We have also used W. Milgate's edition of *The Satires, Epigrams and Verse Letters*, Oxford UP 1967.

5. Grierson, vol. II, 156–7; cf. Milgate, 156–7.

assumes the existence of two worlds or 'climes'. One is a platonic clime in which Lucy exists with platonic forms, and which her usher-exegete has knowledge of. (This world of essences transcends all contingency and relativity, and so supersedes all notions of value deployed by social man.) A second clime is the present historical world, the world of the court, of Mitcham and of Donne's frustrated daily existence, a world where value is a function of contingent market relations, supply and demand, mere 'circumstance'. It is in this second world that the countess is 'worthyest', most valuable, and it is here that Donne so desperately wishes to find employment as the official usher of the valued one. His role is to introduce the myopic courtiers to the rare (and useful?) worthy one. In this he himself gains value as the indispensable spectacles through which courtiers can perceive the rare and hidden riches of that dark text, Lucy. The 'alienated intellectual' overcomes his alienation, finds community, wins employment and use as an essential mediator between the two climes.[6] However, Donne fails to show us why the lower climes should value virtue, why this particular rare commodity should be desired by courtiers at all. The unexamined gap in his argument here is simply leapt over as he assumes, optimistically, that the second clime must find use and market value for representatives of the higher world.

Donne does not resolve the paradox in the way we have been doing, but wisely leaves it in its highly compressed form, with only hints that the very absence of virtue at the court makes the countess 'worthyest' and endows both her and her usher-exegete with value. It is understandable enough that Donne should not have wanted to express these views in such plain form, so we already have sound reasons for his wish to darken the text. Of course Donne need not have introduced the double-edged paradoxical compliment to the countess, and could have avoided the danger of relativising the countess's virtue. But this would not have permitted him to introduce the important self-reference, so well worked into a complex image of the relations between poet, patroness, society and ethical idealism. Here we have a nontrivial explanation for his desire to keep the text dark, one which offers an account of verbal processes and of relevant social and psychological motivations.

We mentioned the significant degree of self-reference in the poem; this invites some further consideration, especially in the light of Donne's 'egocentricity', widely commented on by critics.[7] The expression of this egocentricity is inevitably more complex here than in many of the *Songs and Sonnets*, where the poet-lover focuses on himself and his relations with a lover. This poem, however, is focused on the patroness, and since he delicately seeks patronage the relationship is one which needs most careful handling; not the time, one would think, for an overt display of

6. See M. H. Curtis, 'The Alienated Intellectuals of Early Stuart England', *Past and Present*, 23 (1962), reprinted in *Crisis in Europe* ed. T. Aston, London: Routledge 1965. On Donne's desperate wish for 'incorporation' see the letter to Goodyer in Gosse, vol. I, 191–2.

7. One of the best studies of this issue is by R. Ellrodt, *L'inspiration personnelle et l'esprit du temps chez les poètes metaphysiques anglais*, 3 vols., Paris 1960, see vol. I, especially chapters 3–4.

egocentricity. And yet the poem begins with a reference to himself. It certainly bestows credit on the countess—she, as alchemist, has succeeded in refining him. But the image turns Donne into the central object of attention, just as the alchemist's attention focuses on the materials he desires to transform. And as the success of the alchemist is defined by his success in refining the material, so the countess's success is defined in terms of her effectiveness in working on the present material, the poet. Thus at the very opening of the poem the overt focus on the patroness has been inverted and become part of a rather complicted self-referring process. Lines two and eight (the self-mentioning, which Grierson found 'irrelevant') again refer to him; so do lines nine, eleven and twelve. Without doubt there is a large enough amount of self-reference in the opening stanzas at least to attract one's curiosity.

In addition there are some peculiarities of reference, predominantly in the pronouns. Line one contains the two pronouns, 'you' and 'mee': in the same line there is the 'pronoun' 'worthyest things'. Its reference is ambiguous: Donne has just been refined, so that one possible reference is 'mee'. If he is included in the category of 'worthyest things', then he belongs to the same class as Lucy ('you'), another possible referent of this phrase. 'Worthyest things' is plural in number, and so it can indeed refer to both Lucy and the poet. Presumably Donne intended the reference to be ambiguous; at any rate it is not immediately clear, and in searching for an appropriate and permitted referent, the reference to the poet will arise and need to be assessed, and decided on. The fact that in the next line Donne glosses 'worthyest things' as 'Vertue, Art, Beauty, Fortune' shows that he acknowledged the need to provide a gloss. As we pointed out above, this list collapses platonic categories into the social and contingent clime of 'Fortune', relativising and undercutting the platonic model. By the time we reach the end of the second line 'worthyest things' has accumulated a wide range of possible references: 'you,' 'mee', 'you and mee', 'Vertue, Art, Beauty, Fortune'. All of these lead into 'Fortune' and are placed in the same category as Fortune, so that the relativising tendency has become thoroughly pervasive.

The fourth line of the poem continues to draw on this multiple ambiguity: 'And such, as they are circumstanc'd, they bee'. Here 'they' may refer to all the referents mentioned. Another pronoun, 'such', is introduced. It in turn may refer to all three and to 'they'; or it may pick up just one of these. If the latter, then we at least the following readings: (1) Lucy (such → worthiest things → You), the countess, such as she is circumstanced so she is—as she is placed in the contingent social market of fortune, so she is valued, worthiest. (2) Donne (such → worthiest thing → me → refined), the poet, such as he is circumstanced so he is—as he is placed in Lucy's platonic world, as a new creature, so he is valued, worthiest. As he is placed in the contingent social market, so he is valued, as nothing. His appeal to Lucy is therefore that she should 'translate' his worth in her platonic world, into a recognised use and hence value in the market, in the appropriate place; as an indispensable usher. The countess is well able to do this. So the reading as it stands is: I, as I am circumstanced so I am, as I am *now* placed in the social market of fortune so I am currently valued—as nothing.[8] At this point the paradox, deploying the model of two climes, functions to give line four another, Donne's real, though covert, reading: I am (not as I *am*, but) as I am *circumstanced*. The paradox enables Donne to present simultaneously two versions of the self here: one, the platonic one covertly (I am as I am regardless of social valuation and placing); the other, the one constructed according to market values overtly (I am as I am circumstanced). He puts one against the other in a most complex and rather disturbing form, and asks Lucy to realise his worth in one 'clime', the platonic, as 'value through use' in the other 'clime', that of contingent social situation and of fortune.

On the surface the statement is of course less complicated: the countess has refined him and now he sees that either rareness or use (being used by or of use to someone) brings value. It is precisely the patronage relationship which makes the poet useful to someone who can use him, and therefore valuable. Until he is used his identity is bestowed by his circumstances and, through no fault of his, or of nature, he is circumstanced such that he has no value.

Stanza two now becomes clearer. It refers to the countess but it also refers to Donne. At court he does not appear (either he is physically absent through having no position, or, if there, is not noticed) because he currently has no value. He places himself in a revealing structural relationship with the countess: her value does not appear at court owing to transcendent height, while his does not appear at court owing to *lownesse*. So the structural opposition links him firmly with her, in a link which comes close to an equation. This provides a perfect explanation for the difficulty Grierson recorded, and indeed it would be most odd if such a phrase appeared in one of Donne's patronage poems without precise significance and motivation. The concluding couplet gives us a final confirmation: this is about her and about him. She is the 'darke text' (as is the pòem, as is his motivation) and 'darke texts need notes'.

We should ask what or whose need this is. As we noticed earlier, it is most obviously a need of the potential audience of the text, the benighted courtiers. It is also the countess's need; she who is the 'darke text' needs to be explicated if she is to be truly valued in the lower 'clime'. She needs an exegete, like Donne. Lastly, it is Donne's need: exegetes need 'darke texts', and above all Donne needs to be an exegete, he needs to be of specific use to the countess and the community. Just as the 'need' has to be explained, so too with the 'must' in the same line. 'Some must

8. As Danby suggested, Donne is obsessed with his nothingness (note 2, above). For examples of the explicit social causes of his sense of being *nothing*, and its remedies, see especially prose letters in Gosse, vol. I, 181, 167, 191–2; and on loss of employment as death, for example, 291; also volume II, 28, 42; and the verse epistles to the Countess of Bedford and the Countess of Salisbury.

bee' refers to the exegete, implicitly Donne himself, so that this 'must bee' seemingly has the force of an existential imperative, and it echoes the 'not be' of line nine. That 'not be' takes in both Lucy and Donne; how does the non-existent poet of line nine come into existence as the necessary exegete-usher of line eleven? By being employed: and this employment not only brings him into existence, creates him indeed (as lines 21–2 make explicit),[9] but also brings the countess's virtue into the social world, thus indirectly giving her existence and, as we saw earlier, value. This is an astonishingly delicate combination of begging and self-assertion, and the relations hinted at are very complex.[1] Donne is the created creature, she the creator; he low, she high; he patronised, she patron; he exegete, she dark text; he usher, she virtue; he excluded, she included. Yet she too is excluded until he realises her social potential and value for her. Structurally Lucy and Donne are opposed and yet equated, transforms of each other creating each other from shared invisibility into apparent existence and social value.

We have by now accounted for the text's darkness. It lies in the double-layered model Donne uses to understand his complex relationship with the patroness and their mutual relations to the social world and to value. But we need to go further. On this level the explanation has entailed an account of the supplicant's perception of himself, and we now wish to explore this perception in more depth. We have made clear the way the first two stanzas offer distinct and contrasting versions of the self. To recapitulate, One version of self refers an autonomous self to inherent values which would doubtless be recognised in a platonic utopia or by stoic and platonic individuals who have detached themselves from existing societies and are strong enough to pursue a Crusoe-like existence (without dog or man Friday of course). The other version of self sees it as socially constructed and dependent, either through equal relationships (as those between friends) or through the social relations of the market based on rareness, use and contingency. It is not difficult to believe that Donne could see these two versions of the self as competing and contradictory. But then, it is also plausible to see them as complementary, so that only those who do have inherent worth, participating in the platonic forms, *ought* to be usable, find employment and value. Such, however, is obviously not the case in the world which Donne strove so hard to convince about his marketable potential and use. For Donne these competing versions of self-identity became highly problematic and a constant, often agonised, preoccupation, in the period before his ordination.

The two stanzas with which we opened our discussion are thus legitimately seen as explorations of the self. The question of the poet's con-

9. See previous note.
1. In contrasting Donne with Jonson, very much at Donne's expense, Danby, like other commentators, misses these rich complexities in Donne's stance.

sciousness of this exploration is one which we have not treated here. Nor do we exlude a range of other possible readings of these stanzas, or for the rest of the patronage poems. But we are suggesting that this reading goes to the heart of these poems and points up their place in Donne's central preoccupations and problems. We believe these neglected poems have much to teach us about these preoccupations and the poetic and intellectual strategies with which Donne confronted them.[2]

The double version of self certainly connects most of the verse epistles, for they are attempts to work out self-identity, polarising or clustering around one or other of these two basic stances. Above all, it invites us to link abstract metaphysical problems with the concrete reality and pressures of the poet's existence.

One important feature that we have touched on in our depiction of the versions of the self in 'You have refin'd mee' can now be brought into prominence. We noted that in presenting contrary versions of self-identity and evaluation Donne envisaged his own level of being in a necessarily equivocal way. He does exist in some mode, but he needs refining, and even creation by a patroness-alchemist; he does not exist or is not visible (lines 7–12) at court, yet he, or some, 'must bee To usher vertue'. Later in the poem he defines himself as one of Lucy's 'new creatures', part of a 'new world' created by her (lines 21–2). In other poems to patronesses this tendency becomes an overt assertion by Donne: that he is nothing. In 'T'have written then' he says (again to the Countess of Bedford), '*nothings*, as I am, may/Pay all they have, and yet have all to pay' (lines 7–8). Of course, line seven is paradoxical: the 'am' asserts existence, 'I am'; and syntactically the verb *to be* functions to relate entities to other entities or to qualities. That second function is prominent here: the classification of an individual, though he exists, as *a nothing*. Classifications are culturally and socially given, conventional and subject to historical change. But for an individual they tend to assume the force of external, changeless forms. This is particularly so as the syntactic form X is Y is used to make classifications which are established by changing cultures and conventions (e.g. 'I am a ratepayer'), as well as those relating to the impersonal, natural order (e.g. 'The sun is a star'). In this way language blurs the distinction between the two kinds of statements and their reality-status. But over and above that, any member of a society is socialised into sets of value systems which become 'reality'. In other words, if we look at Donne's 'actual' situation, even at this, his worst time, we cannot by any stretch of the imagination see him as nothing: a reasonably comfortable house in Mitcham, one or two servants, frequent trips to London, to influential friends who remain

2. Nor is the manner in which the concept of self is being explored in these poems confined to Donne. That questions about value in just the way we are discussing were current in the milieu from which Donne received his training, are suggested by Shakespeare's *Troilus and Cressida* which includes, among its central preoccupations, a study of conflicting versions of value and their relation to social fabric and metaphysical frameworks.

loyal and help in a host of ways, access to books, writing poetry which has an appreciative audience, no hunger . . . to the landless labourer in Mitcham Donne would have seemed the opposite of 'nothing'. But this only confirms the strength of the conventionally given perception, which meant in Donne's case that not being of the court group was not being at all. For Donne therefore these lines do not have the force of paradox: *being* is defined in terms of membership of the group to which he aspires: creation is therefore a social act, the act of admitting, drawing in the individual to the group.

Nevertheless, no sooner has Donne offered a negative version of self reflecting his present social situation than he proposes a contrary version of the self as having a transcendental and valuable identity:

> Yet since rich mines in barren grounds are showne
> May not I yeeld (not gold) but coale or stone?
> (lines 11–12)

Donne is certainly barren ground at the moment, in so far as he is anything at all. Yet in the same breath he *assumes* that he is also a rich mine. This draws, precisely in the ways we have shown before, on the versions of the self as having intrinsic value, whatever the social market value. But the image is most subtly chosen, for it also informs the patron of the self's potential market value, however hidden that may be. The intrinsically valuable platonic, private and independent self turns out to be as much the property of the patron as the public social self. In specifying the kind of rich mine (line 12) it may be that Donne loses confidence, moving from coal to stone. But whatever the exact market value, this hidden self is certainly cashable. Indeed, he suggests the most valuable kind of mine: a gold mine (negation being the permissible way of articulating the nearly forbidden). Still, however high his self-estimation, however much he feels he has a self beyond the *nothing* which he is socially, the clash between secret hidden core and apparent social identity forces him to invoke an external agent to strip away this surface (where before it was to burn away impurities), to dig up the riches, so that he may 'yeeld' the riches to someone else. Syntactically *yield* always occurs in forms such as '*yielded* something for/to someone', where the *someone* is never *I*. Thus the image and the syntax are tied absolutely into *use*, commerce and markets. The social creator is revealed as a potential and willing social user and exploiter, while creation turns out to be the discovery of market value in the human being. Conversely, the sense of nothingness, negation, has a social origin—namely the absence of such exploitive use. Again, the metaphysics of annihilation, of being and of nothingness, the fundamental questions of identity raised in these poems, find very tangible social explanation.

'Creation' becomes a specific term here, meaning admission to the desired social group. Some present members of such groups had membership from the beginning and did not need creation. But the process is a general one and may apply to any individual at any social level in relation to any coveted group. The only exception to this is the king–hardly surprising in the time of James I. Donne's ultimate patron–who proclaimed that kings 'are not onely Gods Lieutenants vpon earth, and sit vpon Gods throne, but even by God himselfe they are called Gods'.[3] In the poem 'To Sir H.W. at his going Ambassador to *Venice*', the king fulfills the role of creator for Wotton:

> And (how he may) makes you almost the same,
> A Taper of his Torch, a copie writ
> From his original . . .
>
> (lines 4–6)

This view of the individual and society encourages one to ask whether it was a common mode of perception at that time, or especially found in any specific group; or whether, for example, Donne's origins in an institutionally excluded group—the community of Roman Catholics—disposed him to view self in this way. Much more work on the lines we are suggesting will be necessary before satisfactory answers can be given.

The source of the creator's credentials could become problematic for anyone who is not totally content to accept the social order and the processes maintaining it. This is in fact a constant concern in the epistles, and is the obverse of his anxiety about his own lack of being, his own lack of credentials. In the light of this consideration, lines such as these from the opening of 'You have refin'd mee' take on a peculiarly bitter and ironic tone:

> now I see
> Rareness, or use, not nature value brings;
> And such, as they are circumstanc'd, they bee.

It is the removal of his blindness which makes him see this unpalatable truth; the countess is indeed creator, though not because of her inherent virtues or nature but because this is how she happens to be circumstanced. The removal of his own blindness makes him see the more massive blindness of the social system to which he seeks admission. Donne's reiteration of the theme that the countess's virtue might go unrecognised (and so her value diminish) except for his good offices takes on a somewhat darker note in this context: Donne covertly assumes for himself the role of creator. The situation is complex enough for Donne to see himself as nothing, as inherently valuable, and possibly as creator, all simultaneously. All these involved shifts are firmly related to a highly specific set of social relationships. Discussions which perpetually divorce the literary language, the psychological, and the social, will inevitably introduce grave distortions and prove limiting in disabling ways.

* * *

3. James I, 1609 speech to Parliament, in *The Political Works of James I*, ed. C. H. McIlwain, Cambridge, Mass. 1918, reprint 1966, 307.

Donne sees the patronage situation in this way, at least in part. In his quest for incorporation he reluctantly accepts the necessity of turning himself, his abilities, and certain of his poems which are overt tokens of exchange—witness the usher and mine images—into commodities. Alienated and critical intellectual that he was, he had no wish to be excluded from the traditional ruling circles, and no ideology to encourage an oppositional stance which would entail action with new associations; and he certainly had no wish to be a 'troublemaker'. Our approach to Donne from this perspective suggests to us that the whole issue of 'the alienated intellectual' in this period needs considerably more research done on it. Such research would develop the lines of inquiry and methods of analysis which we are applying to Donne's verse epistles in a collective enterprise bringing together historians, linguists, and literary critics. One important general question which would be focal in such an inquiry would be at what times certain intellectuals became alienated *and* sufficiently organised to form radical, highly critical groups, acting for change against the reigning hegemony.[4]

We conclude this study by looking at three verse epistles which were *not* written to patronesses. The first two we consider, 'Sir, more then kisses' ('To Sir Henry Wotton') and (Like one who in her third widdowhood' ('To Mr Rowland Woodward') were probably written around 1597–1598, a decade before the poems which we have just considered and, significantly, before Donne was dismissed by Egerton and ejected into the social wilderness inhabited by the various 'alienated' intellectuals.

It is striking that in these two poems Donne assumes a simple version of the self, one having a virtually autonomous existence, identity without social relationships, and certainly without 'creators'. The disturbing issues about alternative versions of the self and its value, central in the later patronage poems are, at least on the surface, conspicuous by their absence. Donne assumes that the individual can retreat into a safe, inherently and unproblematically valuable core. The world around may be obnoxious but the individual has his own mental and moral edifice into which he may retreat, like the snail ('To Sir Henry Wotton', lines 49–52).

Given this stance, it is not surprising that Lawrence Stapleton, one of the few critics to attend to the verse epistles with seriousness, should claim that in those letters, written before 1600, Donne reveals 'the assumptions by men of his circle, of a stoical attitude of detachment . . . man must dwell in himself, to house his spirit, as the snail his body'.[5] Nevertheless, the same critic registers something odd about these apparently stoic poems:

4. Michael Walzer has some suggestive speculations on this topic in his conclusion to *The Revolution of the Saints*. [London: Weidenfeld, 1966.]
5. L. Stapleton, 'The Theme of Virtue in Donne's Epistles', *Studies in Philology* 55 (1958), 187–200, reprinted in *Essential Articles for the Study of John Donne's Poetry*, ed. J. R. Roberts, Sussex: Harvester Press 1975, 451–2. On the date of 'Sir, more then kisses', see Milgate, op cit., 227–8, and Grierson, op. cit., vol. II, 140–1.

> The reader feels indeed that in such verses as this Donne is but conning over, genuinely enough, the social lessons of self-mastery . . . Donne had not, of course retired to any of the uncongenial country residences that he later owed to the help of relatives or friends and resorted to through necessity. He was fashioning an attitude of detachment which might save him from corruption in the world of affairs.[6]

Stapleton leaves the issue there; in the context of our study we wish to look more closely at the 'stoical attitude' and the stoic self which Donne seems to be cultivating here.

Having roundly abused the whole social world, countries, courts and towns, Donne offers Henry Wotton the following advice:

> Be thou thine owne home, and in thy selfe dwell;
> Inne any where, continuance maketh hell.
> And seeing the snaile, which every where doth rome,
> Carrying his own house still, still is at home.
> Follow (for he is easie pac'd) this snaile,
> Bee thine owne Palace, or the world's thy gaile,
> And in the world's sea, do not like corke sleepe
> Upon the waters' face: nor in the deepe
> Sinke like a lead without a line; but as
> Fishes glide, leaving no print where they passe,
> Nor making sound; so closely thy course goe,
> Let me dispute, whether thou breathe, or no.
> (lines 47–58)

Stapleton's feeling that Donne is here 'but conning over . . . social lessons of self-mastery' seems to be a response to the flaccid, simpleminded version of the self informing this passage. There is no recognition that the self may well have internalised unpleasant aspects of the social world which Donne attacks (but inhabits—and ambitiously so), no acknowledgment of the individual's complicity in the state of the society to which he owes his continuing work and existence, no sign that there is any tension between participation and retreat.[7] In Christian terms, one might add, such 'stoical' stances are surprisingly blind to the effects of the fall—the corruption of the will and blindness of the intellect. There are one or two hints of these vital problems: 'Let no man say there, Virtues flintie wall/shall locke vice in mee, I'll do none but know all' (lines 35–6); and at line forty-eight: 'Inne any where, continuance maketh hell'. This suggests that retreat into the self will have to come to terms precisely with evil inside. But this hint is not developed and these earlier poems are innocent of the real difficulties involved in questions of identity discussed above.

Nevertheless, while the surface suggests no complexities, when we

6. Stapleton, article cit., 452.
7. There is no space here to contrast the profound explorations of such issues in Marvell's *Upon Appleton House*.

look at the poems more closely they reveal movements which make us doubt that the stoic stance was ever at all congenial to Donne, let alone seriously held as a conviction to live by.

The version of self in the poem 'To Sir Henry Wotton' advocates retreat leading to stasis and peace. The external world's instability does provide a threat, and we noted the hinted threat from internal vice. But no change of self is envisaged or demanded: the snail remains a snail within the house, the fish glides along leaving no print and remains exactly the fish it has always been. In the poem to Mr Rowland Woodward, the beginnings of an analysis of self are evident. It has been spatialised so that 'wee' may turn into 'our selves';

> So wee, if wee into our selves will turne,
> Blowing our sparkes of vertue, may outburne
> The straw, which doth about our hearts sojourne.
> (lines 22–4)

That is, the self has become an inner and outer self, with the inner seen as the heart around which there is the straw of the outer self. The latter can be burned off. Here then is an advocacy of change.

However, if we consider the interactional structures of the poem to Sir Henry Wotton we find the stasis we described rather undercut. The whole poem is organised as a dialogue. Overtly it begins with an address to a friend, in a formal tone; it ends in a gently earnest plea for the friend's love. The overall frame of the poem is thus address and plea, an interaction, and the overt content of the poem needs to be read within this context: retreat which is in tension with the interaction of the friend. Contained within this overall frame are the linguistic forms of interaction: commands, questions, statements, mirroring the alternating forms of conversation. Furthermore, they are conducted in the form of intimate address: thou, thine, thy.

In other words, in its formal structure the poem is the very antithesis of retreat: it is constructed around the core forms of the language of social interaction, and whatever version of self is depicted in the apparent stoic pose, there is a deeper version where the self is defined in interaction with others. The others are friends, intimate, and the poet seeks their love, which seems essential to him. With this in mind we can see how the disturbance at lines thirty-five, thirty-six and forty-eight reflects the way the retreat is a very limited one, with the continuing and sought after support of friends. So the two versions of self in the poem to Wotton are straightforwardly contradictory.

Yet we are struck by the amazing confidence with which, despite this, Donne's poem exhorts his friend to behave and act in ways which seemingly follow from an uncomplicated stoic stance towards the world. This combination of confusion and confident advice urges us to examine the underlying view of social processes that allows such contradictions and even makes them seem unproblematic. To do so we shall look at the syntactic forms, first pointing out the agents operating in the poem. A selection serves to indicate the kind of agents they are. Initially, some non-human ones: *They* (Rockes, Remoraes) break or stop ships (lines 7–9); *Virtue's flintie wall* shall lock vice in me (lines 35–6). Then some human ones: *men* play princes (lines 23–4); *men* retrieve and greet themselves (lines 43–5). Some passives, with the agent deleted: two temperate regions *girded in* (line 13); you, *parch'd* in court, in the country *frozen* (line 15); shall cities *be chosen* (line 16); falsehood *is denizon'd* (line 34). In the first group, non-human agents act concretely on other entities; the actions are physical ones, 'making', 'breaking', 'curing', 'locking'. In the second list, human agents act, but significantly the actions are not direct, concrete, nor do these agents act on other entities. Instead the actions are reflexive (e.g. 'retrieve and greet themselves') or non-physical actions, 'see', 'know', ('play-actions' literally, such as 'playing princes'). In the last group, the passives, we have no way of recovering who the agents were—who 'froze', 'parch'd', 'built', 'denizon'd' whom.

Without further analysis we think it sound to claim that *men* are perceived and presented as peculiarly inactive, passive, reflexive; the real agents are non-human, concrete or abstract. The imperatives from line forty-seven onwards ('Be thou thine owne home, and in the selfe dwell . . . Follow . . . this snaile . . . Bee thine owne Palace . . .') are no exception, for while they do advocate actions by human agents they are figurative actions which are difficult to understand precisely or to perform: they exhort the addressee to be in a certain kind of state, rather than indicating the processes which would lead someone to be in that state. The poem discloses a failure to grasp specific and relevant agents, an inability to specify the processes and agents by which or by whom the new state is to be implemented. In short, there is a marked lack of understanding of processes, agents, and causation in the social world. Yet Donne has superimposed a seemingly confident stoic stance on this uncertainty. His shaky perception of agency and process explains the presence of the non-stoic formal frame and the plea for friendship, a call for support. The underlying content of this poem might then be described as being about interaction, but one which proceeds without clear grasp of the 'ground rules' of processes in the social world.

The second of the pre-1600 poems we are considering is to Mr Rowland Woodward, 'Like one who'in her third widdowhood'. It has many elements in common with the poem to Sir Henry Wotton just discussed and is open to very similar comment. Donne advises, 'Seeke wee then our selves in our selves' (line 19). We see that the active self is still envisaged as unproblematic in its autonomy, the complicated perceptions of the patroness poems are absent. Lines thirty-one onwards may appear to contradict our judgment:

> Wee are but farmers of our selves, yet may,
> If we can stocke our selves, and thrive, unplay
> Much, much deare treasure for the great rent day.

Farming, thriving, stocking and unplaying treasure may seem to be the very stuff of known social practice and relationships. We believe not, for the field and its cultivation is figured as purely individualistic and autonomous while the market in which the produce can be cashed for payment of rents is a heavenly one, located outside society and beyond history, at the Last Judgment. Despite the apparent Christian dimension here, and despite the explicit mention of original sin and the doctrine of imputed merit (lines 13–18), the self is again envisaged in such a way that the problems about corruption of the will and intellect, or the need for grace in farming the self, let alone questions about the complex interactions between individual and sociey, cannot arise. Nevertheless, as in the poem to Sir Henry Wotton, the poem has an interactional structure. It begins with a form of address which assumes shared knowledge and belief between speaker and addressee, '*You know*, Physitians, when they would infuse' (line 25, our italics) and ends not only with the assurance of Donne's love for Woodward, but a strong statement of his need for Woodward's love in return: 'But to know, that I love thee' and would be lov'd' (line 36). The intense need for love is expressed in a command to Woodward to love him, a most un-stoic conclusion.[8]

Clearly, there are continuities between the poem to Wotton and this one; the version of the self is a little more elaborate here and the 'stoicism' a little more openly uncertain. If we look at agency, as we did in the other poem, interestingly enough we find a large number of the human agents involved in real, physical processes (though 'metaphorically' used to indicate psychological processes): gathering the sun's beams, blowing sparks, outburning straw (lines 20–24). There are far fewer passives, and the deleted agents is in all cases Donne himself (or one of his attributes): *tyed* to retiredness (line 2); seeds *were sown* (line 6); *betroth'd* (line 8). The imperatives are commands to perform actions: manure thy self; with vain outward things be no more moved; to thyself be approved (lines 34–5). Compared with the poem to Wotton there is an increase of agentiveness, awareness of agency, and the realisation of what are possible processes which men may carry out to reach a desired state. This increase in the poet's awareness of what social interaction and change could be about is accompanied by signs of a decrease in emphasis on the linguistic forms of interaction, as though a progress in understanding the causes of action leads to a progress from talk to action.

Of course, the stoic stance is classically one which the alienated intellectual may assume. We are interested to note—beyond the versions of self revealed—the uncertainty with which Donne holds this stance, an uncertainty which, as our analysis reveals, is based on his wish for incorporation (the plea for friendship, the interactional forms) and an insufficient understanding of social processes. The latter may be a direct consequence of the fact that he was not, as we have pointed out, com-

8. The conclusion of a classic contemporary stoic poem, Ben Jonson's fine *To the World* ('False world, good night') provides an essential contrast here.

mitted to an ideologically based critique of his society.

In conclusion we turn briefly to a poem written in the period of the patroness poems discussed above. In 1610 Donne addressed 'Man is a lumpe' to Sir Edward Herbert, the son of one of his patronesses. The shifts in Donne's approach to the self, which had taken place over the preceding ten years in his drastically changed circumstances of renewed 'exile', are clear. They link up with the attitudes to self we discussed in relation to his patronage poems. This poem, written to a friend, fellow poet, and fellow philosopher, shows much of the obsession with negativity and annihilation (social and metaphysical) so marked in the patroness poems. The possibility of a virtuous and unequivocally valuable inner core, held out to Wotton and Woodward earlier, is now much further removed as he offers a traditional, compound platonic-Christian image of man composed of destructive and warring beasts which can only be controlled by equally destructive energies directed against the self, and a vision of a Christian God viciously indifferent to the fate of his creatures. Despite some surface suggestions that man may act autonomously to transcend internal wars and external social relations, in fact we get a version of the self and of society which is extremely close to that we described in the contemporary poems. Man in general only acts reflectively—given that 'the beasts' and 'nature' are his *own* beasts and his *own* nature. And though his 'businesse is, to rectifie/Nature, to what she was' (lines 33–4), we note that immediately Donne shows that this is not what man does, for 'wee'are led awry'. In all this Donne seemingly presents the friend as a means of overcoming the viciousness of man's existence. However, the last lines of the poem undercut any such reading decisively:

> You have dwelt upon
> All worthy bookes, and now are such an one.
> Actions are authors, and of those in you
> Your friends finde every day a mart of new.
> (lines 47–50)

The friend produces, every day, actions, which are authors, which are books. And every day there is a market of these actions/authors/books. The principle of commodification is applied to the actions of the friend/patron; his friends, the real authors, may buy and may plagiarise. If the friends are poets in need of patronage they buy the already written texts; so the book or poem which Donne writes to the friend is not in fact written by Donne the poet, but by the friend/patron. Here the friend acts analogously to the patroness/creator, for while she creates the poet and with him his future actions and values, the friend in appropriating the very labour of the poet creates him as poet. The reality, as Donne presents it, is that the friend negates the actions of the poet and thereby the poet. The implications of this stance are if anything an even more savage comment by Donne on his society, where even those whom he calls his friends and lovers reduce him to powerlessness and inferiority. Here the friend is like the creator of the patroness poems; despite the negative view which Donne presents of this friendship, he needs it, either to be created, or to be written into the social world which he views so critically.

FRANK MANLEY

John Donne: The Anniversaries †

The *Anniversaries* were never very popular. As early as April, 1612, Donne received letters from England criticizing them in the same way they have been criticized ever since: that they say too much, that the praise is too fulsome, the imagery too extravagant. Ben Jonson summed it up in his classic remark to William Drummond of Hawthornden: "that Dones Anniversarie was profane and full of Blasphemies/that he told Mr Donne, if it had been written of ye Virgin Marie it had been something. . . ." Yet Donne always defended the poems. He replied to the criticism in his letters:

> I hear from England of many censures of my book of Mistress Drury; if any of those censures do but pardon me my descent in printing anything in verse (which if they do they are more charitable than myself. . . , I doubt not but they will soon give over that other part of that indictment, which is that I have said so much; for nobody can imagine that I who never saw her, could have any other purpose in that, than that when I had received so very good testimony of her worthiness, and was gone down to print verses, it became me to say, not what I was sure was just truth, but the best that I could conceive; for that had been a new weakness in me, to have praised anybody in printed verses, that had not been capable of the best praise that I could give.[1]

And he told Jonson, in what is undoubtedly the most acute defense of the poems ever made, "that he described the Idea of a Woman and not as she was." The purpose of this introduction will be in great part to expand the implications of that statement:

Later in the century the *Anniversaries* were imitated a number of times, though none of the imitations implies a very profound criticism of the poems. Almost immediately after they were written, they were used by Webster in his *Duchess of Malfi* (1613), to help build up the context of allusion, the air of mystery and sanctify surrounding his central character.[2] William Drummond of Hawthornden imitated a number of pas-

† From Frank Manley, *John Donne: The Anniversaries*, copyright 1963. Pp. 6–10, 16–20, 40–50. Reprinted by permission of the publishers, The John Hopkins Press.

1. Edmund Gosse, *The Life and Letters of John Donne* (London, 1899), I, 305–6.

2. Most of the allusions are pointed out by Charles Crawford, *Collectanea* (Stratford-on-Avon, 1907), I, 50–65.

sages of *The First Anniversary*, particularly the new philosophy section, in his prose meditation on death, *The Cypresse Grove* (1623). And some years later, in 1692, John Dryden celebrated the death of the Countess of Abdingdon in a "panegyrical" elegy entitled *Eleonora*, written directly in imitation of Donne's "admirable *Anniversaries*." Dryden never saw the Countess of Abdingdon and therefore took the *Anniversaries* as the solution to the problem of how to write an elegy about someone of whom he knew nothing. In his hands, however, Donne's "Idea of a Woman" lost all its numen and became reduced to a flat, abstract pattern of virtue. As Dryden explained in the Preface to the poem:

> I have followed his [Donne's] footsteps in the design of his panegyric, which was to raise an emulation in the living, to copy out the example of the dead. And therefore it was that I once intended to have called this poem 'The Pattern;' and though, on a second consideration, I changed the title to the name of that illustrious person, yet the design continues, and Eleonora is still the pattern of charity, devotion, and humility; of the best wife, the best mother, and the best of friends.[3]

In the eighteenth century the *Anniversaries* were largely forgotten, along with the rest of Donne. They were remembered, if at all, primarily through an allusion in *Spectator Paper, No. 41*, which quoted a few lines and remarked that they referred to one of Donne's mistresses. The error echoed through the century. Fielding, for example, picked it up in *Tom Jones* (IV, ii), where he has the same lines refer to Tom's mistress, Sophia. By the nineteenth century even the mistake in the *Spectator Papers* was forgotten.

In the twentieth century, however, the *Anniversaries* shared in the general rehabilitation of Donne, though they were not read as enthusiastically or as carefully as the *Songs and Sonets* or the *Divine Poems*. The general feeling was that despite a number of passages as brilliant and complex as Donne ever wrote, the poems as a whole left one curiously unsatisfied and confused. Fifteen years ago, however, Louis L. Martz discovered that "the full meaning of each [of the *Anniversaries*] grows out of a deliberately articulated structure" and that the structure is not essentially elegiac, but meditative, based on the strict principles of meditation established by Ignatius Loyola.[4] The discovery was extremely important. It established the process by which Donne transforms the death of Elizabeth Drury into an image of his own heart's loss of wisdom. But Martz failed to do anything with it. He regarded the poems as only partially successful. In *The Second Anniversary*, according to Martz, the meditative structure is organic; in *The First*, it is mechanical. One poem therefore is a success, the other a qualified failure.

The second major contribution to the study of the *Anniversaries* in

3. *Works*, ed. Sir Walter Scott, rev. George Saintsbury (Edinburgh, 1885), XI, 124.

4. "John Donne in Meditation: *The Anniversaries*," *ELH*, XIV (1947), 247–73, reprinted in *The Poetry of Meditation* (New Haven, 1954), pp. 219–48.

this century was made by Marjorie Nicolson, who discovered that the poems are not two, but one: the antithetical poles of the same logical unit:

> The *Anniversaries* are . . . as artfully though not so obviously articulated as 'L'Allegro' and 'Il Penseroso.' The first is a lament over the body—the body of man and the body of the world—a meditation upon death and mortality. The second is a vision of the release of the soul from its prison. The whole, with antitheses of doubt and faith, despair and hope, death and the triumph of immortality, is a great symphony in which the harmony is more profound because of cacophony.[5]

The discovery was vitiated somewhat by Miss Nicolson's fantastic theory of the "Double Shee," but even there she was correct in recognizing some obscure symbolic process at work in the poems.

As a result of the work of Martz and Nicolson the *Anniversaries* have come to be regarded with something like respect, though no one purports to know precisely what they are about. Everyone agrees that they are meditations, that they have something to do with religion, and that they are in some way a bridge between Donne's early and late verse, his love poetry and the *Divine Poems.* But other than that the criticism remains the same as it was in the seventeenth century: that the *Anniversaries* are "profane and full of Blasphemies." And the answer remains the same too, if we could once discover what it means: that they are about "the Idea of a Woman and not as she was."

* * *

But the problem then becomes, what is she a symbol of? And the answer is not easy, any easier than it is with Beatrice. The general area seems clear enough. She has to do with the state of our own souls. As Donne explains in the very first lines of the poem:

> When that rich soule which to her Heauen is gone
> Whom all they celebrate, who know they haue one,
> (For who is sure he hath a soule, vnlesse,
> It see, and Iudge, and follow worthinesse,
> And by Deedes praise it? He who doth not this,
> May lodge an In-mate soule, but tis not his.)
> [1–6]

She is not only directly identified as a "rich soule" herself, but she is celebrated only by those who know they have a soul; and *celebrated* in this sense means not only *memorialized* but also *reinacted, reperformed,* as in the celebration of the mass. As Donne explains a little later on (lines 67–78), "the matter and the stuffe" of the new world created in her memory is her virtue, but "the forme our practise is." She has to do

5. *The Breaking of the Circle* (Evanston, Ill., 1950), pp. 65–66.

with the *possibilitatem boni* Augustine thought was lost in the fall, the innate uprightness of the soul which is restored only by grace.[6] She is the soul's likeness to God, the "intrinsique balme" that preserves it from the putrefaction of spiritual death:

> Physitians say, That man hath in his Constitution, in his Complexion, a natural vertue, which they call *Balsamum suum*, his owne Balsamum, by which, any wound which a man could receive in his body, would cure it selfe, if it could be kept cleane from the anoiances of the aire, and all extrinsique encumbrances. Something that hath some proportion and analogy to this Balsamum of the body, there is in the soule of man too. The soule hath *Nardum suam*, her Spikenard. . . , a naturall disposition to Morall goodnesse, as the body hath to health. But therein lyes the souls disadvantage, that whereas the causes that hinder the cure of a bodily wound, are extrinsique offences of the Ayre, and putrefaction from thence, the causes in the wounds of the soule, are intrinsique, so as no other man can apply physick to them; Nay, they are hereditary, and there was no time early inough for our selves to apply any thing by way of prevention, for the wounds were as soone as we were, and sooner.[7]

But all that remains metaphoric and vague. There is no clear, explicit identification of the symbolism in the poem, and for that reason it has run off in the minds of critics to Jesus Christ or the Catholic Church, Queen Elizabeth, the Virgin Mary, the Logos, Astraea. There is nothing to bring it into sharp focus, and we are left with a feeling of incompleteness.

I am not certain that any sharp focus is possible. The symbol is too complex for all its parts to be held in the mind at once discursively. Moreover, it is the nature of symbols to suggest more than they seem to contain. They resist all efforts at precise, intellectual definition. But in present-day terms perhaps a vague idea of what Donne was getting at is available in C. G. Jung's concept of the *anima*, which is in itself vague, but which in general represents the "Idea of a Woman" in man, the image of his own soul, his own deepest reality. It is a universal symbol of otherness in man, either of desire, the completion of one's own androgynous self, as in the Platonic myth, or of strange intuitive knowledge otherwise unavailable to him, "a source of information about things for which a man has no eyes."[8] In Donne's own time, however, the clearest formulation was in terms of the traditional concept of Wisdom,

6. Cf. Donne, *Sermons*, ed. George R. Potter and Evelyn M. Simpson (Berkeley and Los Angeles, 1953–62), II, 55; "in that wound, as wee were all shot in *Adam*, we bled out *Impassibilitatem*, and we sucked in *Impossibilitatem*; There we lost our *Immortality*, our *Impassibility*, our assurance of Paradise, and then we lost *Possibilitatem boni*, says S. *Augustine*: all possibility of recovering any of this by our selves." Hereafter cited as *Sermons*.

7. *Sermons*, V, 347–49.

8. *The Collected Works of* C. G. *Jung*, ed. H. Read, M. Fordham, and G. Adler (New York, 1953), VII, 186.

which, like the *anima*, was almost always symbolized by woman, who represented the subconscious, intuitive, feminine intelligence of the heart as opposed to the active, conscious, masculine intelligence of the mind. "What is Wisdome?" Donne asks, modifying the ancient Stoic definition:

> we may content our selves, with that old definition of Wisdome, that it is *Rerum humanarum, & divinarum scientia*; The Wisdome that accomplishes this cleannesse, is the knowledge, the right valuation of this world, and of the next; To be able to compare the joyes of heaven, and the pleasures of this world, and the gaine of the one, with the losse of the other, this is the way to this cleanenesse of the heart; because that heart that considers, and examines, what it takes in, will take in no foule, no infectious thing [*Sermons*, VII, 336].

It is that Wisdom that the total experience of the *Anniversaries* presents. Donne says in effect:

> Looke then upon the greatnes of God and the smalnesse of man; the goodnes of God, and the vilenesse of man; the wisdome of God, and the folly of man; the love of God, and the hate of man; the grace of God, and the disgrace of man; the mercy of God, the tyranny of man; and the glory of God, and the infamy of man: and fixing the eye of the heart upon the one and the other, how canst thou but to the glory of God, and shame of thy selfe . . . cry with the Prophet David, *Oh Lord what is man that thou doest visit him?*[9]

It forms the essential structure of each poem—the alternation of contempt for the world (meditation) and praise of virtue (eulogy)—as well as the total structure of both poems taken together as a unit. In the first Donne realizes imagistically, through the death of a girl he never saw, the grace and the indwelling widsom of God, *sapientia creata*, that was lost in the fall; and the entire movement is downward to decay. In the second, however, he has found his direction; through the realization of his soul's loss he has regained the wisdom that orients him toward God, and the entire poem surges upward toward eternal life. It is as a concrete image of that Wisdom, its direct emotional apprehension, that the mysterious figure of woman at the center of the poem is best understood. She is in herself both the object and the wit: the realization as well as the means to realize it, for the only way to understand the *Anniversaries* is intuitively, through symbolic understanding. The poems make sense only to those who realize, with Donne, that

> no thing
> Is worth our trauaile, griefe, or perishing,

9. Nicholas Breton, *Divine Considerations of the Soule* (1608), cited in Martz, *op. cit.*, pp. 227–28.

But those rich ioyes, which did possesse her hart,
Of which shee's now partaker, and a part.
[*The First Anniversary*, 431–434]

According to Augustine, in a phrase echoed by Donne in the opening lines of the poem, they only know they have a soul who see *(meminit)*, judge *(intelligit)* and follow *(diligit)* God; and "that is true wisdom": *quod est sapientia.*[1]

* * *

Considered in terms of the tradition of Wisdom, certain things about the *Anniversaries* become immediately clear. I have already mentioned the fundamental structure of the poems, the alternation of contempt and glorification based on the definition of wisdom as "the right valuation of this world, and of the next." As Donne explained in *The First Anniversary*, the purpose of the poem was to demonstrate to the "new world"

The dangers and diseases of the old:
For with due temper men do then forgoe,
Or couet things, when they their true worth know.
[88–90]

The tradition also explains why the poems were written in the form of traditional Ignatian meditations. As Louis L. Martz has pointed out, each of the *Anniversaries* is divided into various large structural units, or meditations, each of which in turn is divided into three main parts. In *The First Anniversary* they are: (1) a meditation on the decay of the world and the effects of original sin on man and the entire frame of the universe; (2) a eulogy of Elizabeth Drury as a lost pattern of virtue; and (3) a refrain and moral, urging us to forget this crippled, dying world. Martz's divisions, I think, are entirely correct, but what he has failed to notice, though he mentions it in other parts of his book,[2] is that these three recurrent parts of the poem correspond to the three traditional parts of the rational soul—memory, understanding, and will. In what Martz terms the *meditations*, Donne sends his mind back in time toward Eden. Through the tradition of the decay of the world, which, as a tradition, represents the collective memory of man, he "remembers" imaginatively the perfection of the first days of the earth and searches out the cause for the present decay. He then turns to the intellect. In the so-called *eulogies*, he probes the significance of a young girl's recent death and discovers in it an answer to what caused the decay. She is a way of comprehending the lost perfection of man's soul, the grace of God in Paradise—not logically, but emotionally, in symbolic terms. And finally, from this combination of memory and understanding, Donne arrives at an act of will: to forget this rotten world now that she is dead.

The most important of these three recurrent parts of the poem is the

1. *De Trinitate*, *PL* 42, 1047.
2. Martz, *op. cit.*, pp. 34–36.

last, the ultimate act of will; for the will, as Donne pointed out in his sermons, has a certain *Virtus transformativa:* "by it we change our selves into that we love most" (*Sermons*, IX, 373):

> *Primus actus voluntatis est Amor:* Philosophers and Divines agree in that, That the will of man cannot be idle, and the first act that the will of man produces, is Love; for till it love something, prefer and chuse something, till it would have something, it is not a Will; neither can it turn upon any object, before God. So that this first, and general, and natural love of God, is not begotten in my soul, nor produced by my soul, but created and infus'd with my soul, and as my soul; there is no soul that knows she is a soul, without such a general sense of the love of God [*Sermons*, VI, 361].

It echoes in the very first lines of the poem:

> For who is sure he hath a soule, vnlesse
> It see, and Iudge, and follow worthinesse,
> And by Deedes praise it?
>
> [3–5]

And ultimately that is what the *Anniversaries* perform. They detach our love from this world and direct it toward the next, toward the luminous "Idea of a Woman," who represents the image of God in man.

But the will is not capable of acting alone. "All sin is from the perverseness of the will," Donne noted, but "all disorder in the will [is] from errour in the understanding" (*Sermons*, VIII, 364–365). All three faculties of the soul must flow together to form one total act of love, for all three were thought to be analogous to the Trinity, though three, yet one. In traditional Augustinian psychology the memory, understanding, and will constitute potentially the Image of God in man. When directed toward their proper goal, they enter into what they love and restore the lost likeness of the soul to God. They become in themselves Wisdom, *sapientia creata*, the image of the increate Wisdom of God:

> The Trinity in the mind itself is the Image of God, by which it remembers, understands, and loves God—which is true wisdom *(sapientia)*. This Trinity of the mind therefore is the Image of God not because the mind remembers, understands, and loves itself, but because it remembers, understands, and loves the one by whom it was made. When it does that, it is wise *(sapiens)*. If it does not, . . . it is stupid *(stulta)*. . . . In brief, it should worship the uncreated God, who made it capable of himself *(cujus ab eo capax est facta)* and capable of being a partaker of himself *(et cujus particeps esse potest)*; according to which it is written, 'Behold, the love of God *(Dei cultus)*, that is wisdom' (*Job*, 28:28). And not by its own light, but by participation in the highest light will it become wise, and where eternal, there will it reign blessed.[3]

3. Augustine, *De Trinitate*, *PL* 42, 1047.

* * *

It is impossible to express in discursive language, but at this point it becomes apparent that the tripartite structure of the *Anniversaries* is identical with the central symbol that rises from it. Put into Aristotelian terms, it is the same as the relationship between efficient and final cause. The symbol is the principle because of which the poem moves toward the production of its effect. It is the form. But at the same time, seen from a slightly different perspective, the symbol is also the process itself that produces the effect. It is both the object and the wit. More concretely, if through the process of the poem—the threefold act of memory, understanding, and will—we arrive at the right valuation of this world and the next, we will have achieved within ourselves the Image of God that was lost. Our souls will have become transformed into the mysterious symbol at the center of the poem:

> Love is a Possessory Affection, it delivers over him that loves into the possession of that that he loves; it is a transmutatory Affection, it changes him that loves, into the very nature of that that he loves, and he is nothing else [*Sermons*, I, 184–185].

In the second place, the tradition of Wisdom helps put into proper perspective the celebrated "new philosophy" section of *The First Anniversary*:

> And new Philosophy calls all in doubt,
> The Element of fire is quite put out;
> The Sunne is lost, and th'earth, and no mans wit
> Can well direct him, where to looke for it.
> And freely men confesse, that this world's spent,
> When in the Planets, and the Firmament
> They seeke so many new; they see that this
> Is crumbled out againe to his Atomis.
> 'Tis all in pieces, all cohaerence gone;
> All iust supply, and all Relation.
>
> [205–214]

The passage is usually taken out of context to illustrate the impact of scientific rationalism on the Medieval world picture and the consequent unsettling of the Renaissance mind. "Donne," according to Douglas Bush, echoing Coffin, Nicolson, and others, "is wandering between two worlds, that of cosmic unity and that of meaningless disorder and decay, and he cannot resolve the conflict."[4] Such a conflict undoubtedly stands somewhere behind the *Anniversaries*—as it does behind every other poem in the Renaissance—and helps explain why they were written. But it is not the statement that the poems themselves make. The *Anniversaries* are not simply a symbolic action, an elaborate gesture of intellectual despair.

4. *English Literature in the Earlier Seventeenth Century*, 1600–1660 (Oxford, 1945), p. 132.

Nor, on the other hand, are they Menippian satires, as Northrop Frye recently claimed: "where the death of a girl expands into a general satire or 'anatomy'."[5] In Frye's elaborate and suggestive system of genres the anatomy, or Menippian satire, is directed not against people themselves, but against mental attitudes or types—"Pedants, bigots, cranks, parvenus, virtuosi, enthusiasts, rapacious and incompentent professional men of all kinds." Evil and absurdity are regarded not as moral or social phenomena, but intellectual, "a kind of maddened pedantry which the *philosophus gloriosus* at once symbolizes and defines." According to this view, Donne overwhelms "his pedantic targets with an avalanche of their own jargon."[6] He hoists them on their own petard by using the most famous discoveries of the day only to prove the decay of the world. The new medicine of Paracelsus, for example, is equated with the new disease of syphilis:

> With new diseases on our selues we warre,
> And with new phisicke, a worse Engin farre.
> [159–160]

And of course Frye is correct. *The First Anniversary* is shot through with satire of that sort. But again the danger is in reading the part for the whole: a complexity of tone for formal satire. The *Anniversaries* contain satire, but they are not themselves contained by it. In terms of Renaissance poetic theory they are formal *epitaphia*, one *recens*, the other, *anniversarium*, written in the mode of Ignatian meditations.

There is, however, a third alternative, which subsumes the previous two. For if the *Anniversaries* are a lament for the loss of Wisdom, *sapientia creata*, then the learning of the new philosophy as well as Donne's own hypothetical disillusion are simply forms of false wisdom that stand in contrast to it. Instead of proving the glory of man, they reveal only further the hideous deformity and decay of the world:

> Those therefore who are wise in and concerning visible things (as are all those outside the Faith and those who are ignorant of God and a future life) understand nothing and are wise in nothing, that is, they are neither intelligent *(intelligentes)* nor wise *(sapientes)*, but foolish and blind. And though they may think themselves wise men, yet they have become fools. For they are wise, not in the wisdom of secret, hidden things, but of that which can be found in a human way.[7]

The distinction was traditional and ultimately goes back to Augustine:

> It is written concerning our Lord Jesus Christ that in him 'are hid all the treasures of wisdom and knowledge' (*Coloss.*, 2:3). The eloquence of Scripture also indicates, however, that these two—that

5. *Anatomy of Criticism: Four Essays* (Princeton, 1957), p. 298.
6. *Ibid.*, pp. 309; 311.
7. Luther, cited in Rice, *The Renaissance Idea of Wisdom*, p. 139; see also the entire chapter, pp. 124–48.

> is, wisdom *(sapientiam)* and knowledge *(scientiam)*—are different from one another, and in particular the holy words of Job, where each is defined to a certain extent. For he says, 'Behold, the love of God *(pietas)*, *that* is wisdom; to refrain from evil, however, is knowledge' (*Job*, 28:28). Not incorrectly we perceive *(intelligimus)* wisdom in understanding *(cognitione)* and in love *(dilectione)* of the one who always is and who remains immutable, that is God. *To refrain from evil*, however, which he says is knowledge, what is that but to be cautious and prudent in the midst of a crooked and perverse nation, as in the night of this century. . . .[8]

Scientia is the knowledge of this world only.[9] It is limited to what is perceived by the senses and represents the extent of man's wisdom in a state of nature.[1] *Sapientia*, on the other hand, is the knowledge of this world and of the next. It is a supernatural gift of God, *de sursum descendens:* the direct intellectual comprehension of eternal things.[2] In *The Second Anniversary*, for example, the satire and the agonized anatomy of the world gives way to a harmonious *docta ignorantia*, which forms the prelude to true wisdom:

> In this low forme, poore soule what wilt thou doe?
> When wilt thou shake off this Pedantery,
> Of being taught by sense, and Fantasy?
> Thou look'st through spectacles; small things seeme great,
> Below; But vp vnto the watch-towre get,
> And see all things despoyld of fallacies:
> Thou shalt not peepe through lattices of eies,
> Nor heare through Laberinths of eares, not learne
> By circuit, or collections to discerne.
> In Heauen thou straight know'st all, concerning it,
> And what concerns it not, shall straight forget.
>
> [290–300]

It suffuses the entire poem:

> Forget this world, and scarse thinke of it so,
> As of old cloaths, cast of a yeare agoe.
> To be thus stupid is Alacrity;
> Men thus lethargique haue best Memory.
> Looke vpward; that's toward her, whose happy state
> We now lament not, but congratulate.
>
> [61–66]

Finally, the tradition of Wisdom helps explain the fundamental difference between the two poems: they stand in the same relation to one another as *scientia* to *sapientia*. As Donne explained in one of his sermons,

8. Augustine, *PL* 37, 1760.
9. *PL* 42, 1037.
1. *PL* 40, 139.
2. *PL* 42, 1012.

a regenerate Christian, being now a *new Creature,* hath also *a new facultie of Reason*. . . . Divers men may walke by the Sea side, and the same beames of the Sunne giving light to them all, one gathereth by the benefit of that light pebels, or speckled shells, for curious vanitie, and another gathers precious Pearle, or medicinall Ambar, by the same light. So the common light of reason illuminates us all; but one imployes this light upon the searching of impertinent vanities, another by a better use of the same light, finds out the Mysteries of Religion; and when he hath found them, loves them. . . . Some men by the benefit of this light of Reason, have found out things profitable and usefull to the whole world; As in particular, *Printing* . . . [and] *Artillery*, by which warres come to quicker ends then heretofore, and the great expence of bloud is avoyded. . . . But . . . their light seems to be great out of the same reason, that a Torch in a misty night, seemeth greater then in a clear, because it hath kindled and inflamed much thicke and grosse Ayre round about it. . . .

But, if you canst take this light of reason that is in thee, this poore snuffe, that is almost out in thee, thy faint and dimme knowledge of God, that riseth out of this light of nature, if thous canst in those embers, those cold ashes, finde out one small coale, and wilt take the paines to kneell downe, and blow that coale with thy devout *Prayers*, . . . if . . . thou canst turne this little light inward, and canst thereby discerne where thy diseases, and thy wounds, and thy corruptions are, and canst apply those teares, and blood and balme to them, . . . thou shalt never envy the lustre and glory of the great lights of worldly men. . . . Their light shall set at noone; even in their heighth, . . . and thy light shall grow up, from a *faire hope*, to a modest assurance and *infallibility*, that that light shall never go out. . . ; as thy light of *reason* is exalted by *faith* here, so thy light of *faith* shall be exalted into the light of *glory*, and fruition in the Kingdome of heaven. . . ; in a man regenerate by faith, that light does all that reason did, *and more* [*Sermons*, III, 359–362].

The First Anniversary is concerned only with the light of reason, unaided by faith. Its tone, therefore, is analytic and satirical; through the use of reason it explores the limits of reason. It proceeds "punctually" from part to part in rigid logical sequence, but its overall movement is downward to decay. Its ultimate discovery is a universe of death. At the same time, however, proceeding from the operation of reason in the poem is the silent process of transformation by which the soul is changed into the very nature of that which it loves. As Donne explains toward the end of the poem, he has rewritten the Song of Moses for his own times, traditionally regarded as the complete summary of the Law, teaching the fear of the Lord and the severity of judgment. It marked the furthest extent to which man could proceed by human reason alone; beyond lay the dispensation of Grace. Therefore, after delivering the Song to his people, Moses ascended Mount Nebo with the Lord and from the top of Pisgah looked over into the Promised Land. But he was not able to enter.

In *The Second Anniversary*, however, Donne crossed over, and the entire poem surges upward toward eternal life:

> Looke vpward; that's towards her, whose happy state
> We now lament not, but congratulate.
>
> [65–66]

The meditations begin with death ("Thinke then, My soule, that death is but a Groome"), the point at which *The First Anniversary* and natural man end, and proceed beyond:

> But thinke that Death hath now enfranchis'd thee,
> Thou hast thy'expansion now and libertee;
> Thinke that a rusty Peece, discharg'd, is flowen
> In peeces, and the bullet is his owne,
> And freely flies: This to thy soule allow,
> Thinke thy sheell broke, thinke thy Soule hatch'd but now.
>
> [179–184]

The symbolism diminishes. Elizabeth Drury becomes more and more recognizable as an idealized pattern of virtue. For the soul itself has now attained the Wisdom that was lost. It has become internalized, and the emotions that were once concentrated within the symbol have now become diffused throughout the entire poem. The total movement of *The Second Anniversary* is harmonious and organic not, as is usually believed, because it is a success and *The First Anniversary* a failure, but because through the purgative process of *The First Anniversary* the soul has at last arrived at a right valuation of this world, and of the next, and rests secure in the love of God. As Dante remarked, commenting on the phrase, "When Israel went out of Egypt":

> If we regard the *literal* sense alone it signifies the departure of the sons of Israel from Egypt in the time of Moses; *allegorically*, it signifies our redemption through Christ; *morally*, it signifies the conversion of the soul from the grief and misery of sin to the state of grace; *anagogically*, it signifies the departure of the blessed soul from the slavery of this corruption to the freedom of everlasting glory.[3]

3. *Opere*, ed. Moore, p. 415.

Donne's Divine Poems

HELEN GARDNER

The Religious Poetry of John Donne †

* * *

Most critics have agreed in regarding '*La Corona*' and 'A Litany' as inferior to the 'Holy Sonnets', which give an immediate impression of spontaneity. Their superiority has been ascribed to their having been written ten years later, and their vehemence and anguished intensity have been connected with a deepening of Donne's religious experience after the death of his wife. There can be no question of their poetic greatness, nor of their difference from '*La Corona*' and 'A Litany'; but I do not believe that greatness or that difference to be due to the reasons which are usually given. The accepted date rests on an assumption which the textual history of the sonnets does not support: the assumption that the three 'Holy Sonnets' which the Westmoreland manuscript alone preserves were written at the same time as the other sixteen. These three sonnets are, as Sir Herbert Grierson called all the 'Holy Sonnets', 'separate ejaculations'; but the other sixteen fall into clearly recognizable sets of sonnets on familiar themes for meditation. They are as traditional in their way as '*La Corona*' and 'A Litany' are, and as the three Hymns are not. The Hymns are truly occasional; each arises out of a particular situation and a personal mood. But in theme and treatment the 'Holy Sonnets', if we ignore the three Westmoreland sonnets, depend on a long-established form of religious exercise: not oral prayer, but the simplest method of mental prayer, meditation. To say this is not to impugn their originality or their power. Donne has used the tradition of meditation in his own way; and it suits his genius as a poet far better than do the more formal ways of prayer he drew upon in '*La Corona*' and 'A Litany'. Yet although, with the possible exception of the Hymns, the 'Holy Sonnets' are his greatest divine poems, I do not myself feel that they spring from a deeper religious experience than that which lies behind 'A Litany'. The evidence which points to a date in 1609 does not seem to me to conflict with their character as religious poems; on the contrary it accords rather

† From Helen Gardner, *John Donne: The Divine Poems*. Pp. xxix–xxxv, 1–lv, copyright 1952. Reprinted by permission of the publishers, the Clarendon Press, Oxford.

better with it than does the hitherto accepted date.

Many readers have felt a discrepancy between the 'Holy Sonnets' and the picture which Walton gives of Donne's later years, and between the 'Holy Sonnets' and the sermons and Hymns. There is a note of exaggeration in them. This is apparent, not only in the violence of such a colloquy as 'Batter my heart', but also in the strained note of such lines as these:

> But who am I, that dare dispute with thee?
> O God, Oh! of thine onely worthy blood,
> And my teares, make a heavenly Lethean flood,
> And drowne in it my sinnes blacke memorie.
> That thou remember them, some claime as debt,
> I thinke it mercy, if thou wilt forget.

At first sight the closing couplet seems the expression of a deep humility; but it cannot be compared for depth of religious feeling with the 'Hymn to God the Father', where, however great the sin is, the mercy of God is implied to be the greater, or with such passages as the following on the phrase *virga irae*:

> But truely, beloved, there is a blessed comfort ministred unto us, even in that word; for that word *Gnabar*, which we translate *Anger*, *wrath*, hath another ordinary signification in Scripture, which, though that may seem to be an easier, would prove a heavier sense for us to beare, than this of *wrath* and *anger*; this is, *preteritio*, *conniventia*, Gods forbearing to take knowledge of our transgressions; when God shall say of us, as he does of *Israel*, *Why should ye be smitten any more?* when God leaves us to our selves, and studies our recovery no farther, by any more corrections; for, in this case, there is the lesse comfort, because there is the lesse *anger* show'd. And therefore, *S. Bernard*, who was heartily afraid of this sense of our word, heartily afraid of this preterition, that God should forget him, leave him out, affectionately, passionately embraces this sense of the word in our Text, *Anger*; and he sayes, *Irascaris mihi Domine*, *Domine mihi irascaris*, *Be angry with me O Lord*, *O Lord be angry with me, lest I perish!*[1]

This is the tone of the last lines of 'Good Friday':

> O thinke mee worth thine anger, punish me,
> Burne off my rusts, and my deformity,
> Restore thine Image, so much, by thy grace,
> That thou may'st know mee; and I'll turne my face.

Both make the close of the sonnet seem facile.

1. *Fifty Sermons*, xlviii. 455.

The almost histrionic note of the 'Holy Sonnets' may be attributed partly to the meditation's deliberate stimulation of emotion; it is the special danger of this exercise that, in stimulating feeling, it may falsify it, and overdramatize the spiritual life. But Donne's choice of subjects and his whole-hearted use of the method are symptoms of a condition of mind very different from the mood of '*La Corona*' or even from the conflicts which can be felt behind 'A Litany'. The meditation on sin and on judgement is strong medicine; the mere fact that his mind turned to it suggests some sickness in the soul. The 'low devout melancholie' of '*La Corona*' the 'dejection' of 'A Litany' are replaced by something darker. In both his preparatory prayers Donne uses a more terrible word, despair. The note of anguish is unmistakable. The image of a soul in meditation which the 'Holy Sonnets' present is an image of a soul working out its salvation in fear and trembling. The two poles between which it oscillates are faith in the mercy of God in Christ, and a sense of personal unworthiness that is very near to despair. The flaws in their spiritual temper are a part of their peculiar power. No other religious poems make us feel so acutely the predicament of the natural man called to be the spiritual man. None present more vividly man's recognition of the gulf that divides him from God and the effort of faith to lay hold on the miracle by which Christianity declares that the gulf has been bridged.

Donne's art in writing them was to seem 'to use no art at all'. His language has the ring of a living voice, admonishing his own soul, expostulating with his Maker, defying Death, or pouring itself out in supplication. He creates, as much as in some of the *Songs and Sonnets*, the illusion of a present experience, throwing his stress on such words as 'now' and 'here' and 'this'. And, as often there, he gives an extreme emphasis to the personal pronouns:

> Take mee to you, imprison mee, for I
> Except you'enthrall mee, never shall be free,
> Nor ever chast, except you ravish mee.

The plain unadorned speech, with its idiomatic turns, its rapid questions, its exclamatory Oh's and Ah's, wrests the movement of the sonnet to its own movement. The line is weighted with heavy monosyllables, or lengthened by heavy secondary stresses, which demand the same emphasis as the main stress takes. It may be stretched out to

> All of whom warre, dearth, age, agues, tyrannies,

after it has been contracted to

> From death, you numberlesse infinities.

Many lines can be reduced to ten syllables only by a more drastic use of elision than Donne allowed himself elsewhere, except in the *Satires*; and others, if we are to trust the best manuscripts, are a syllable short and fill out the line by a pause. This dramatic language has a magic that is unanalysable: words, movement, and feeling have a unity in which no element outweighs the other.

The effect of completely natural speech is achieved by exploiting to the full the potentialities of the sonnet.[2] The formal distinction of octave and sestet becomes a dramatic contrast. The openings of Donne's sestets are as dramatic as the openings of the sonnets themselves: impatient as in

Why doth the devill then usurpe in mee?

or gentle as in

Yet grace, if thou repent, thou canst not lacke;

or imploring as in

But let them sleepe, Lord, and mee mourne a space.

Though the *turn* in each of these is different, in all three there is that sudden difference in tension that makes a change dramatic. Donne avoids also the main danger of the couplet ending: that it may seem an afterthought, or an addition, or a mere summary. His final couplets, whether separate or running on from the preceding line, are true rhetorical climaxes, with the weight of the poem behind them. Except for Hopkins, no poet has crammed more into the sonnet than Donne. In spite of all the liberties he takes with his line, he succeeds in the one essential of the sonnet: he appears to need exactly fourteen lines to say exactly what he has to say. Donne possibly chose the sonnet form as appropriate for a set of formal meditations, but both in meditation and in the writing of his sonnets he converts traditional material to his own use. He was not, I believe, aiming at originality, and therefore the originality of the 'Holy Sonnets' is the more profound.

With the exception of 'The Lamentations of Jeremy', in which Donne, like so many of his contemporaries, but with more success than most, attempted the unrewarding task of paraphrasing the Scriptures, the remainder of the *Divine Poems* are occasional. The poem 'Upon the Annunciation and Passion' is very near in mood and style to '*La Corona*'. As there, Donne writes with strict objectivity. He contemplates two mysteries which are facets of one supreme mystery, and tries to express what any Christian might feel. On the other hand, 'Good Friday, Riding Westward' is a highly personal poem: a free, discursive meditation arising out of a particular situation. The elaborate preliminary conceit of the contrary motions of the heavenly bodies extends itself into astronomical images, until the recollection of the Passion sweeps away all thoughts but penitence. As in some of the finest of the *Songs and Sonnets*, Donne draws out an initial conceit to its limit in order, as it seems, to throw it away when "to brave clearness all things are reduc'd'. What he first sees

2. As in '*La Corona*', Donne keeps to two rhymes in the octave, and varies his sestet, using either *cddcee* or *cdcdee*. No general plan governs his choice here of which type of sestet he uses.

as an incongruity—his turning his back on his crucified Saviour—he comes to see as perhaps the better posture, and finally as congruous for a sinner. The poem hinges on the sudden apostrophe:

> and thou look'st towards mee,
> O Saviour, as thou hang'st upon the tree.

After this, discursive meditation contracts itself to penitent prayer. The mounting tension of the poem—from leisurely speculation, through the imagination kindled by 'that spectacle of too much weight for mee', to passionate humility—makes it a dramatic monologue. So also does the sense it gives us of a second person present—the silent figure whose eyes the poet feels watching him as he rides away to the west.

'Good Friday' is the last divine poem Donne wrote before his ordination and it points forward to the Hymns. They also arise from particular situations, are free, not formal meditations, and have the same unforced feeling. They are the only lyrics among the *Divine Poems*, and it is not only in their use of the pun and conceit that they remind us of the *Songs and Sonnets*. They have the spontaneity which '*La Corona*' and 'A Litany' lack, without the overemphasis of the 'Holy Sonnets'. In them Donne's imagination has room for play. Each sprang from a moment of crisis. The 'Hymn to Christ' was written on the eve of his journey overseas with Doncaster, a journey from which, as his Valediction Sermon shows, he felt he might not return. It is a finer treatment of the subject of the sonnet written after his wife's death in the Westmoreland manuscript. While the sonnet is general and reflective, in the.Hymn his imagination is fired by his immediate circumstances and he translates his thoughts into striking and moving symbols. The 'Hymn to God the Father' was written, according to Walton, during Donne's grave illness of 1623, and the 'Hymn to God my God, in my sickness', whether it should be dated during the same illness or in 1631, was written when he thought himself at the point of death. In both the conclusion is the same: 'So, in his purple wrapp'd receive mee Lord', and 'Sweare by thy selfe'. Donne's earliest poem on religion, the third Satire, ended with the words 'God himselfe to trust', and it is fitting that what is possibly his last divine poem, and certainly one of his best known, should end with the memory of the promise to Abraham, the type of the faithful.[3] For the *Divine Poems* are poems of faith, not of vision. Donne goes by a road which is not lit by any flashes of ecstasy, and in the words he had carved on his tomb 'aspicit Eum cujus nomen est Oriens'. The absence of ecstasy makes his divine poems so different from his love poems. There is an ecstasy of joy and an ecstasy of grief in his love poetry; in his divine

3. Cf. Gen. xxii. 15: 'By myself have I sworn, saith the Lord'; and Heb. vi. 13–18: 'For when God made promise to Abraham, because he could swear by no greater, he sware by himself. . . . For men verily swear by the greater: and an oath for confirmation is to them an end of all strife. Wherein God, willing more abundantly to shew unto the heirs of promise the immutability of his counsel, confirmed it by an oath: that by two immutable things, in which it was impossible for God to lie, we might have a strong consolation, who have fled for refuge to lay hold upon the hope set before us.'

poetry we are conscious almost always of an effort of will. In the 'Holy Sonnets' there is passion and longing, and in the Hymns some of the 'modest assurance' which Walton attributed to Donne's last hours, but there is no rapture.

* * *

The meditation is a very old religious exercise. Its essence is an attempt to stimulate devotion by the use of the imagination. The method of meditation was systematized in the sixteenth century by St. Ignatius Loyola, whose *Exercitia Spiritualia* was printed with Papal approval in 1548. A meditation on the Ignatian pattern, employing the 'three powers of the soul', consists of a brief preparatory prayer, two 'preludes,' a varying number of points, and a colloquy. The preparatory prayer is 'to ask God our Lord for grace that all my intentions, actions and operations may be ordered purely to the service and praise of His divine Majesty'.[4] The first prelude is what is called the *compositio loci*: the seeing 'with the eyes of the imagination' either a place 'such as the Temple or the mountain where Jesus Christ is found', or, if the meditation is of an invisible thing such as sin, a situation: 'that my soul is imprisoned in this corruptible body, and my whole compound self in this vale [of misery] as in exile amongst brute beasts.' The second prelude is a petition 'according to the subject matter'; thus, if the meditation is of the Passion, the petition will be for 'sorrow, tears, and fellowship with Christ in his sufferings'; if the meditation is of sin, the petition will be for 'shame'. The meditation proper follows, divided into points, usually three or five. Lastly, the memory, the storehouse of images, having been engaged in the preludes, and the reason in the points, the third power of the soul, the will, is employed in the colloquy, which is a free outpouring of the devotion aroused.

The Ignatian method can be applied to any topic and was widely popular. Donne, with his Jesuit uncles, his pious mother, and his tutors who were of her faith, must have been familiar as a boy and young man with systematic meditation. His teachers probably took the advice of St. Peter of Alcantara, who taught that beginners should specially practice two kinds of meditation: on the Last Things, 'which like sharpe prickes doe spurre us on to the love and feare of God', and on the life and Passion of our Lord, 'which is the springe and fountaine of all our good'.[5] Donne begins his set of sonnets on the Last Things in the proper manner with a preparatory prayer. In the octave of the first sonnet he recollects himself, remembers his creation and redemption and that he has received

4. Quotations are taken from *The Spiritual Exercises*, translated from the Spanish with a Commentary, by W. H. Longridge, S.S.J.E. (1930).

5. See *A Golden Treatise of Mental Prayer*, translated by G. W. (Brussels, 1632), pp. 6–8. The original was written about 1558. St. Peter provides two sets of seven meditations to be used either on the mornings and evenings of one week, or in successive weeks. The first set are on Sin, the Miseries of Life, Death, the Judgement, Hell, Heaven, the Blessings of God; the second on the events of the Passion, the Resurrection, and Ascension. Similar sets can be found in another popular book of devotion: *The Exercise of a Christian Life*, by the Italian Jesuit, Gaspar Loarte, written in 1569 and translated into English in 1584.

the gift of the Holy Spirit; in the sestet he laments the power of the devil upon him and asks for grace. The next three sonnets show very clearly the two preludes of a meditation, which correspond neatly to the two parts of a sonnet: the *compositio loci* occupying the octave, and the 'petition according to the subject' the sestet. In his second sonnet, where he imagines himself dangerously ill, Donne uses a pair of vivid images to make himself realize the situation. He is here doing what St. Ignatius advised in the 'Additions for the purpose of helping the exercitant to make the Exercises better':

> setting before myself examples, e.g. as if a knight were to find himself in the presence of his king and all his court, covered with shame and confusion because he has grievously offended him from whom he has first received many gifts and favours. Likewise in the second Exercise, considering myself a great sinner, bound with chains, and about to appear before the supreme eternal Judge, taking as an example how prisoners in chains, and worthy of death, appear before their temporal judge.

These examples, or 'congruous thoughts' as they are sometimes called, were regarded as an important element in meditation. Donne's pilgrim, who has done treason abroad, and his thief, who on the way to execution longs for the prison from which he had wished to be delivered, are excellent examples of 'congruous thoughts'. These brief, vivid, realistic images from human life are very characteristic of 'Holy Sonnets', which show none of that elaboration of a simile or an analogy into a conceit which is characteristic of the *Songs and Sonnets.* After imagining the sick man's predicament, Donne in the sestet draws out the moral: that grace will follow repentance, and that grace is needed to repent. This is hardly a petition, though it comes near to one; but in the third and fourth sonnets a true 'petition according to the subject' follows a brilliant first prelude. In the third sonnet, the actual moment of death is imagined and the prayer is for a 'safe issue' from death. In the fourth, the *compositio loci* is a picture of the Last Judgement, when those who have met death in such diverse ways and distant ages rise together at the Trump; this is followed by the petition to the Lord to delay the summons and teach a present repentance. The fifth sonnet, on the other hand, has no *compositio loci*—its octave is more like a 'point' drawn out from a meditation on hell—though its sestet contains a striking petition; while the sixth, the sonnet to Death, is only linked to the others by its subject; in manner and temper it is quite undevotional. This is what we should expect with Donne, who always as he writes develops his material in his own way. He is a poet using for his own purposes various elements from a familiar tradition; not a pious versifier, turning common material into rhyme.

The last six sonnets of the twelve printed in 1633 depend less on the preludes of the Ignatian meditation than on the colloquy. They serve the purpose of the second set of meditations suggested by St. Peter of Alcantara and others, in that they fix the mind on the saving love of God in Christ; but they handle the subject with the discursive freedom of a colloquy. The eleventh sonnet, the 'wholsome meditation', which along with the twelfth appears to have been Donne's original pendant to his set on the Last Things, recalls the colloquy with which St. Ignatius concludes the first exercise, on sins:

> Imagining Christ our Lord present before me on the Cross, to make a colloquy with Him, asking Him how it is that being the Creator, He has come to make Himself man, and from eternal life has come to temporal death, and in this manner to die for my sins. Again, reflecting on myself, to ask what have I done for Christ, what am I doing for Christ, what ought I to do for Christ. Then beholding Him in such a condition, and thus hanging upon the Cross, to make the reflections which may present themselves.

In these last sonnets, the influence of the meditation is felt, not in the structure of the sonnets, but in such things as the vivid sense of the actualities of the Passion in 'Spit in my face', the imagining of the face of Christ on the Cross in 'What if this present were the worlds last night', and the use of 'congruous thoughts' in this last sonnet and in the one that follows it, 'Batter my heart'.

The four penitential sonnets are less obviously meditations, because their subject is an invisible thing, sin. There is, therefore, less scope for a recognizable *compositio loci.* In the order in which they are printed here they form a brief sequence, beginning with the regular preparatory prayer. The sonnet which I have placed second, 'I am a little world', is a general meditation, with a very short *compositio loci,* in which Donne reminds himself, as St. Ignatius advised in meditating on sin, that both body and soul are given over to sin. This is followed by a long second prelude asking for repentance. The sonnet which I have placed third, 'O might those sighes and teares', specifies a particular sin, 'sufferance', in the sense of indulgence in excessive and misdirected grief. Its particularity makes it more suitably follow than precede the sonnet on sin in general. It also leads on to the last, 'If faithful soules be alike glorifi'd', which develops a subsidiary point, arising out of the likeness and contrast between the tears he shed as a lover and the tears he sheds as a penitent: tears may be the signs of many kinds of grief, and only God, the giver of true grief, can know if grief is true. The four sonnets are closely linked together. It is the sin in his 'feebled flesh' that weighs him down in the opening prayer, 'lust and envie' that have burned his little world in the second sonnet: indulgence which has caused him mourning that he mourns in the third. The meditation on sin is the opening exercise of the *Spiritual Exercises* and Donne develops the subject on the lines suggested there. But here again he writes with the freedom of a poet whose imagination is not tied to an initial plan. The second sonnet has only a very short *compositio loci*; the third expands the *compositio* to fill the whole sonnet, which is wholly given up to the imagining of his predicament and contains no petition; while the fourth has no relation to the form of a meditation, but is an individual moralization, containing neither *compositio* nor petition.

The influence of the formal meditation lies behind the 'Holy Sonnets', not as a literary source, but as a way of thinking, a method of prayer. Mr. Louis Martz has recently shown that the Ignatian method of meditating by points and the use of parallel sets of meditations for mornings and evenings of a week provided Donne with the structure of the two *Anniversaries*.[6] That such different works as the 'Holy Sonnets' and the *Anniversaries* can be shown to depend on the same exercise points to real familiarity with the method. When we are genuinely familiar with something we can use it with freedom for our own purposes. There is no need to feel surprise that Donne, at a time when he was engaged in bitter controversy with the Jesuits, should be drawing on Jesuit spirituality in his poetry, and presumably had continued to use a Jesuit method of prayer. He would be making a distinction here which Protestants made without difficulty—taking the corn and leaving the chaff. At the close of the sixteenth century perfectly orthodox Protestant works of devotion made use of contemporary Catholic devotional works, inspired by the Jesuit revival. Many Protestants felt that, in the bitter theological controversies of the time, the Christian life of prayer and devotion was in danger of perishing. They could not recommend the great medieval works of devotion, for these were almost all written for members of religious communities, and Protestants rejected the life of the cloister. But books such as Loarte's *The Exercise of a Christian Life*, which in its Protestant English dress converted Robert Greene, were, with judicious pruning, easily made suitable for devout Protestants.[7]

As in '*La Corona*' and 'A Litany', so in the 'Holy Sonnets', Donne is using as the material of his poetry ways of devotion he had learnt as a child. We have not accounted for the 'Holy Sonnets' if we say that he wanted to write sets of meditations in sonnet form, any more than we have accounted for *Paradise Lost* if we say that Milton wished to write a classical epic on a Christian subject. But recognition of a poet's conscious intentions takes us some way towards appreciation of his achievement, and can save us from too simple a correlation between the experience of the poet and his translation of it into poetry.

6. See Louis L. Martz, 'John Donne in Meditation: the *Anniversaries*' (*E. L. H.*, December 1947). It was after I had come to my own conclusions on the date and origins of the 'Holy Sonnets' that I read Mr. Martz's article. It was encouraging to find that we had independently arrived at similar conclusions with such different poems.

7. See Helen C. White, 'Some Continuing Traditions in English Devotional Literature' (*P.M.L.A.* lxvii, 1942, pp. 966–80). The one medieval work which never lost its hold was the *Imitation of Christ*, which as Miss White rightly points out is the most deeply Scriptural of devotional works. This, for Protestants, outweighed the fact that it is impregnated with the spirit of the cloister.

LOUIS L. MARTZ

[Donne's "Holy Sonnets" and "Good Friday, 1613"] †

What I should like to stress at this point is the way in which the total movement of these poems [of Southwell] resembles, in its rudiments, the "intellectual, argumentative evolution" of Donne's or Herbert's poetry: the "strain of passionate, paradoxical reasoning which knits the first line to the last," and performs this knitting through close analysis and elaboration of concrete imagery. Southwell seems to be struggling toward the qualities that Hutchinson has thus accurately described as the dominant characteristic of Herbert: "Almost any poem of his has its object well defined; its leading idea is followed through with economy and brought to an effective conclusion, the imagery which runs through it commonly helping to knit it together." Southwell's poems give that impression of a "predetermined plan" which Palmer has noted as a characteristic of many of Herbert's poems,[1] and which is also, I think, a strong characteristic of Donne's. May it not be that all three poets are working, to some extent, under the influence of methods of meditation that led toward the deliberate evolution of a threefold structure of composition (memory), analysis (understanding), and colloquy (affections, will)?

The "Holy Sonnets" seem to bear out this conjecture. Holy Sonnet 12 bears a very close resemblance to the conclusion of St. Ignatius Loyola's second exercise for the First Week, a "meditation upon sins," where the fifth and last point is:

> an exclamation of wonder, with intense affection, running through all creatures in my mind, how they have suffered me to live, and have preserved me in life; how the angels, who are the sword of the Divine Justice, have borne with me, and have guarded and prayed for me; how the saints have been interceding and praying for me; and the heavens, the sun, the moon, the stars, and the elements, the fruits of the earth, the birds, the fishes, and the animals; and the earth, how it is it has not opened to swallow me up. . . .
>
> The whole to conclude with a colloquy of mercy, reasoning and giving thanks to God our Lord, for having given me life till now, and proposing through His grace to amend henceforward. (pp. 24–5)[2]

In Sonnet 12 this problem, simply and firmly proposed in the opening line, is elaborated with a single, scientific instance in the first quatrain:

† From Louis L. Martz, *The Poetry of Meditation*, copyright 1954. Pp. 43–56. Reprinted by permission of the publishers, The Yale University Press.

1. *The Works of George Herbert*, ed. F. E. Hutchinson (2nd ed., Oxford Clarendon Press, 1945), p. xlix; *The English Works of George Herbert*, ed. George Herbert Palmer (3 vols., Boston and New York, Houghton Mifflin, 1905), I, 142.

2. *The Text of the Spiritual Exercises of St. Ignatius, Translated from the Original Spanish*, with preface by John Morris (4th ed., Westminster, Md., 1943).

Why are wee by all creatures waited on?
Why doe the prodigall elements supply
Life and food to mee, being more pure then I,
Simple, and further from corruption?

The problem is then examined in greater detail through a shift to direct questioning of the animals, which runs through the next six lines:

Why brook'st thou, ignorant horse, subjection?
Why dost thou bull, and bore so seelily
Dissemble weaknesse, and by'one mans stroke die,
Whose whole kinde, you might swallow and feed upon?
Weaker I am, woe is mee, and worse then you,
You have not sinn'd, nor need be timorous.

The "colloquy of mercy" then appears to follow, as the speaker addresses himself, the representative of all mankind, "reasoning," developing the sense of "wonder," and implicity "giving thanks":

But wonder at a greater wonder, for to us
Created nature doth these things subdue,
But their Creator, whom sin, nor nature tyed,
For us, his Creatures, and his foes, hath dyed.

Puente's development of this Ignatian topic will provide, perhaps, a more convincing proof of our argument for Jesuit influence here:

> The fourth pointe, shall bee, to breake out with these considerations into an exclamation, with an affection vehement, and full of amazement; As, that the creatures have suffered me, I having so grievously offended their Creator, and benefactor. . . . That the elements, the birdes of the aire, the fishes of the sea, the beastes, the plantes of the earthe have helped to sustaine mee. I confesse that I deserve not the breade I eate, nor the water I drinke, nor the aire I breathe in: neither am I worthy to lift up myne eyes to heaven. . . . (1, 70–1)[3]

At the same time, it seems that Holy Sonnet 15 bears some general relation to St. Ignatius' "Contemplation for obtaining love," a special meditation, annexed to the Fourth Week, which aims at achieving "an interior knowledge of the many and great benefits I have received, that, thoroughly grateful, I may in all things love and serve His Divine Majesty." The meditation opens by calling to mind

> the benefits received, of my creation, redemption, and particular gifts, dwelling with great affection on how much God our Lord had done for me, and how much He has given me of that which He has; and consequently, how much He desires to give me Himself

3. Luis de la Puente, *Meditations upon the Mysteries of our Holie Faith, with the Practice of Mental Prayer touching the same,* [trans. John Heigham], (2 vols., St. Omer, 1619). The original work appeared in 1605.

> in so far as He can according to His Divine ordinance; and then to reflect in myself what I, on my side, with great reason and justice, ought to offer and give to His Divine Majesty. (pp. 74–5)

This seems to be exactly what the speaker is so deliberately telling himself to do in Sonnet 15:

> Wilt thou love God, as he thee! then digest,
> My Soule, this wholsome meditation,
> How God the Spirit, by Angels waited on
> In heaven, doth make his Temple in thy brest.
> The Father having begot a Sonne most blest,
> And still begetting, (for he ne'r begonne)
> Hath deign'd to chuse thee by adoption,
> Coheire to'his glory, 'and Sabbaths endlesse rest.
> And as a robb'd man, which by search doth finde
> His stolne stuffe sold, must lose or buy'it againe:
> The Sonne of glory came downe, and was slaine,
> Us whom he'had made, and Satan stolne, to unbinde.
> 'Twas much, that man was made like God before,
> But, that God should be made like man, much more.

In lines 3 and 4 there may be a reminiscence of a part of the "second point" of this exercise, where one is advised to "consider how God dwells in creatures . . . and so in me, giving me being, life, feeling, and causing me to understand: making likewise of me a temple. . . ." But the resemblances are only general, and of course the sonnet does not trace the progress of a complete exercise: it is analysis only, understanding; part of a complete exercise.

This, I believe, is what we should expect to find in most of the "Holy Sonnets" (and in most of the other religious poems of the time related to the art of meditation): a portion of an exercise which has been set down in explicit poetry; especially the colloquy, in which the "three powers" fuse, become incandescent, as Fray Luis de Granada says: "When we talke unto almightie God, then the understanding mounteth up on highe, and after it followeth also the will, and then hath a man commonly on his parte greater devotion, and attention, and greater feare, and reverence of the majestie of almightie God, with whom he speaketh. . . ." (p. 309)[4] The complete exercise was long—an hour or more in duration—and its deliberate, predominantly intellectual method would not, for most of its course, provide material for poetry. Now and then a poet might recapitulate an exercise in miniature, or compose a poem that developed under the impulse of his frequent practice of the stages in a full sequence; but more often we should expect the poetry to reflect chiefly the final stages of the sequence. Furthermore, the formal procedure for a full exercise was not by any means necessarily followed on

4. *Of Prayer and Meditation*, [trans. Richard Hopkins], (Douay, 1612).

every occasion. All the meditative treatises explain that this full framework is provided as an aid for beginners or as a method to fall back upon in times of spiritual dryness. Even the Jesuit exercises, which might appear to prescribe the most rigorous of all plans, are actually very flexible, for St. Ignatius expects them to be performed under the direction of a priest who will adapt them to the needs and capacities of each individual. Adepts in meditation are encouraged, both by the Jesuits and by other writers, to follow the lead of their affections. Thus we find Tomás de Villacastín warning that "the infinite goodness and liberality of God is not tyed to these rules" (p. 55)[5]; Fray Luis de Granada explaining that he has set down "diverse and sundrie poyntes, to the intent, that emonge so great varietie of considerations, everie one might make his choice of such thinges, as might best serve his devotion" (p. 49); and St. François de Sales urging the reader to "take this for a generall rule, never to restraine, or with-hold thy affections once inflamed with any devout motion, but let them have their free course." (p. 138)[6]

In accordance with this freedom of procedure we find that colloquies may be made not at the end of the set sequence but at any time during an exercise: indeed, the Jesuit Gibbons says "it will be best, and almost needful so to do" (§2, ¶25)[7]; and Puente proves the point by scattering colloquies frequently throughout the course of his meditations. In these colloquies of Puente we find something very close to the tone and manner of Donne's religious poetry: subtle theological analysis, punctuated with passionate questions and exclamations:

> O my soule, heare what this our Lord saieth: Which of you can dwell with devouring fier? O who shallbee able to dwell in these perpetuall ardours? If thou darest not touche the light fier of this life, why doest thou not tremble at the terrible fier of the other? Contemplate this fier with attention, that the feare thereof may consume the fier of thy insatiable desire, if thorough thy want of fervent zeale, the fier of God's love bee not sufficient to consume them. (1,144)

> O God of vengeance, how is it that thou hast not revenged thy selfe on a man so wicked as I? How hast thou suffred mee so long a time? Who hath withhelde the rigour of thy justice, that it should not punish him, that hath deserve[d] so terrible punishment? O my Soule, how is it, that thou doest not feare, and tremble, considering the dreadefull judgement of God against his Angells? If with so great severitye hee punished creatures so noble, why should not so vile, and miserable a creature as thou, feare the like punishment? O my Soule, how is it, that thou doest not feare, and tremble,

5. A *Manual of Devout Meditations and Exercises* . . . [trans. H. More], (St. Omer, 1618). The original appeared c. 1610.

6. *An Introduction to a Devoute Life*, [trans. John Yakesley], (3rd ed., Rouen, 1614).

7. Richard Gibbons, "The Practical Methode of Meditation," prefixed to Gibbons' translation: *An Abridgement of Meditations of the Life, Passion, Death and Resurrection of our Lord and Saviour Jesus Christ* . . . [St. Omer], 1614.

> considering the dreadefull judgement of God against his Angells? If with so great severitye hee punished creatures so noble, why should not so vile, and miserable a creature as thou, feare the like punishment? O most powerful creator, seeing thou hast shewed thy selfe to mee not a God of vengeance, but a father of mercye, continue towardes mee this thy mercye, pardonning my sinnes, and delivering mee from hell, which most justly for them I have deserved. (1, 55)

More specific similarities are found in the passage where Puente urges that in addressing colloquies to God, or Christ, or the Trinity we should offer "titles and reasons, that may move them to graunt us what wee demand." In Christ, he says, we may claim such titles as his sufferings and his love,

> Sometimes speaking to the eternall Father, beseeching him to heare mee for the Love of his Sonne; for the Services hee did him; and the Paines that for his love hee endured. Other times speaking to the Sonne of God: alledging unto him the love that hee bare us, the Office that hee holdeth of our Redeemer, and Advocate; and the greate Price that wee cost him. . . .
>
> Other Titles there are on the part of our Necessitye, and Miserye, alledging before our Lord; like *David*, that wee were conceived in Sinne, that wee have disordered passions, strong enemies . . . and that without him wee are able to doe nothing. That we are his Creatures made according to his owne Image, and Likenesse, and that for this cause the devill persecuteth us to destroye us, and that therefore it appertayneth to him to protect us. (1, 4–5)

Donne's Sonnet 2 certainly looks like a colloquy stemming from such advice as this:

> As due by many titles I resigne
> My selfe to thee, O God, first I was made
> By thee, and for thee, and when I was decay'd
> Thy blood bought that, the which before was thine;
> I am thy sonne, made with thy selfe to shine,
> Thy servant, whose paines thou hast still repaid,
> Thy sheepe, thine Image, and, till I betray'd
> My selfe, a temple of thy Spirit divine;
> Why doth the devill then usurpe on mee?
> Why doth he steale, nay ravish that's thy right?
> Except thou rise and for thine owne worke fight,
> Oh I shall soone despaire, when I doe see
> That thou lov'st mankind well, yet wilt'not chuse me,
> And Satan hates mee, yet is loth to lose mee.

Such general or fragmentary parallels between Donne's poetry and Jesuit methods of meditation are strongly supported by the fact that at least four of the "Holy Sonnets" appear to display, in their total movement, the method of a total exercise: they suggest the "premeditation" or the recapitulation, in miniature, of such an exercise; or, at least, a poetical structure modeled on the stages of a complete exercise. Such a threefold structure, of course, easily accords with the traditional 4-4-6 division of the Petrarchan sonnet, and thus provides a particularly interesting illustration of the way in which poetical tradition may be fertilized and developed by the meditative tradition. Perhaps the clearest example is found in Holy Sonnet 11, which suggests the traditional meditative procedure briefly described by Antonio de Molina: ' Thus when we see our Saviour taken prisoner, and used so ill, whipped and nayled on the Crosse; we must consider that we be there present amongst those villaines, and that our sinnes be they who so abuse him, and take away his life";[8] and developed with dramatic detail by Puente:

> Then I am to set before mine eyes Christ Jesus crucified, beholding his heade crowned with thornes; his face spit upon; his eyes obscured; his armes disioincted; his tongue distasted with gall, and vineger; his handes, and feete peerced with nailes; his backe, and shoulders torne with whippes; and his side opened with a launce: and then pondering that hee suffereth all this for my sinnes, I will drawe sundrye affections from the inwardest parte of my heart, sometimes trembling at the rigour of God's iustice . . . sometimes bewailing my sinnes which were the cause of these dolours: and sometimes animating myselfe to suffer somewhat in satisfaction of myne offences, seeing Christ our Lord suffered so much to redeeme them. And finally I will beg pardon of him for them, alledging to him for a reason, all his troubles, and afflictions, saying unto him in amorous colloquie.
>
> O my most sweete Redeemer, which descendest from heaven, and ascendest this Crosse to redeeme men, paying their sinnes with thy dolours, I present myselfe before thy Majestie, grieved that my grievous sinnes have been the cause of thy terrible paines. Upon mee, O Lord, these chastizements had been iustlie imployed, for I am hee that sinned, and not upon thee that never sinnedst. Let that love that moved thee to put thyselfe upon the Crosse for mee, move thee to pardon mee what I have committed against thee. (1, 59–60)

Similarly, in Donne's sonnet, the speaker has made himself vividly present at the scene, so dramatically conscious of his sins that he cries out to Christ's persecutors in lines that throw a colloquial emphasis on the words "my," "mee," and "I":

> Spit in my face, you Jewes, and pierce my side,
> Buffet, and scoffe, scourge, and crucifie mee,

8. Antonio de Molina, A *Treatise of Mental Prayer*, [trans. J. Sweetman], ([St. Omer], 1617), pp. 60–1. The original appeared in 1615.

For I have sinn'd, and sinn'd, and onely hee,
Who could do no iniquitie hath dyed:

but after this passionate outcry the tone of the next quatrain shifts to one of tense, muted, intellectual brooding, as the understanding explores the theological significance of the scene:

But by my death can not be satisfied
My sinnes, which passe the Jewes impiety:
They kill'd once an inglorious man, but I
Crucifie him daily, being now glorified.

And then, with another marked shift in tone, the speaker turns to draw forth in himself the appropriate "affections," suffusing intellectual analysis with the emotions of love and wonder:

Oh let me then, his strange love still admire:
Kings pardon, but he bore our punishment.
And *Iacob* came cloth'd in vile harsh attire
But to supplant, and with gainfull intent:
God cloth'd himselfe in vile mans flesh, that so
Hee might be weake enough to suffer woe.

Likewise, in the first quatrain of Sonnet 7 we may see the dramatic operations of both imagination and memory, for here the speaker remembers the description of Doomsday in the book of Revelation, especially the opening of the seventh chapter: "I saw four angels standing on the four corners of the earth"; and he cries out, seeing them there in a vivid composition of place:

At the round eaths imagin'd corners, blow
Your trumpets, Angells, and arise, arise
From death, you numberlesse infinities
Of soules, and to your scattred bodies goe. . . .

With the "matter" of the meditation thus "composed" and defined, the understanding then performs its analysis in the second quatrain, "discoursing" upon the causes of death throughout human history: a summary of sin and a reminder of its consequences:

All whom the flood did, and fire shall o'erthrow,
All whom warre, dearth, age, agues, tyrannies,
Despaire, law, chance, hath slaine, and you whose eyes,
Shall behold God, and never tast deaths woe.

Finally, in the sestet, the will expresses its "affections" and "petitions" in colloquy with God, "as one friend speaks to another, or as a servant to his master":

But let them sleepe, Lord, and mee mourne a space,
For, if above all these, my sinnes abound,
'Tis late to aske abundance of thy grace,

When wee are there; here on this lowly ground,
Teach mee how to repent; for that's as good
As if thou'hadst seal'd my pardon, with thy blood.

"When wee are there"—those words which so puzzled I. A. Richards' students[9] may be explained if we realize that this is part of a traditional colloquy with God after a visualization of the Day of Doom. "Wee," though no doubt including all sinners, suggest primarily God and the individual speaker's soul; "there" refers to the throne of Judgement in the heavens, as presented in the book of Revelation; "there" is thus in sharp contrast with the "lowly ground" where the soul now prays for grace, with theological overtones relating to the Catholic sacrament of Penance.

Somewhat the same procedure appears also to be operating in Holy Sonnet 9, where an example of Donne's besetting sin of intellectual pride is "proposed" in an audacious, blasphemous evasion of responsibility:

If poysonous mineralls, and if that tree,
Whose fruit threw death on else immortall us,
If lecherous goats, if serpents envious
Cannot be damn'd; Alas; why should I bee?

The problem thus set forth concretely is then pursued abstractly in the second quatrain, which reveals the speaker's knowledge of the proper theological answer to his question, but he continues the evasion and increases the blasphemy by first an implied ("borne in mee"), and then a direct, attack on God's justice:

Why should intent or reason, borne in mee,
Make sinnes, else equall, in mee more heinous?
And mercy being easie, and glorious
To God; in his sterne wrath, why threatens hee?

But at last, and very suddenly, the thin wall of this uneasy argument collapses and the poem concludes with one of Donne's most vehement colloquies, giving the answer that has been implicit and premeditated throughout:

But who am I, that dare dispute with thee
O God? Oh! of thine onely worthy blood,
And my teares, make a heavenly Lethean flood,
And drowne in it my sinnes blacke memorie;
That thou remember them, some claime as debt,
I thinke it mercy, if thou wilt forget.

9. I. A. Richards, *Practical Criticism* (New York, Harcourt, Brace, 1935), pp. 44–5. Miss Gardner would interpret this sonnet as developing in accordance with the two preludes of the Ignatian method, the octave giving the "composition" and the sestet the petition "according to the subject-matter." This seems to me a valid interpretation: since the whole progress of the exercise would have been "premeditated" and foreseen, the action of the "three powers" would be anticipated in the preludes. See her excellent analysis of this and other "Holy Sonnets" in John Donne, *The Divine Poems*, ed. Helen Gardner (Oxford, Clarendon Press, 1952), pp. l-liv.

And fourthly, with a slightly different division of lines, I believe that we can follow the same movement in Sonnet 5, which presents in its first four lines a "composition by similitude" defining precisely the "invisible" problem to be considered:

> I am a little world made cunningly
> Of Elements, and an Angelike spright,
> But black sinne hath betraid to endlesse night
> My worlds both parts, and (oh) both parts must die.

The next five lines form a unit overflowing the usual Petrarchan division; and appropriately, since the intellect is here using a mode of violent hyperbole:

> You which beyond that heaven which was most high
> Have found new sphears, and of new lands can write,
> Powre new seas in mine eyes, that so I might
> Drowne my world with my weeping earnestly,
> Or wash it, if it must be drown'd no more:

and then, inevitably, the last five lines, another firm unit, show the passionate outburst of the affections thus aroused, ending with a petition in colloquy with God:

> But oh it must be burnt! alas the fire
> Of lust and envie have burnt it heretofore,
> And made it fouler; Let their flames retire,
> And burne me ô Lord, with a fiery zeale
> Of thee and thy house, which doth in eating heale.[1]

We can see then why, as Grierson records, three manuscripts of the "Holy Sonnets" entitle them "Devine Meditations."[2] They are, in the most specific sense of the term, meditations, Ignatian meditations: providing strong evidence for the profound impact of early Jesuit training upon the later career of John Donne.

Finally, let us turn to examine the adumbrations of this method of meditation in one of Donne's longest, greatest religious poems, one for which, unlike the "Holy Sonnets," we can give the precise date and occasion: "Goodfriday, 1613. Riding Westward." The manuscript headings recorded by Grierson fill out our information: "Riding to Sr Edward Harbert in Wales"; "Mr J. Dun goeing from Sir H. G. on good friday sent him back this meditation on the way."[3] The first ten lines of this meditation form an elaborate, deliberately evolved "composition by similitude":

1. Cf. Puente, *1*, 88: "O most just judge, and most mercifull Father, I confesse that I am thorough my sinnes a blacke, and filthy cole, and halfe burnt with the fier of my passions, washe mee, o Lord, and whiten mee with the living water of thy grace, and therwith quenche this fier that burneth mee. . . ." Also Puente, *1*, 274: "in steede of drowning the worlde againe with another deluge; or burning it with fier like Sodom; hee [God] would drowne it with abundance of mercies, and burne it with the fier of his love. . . ."

2. *The Poems of John Donne*, ed. Herbert J. C. Grierson (2 vols., Oxford, Clarendon Press, 1912), *1*, 322.

3. *Idem*, *1*, 336.

Let mans Soule be a Spheare, and then, in this,
The intelligence that moves, devotion is,
And as the other Spheares, by being growne
Subject to forraigne motions, lose their owne,
And being by others hurried every day,
Scarce in a yeare their naturall forme obey:
Pleasure or businesse, so, our Soules admit
For their first mover, and are whirld by it.
Hence is't, that I am carryed towards the West
This day, when my Soules forme bends toward the East.

The composition has thus precisely set the problem: profane motives carry the soul away from God, while the soul's essence ("forme"), *devotion*, longs for another, greater object. The speaker then proceeds, by intellectual analysis, to develop (lines 11–32) this paradox of human perversity, by playing upon the idea that the speaker, in going West on human "pleasure or businesse," is turning his back upon the Cross. He is thus refusing to perform the devotion proper to the day; he is refusing, that is, to *see* the place and participate in its agony as if he were "really present":

There I should see a Sunne, by rising set,
And by that setting endlesse day beget;
But that Christ on this Crosse, did rise and fall,
Sinne had eternally benighted all.
Yet dare I'almost be glad, I do not see
That spectacle of too much weight for mee.
Who sees Gods face, that is selfe life, must dye;
What a death were it then to see God dye?

Nevertheless, in the very act of saying that he does not see these things, he develops the traditional paradoxes of the scene in lines that echo the meditative treatises:

Could I behold those hands which span the Poles,
And turne all spheares at once, peirc'd with those holes?
Could I behold that endlesse height which is
Zenith to us, and our Antipodes,
Humbled below us? or that blood which is
The seat of all our Soules, if not of his,
Made durt of dust, or that flesh which was worne
By God, for his apparell, rag'd, and torne?[4]

4. Cf. Luis de Granada, pp. 288–9: "Lift up thyne eies unto that holie roode, and consider all the woundes, and paines, that the Lorde of maiestie suffereth there for thy sake . . . Beholde that divine face (which the Angels are desirous to beholde) how disfigured it is, and overflowed with streames of bloude. . . .
"That goodly cleare forhead, and those eies more bewtifull than the Sunne, are now dimned and darkened with the bloude and presence of deathe. Those eares that are wonte to heare the songes of heaven, doe now heare the horrible blasphemies of synners. Those armes so well fashioned and so large that they embrace all the power of the worlde, are now disioynted, and stretched out upon the crosse. Those handes that created the heavens, and were never injurious to anie man, are now nayled and clenched fast with harde and sharpe nayles."

And next, as we should expect of one reared in the Catholic meditative tradition, he considers the sorrows of the Virgin:

> If on these things I durst not looke, durst I
> Upon his miserable mother cast mine eye,
> Who was Gods partner here, and furnish'd thus
> Halfe of that Sacrifice, which ransom'd us?

And now, with the analysis completed, the speaker ends his meditation, with perfect symmetry, in a ten-line colloquy which accords with the directions of St. Ignatius Loyola:

> Imagining Christ our Lord before us and placed on the Cross, to make a colloquy with Him . . . Again, to look at myself, asking what I have done for Christ, what I am doing for Christ, what I ought to do for Christ; and then seeing Him that which He is, and thus fixed to the Cross, to give expression to what shall present itself to my mind. (p. 23)

> Though these things, as I ride, be from mine eye,
> They'are present yet unto my memory,
> For that looks towards them; and thou look'st towards mee,
> O Saviour, as thou hang'st upon the tree;
> I turne my backe to thee, but to receive
> Corrections, till thy mercies bid thee leave.
> O thinke mee worth thine anger, punish mee,
> Burne off my rusts, and my deformity,
> Restore thine Image, so much, by thy grace,
> That thou may'st know mee, and I'll turne my face.

Thus similitude, visualization, theological analysis and the eloquent motions of the will have all fused into one perfectly executed design—a meditation expressing the state of devotion which results from the integration of the threefold Image of God: memory, understanding, will. And thus once again the process of meditation appears to have made possible a poem which displays this "articulated structure," this "peculiar blend of passion and thought":[5] the perfect equipoise of carefully regulated, arduously cultivated skill.

5. *Works of Herbert*, ed. Palmer, *I*, 140; *Metaphysical Lyrics and Poems*, ed. Herbert J. C. Grierson (Oxford, Clarendon Press, 1921), p. xvi.

STANLEY ARCHER

Meditation and the Structure of Donne's "Holy Sonnets" †

In recent years two important works dealing with Donne's "Holy Sonnets" have appeared. I am referring of course to Miss Gardner's edition of *The Divine Poems* and to *The Poetry of Meditation* by Professor Louis L. Martz. Mr. Martz moves far beyond the scope of Miss Gardner's critical work, tracing the meditative tradition in poetry throughout the seventeenth century. The chief accomplishments of Miss Gardner's work are a regrouping of the poems and a thorough annotation. It is interesting to note that both Miss Gardner and Professor Martz reached independently several conclusions in regard to the structure of the "Holy Sonnets":

1. Their structure was influenced by meditative literature or by the meditative tradition as it was expressed during the Counter Reformation, probably from the *Spiritual Exercises* of St. Ignatius Loyola.
2. Donne more than likely received such influence during his childhood from his family environment.
3. Such structure cannot be accounted for in the poetic tradition, but it is a result of a fusion of both the poetic and meditative traditions.

The evidence provided by these two important scholars of Donne in support of these conclusions is indeed impressive. And indeed one would ordinarily accept it without critical examination, thinking it naïve of him to imagine any longer that in the "Holy Sonnets" Donne is attempting to write poetry by anything other than the "predetermined plan" of the spiritual exercises.[1] However, in this instance, there is an interesting discrepancy in the way each writer demonstrates his hypothesis.

Professor Martz tells the reader that one need not expect to find an entire meditation according to the threefold Ignatian plan in many of the "Holy Sonnets," the reason for this being that the sonnets are short whereas the exercise covered a long period of time. Such poems correspond to merely a fragment of the meditation, usually the colloquy, or conclusion.[2] But as his chief internal evidence for relating the sonnets to the *Spiritual Exercises* he examines four sonnets which capture an entire exercise—Sonnets 11, 7, 9, and 5.[3] These and Sonnet 12 he

† From *English Literary History*, XXVIII (June, 1961), 137–47. Reprinted by permission of the publishers, The Johns Hopkins Press, and Stanley Archer.

1. See Louis L. Martz, *The Poetry of Meditation* (New Haven, 1955), p. 43.
2. *Ibid.*, p. 46.
3. Since Professor Martz uses Sir Herbert Grierson's grouping, and since I shall deal in more detail with his discussion, I have retained his numbering rather than Miss Gardner's.

separates into three parts to show their threefold structure corresponding to the three parts of the meditation.

Now let us examine what Miss Gardner says about these particular sonnets. Of Sonnet seven she writes:

> in the fourth [i.e., according to her grouping] the *composito loci* is a picture of the Last Judgment; . . . this is followed by the petition to the Lord to delay the summons and teach a present repentance.[4]

It is clear that she does not stress the threefold structure emphasized by Professor Martz, but rather sees the meditation as twofold. But she does agree that this is a meditative sonnet. Of Sonnet nine she writes:

> The fifth sonnet, on the other hand, has no *composito loci*—its octave is more like a 'point' drawn out from a meditation on hell.[5]

She adds that in this sonnet Donne has taken great liberty with the material of meditation. But of Sonnets eleven and twelve she writes:

> The last six sonnets of the twelve printed in 1633 depend less on the preludes of the Ignatian meditation than on the colloquy. They serve the purpose of the second set of meditations of St. Peter of Alcantra and others, in that they fix the mind on the saving love of God in Christ; but they handle the subject with the discursive freedom of the colloquy.
>
> In these last sonnets the influence of meditation is felt, not in the structure of the sonnets, but in such things as the vivid sense of the actualities of the Passion in "Spit in my face." . . .[6]

It will be remembered that Professor Martz demonstrates the threefold structure of the meditation in two of these very sonnets. The last sonnet used by Professor Martz Miss Gardner styles a "general meditation, with a very short *compositio loci*."[7]

Thus we note that two scholars, in applying the same hypothesis, have arrived at dissimilar conclusions. The difference seems to lie in the concept of the meditative process as held by each. From this one gathers that varied conclusions may be reached, according to which meditative writer influences the critic. When ideas about a work of art bear such diverse results, there is some warrant for a re-examination of the evidence which led to the idea.

Since Professor Martz examines the question at greater length than does Miss Gardner, it is necessary to examine his discussion in some detail. He conjectures that Donne was influenced by the structure of the meditation and notes, "The 'Holy Sonnets' seem to bear out this conjec-

4. Helen Gardner, ed., John Donne: *The Divine Poems* (Oxford, 1952), p. lii.
5. *Ibid.*
6. *Ibid.*, p. liii.
7. *Ibid.*

ture."[8] Before the examination is complete this statement takes on enormous proportions:

> They [the "Holy Sonnets"] are, in the most specific sense of the term, meditations. Ignatian meditations: providing strong evidence for the profound impact of early Jesuit training upon the later career of John Donne.[9]

The reader is not unprepared for such a conclusion. Professor Martz has reminded us, as did Miss Gardner, of Donne's Jesuit uncles, his Catholic upbringing, and his own statement about the influence of his early training. Meditative literature was popular during Donne's day, and there can be little doubt that in his delving into theology Donne read a good deal of it. It will be necessary to return to this evidence later on. Now I shall consider another matter concerning Professor Martz's argument.

From his analogy between Donne and Joyce,[1] Mr. Martz apparently does not believe that Donne was consciously copying the structure of a meditation in many of the sonnets, since only a few of the sonnets follow this structure. In others there is matter unsuitable for formal meditation,[2] as in the second quatrain of "If Poysonious Mineralls" in which Donne with the intellect imagines that God's decrees are unjust. But Mr. Martz points out that the threefold structure of certain ones of the sonnets is analogous to that of the Ignatian meditation, as found in the *Meditation upon the Mysteries of our Holie Faith, with the Practise of Mental Prayer touching the same* by the Spanish Jesuit, Luis de la Puente, which appeared in 1605 (English translation, 1619). Furthermore, according to St. François de Sales, the beginning of a meditation should be a dramatic one, wherein one imagines himself in intimacy with the matter of meditation, and such dramatic beginnings are common in the "Holy Sonnets": "Oh my blacke Soule!," "Spit in my face, you Jewes," "At the round earth's imagin'd corners."[3] One wonders why it is necessary to attribute the dramatic openings of these specific poems to the meditative tradition, for they abound in the earlier poems of Donne as well.

From the opening, corresponding to the memory, "the meditation" develops by means of the other two "powers of the soul," reason or understanding and will, as described by Puente.[4] One gets a subject, a mystery of faith, or other such appropriate subject. This the memory sets forth imaginatively; the reason or understanding studies the implications; and the will draws forth religious affection, or is turned to praise of God. In short, the will poses some application or conclusion for the matter.

8. Martz, p. 43.
9. *Ibid.*, p. 53.
1. *Ibid.*, p. 146.
2. Professor Martz criticizes Donne for his departure in this. Of Sonnet 13 he writes (p. 84): "Unfortunately, the sestet of this sonnet is unworthy of this opening: the reference to 'all my profane mistresses' is in the worst of taste: there is almost a tone of bragging here."
3. *Ibid.*, p. 51.
4. *Ibid.*, pp. 34–35.

It will be seen that the structure of Sonnet seven, analyzed in the manner of Mr. Martz, corresponds to the structure of the meditation.

At the round earths imagin'd corners, blow
Your trumpets, Angells, and arise, arise
From death, you numberlesse infinities
Of soules, and to your scattred bodies goe,

All whom the flood did, and fire shall o'erthrow,
All whom warre, dearth, age, agues, tyrannies,
Despaire, law, chance, hath slaine, and you whose eyes,
Shall behold God, and never tast deaths woe.

But let them sleepe, Lord, and mee mourne a space,
For, if above all these, my sinnes abound,
'Tis late to aske abundance of thy grace,
When wee are there; here on this lowly ground,
Teach mee how to repent; for that's as good
As if thou hadst seal'd my pardon, with thy blood.

The first section sets forth dramatically the matter of meditation, the day of judgment, though in this sonnet, as in others, the imagination rather than the memory presents the subject. The subject is also set forth in the form of a petition. In the second, the understanding reasons about death. Actually, this quatrain seems more an afterglow of the imagination in the first, though in other sonnets the break between memory and reason is more pronounced. And in the sestet there is a prayer or petition to God dealing with the implications drawn from the preceding meditation. Professor Martz shows this basic structure in four other sonnets.

But is there perhaps another source or other sources for such structure other than the meditative literature of the Counter Reformation? Must one conclude with Professor Martz that it demonstrates a fusion of the poetic and meditative traditions?

In reading Donne's *Songs and Sonnets* one is struck by the number of poems written in three stanzas. There are eighteen to be exact. Let us examine one of them. "A Valediction: Of Weeping" will do:

Let me powre forth
My teares before thy face, whil'st I stay here,
For thy face coines them, and thy stampe they beare,
And by this Mintage they are something worth,
For thus they bee
Pregnant of thee;
Fruits of much griefe they are, emblemes of more,
When a teare falls, that thou falls which it bore,
So thou and I are nothing then, when on a divers shore.

On a round ball
A workeman that hath copies by, can lay

An Europe, Afrique, and an Asia,
And quickly make that, which was nothing, *All*:
So doth each teare,
Which thee doth weare,
A globe, yea world by that impression grow,
Till thy teares mixt with mine doe overflow
This world, by waters sent from thee, my heaven dissolved so.

O more than Moone,
Draw not up seas to drowne me in thy spheare,
Weepe me not dead, in thine armes, but forbeare
To teache the sea, what it may doe too soone;
Let not the winde
Example finde,
To doe me more harme, than it purposeth;
Since thou and I sigh one anothers breath,
Who e'r sighes most, is cruellest, and hastes the others death.

In the first stanza, the situation is dramatically set forth, reconstructed, of course, from the memory. The scene is the parting of the two lovers, and the poet is particularly concerned with the tears they are shedding at parting. The reader gets a picture of these tears in the first stanza. In the second stanza the reasoning is about the significance of these tears. The reasoning in this stanza is hyperbolic, much the same as that of Sonnet 5.[5] In the last stanza the will presents a petition, to the love of the poet rather than to God, but none the less a petition.

The "Sunne Rising" is another example of a similar structure. In the first stanza, the subject of the poem, love, is dramatically set forth by means of a petition to the sun. In the second stanza the poet reasons about the nature, and, particularly, the power of this love. The last stanza represents "affections" drawn from the subject. In the conclusion of the poem the poet affirms the value of love.

Such is the structure of others of the *Songs and Sonnets*, indicating that the structure of the "Holy Sonnets" derives from Donne the poet rather than Donne the religious. It is highly doubtful that Donne was influenced in these early and profane poems by the meditative literature of the day, though he was reading a great deal of the Fathers and of polemic literature.

Yet one may object to the above conclusions on the grounds that the *Songs and Sonnets* conceivably may have been written later than or contemporary with the "Holy Sonnets" and therefore cannot have influenced their structure. Although it seems unlikely that the same environment could have given rise to the two groups, it is necessary to deal with the argument. Fortunately, certain of Donne's poems can be dated with some exactness, particularly the satires, the earlier of which were written

5. *Ibid.*, p. 53.

in the years 1593–1594.[6] Let us then examine "Satyre I" to see whether it has the same threefold structure and the dramatic portrayal of the subject.

The beginning presents the dramatic conflict. The poet is being enticed from his study, and he blurts out:

> Away thou fondling motley humorist,
> Leave me, and in this standing woodden chest,
> Consorted with these few bookes, let me lye
> In prison, and here be confin'd, when I dye.

The situation and subject matter for the poems are here set forth by the imagination.

> Here are Gods conduits, grave Divines; and here
> Natures Secretary, the Philosopher;
> And jolly Statesmen, which teach how to tie
> The sinewes of a cities mistique bodie;
> Here gathering Chroniclers, and by them stand
> Giddie fantastique Poëts of each land.

In these lines the reason explores the benefits of the library, just as the poet explores death and its causes in the second quatrain of "At the round earths imagin'd corners." The conclusion which follows affects the will:

> Shall I leave all this constant company,
> And follow headlong, wild uncertaine thee?

At the next line another threefold structure begins, and they are repeated in the poem. The one beginning at line forty-two is interesting. In the preceding group the poet has reproached the humorist for his lack of virtue and his rich attire.

> At birth, and death, our bodies naked are;
> And till our Soules be unapparrelled
> Of bodies, they from bliss are banished.

The subject as set forth is the state of man's soul. The reason then examines the cause:

> Mans first blest state was naked, when by sinne
> Hee lost that, yet hee was cloath'd but in beasts skin,
> And in this course attire, which I now weare,
> With god, and with the Muses I conferre.

The poet's instruction, by the time of the last division, has taken effect. The humorist repents, and the poet's will is swayed:

> But since thou like a contrite penitent,
> Charitably warn'd of thy sinnes, dost repent

6. Sir Edmund Gosse, *Life and Letters of John Donne* (New York 1899), Vol. I, pp. 36–40.

These vanities, and giddinesse, loe
I shut my chamber doore, and come, lets goe.

This threefold structure may be found in many others of the poems—the *Songs and Sonnets*, and *Elegies*, the *Satyres*.

The picture is now clear in regard to the structure of the "Holy Sonnets." Similar structure is found in Donne's poetry from the first poems to the last. Therefore, the explanation that the structure of the "Holy Sonnets" was patterned upon the formal exercises of "meditation" found in the literature of their day is not the better explanation. They are poems which in their structure fit neatly into the entire pattern of Donne's poetry. As he grew older, his environment and interests changed, but his poems kept their same fundamental structure and dramatic tone.

There is however one major objection to this argument. Perhaps Donne was introduced to meditation in his childhood. Such training might have served as an unconscious influence upon his poetic style throughout his life and culminated in the "Holy Sonnets." It is a considerable argument, not easily refuted. Let us examine the facts, such as they are. Gosse expresses them this way.

> An exciting event in the family must have been the appearance of the boy's uncle, Father Jasper Heywood, on a mission to England from Rome. He arrived in the summer of 1581, when Donne was eight years old, in company with Father William Holt. The severity with which the Heywoods had been used had always been somewhat relaxed in the case of Jasper, who was understood not to belong to the extreme party. He was allowed to leave Dillingen, and become Superior of the English Jesuits in succession to Parsons. He must have been a quaint, fantastic person. He appeared to have no sense of the delicacy of his position in England. He assumed the perilous airs of a Papal Legate, and was positively accused of a parade of wealth and pomp in his private life in London. He had lax views of discipline, and quarrelled with the austerer section of his co-religionists to such an extent that he was recalled by Rome in 1583, after having outraged the commonest prudence by summoning a Council under the style of Provincial of the Jesuits in England.[7]

Gosse goes on to say that Father Heywood was permanently exiled in January 1585, at which time Donne had been in Hart Hall, Oxford, for three months. This picture of Father Heywood is not that of a man who would suffer the little children. He might be expected to insist with some severity that they know their catechism.[8] But to suppose that he spent time teaching them the meditations designed especially for the Society

7. *Ibid.*, p. 13.

8. "*En tête de son programme pédogogique il (le jésuite) plaça la religion, et dans ce programme la primère étude fut celle du catéchisme.*" Rochemontieux, *Un Collège au XVIIe et XVIIIe Siècles* (1889), quoted in M. P. Ramsay, *Les Doctrines Médiévales Chez Donne* (Paris, 1924), pp. 35–36.

of Jesus is to hazard an unlikely guess. Further, to suppose that such meditation, had it been taught, could have had such a lasting influence that it shaped the poet's later thought to a great extent is difficult indeed.

A fascinating account of Jesuit activity in England during this period is the autobiography of the Jesuit Father John Gerard. Father Gerard was sent to England by the Society of Jesus to minister to the Catholics there and to recruit young Englishmen for the order. In reading through this book one is struck by the number of times the author refers to the *Spiritual Exercises*. As far as he himself is concerned, it seems that his practice of these meditations was not consistent in degree. For when he is in prison, they become much more important in his life than when he is out.[9] But there are many to whom he teaches these exercises. He teaches them to mature prospective seminarians, and older, staunch Catholics who wish to progress toward spiritual perfection. These people are well-educated and usually of high birth. An example is Robert Lee:

> He was a gentleman of good family and a very fine character and his charming manners made him a favorite with everyone. . . . Everything he did, he did well, and he was a Catholic too; in fact he was such a good man that he was thinking of withdrawing from the world to follow Christ more closely. When I was in the Clink, he came to visit me frequently, and it was easy to see that he was called to higher things than catching birds. . . . I had, therefore, fixed a date to give this good friend of mine a retreat, for I wanted him to discover by means of the Exercises the straight road that leads to life. . . .[1]

The conditions which Father Gerard lists preceding his decision to instruct Lee in the *Exercises* indicate that he used some degree of reticence in teaching them. Such instruction required time which could be devoted to more practical teaching; moreover, it was not necessary for salvation.

While he instructed many in the *Spiritual Exercises*, he gave instruction of a different nature to others. It is clear that he distinguishes between these exercises and the art of meditation by this quotation concerning Lee's friend, Hart, who was to become a Jesuit:

> . . . in place of the Exercises, I taught him the method of daily meditation.[2]

This art of meditation Father Gerard taught to many—among them women. Yet he never mentions having taught a woman the *Spiritual Exercises*. The method of meditation itself was not taught to all his acquaintances. It too was for people with more than a practical interest in religion. He mentions teaching it to Lady Vaux:

9. John Gerard, *The Autobiography of a Hunted Priest*, trans. by Philip Caraman (New York, 1952), pp. 72, 116.

1. *Ibid.*, p. 151.

2. *Ibid.*, p. 173.

> Then I taught her how to meditate, for she was capable of it—in fact she had intelligence and talents of a high order.[3]

Again, the reader is assured that this is not instruction for everyone.

Among the thirty or more candidates for the priesthood whom Father Gerard sends to the Continent some are "boys." We do not know how old they were, but they must have been old enough to travel alone for a great distance. Now while many of the candidates had received instruction from the *Spiritual Exercises*, apparently these "boys" did not. Father Gerard mentions giving them letters and instruction, but nowhere does he mention having taught them the *Spiritual Exercises* or the meditations. Nor is there any record in the entire book of his having taught either of these to a boy or a girl. Thus it seems apparent that Father Gerard's attitude toward these disciplines was that they were for people who had reached a spiritual plateau and were ready to advance to one much higher.

It cannot of course be proved that Donne did not receive such instructions in meditation at the age of eleven, or before. However, in view of Father Gerard's attitude toward instruction in them, it seems highly improbable that he did.

If the meditative influence is discounted in the structure of the "Holy Sonnets," one is faced with the problem of determining another source for their structure. Long ago Gosse suggested that Donne in his satires imitated Persius, and certainly the dramatic tone in the first lines of some of the Persius poems is similar to that of Donne, indicating a possible influence of the Latin poet. I have shown that the threefold structure of the sonnets is found in the earlier poems of Donne as well. The ultimate source of the threefold structure in the work of Donne is not easily determined. I believe that it is highly probable that this structure can be traced in poems of Donne's time and in forms other than the Petrarchan structure of the sonnet. This threefold structure recalls the strophe, antistrophe, and epode of the Greek chorus, a form almost as old as poetry itself. But such a study would extend far beyond the scope of this paper. Even if it is not made, it would not be too surprising to find that Donne, who is novel in his use of imagery and diction, makes some contribution to structure as well. Such a conclusion would be more reasonable than trying to account for the structure of the "Holy Sonnets" through the impressions received by a child of eleven or younger. The evidence presented here has shown that this structure, continuing throughout the poems of Donne, should not surprise when it appears in the "Holy Sonnets." One need not explore the mass of "meditative" literature to explain its presence there.

3. *Ibid.*, p. 147.

R. V. YOUNG

Donne's Holy Sonnets and the Theology of Grace†

The flowering of the English devotional lyric, long treated as an Anglican phenomenon with Catholic overtones distinct from Puritanism[1] is now widely regarded as unambiguously Protestant, with negligible debts to Continental Catholicism. With increasing frequency in recent years, a distinctively Protestant poetics has been designated the source of the English tradition of devotional poetry.[2] The Holy Sonnets of John Donne have furnished especially fertile ground for theological speculation. Once seen as examples of the influence of Ignatian meditation on Anglican poetry, the Holy Sonnets are now more often interpreted as an expression of the final crisis in the poet's conversion from Catholic recusancy to a Calvinist orientation consistent with Anglican orthodoxy. Despite the broad acceptance it now enjoys, this view of the Holy Sonnets is flawed in several ways. First, it is based on a simplistic and inaccurate view of the theological issues of Donne's era. Second, it attempts to establish the existence of an exclusively Protestant mode of poetry without determining whether the same features of theme and style are available in contemporaneous Catholic poetry. Finally, it forces the Holy Sonnets into a doctrinal frame that often overlooks the equivocal resonance and play of wit in Donne's poetry.

Scholars who espouse the notion of Protestant poetics are fond of observing that the Reformation maintained that man's justification begins with what is called *prevenient grace.* William Halewood quotes one of Donne's sermons on this point: "He is as precise as Taylor in his use of the nomenclature of Reformation theology," Halewood writes. "The grace which provokes the faith which leads to justification is *preventing* or *prevenient:* 'no man can prepare that worke, no man can begin it, no man can proceed in it of himselfe. The desire and the actual beginning is from the preventing grace of God' (*Sermons*, 2:305)."[3] Barbara Lewalski is even more emphatic:

† From *"Bright Shootes of Everlastingnesse": The Seventeenth-Century Religious Lyric* edited by Claude Summers and Ted-Larry Pebworth, by permission of the University of Missouri Press. Pp. 20–39.

1. See especially Helen C. White, *The Metaphysical Poets* (1936; rpt. New York: Collier, 1962); Helen Gardner, ed., *John Donne: The Divine Poems*, 2d ed. (Oxford: Clarendon, 1978); Louis L. Martz, *The Poetry of Meditation*, 2d ed. (New Haven: Yale University Press, 1962); and Anthony Low, *Love's Architecture: Devotional Modes in Seventeenth-Century English Poetry* (New York: New York University Press, 1978).

2. See especially William Halewood, *The Poetry of Grace: Reformation Themes and Structures in English Seventeenth-Century Poetry* (New Haven: Yale University Press, 1970); Barbara K. Lewalski, *Donne's Anniversaries and the Poetry of Praise* (Princeton: Princeton University Press, 1973); Andrew Weiner, *Sir Philip Sidney and the Poetics of Protestantism: A Study of Contexts* (Minneapolis: University of Minnesota Press, 1978); and Lewalski, *Protestant Poetics and the Seventeenth-Century Religious Lyric* (Princeton: Princeton University Press, 1979). "Protestant Poetics" was the topic of a special session at the 1983 MLA convention in New York.

3. *The Poetry of Grace*, pp. 62–63.

> Because man's natural state is so desperate, there can be no question (as in some Roman Catholic formulations) of man's preparing himself through moral virtue for the reception of grace, or of performing works good and meritorious in themselves; everything that he does himself is necessarily evil and corrupt. As the tenth of the Thirty-nine Articles of the established church put it, "The condition of man, after the fall of Adam is such that he cannot turne, and prepare himselfe by his owne naturall strength, and good workes, to faith, and calling upon God, wherefore we have no power to doe good workes pleasant, and acceptable to God, without the grace of God preventing us, that we may have a good will, and working with us when we have that good will."[4]

Now this is all very puzzling. "Prevenient grace" hardly seems to qualify as a decisive example of "the nomenclature of Reformation theology" since the term is used in the Council of Trent's *Decree on Justification* (1547), which states quite explicitly that the work of salvation begins not with man's efforts, but with the unmerited grace of God:

> [The Council] declares further that the beginning of this same justification in adults must be received from the prevenient grace of God through Christ Jesus; that is, from his call, by which they are called for no existing merit of their own, in order that those who have sins turned away from God, might be disposed through his awakening and help to turn to their own justification, by freely assenting to and cooperating with that grace. Thus as God touches the human heart with the light of the Holy Spirit, the man himself is not wholly inactive, inasmuch as he might cast it aside. Nonetheless, without God's grace he cannot move himself toward justice in God's sight by his own free will. Hence when it is said in Sacred Scripture, "Turn toward me and I shall turn toward you" (Zach. 1:3), we are reminded of our freedom; and when we respond, "Convert us, Lord, to you and we shall be converted" (Lam. 5:21), we confess that we are anticipated by God's grace.[5]

This is not a Tridentine novelty. St. Thomas Aquinas makes it clear that the "preparation for grace" attributed by Lewalski to "some Roman Catholic formulations" can only come after and as a result of God's prior gift of grace: "But if we speak of grace as it signifies a help from God moving us to good, no preparation is required on man's part anticipating, as it were, the divine help, but rather, every preparation in man must be by the help of God moving the soul to good."[6] Or as the mystic, St. John of the Cross, succinctly puts it, "without his grace one is unable to merit his grace."[7]

4. *Protestant Poetics*, pp. 15–16.

5. Quoted from *Enchiridion Symbolorum, Definitionum et Declarationum de rebus fidei et Morum*, ed. Henr. Denzinger and Clem. Bannwart, S.J., 17th ed. (Fribourg: Herder, 1927), 797: • • •

6. *Summa Theologica*, 1–2.112.2: • • •

7. *Cántico espiritual*, 32.5: "sin su gracia no se puede merecer su gracia." *Vida y obras completas*

There are, to be sure, significant differences between Protestant and Catholic versions of justification; the insistence of the Council of Trent on the cooperation of man's free will with God's grace is an example, and will presently receive further consideration. But there is no basis for suggesting that the concept of prevenient grace was a discovery, even a rediscovery, of the Reformation. At times it appears that the proponents of Protestant poetics have derived their concept of Catholic theology wholly from Reformation polemics. In any case, many commentators of recent years have read Donne's devotional poems, along with those of his English contemporaries, as expositions of an exclusively Protestant, indeed a Calvinist, view of election and grace. According to one critic, Donne's Holy Sonnets "yield more fully to an analysis of their biblical motifs, their anguished Pauline speaker, their presentation of states of soul attendant upon the Protestant drama of regeneration, than they do to any other meditative scheme," and the first of these sonnets, "As due by many titles," has been called a treatment of "the problem of election."[8]

Here and there in the Holy Sonnets there are explicitly Calvinist terms, as well as passages that suggest a Calvinist theology of grace—the phrase "Impute me righteous" in Sonnet 3, for instance, or the famous paradox that closes "Batter my heart," Sonnet 10. But neither the first sonnet, "As due by many titles," nor the Holy Sonnets generally can be read as a specifically Calvinist, nor even Protestant, exposition of grace. In fact, the persona of the Holy Sonnets seems almost to be "trying out" different versions of grace in order to arrive at a theologically moderate position. We know from his letters that Donne inclined this way. Writing to Henry Goodyere within a year of the time he is believed to have composed most of the Holy Sonnets, he praises his own verse litany, "That neither the Roman Church need call it defective, because it abhors not the particular mention of the blessed Triumphers in heaven; nor the Reformed can discreetly accuse it, of attributing more then a rectified devotion ought to doe"; and in another letter to Goodyere, written about the same time, he says of Catholic and Protestant churches, "The Channels of God mercies run through both fields; and they are sister teats of his graces, yet both diseased and infected, but not both alike."[9] This is hardly the attitude of militant Calvinism.

Donne's "ecumenical" inclination is further developed in his *Essays in Divinity*, probably composed during the three or four years before his ordination. As Evelyn Simpson observes, this work would hardly have

---

de San Juan de la Cruz, ed. Crisógono de Jesús, O.C.D., Matías del Niño Jesús, O.C.D., and Lucinio del SS. Sacramento, O.C.D., 5th ed. (Madrid: BAC, 1964), p. 718.

8. Lewalski, *Protestant Poetics*, pp. 265–66. Unlike Lewalski, I follow the order of the first twelve sonnets in the Gardner edition of the *Divine Poems*, which seems to have been vindicated by Patrick F. O'Connell, "The Successive Arrangements of Donne's 'Holy Sonnets,'" *Philological Quarterly* 60 (1981): 323–42, esp. p. 334.

9. *Letters to Severall Persons of Honour* (1651), introd. M. Thomas Hester (fac. rpt.; New York; Delmar, 1977), pp. 34, 102. Hester gives as the dates of these letters 1608 and 1609 respectively, in the Schedule, pp. xviii–xxii.

commended Donne to Anglican orthodoxy, as represented by the Calvinist archbishop of Canterbury, George Abbot, since "Abbot was a narrow-minded man, bitterly hostile to the Church of Rome."[1] In the *Essays* Donne maintains, however, that despite sharp differences between the Anglican and Roman communions, they share the same foundation: "yet though we branch out *East* and *West*, that Church concurs with us in the root, and sucks her vegetation from one and the same ground, *Christ Jesus*." Donne continues, "so Synagogue and Church is the same thing, and of the Church, *Roman* and *Reformed*, and all other distinctions of place, Discipline, or Person, but one Church, journying to one *Hierusalem*, and directed by one guide, Christ Jesus." Most remarkably, Donne even goes so far as to prefer a unity based on the form of *any* of the principal churches—Roman, Genevan, or Anglican—to the disunity prevailing in his day:

> And though to all my thanksgivings to God, I ever humbly acknowledg, as one of his greatest Mercies to me, that he gave me my Pasture in this Park, and my milk from the brests of this Church, yet out of a fervent, and (I hope) not inordinate affection, even to such an Unity, I do zealously wish, that the whole catholick Church, were reduced to such Unity and agreement, in the form and profession Established, in any one of these Churches (though ours were principally to be wished) which have not by any additions destroyed the foundation and possibility of salvation in Christ Jesus; That then the Church, discharged of disputations, and misapprehensions, and this defensive warr, might contemplate Christ clearly and uniformely.[2]

Again, this is not the tone of Calvinist rigor, and the emphasis on the corporate unity of the Church seems incompatible with the stress on individual election urged by Calvin and his more vociferous English followers.

Hence when Donne plainly repudiates Calvin on the specific matter of grace in a subsequent passage of the *Essays in Divinity*, his theology is perfectly consistent. Although in his reply to Cardinal Sadoleto, Calvin names "justification by faith, the first and keenest subject of controversy between us,"[3] his own *Antidote to the Council of Trent* clearly establishes that the central theological issue of the Protestant Reformation was freedom of the will. Calvin says "amen" to the Council's first three canons on justification, which stipulate, respectively, that man cannot be justified by his own human works or the law without the grace of Christ; that this grace does not merely make salvation easier, but is absolutely necessary; and that prevenient grace is requisite to dispose

1. See the Introduction to her edition of Donne's *Essays in Divinity* (Oxford: Clarendon, 1952), p. xi.

2. *Essays in Divinity*, pp. 50, 51, 51–52.

3. *John Calvin: Selections from His Writings*, ed. John Dillenberger (New York: Doubleday, 1971), p. 95.

man even to desire salvation. Calvin only begins to take exception with the fourth canon, which says, "If anyone say that the free will of man, moved and excited by God, in no way cooperates by assenting to God's stimulus and call, by which it disposes and prepares itself for receiving the grace of justification, and that it is unable to resist, if it would, but that as a thing inanimate it is able to do nothing and is held merely passive, let him be anathema."[4] Calvin's rejoinder: "the efficacy of divine grace is such, that all opposition is beaten down, and we who were unwilling are made obedient, it is not we who assent, but the Lord by the Prophet, when he promises that he will make us to walk in his precepts."[5] Calvin raises similar objections to canons 5 through 7, which assert that Adam's sin did not obliterate free will; that man does evil only on his own with God's permissive will and not his proper consenting; and that man is not utterly incapable of doing good before justification.

When Donne meditates on God's mercy in the *Essays in Divinity*, his discussion of grace and nature is Thomistic, his view of the human will far more Tridentine than Calvinist:

> in our repentances and reconciliations, though the first grace proceed only from God, yet we concurr so, as there is an union of two Hypostases, *Grace* and *Nature*. Which, (as the incarnation of our Blessed Saviour himself was) is conceived in us of the Holy Ghost, without father; but fed and produced by us; that is, by our will first enabled and illumined. For neither God nor man determine mans will; (for that must either imply a necessiting therof from God, or else *Pelagianisme*) but they condetermine it.

Above all Donne denies Calvin's notion of irresistible grace by which "all opposition is beaten down": "And yet we may not say, but that God begins many things which we frustrate; and calls when we come not."[6] The issue would not go away for Donne, even after his ordination. Of course, in his very public sermons far more discretion was required than in his letters or *Essays*, which remained unpublished during his lifetime. Still, Donne clung consistently to an un-Calvinist belief in freedom of the will. In a sermon of 1626, for example, he affirms what seems to be predestination: "Christ doth not now begin to make that man his, but now declares to us, that he hath been his from all eternity. . . ." But a few pages further, immediately after referring to "the Eternal Decree of my Election," he attacks what—for Calvin—seems the necessary corollary, the doctrine of irresistible grace (which Donne attributes to "the later School"): "He came not to force and compel them, who would not be brought into the way: Christ saves no man against his will."[7] Like

4. *Enchiridion Symbolorum*, ed. Denzinger and Bannwart, 814: * * *
5. *Calvin: Selections*, ed. Dillenberger, p. 194.
6. *Essays in Divinity*, pp. 80, 81.
7. "A Sermon Preached to the Household at White-hall, April 30, 1626," in *The Sermons of John Donne*, ed. George R. Potter and Evelyn M. Simpson, 10 vols. (Berkeley: University of California Press, 1953–1962), 7:153, 156.

the fathers of the Council of Trent, Donne seeks to formulate the delicate balance between grace and nature, predestination and free will. If his conclusions differ from theirs, they likewise differ from Calvin's.

It is not surprising, therefore, to find many of the theological features of the Holy Sonnets paralleled in the devotional poems of Donne's Catholic contemporaries, who exhibit an equal concern over the problem of election and grace. A good example is furnished by the *Hexáclito cristiano* (*Christian Heraclitus*, 1613) by Francisco de Quevedo (1580–1645). Like Donne's Holy Sonnets, it is a collection of penitential lyrics that focus on the spiritual condition of the poetic persona. The parallels begin to emerge with the first poem of each set. The octave of Donne's "As due by many titles" establishes the misery of man's natural condition by seeing his situation as that of an unreliable debtor who tries to cancel his debts by inviting God to foreclose on his hopelessly overmortgaged self:

> As due by many titles I resigne
> My selfe to thee, O God, first I was made
> By thee, and for thee, and when I was decay'd
> Thy blood bought that, the which before was thine,
> I am thy sonne, made with thy selfe to shine,
> Thy servant, whose paines thou hast still repaid,
> Thy sheepe, thine Image, and till I betray'd
> My selfe, a temple of thy Spirit divine. . . .[8]

The proliferation of metaphors, suggesting various relationships with God, is an indication of the speaker's uncertainty and the feebleness of his position. Hence it is not surprising that the sestet dwells queasily on the prospect that the proffered self may not be worth the cost of refurbishing, that only the devil is still interested:

> Why doth the devil then usurpe in mee?
> Why doth he steale, nay ravish that's thy right?
> Except thou rise and for thine owne worke fight,
> Oh I shall soone despaire, when I doe see
> That thou lov'st mankind well, yet wilt'not chuse mee,
> And Satan hates mee, yet is loth to lose mee.

Like this first of the Holy Sonnets, the first poem of Quevedo's *Heráclito* is an intense reflection of the poet's fearful sense of his utter dependence on divine grace:

> A new heart, a new man, Lord,
> Are what my soul has need of;
> Strip me of myself, for it could be
> That in your pity you might pay what I owe.
> I take doubtful steps in the blind night,
> For already I have come to hate the day,

8. The Holy Sonnets are quoted from Gardner's second edition of the *Divine Poems*.

And I fear that I shall find cold death
Wrapped in a deadly bait (although sweet).
I am of your making; your image, Father, I have been,
And, if you have no concern for me, I believe
That nothing else will take my part.[9]

Donne describes himself as "due by many titles" to God; Quevedo mentions the debt that he "owes" to God, and describes himself as of God's "making" and formerly His "image" until corrupted by sin. Donne says that he is God's "owne worke" and his "image." Both emphasize that God must take their part and "fight for" or "defend" the sinner, who is helpless without such assistance. Indeed, the fundamental theme of both poems is the utter hopelessness of the sinner's situation without divine intervention. Donne closes on the brink of despair, awaiting some sign that God will "chuse" him; Quevedo calls upon God to take decisive action on behalf of a sinner who turns away from spiritual health: "Do what is demanded by the way I seem, / Not what I demand; for, like a profligate, / I hide my salvation from my desire."

There are Catholic poets of grace besides Quevedo, and not all are confined to Spain. The Frenchman Jean de la Ceppède (1550–1622), for example, closes one of his *Théorèmes Spirituels* (1613–1621) with the plea of a hapless sinner for divine help: "But it is for you, Lord, to make me capable / Of sharing in your riches: for my guilty soul / Does not know how, without your aid, to return to you."[1] The close of another of La Ceppède's sonnets recalls a figure frequently associated with Luther's view of justification: "Oh Christ, oh holy Lamb, deign to hide / All my scarlet sins, the kindling twigs of the abyss, / Within the bloody folds of the cloak of your flesh."[2] These lines suggest that a Catholic poet can use the metaphor of having his sins covered by the righteous blood of Christ without invoking the Reformation doctrine of imputed, rather than infused, grace. Hence there is little reason to find anything specifically Protestant in the closing lines of Donne's "Hymne to God my God, in my sicknesse":[3]

Looke Lord, and finde both *Adams* met in me;
As the first *Adams* sweat surrounds my face,
May the last *Adams* blood my soule embrace.

9. Quevedo is quoted from Francisco de Quevedo, *Obras completas*, ed. José Manuel Blecua (Barcelona: Editorial Planeta, 1963), 1:20: * * *

1. Quoted from *European Metaphysical Poetry*, ed. Frank Warnke (New Haven: Yale University Press, 1961), p. 104: * * *

2. Quoted from *The Baroque Poem*, ed. Harold B. Segel (New York: Dutton, 1974), p. 172: * * *See Luther's *Commentary on Galatians*, in *Martin Luther: Selections from His Writings*, ed. John Dillenberger (New York: Doubleday, 1961), p. 129: "So we shroud ourselves under the covering of Christ's flesh, . . . lest God should see our sin."

3. Cf. Lewalski, *Protestant Poetics*, pp. 16–17; and Richard Strier, *Love Known: Theology and Experience in George Herbert's Poetry* (Chicago: University of Chicago Press, 1983), p. 130. On La Ceppède's relation to the Counter-Reformation, see P. A. Chilton, *The Poetry of Jean de la Ceppède: A Study in Text and Context* (Oxford: Oxford University Press, 1977), pp. 24, 50–52. Terence Cave, *Devotional Poetry in France, c. 1570–1613* (Cambridge: Cambridge University Press, 1969), pp. 22–23, observes that the differences between Catholic and Protestant poetry in France are largely negative; i.e., some subjects available to Catholics are not available to Protestants.

So, in his purple wrapp'd receive mee Lord,
By these his thornes give me his other Crowne
(11. 23–27)

Obviously here, as in the Holy Sonnets, Donne is concerned with the problem of grace, conceived in terms of Pauline typology; however, this is hardly a theme unique to the Protestant Reformation. As the examples of Quevedo and La Ceppède indicate, Continental Catholic poets were equally sensitive to man's hopeless sinfulness before God and radical dependence on his grace. In all of these poems the expression of Christian experience seems more important than the articulation of theological distinctions.

Even in those Holy Sonnets that seem to display most explicitly the severities of Calvinism, it is difficult to find in Donne an uncritical propounder of Reformation theology. At first glance the famous conclusion to Sonnet 10, "Batter my heart," suggests nothing so much as the effects of Calvinist "irresistible" grace: "Take mee to you, imprison mee, for I / Except you'enthrall mee, never shall be free, / Nor ever chast, except you ravish mee." But even the critic who has recently been most resolute in turning up Calvinism in the Holy Sonnets finds it hedged in by important reservations. John Stachniewski writes that "the essential subject matter" of Sonnet 10 is "the conflict between [Donne's] personal integrity and the demands of a theology which brutalized self-esteem." Stachniewski concludes that Donne's Calvinism in the Holy Sonnets is a temporary phase in his transition from Catholic to High Anglican, arising from his sense of worldly disappointment at the time of the poems' composition: "Donne felt his dependence on God to resemble his dependence on secular patronage with its attendant frustration, humiliation, and despair."[4]

It is not necessary, however, to turn the Holy Sonnets into a sublimated manifestation of the poet's socioeconomic frustration to question whether a few scattered suggestions of Calvinism make the poems a Calvinist work. "Batter my heart" is precisely a prayer to God for grace, which, if the Calvinist notion of the irresistibility of grace be true, is essentially pointless. However inappropriate the use of quasi-mystical imagery at the end of Donne's sonnet may be, Hugh Richmond has pointed out a striking parallel in a similar sonnet by the French Catholic poet Ronsard.[5] In any case, Donne pleads that God stop tinkering with him ("for, you / As yet but knocke, breathe, shine, and seeke to mend") and instead reforge him altogether: "That I may rise, and stand, o'erthrow mee,' and bend / Your force, to breake, blowe, burn and make

4. "John Donne: The Despair of the 'Holy Sonnets,' " *ELH* 48 (1981): 690, 702–3. See also Wilbur Sanders, *John Donne's Poetry* (Cambridge: Cambridge University Press, 1971), pp. 120–31; Lewalski, *Protestant Poetics*, pp. 120–31; John Carey, *John Donne: Life, Mind, and Art* (New York: Oxford University Press, 1981), pp. 51–59. There is a similar politicizing of Donne's *Songs and Sonets* and his *Devotions* in Jonathan Goldberg, *James I and the Politics of Literature* (Baltimore: Johns Hopkins University Press, 1983), pp. 66–67, 80–83, 107–12, 211–19.

5. *Divine Poems*, ed. Gardner, pp. 152–53.

me new" (ll. 1–4). Now this may quite plausibly be read as a plea for infused sanctifying grace *(gratia gratum faciens)* which, as Barbara Lewalski insists, is an idea contrary to the Protestant Reformation: "The Reformers were adamant in their insistence that this justification is only imputed to the sinner, not infused into him as the Roman Catholics held, so as actually to restore God's image in him; however, the imputed righteousness is really his because he is joined to Christ as body to head."[6] Of course, there is no denying that Donne's sonnet expresses a sense of profound depravity and fear of damnation—not without Calvinist reverberations—for the very reason that the poet has abandoned Catholic sources of consolation without yet discovering or devising acceptable alternatives. This is a matter of rather delicate discriminations, however, and it is questionable whether the close of "Batter my heart" yields a clear theological resolution.

The trouble with theological categorizing of the Holy Sonnets is that it is likely to flatten out the wit and daring that are characteristic of Donne's poetry. The equivocal implication of the third of these sonnets, "This is my playes last scene," with its explicit reference to imputed righteousness, furnishes a good example. The octave presents a traditional meditative theme, the deathbed:

> This is my playes last scene, here heavens appoint
> My pilgrimages last mile; and my race
> Idly, yet quickly runne, hath this last pace,
> My spans last inch, my minutes last point,
> And gluttonous death will instantly unjoynt
> My body,'and soule, and I shall sleepe a space,
> But my'ever-waking part shal see that face,
> Whose fear alredy shakes my every joynt.

Clearly this poem is based on the standard Ignatian meditative topos of the Four Last Things.[7] Even as the octave evokes death and judgment, so the sestet adds heaven and hell:

> Then, as my soule, to'heaven her first seate, takes flight,
> And earth-borne body, in the earth shall dwell,
> So, fall my sinnes, that all may have their right,
> To where they'are bred, and would presse me, to hell.
> Impute me righteous, thus purg'd of evill,
> For thus I leave the world, the flesh, and devill.

This closing couplet could be seen as turning the Ignatian meditation into something emphatically Calvinist. Yet this almost magical invoca-

6. *Protestant Poetics*, p. 17.

7. *The Spiritual Exercises*, 1st week, 5th exercise, in *Obras completas de San Ignacio de Loyola*, ed. Ignacio Iparraguirre, S.J. (Madrid: BAC, 1963), pp. 214–16. Lewalski, *Protestant Poetics*, p. 268, argues that the use of the pilgrimage and race tropes in the opening lines of this sonnet make it Protestant in mood. But the notion of life as a pilgrimage is too familiar an idea in the Middle Ages to require illustration. St. Thomas More combines the theme of life as a pilgrimage with the contemplation of death in a Latin epigram. *Vita Ipsa cursus ad mortem est*, in Fred Nichols, ed., *An Anthology of Neo-Latin Poetry* (New Haven: Yale University Press, 1979), p. 462.

tion of the Calvinist dogma has troubled more than one critic. Wilbur Sanders calls these lines "blatant theological sophistry" and adds that "the spiritual malady so obviously won't give way to the patent medicine applied to it, that it seems almost to be a part of the poetic strategy to make us aware of this fact."[8] There is perhaps more to what Sanders says than he realizes: it is quite as likely that Donne is playing with a theological concept in a dramatic and witty fashion as it is that he is writing bad verse theology.

With this approach in mind, it is instructive to consider two other references to "imputation" in the Donne canon. The first comes from Satyre III, "Of Religion":

> and shall thy fathers spirit
> Meete blinde philosophers in heaven, whose merit
> Of strict life may be imputed faith, and heare
> Thee, whom hee taught so easie wayes and neare
> To follow, damn'd? (11. 11–15)[9]

In raising the theme of the virtuous heathen—a lively topic in the Middle Ages and among Renaissance humanists—Donne simply stands Calvinism on its head: instead of Christ's righteousness imputed to a man on the basis of his faith, Donne speculates that virtuous pagans might have faith imputed to them on the basis of righteousness. This passage comes in a poem that questions Catholicism, Calvinism, Anglicanism, and indifferentism alike on behalf of the sincere individual believer, who is exhorted to "doubt wisely" (1. 77). Thus the severe Calvinist version of grace is subverted by a witty turn growing out of a moderate Erasmian attitude amidst the horrors of sixteenth-century religious strife.[1]

The Calvinist concept of imputed righteousness is subjected to an especially extravagant outburst of Donne's wit in Elegy 19, the notorious "Going to Bed," in which the poetic persona is occupied with getting his mistress undressed and into bed as quickly as possible:

> Like pictures, or like bookes gay coverings made
> For laymen, are all women thus arraid;
> Themselves are mystique bookes, which only wee
> Whom their imputed grace will dignify
> Must see reveal'd. (11. 39–43)[2]

Like his principal classical model, Ovid, Donne uses the erotic elegy as a vehicle for ridiculing the most revered ideals and institutions of respectable society. Amatory figures become quick thrusts in a perilous antiestablishment poetic game. Here, beneath the surface of outrageous wit and blasphemous sensuality, Donne indulges in a momentary ges-

8. *John Donne's Poetry*, p. 128.

9. Quoted from *The Complete Poetry of John Donne*, ed. John T. Shawcross (Garden City, N.Y.: Doubleday/Anchor, 1967), p. 23.

1. Donne could well have absorbed a pre-Tridentine Erasmian Catholicity from his Jesuit uncle, Jasper Heywood. See Dennis Flynn, "The '*Annales* School' and the Catholicism of Donne's Family," *John Donne Journal* 2 (1983): 1–9.

2. Quoted from *John Donne: The Elegies and the Songs and Sonnets*, ed. Helen Gardner (Oxford: Clarendon, 1965), p. 16.

ture of theological satire. In a context of "imputed grace" and the removal of clothing, it is difficult not to recall how Luther explains God's imputation of righteousness to the sinner, in his *Commentary on Galatians*, by comparing it to *covering* his sin by grace and not *seeing* it.[3] For Donne's speaker the woman's "imputed grace" permits him to *uncover* (or *discover*) and *see*. The implication of the conceit emerges when it is reversed: the justification of the elect, an inscrutable act of divine power according to the Calvinist formulation, makes God's work of salvation as arbitrary and fickle as a woman's choice of the lover admitted to her bed. Hence this risqué poem by a young law student and flamboyant dandy is also a sly send-up of the dominant theology of the Reformation.

To be sure, the Satyres and Elegies, if Dame Helen Gardner's dating is reliable, were written more than ten years before the Holy Sonnets; and when the latter were composed Donne had already undertaken the labor of an Anglican polemicist, and the idea of entering Anglican orders had at least been broached to him. But the Holy Sonnets, like almost all Donne's poetry, are private exercises, circulated for the most part among his friends. There are undeniable marks of the poet's Catholic upbringing in their themes and structures, and the specifically Calvinist elements are handled tentatively, even with an air of provisionality. Sonnet 3, "This is my playes last scene," with its reference to imputed righteousness, a doctrine ridiculed by Donne in other poems, seems to ask, "Does this work? Will my sins simply drop away into hell as I am 'purg'd of evill' by imputation?" There is an air of nervousness here—a result, perhaps, of Donne's embarrassed or even guilty recollection of earlier flippant treatments of matters of eternal life and death. Still, a negative answer is implied in the nine remaining sonnets of the set, which keep seeking different approaches to the problem of justification and grace.

This is not to say that the doctrines of the Reformation, especially Calvin's view of justification, had no bearing on the Holy Sonnets, but that the impact of Calvinism was oblique rather than direct. In fact, there is often a Calvinist subtext, like a magnetic field, exerting a subtle but continuous force over the most unlikely of the Holy Sonnets. For instance, the ninth sonnet, "What is this present were the worlds last night?," discloses under scrutiny the spiritual strains generated by the terrifying yet fascinating concept of irresistible grace.

At first glance the octave of the poem seems an extravagant sacred parody of a Petrarchan love sonnet, done in Continental style. Donne's anguished meditator, recalling the counsel of Astrophil's muse, attempts to convince himself that he need only "looke in [his] heart and write."[4] What he sees there is a graphic, Spanish baroque crucifix:

> What if this present were the worlds last night?
> Marke in my heart, O Soule, where thou dost dwell,

3. *Luther: Selections*, ed. Dillenberger, p. 129.
4. *Astrophil and Stella*, sonnet 1, cited here and below from *The Poems of Sir Philip Sidney*, ed. William A. Ringler, Jr. (Oxford: Clarendon, 1962).

The picture of Christ crucified, and tell
Whether that countenance can thee affright,
Teares in his eyes quench the amasing light,
Blood fills his frownes, which from his pierc'd head fell,
And can that tongue adjudge thee unto hell,
Which pray'd forgiveness for his foes fierce spight?

Even as Astrophil assures "sleepe" that no better image of Stella is available than what is in his mind (*Astrophil and Stella*, sonnet 39), so Donne's speaker assures himself by means of the image of Christ in his mind. Yet the octave ends, literally, with a question mark; and, though Christ "pray'd forgivenesse for his foes fierce spight," when he returns as Judge of the world, some at least will indeed be adjudged "unto hell."

The sestet undertakes a strengthening of the persona's assurance of salvation by encouragement of an emotional and aesthetic response to the interior image of Christ that he has evoked. Again the conventions of Petrarchan/Neoplatonic love poetry are parodied:

No, no; but as in my idolatrie
I said to all my profane mistresses,
Beauty, of pitty, foulness onely is
A signe of rigour: so I say to thee,
To wicked spirits are horrid shapes assign'd,
This beauteous forme assures a pitious minde.

The very slyness of these lines is troubling. In a poem resonant with echoes of Sidney, one can hardly forget that "two Negatives affirme" according to the "Grammer rules" of *Astrophil and Stella*, sonnet 63. Can Donne's "No, no," like Stella's, be construed as an implicit *yes?* The speaker of "What if this present" must fear a certain poetic justice, since as a youthful seducer he seems, like Astrophil, to have distorted the conventions. In his Neoplatonic discourse in the *Book of the Courtier*, Pietro Bembo tells us that a "beauteous forme" is a "signe" not of "a pitious minde" but of a virtuous soul.[5] Samuel Daniel's Delia, after all, was "faire, and *thus* vnkinde."[6] In view of the evident duplicity of the persona's addresses to his "profane mistresses" in the past, his present analogous address to his own soul—patently intended to be overheard by the divine lover—is at best questionable, and a dubious means of assuring oneself of salvation.

In a Calvinist perspective this is a crucial issue, for the interpretation of the "picture" in the persona's heart—is it a "marke" of election or condemnation?—is contingent upon the speaker's emotional response to Christ's countenance. To find this tearful, bloody visage beautiful is not

5. Baldasarre Castiglione, *The Courtier*, book 4, trans. Sir Thomas Hoby, in *Three Renaissance Classics*, ed. Burton A. Milligan (New York: Scribner's, 1953), p. 599: "Whereupon doth very seldom an ill soule dwell in a beautifull bodie. And therefore is the outwards beautie a true signe of the inwarde goodnesse. . . ."

6. *Delia*, sonnet 6, in *Poems and a Defence of Ryme*, ed. Arthur Colby Sprague (1930; rpt. Chicago: University of Chicago Press, 1965): "O had she not been faire, and thus vnkinde, / My Muse had slept, and none had knowne my minde."

a natural response; it requires grace, grace that in Calvin's view is irresistible. The picture of the suffering Christ within will be an image of beauty to the man who has faith, when faith means the subjective, unpremeditated realization that one is in fact saved. "A right definition of faith," Calvin says in *The Institutes* (3.2.7), is "a firm and certain knowledge of God's benevolence toward us, founded upon the truth of the freely given promise in Christ, both revealed to our minds and sealed upon our hearts through the Holy Spirit." Seeking a "signe" of "pitty" instead of "rigour," seeking, that is, the "marke" of his faith and election, a man has nothing to consult but his feelings; for as Calvin adds, in the next section of *The Institutes* (3.2.8), "that very assent itself . . . is more of the heart than of the brain, and more of the disposition than of the understanding."[7] Donne's persona seems to be trying to stimulate in himself the appropriate feelings toward the crucified Christ—a passionate attraction at least as intense as what he once felt for his "profane mistresses." The manipulative insincerity of the erotic analogy, however, infects his expression of desire for Christ.

The air of tentativeness, if not downright factitiousness, in Donne's sonnet becomes apparent when it is set beside an anonymous Spanish sonnet of the same era, "To Christ Crucified":

> (I am not moved, my God, to love you / by the heaven you have promised me; / nor am I moved by fear of hell / to leave off offending you for this. // You move me, Lord; I am moved to see you / nailed to a cross and ridiculed; / I am moved to see your body so wounded; / I am moved by your mistreatment and your death. // Your love, at last, moves me and in a way / that though there were no heaven, I would love you, / and though there were no hell, I would fear you. // You need give me nothing for me to love you; / for though I might not hope as I do hope, / I would love you the same as I do love you.)[8]

Everything about this poem bespeaks a guileless simplicity, a spontaneous and passionate longing for the crucified Christ. The contrast with Donne's sonnet is striking. Although the Donne poem is in many ways compatible with baroque Catholicism and seems, at first, to be on the same theme, Donne introduces an element of uneasy self-consciousness. The Spanish poem addresses Christ on the cross; the speaker of the Donne sonnet addresses his "Soule" with Christ as an inferential overhearer. The speaker of the Spanish poem simply dismisses any consideration of salvation as irrelevant to his exalted love of Christ, while Donne's persona is obsessed with finding sufficient love for Christ in his heart to be assured of salvation. Calvinist notions of grace pervade the Holy Son-

7. *Calvin: Selections*, ed. Dillenberger, pp. 380, 381.

8. *An Anthology of Spanish Poetry, 1500–1700*, ed. Arthur Terry (Oxford: Pergamon, 1968), 2:96–97. The poem was first published in 1628, but, as Terry points out, it could have been written any time after the middle of the sixteenth century. [The Spanish text is here omitted; only the translation reprinted—*Editor*.]

nets in this fashion: not as principal theological inspiration, but as a lingering fear of faithlessness haunting the background of poems that in most of their features resemble the Catholic devotional poetry of the Continent. It is not surprising that Donne should handle such traditional forms with a certain diffidence and trepidation: he was, as he composed the Holy Sonnets, neither still Catholic nor yet Protestant in a settled way that gave his conscience peace; and, as it is phrased in one of his letters, "to be no part of any body, is to be nothing."[9]

But though Donne's persona is hag-ridden by doubts of his own sincerity, and hence by doubts of the validity of his sense of grace, the Calvinist dynamic does not finally dominate the Holy Sonnets. The last sonnet, "Father, part of thy double interest," closes with the law of love—not faith—as the ultimate Christian obligation:

> Yet such are those laws, that men argue yet
> Whether a man those statutes can fulfill;
> None doth, but all-healing grace and Spirit,
> Revive againe what law and letter kill.
> Thy lawes abridgement, and thy last command
> Is all but love; Oh let that last Will stand!

These lines are not notably Catholic or Protestant. Donne is not here taking a position on the theology of justification and grace; he is praying for grace and exhorting himself to love. Herein he is typical of the English devotional poets of the seventeenth century, who, though generally Protestant, are not, *in their poetry*, so much militant proponents of the Reformation as Christians confronting God.

These poets bring to their poetic encounter with God varied experiences and draw upon a number of Christian resources—Catholic and Protestant, Medieval and Renaissance. What is conspicuously missing is a definitely Protestant theology of grace embodied in poems decisively incompatible with Catholic theology. Calvin's presence, like that of other divines of the era, remains marginal when it is not equivocal. Instead of versified theological expositions, marks of the strains exerted by competing versions of grace and salvation ought to be the quarry of the critic. For it is the poets' sensitivity to the theological tensions of the era that generates the urgency peculiar to their poems.

9. *Letters to Severall Persons of Honour*, p. 51.

READINGS OF *HOLY SONNET 10 (XIV)*: A CRITICAL DISCUSSION

J. C. LEVENSON: [The First Quatrain]†

Dramatic immediacy often short-circuits one's literary perception. The first quatrain of Donne's *Holy Sonnet*, XIV exemplifies this for me, since the words reverberated in my mind for a number of years without creating any discomfort at insufficient comprehension. Donne's strong, intimate tone, "agonized and clear," and his explosive shifting from one verb to another, as though no single metaphor could be adequate,—these are the most important characteristics of the first four lines. The switching of verbs conveys the intensity of the poet's emotion, but beneath the changes there is the fundamental consistency of a fully realized conceit. The various metaphors coherently suggest a single situation: God is a tinker, Donne a pewter vessel in the hands of God the artisan. A modern version of the Biblical potter-and-clay image holds together the centrifugal fragments of Donne's expostulation. As in the best dramatic poetry, the major esthetic effect can occur long before one's anatomical curiosity asserts itself and can be reinforced by that same analytic process which leaves merely melodramatic lines in shards.

GEORGE HERMAN: [The Extended Metaphor]††

Mr. J. C. Levenson's interpretation of the first quatrain of Donne's *Holy Sonnets*, XIV (Exp., Mar., 1953, XI, 31) seems to me quite unsatisfactory. It isn't likely that any good poet, much less Donne, limited to fourteen lines, would start by addressing a "three-personed God," shift to "a fully realized conceit" involving God the tinker and Donne the pewter vessel, and then get on to the usurped and besieged town. Donne's extended metaphor seems to me reasonably clear and consistent *throughout* the poem, and it has nothing to do with a tinker or a pewter vessel—though I cannot say that I fully realize it. God the Father as yet but knocks at the gate (or the heart). God the Holy Ghost as yet but breathes upon the heart, which is also the town and a woman; it *may* be that Donne is playing with "breathe" and the phrase "breathe upon," meaning "to taint, corrupt," for which the *NED* gives the following subsidiary quotation: "1591 Shaks. *Two Gent.* v, iv, 131. Take but possession of her, with a Touch: I dare thee, but to breath vpon my Loue." God the Son (Sun) as yet but shines upon the heart-town-woman. The three-

† From J. C. Levenson, "Donne's *Holy Sonnets*, XIV," in *Explicator*, XI (March, 1953), Item 31. Reprinted by permission of *Explicator* and J. C. Levenson.

†† From George Herman, "Donne's *Holy Sonnets*, XIV," in *Explicator*, XII (December, 1953), Item 18. Reprinted by permission of *Explicator* and George Herman.

fold, three-personed effort as yet but seeks to mend the defect. But a greater violence is required: God the Father needs to break instead of merely knock. God the Holy Ghost needs to blow instead of merely breathe; it *may* be that Donne is playing with "blow" and the phrase "blow upon," meaning to "bring into discredit, defame," for which the *NED* gives the following quotation: "1470–85 (ed. 1634) Malory, *Arthur* (1816) II.438. Then Sir Gawaine made many men to blow upon Sir Launcelot, and all at once they called him "False recreant Knight!" God the Son (Sun) needs to burn rather than merely to shine upon. This greater three-fold, three-personed effort would seek to remake her entirely. Clearly, "make" had the appropriate popular meaning in Donne's day that it has today, and it seems to me likely that Donne here consciously employed the pun. (Cf. *Merry Wives of Windsor*, III, iii, 43–47. Also, the phrase "to meddle or make" of *MWW*, I,iv,115; *Troilus and Cressida*, I,i,14, also 87; *Much Ado About Nothing*, III, iii, 55. *NED* gives an obsolete meaning of "meddle" as "To have sexual intercourse (*with*). Also refl [exive]." Cf. *Coriolanus*, IV,v,50.) Eric Partridge calls "make my play," of *Henry VIII*, I, iv, 46–50, "an erotic pun" (*Shakespeare's Bawdy*; cf. entries *thing* and *make one's play*). The besieged and occupied woman-town, despite her better Reason, has acquiesced to her possession by God's enemy and is betrothed to him. She asks God to break that bond ("Divorce me, etc."), to take her, to ravish her, and thereby, paradoxically, to make her chaste.

Incidentally, wouldn't it be rather futile to attempt to shine pewter?

J. C. LEVENSON: [Three Conceits]†

The interpretation of figurative language, when we are prepared to find a great variety of practice, can help us towards an understanding of poetry. Mr. George Herman's comment on Donne's *Holy Sonnets*, XIV (Exp., Dec., 1953, XII, 18) seems to me to err in stating *a priori* that no good poet, "much less Donne," would develop a conceit of metal-working in his first quatrain, a military conceit in his second quatrain, and a sexual conceit in his sestet, given the contracted space of fourteen lines in which to work. This is, of course, precisely what Donne did, apparently satisfied that the unified theme, the common denominator of violence, and the specific verbal linkages established a sufficient connection among his three conceits. The word "o'erthrow" in line 3 makes it seem to have been less of a jump when we have shifted from the artisan's workshop to the beleaguered town; the words "weak and untrue" in line 8 offer an easy transition from thoughts of siege to thoughts of sex; and the word "enemy" in line 10 reaches back in association, even though the enemy is now singular rather than collective.

† From J. C. Levenson, "Donne's *Holy Sonnets*, XIV," in *Explicator* XII (April 1954), Item 36. Reprinted by permission of *Explicator* and J. C. Levenson.

The complexity of Donne's poetic practice is different from that of Mr. Herman's interpretation, and considerably less difficult. The monistic assumption that the three systems of imagery in this sonnet are congruent provides a specious simplification. It is not only not simple, but just about impossible to conceive as an entity one literal and two metaphorical images as disparate as "the heart, which is also a town and a woman." The trouble with this hypothesis is (1) it makes us go through the cycle of changed reference several times instead of only once, (2) it opens a field for scatological interpretation of which Mr. Herman has barely ploughed a corner, and (3) it leads, as Mr. Herman sees, to a notion of God as "corrupting" man, an idea which it is unlikely any good poet, much less Donne, would seriously entertain. On the other hand, Donne's habit of shifting metaphors, common enough in his secular poetry, extends to the *Holy Sonnets*, as in IV, "Oh my black Soule!" where the soul is successively pilgrim, prisoner, and penitent, and even changes color from black to red; IX, "If poysonous mineralls," where the mineral, vegetable, and animal kingdoms are traversed in just three lines; or X, "Death be not proud," in which death is treated as "mighty and dreadfull," as pleasant anodyne, and, in the sestet alone, as slave, criminal, and soporific. As Johnson remarked, "who would imagine it possible that in a very few lines so many remote ideas could be brought together?"

My initial comment on *Sonnet* XIV (Exp., Mar., 1953, XI, 31) dealt with the stylistic obstacles to seeing any conceit at all in the first quatrain, and overcome by the discovery of a single implied metaphor, I rushed into oversimplifications of my own which should be corrected. The argument that Donne's neologism for the potter-and-clay metaphor makes God here a worker in metals seems to me to hold. But even though pewter *can* be shined, there is obviously no authority in the text for saying that Donne the vessel in God's hands is specifically of one metal rather than another. My calling God a "tinker" with reference to this metal vessel was a decidedly poor use of words, since the argument of the first four lines is that God should cease to tinker ("seek to mend") the damaged object, but demolish it, melt it down, and make it new. This conceit fits with Mr. Herman's observation that lines 2 and 4 show a threefold effort that follows from the apostrophe to "three-personed God." (The triple series recurs in line 11 and again in lines 12–14). In each case the three particular verbs are summed up in the abstract unity of the final phrase, and although Mr. Herman's argument that the verbs in triple series refer to Father, Holy Ghost, and Son (in that order!) rests on untenable theological premises and uses tenuous lexicographical methods, his basic observation stands if we see the one-in-threeness as determined here by the vehicle of the metal-working metaphor. The most marked relation which this conceit bears to the next is one of contrast; the novel image drawn from common life is followed in the second quatrain by a conventional, heroic image. Donne brought together in his poetry not only remote ideas, but both "plain" and "elevating" figures.

GEORGE KNOX: [Contemplation of the Trinity]†

I disagree with two recent readings of this sonnet (*Exp.*, Mar., 1953, XI, 31; *Exp.*, Dec., 1953, XII, 18) and offer the following interpretation as more complete. Mr. Levenson's and Mr. Herman's explications seem somewhat oblivious of the obvious. It seems very clear to me that the very first line invites contemplation of the Trinity and that this concept determines the structure of the whole sonnet. Mr. Levenson's God-the-tinker idea does not take us beyond the first quatrain, and Mr. Herman's mention of the Trinity is spoiled by his woman-town ratio. We begin with: "three-personed God," for in the tripartite division the Father is power, the Son the bringer of light (allowing Mr. Herman his "Sun" pun), and the Holy Ghost the infusion of love or Grace. Hence, in the second line, "knock, breathe, shine," reflect these forces as they are contemplated in the poetic invocation. Knocking represents first God's courting, and second the power employed to "break" the hardened human heart and the obdurate walls of the will; the breathing with or through is the interchange or interflowing of infinite and finite substance, a common image in Christian symbology; and shining is the casting and reflecting of the light of divine intelligence. Carried into the violent, immediate secular execution, or rather as interpreted on the material plane of consciousness, and employed against the unregenerate ego, these forces must be translated: "break, blow, burn." The paradox develops thus: in order that the poet (his inner self, his heart first) may be regenerated ("That I may rise, and stand,") the "three-personed God" must "seek to mend" man's being. God must "make me anew" (i.e., remake me).

In the second quatrain the forces are embodied in a military action in the image of a besieged town. God's trinitarian powers labor to enter into possession of His rightful grounds but the poet's Reason ("Your viceroy") which should defend him against his unjust captor (sinful living) is weakened and "untrue." The word "untrue" carries us on from "heart" and further anticipates the love-courtship theme so intensely finalized in the third quatrain. The degenerate will and spirit, though weakened, still love and want to be loved by God; but the poet's being ("usurped town"), although "due" to God ("another") is "betrothed" to Satanic forces ("Your enemy"). Now, since the poem opened with a wish that God batter the heart, it is right that it should be rounded out structurally by a consummation through love.

The necessity of forceful overpowering and violent reshaping (conver-

† From George Knox, "Donne's *Holy Sonnets*, XIV," in *Explicator* XV (October, 1956), Item 2. Reprinted by permission of *Explicator* and George Knox.

sion paradox) means that one dies so that he may live, loses that he may gain. This is made clear in the first quatrain as an invocational demand. The necessity for regeneration through redeemed Reason is indirectly requested in the second. In the third quatrain the sonnet has progressed to the point where a resolution must be achieved in terms equally as violent as those of the first quatrain. The poet's present imprisonment in sinful living must be replaced by a new imprisonment in the triune personality of God. The word "enthrall" carries the meaning of being captivated by love, of being enamored in love, and of being subjugated to love: bent and mended in accordance with God's will, which is complete love. Paradoxically, we have here freedom in enthrallment. Although man is bound anew he is in essence or in substance free.

The triadic division of the sonnet into quatrains follows the extension of the "knock, breathe, shine," and the "break, blow, burn," alignments. The first quatrain calls on God the Father's omnipotence to batter the heart. The second envisions the admission of God through the medium or agency of Rectified Reason, Reason rectified through love. The third exemplifies the reborn understanding (en*light*ened through the Son) conceiving the consubstantiality of man and God through imagery of interpenetration. Man is to be imprisoned in God by being totally inspired (breathed in and into) completely (the town image) and opening and receiving God. That is, the fallen one must be ravished before he become spiritually chaste. I would save Mr. Herman the strain of trying to imagine the poet in the role of woman. The sexual ravishment involves no bisexuality on the part of the poet nor does it require our imagining literally the relation between man and God in heterosexual terms. The traditions of Christian mysticism allow such symbolism of ravishment as a kind of "as if."

JOHN E. PARISH: [The Sonnet's Unity]†

Within the last ten years four critics have published articles about No. 14 of Donne's *Holy Sonnets*. In the first (*Explicator*, March 1953), J. C. Levenson suggested that in the opening quatrain God is compared to a tinker and sinful man to a damaged pewter vessel. Later in the same year (*Explicator*, December 1953) George Herman expressed doubt that the image of a tinker is implied. More likely, he felt, the sonnet is unified by a single extended metaphor which (if it could be realized) would demonstrate the part each Person of the Trinity plays in saving the penitent, since (according to Herman) in the first quatrain God the Father is implored to *breake* rather than merely *knocke*, the Holy Ghost to *blowe* rather than simply *breathe*, and God the Son (Sun) to *burn* rather than

† From John E. Parish, "No. 14 of Donne's *Holy Sonnets*", in *College English*, January, 1963. Reprinted with the permission of the National Council of Teachers of English and John E. Parish.

gently *shine* on the sinner's heart, "which is also the town and a woman." In the words *make me new* Herman believed that all three Persons are beseeched to act on the heart-town-woman and that, as applied to the woman, *make me* is a plea (like that in the sestet) to be violated. "Clearly, *make* had the appropriate popular meaning in Donne's day that it has today, and it seems to me likely that Donne here consciously employed the pun."

After three years George Knox replied to Herman (*Explicator*, October 1956), whom he wished to spare "the strain of trying to imagine the poet in the role of woman." According to Knox, "the traditions of Christian mysticism allow such symbolism of ravishment as a kind of 'as if.' " (One must infer that in Knox's opinion such symbolism shares nothing with metaphor in its effect on the imagination). Describing the interpretations of both Levenson and Herman as "somewhat oblivious of the obvious," Knox claimed to see the unifying conceit that had eluded Herman: "It seems very clear to me that the very first line invites contemplation of the Trinity and that this concept determines the structure of the whole sonnet. . . . The first quatrain calls on God the Father's omnipotence to batter the heart. The second envisions the admission of God through the medium or agency of Rectified Reason, Reason rectified through love [the Son]. The third exemplifies the reborn understanding (en*light*ened through the Son) conceiving the consubstantiality of man and God through imagery of interpenetration [the Holy Ghost]."

Then in 1961 Arthur L. Clements (*Modern Language Notes*, June 1961)—by citing biblical passages associating each of the verbs *knocke*, *breathe* and *shine* with all three Persons of the Trinity—proved beyond doubt (in my opinion) that "the sonnet's structure cannot then be viewed as the development of three quatrains each separately assigned to each of the Three Persons." Contending that "the organizing principle of the poem . . . is the paradox of death and rebirth, the central paradox of Christianity," Clements pointed out further that to illustrate this paradox of destroying in order to revive or throwing down in order to raise Donne employs throughout the sonnet two kinds of figurative language: "one kind is warlike, military, destructive; the other is marital, sexual, or uniting." The two kinds of metaphor are fused in lines 11–14 and are "made to achieve between themselves what Donne wishes to achieve with God."

Like Clements, I must join those whom Knox considered "oblivious of the obvious," those who cannot perceive three divisions of the sonnet devoted respectively to the Father, the Son, and the Holy Ghost. I believe that the sinner's only reason for addressing God as "three person'd" is that he is imploring him to exert all his power, his triple power, to rescue him from Satan. I hope that my interpretation will show, even more clearly than Clements has shown, how the interlocking of the various metaphors and of the stanzaic divisions gives the sonnet its unity.

In the first quatrain, I believe, the repentant sinner compares his heart to a walled town, one of many over which God is the rightful King.

Upon approaching, the King has found this particular town closed to him, a Usurper (Satan) having captured it. Now the King with his army is encamped outside the walls, knocking at the gates and asking to be re-admitted so that he can restore (*mend*) whatever has been demolished in the capture and whatever has deteriorated during the occupation. But, declares the sinner, such gentle overtures will not suffice. The King must burst open the gates with *a battering ram*. (On another level, God *is* the battering ram). Beyond all mending, the town must be completely destroyed, after which a new one will *rise* in its place, built by the King to *stand* forever.

The verbs *batter*, *breake*, and *burn* all suggest storming a citadel; and even *blowe* may be intended to suggest the use of gunpowder to blow up the fortress or blow it into smithereens. One is reminded of the violent scenes described by Aeneas in telling Dido about the fall of Troy and (faintly) of the fact that a new Troy is fated to rise. Even richer and more apt, however, are the allusions to the destruction of Jerusalem by Nebuchadnezzar (God's unwitting agent) and to the many predictions by the Prophets of the New Jerusalem to rise when a chastened people come to deserve it. There are also echoes of "the name of the city of my God, which is new Jerusalem" and of "Behold, I stand at the door and knock: if any man hear my voice and open the door, I will come in to him" (Revelation iii:12, 20).

The sonnet as a whole is unified by a shifting viewpoint which produces the effect of God's boring from the outside into the very center of the human heart. In the first quatrain the perspective is mainly that of the King outside the walls, seeking admission. In the second, the reader is carried inside the usurped town and sees the lamentable state of affairs through the eyes of the populace, rightfully the subjects of the King and of the Princess whom he has appointed as his Viceroy (these subjects being all the forces of man that should be governed by reason, here identified with the soul). In the sestet the point of view is that of the captive Princess herself (Reason, or the Soul), who has entered into a shameful marriage with the Usurper and is held in solitary confinement deep within the citadel.

Still further to invigorate and unify the prayer, Donne personifies the fortified town of the first quatrain as a woman, a woman urging her suitor to take her by force rather than by courtship. (In the Psalms, fallen Jerusalem or Zion is often personified as a mourning woman). This plea of the personified city for violent attack anticipates the similar plea which the dishonored Princess makes in the sestet.[1]

The phrase *usurpt towne* is deliberately ambiguous and transitional, connecting the first and second quatrains. It refers back to the walled town, of course; but simultaneously it designates the wretched people

1. This begging for violation is less shocking when the woman is a personified city than when she is the soul of the repentant sinner. Few readers will detect this imagery in the first quatrain until *after* discovering it in the sestet; but in a re-reading, awareness of its first employment will mollify the shock of the second.

within the town, just as one might have said in 1944 "Paris awaits her deliverers," meaning that the *people* of Paris were hoping soon to be liberated. The complaint of the populace in the second quatrain is that though they acknowledge their duty to the King and labor to admit him, without the guidance of the Princess their efforts are futile. (It is not clear to me how the nonspiritual forces in man, unaided by the reason-soul, can labor at all to admit God). Since the capture of the town, the Usurper has held the Princess incommunicado; and her unhappy people, while aware of her shameful marriage, are unable to pass fair judgment on it, not knowing whether it was forced on her or whether she has voluntarily shifted allegiances to the Usurper and is therefore guilty of treason (*untrue*).

After the prayers of the personified city and of the leaderless people, finally in the sestet the captive Princess is heard from her solitary confinement. In language of almost unendurable anguish, which gives the sonnet much of its tone of passionate sincerity, she beseeches the King to deliver her from shame, declaring paradoxically that she can never be free unless he enthralls her and can never be chaste again unless he ravishes her. Appropriately, since the subject of the sonnet is remorse,[2] Donne is alluding again to the third chapter of Revelation—this time to the nineteenth verse: "As many as I love, I rebuke and *chasten:* be zealous therefore, and repent," and he has in mind two meanings of the verb *chasten*; to castigate and to purify.

Readers like Knox, who find it a strain "to imagine the poet in the role of woman," should remember that with Donne (as with Shakespeare, Spenser and others) the soul is always feminine. For example, in No. 2 of the *Holy Sonnets*, in the first nine lines the penitent describes himself as (among other things) one of God's sons and then as a temple of God's spirit presently usurped by Satan; but in the last five lines the feminine soul urges God to rescue her from Satan, who has kidnaped and ravished her.

To represent man's body as a temple or a castle and his soul as the priestess or governess was conventional.[3] Alma within her beleaguered castle, in Book Two of *The Faerie Queene*, is the most celebrated example; but since Alma has managed to remain chaste, a passage from *The Rape of Lucrece* more closely resembles Donne's sonnet. Shakespeare attributes to Tarquin, after he has committed the crime, something indistinguishable from Christian remorse. He is "a heavy convertite"; both his body (a temple) and his soul (a princess now as dishonored as Lucrece herself) have been polluted by his lustful will. Shakespeare's choice of words is remarkably like Donne's:

2. Here I disagree with Helen Gardner, who regards this sonnet (No. 10 in her arrangement) as one of three "on the love man owes to God and to his neighbour." (*The Divine Poems* [Oxford, 1952], p. xli). Donne's sonnet seems to me to be a sinner's plea that remorse enough be put into his heart to start him on the way to repentance. As such, it would serve admirably as the first of a sequence; but perhaps all the sonnets are what Grierson called them—"separate ejaculations."

3. During Elizabeth's long reign, English poets must have found new value in the old conceit, since a flesh-and-blood Princess was God's viceroy over them and sole head (under God) of their church.

Besides his soules faire temple is defaced,
  To whose weake ruines muster troopes of cares,
  To aske the spotted Princesse how she fares.
Shee sayes her subjects with fowle insurrection,
Haue batterd downe her consecrated wall,
And by their mortall fault brought in subjection
Her immortalitie, and made her thrall,
To liuing death and payne perpetuall.
  Which in her prescience shee controlled still,
  But her foresight could not forestall their will. (719–728)

But if the exhausted metaphor of the castle-body and the princess-soul was anemic by the 1590s, until Donne wrote his *Holy Sonnets* no poet had thought of wedding it to the equally weary and thinblooded convention of comparing a cold mistress to a castle and her lover to the general of an army besieging it. Miraculously, this marriage of two ancient weaklings produced an abnormally vigorous offspring, a sonnet in which Donne, with his accustomed daring, requires the reader to see God wearing (with a difference) the rue of a Petrarchan lover.

R. D. BEDFORD [The Potter-Clay Image]†

Some twenty five years ago there was an extraordinary flurry of critical activity around the opening lines of Donne's 'Batter my heart' sonnet:

Batter my heart, three person'd God; for, you
As yet but knocke, breathe, shine, and seeke to mend;
That I may rise, and stand, o'erthrow mee, 'and bend
Your force, to breake, blowe, burn and make me new.

The discussions (which were never adequately resolved) seem to have been sparked off by an innocent enough remark by J. C. Levenson that he had read the first quatrain for years without feeling 'any discomfort at insufficient comprehension'. But whereas the conceit of the second quatrain (the usurped town) and of the sestet (the divorce and ravishment) are clear enough, the opening lines seem to show Donne writing 'as though no single metaphor could be adequate'.[1] The sonnet *as a whole* was rigorously explored,[2] but uncertainty, hesitancy and a sense or either insufficient comprehension on the reader's part or, more likely, an insufficient control on Donne's part, still shrouds the opening in mystery. Most readers are pretty clear about the general drift, the kind of gesture that is being made, but as to what *exactly* Donne is talking about

† From *Notes and Queries* 29 (1982): 15–19. © Oxford University Press 1982. Reprinted from *Notes and Queries* vol 29 No. 1 (1982) by permission of Oxford University Press.

1. J. C. Levenson, 'Donne's *Holy Sonnets*, XIV', *The Explicator* 11, March 1953, item 31.

2. George Herman, 'Donne's *Holy Sonnets*, XIV', *The Explicator* 12, Dec. 1953, item 18; J. C. Levenson, 'Donne's *Holy Sonnets*, XIV', *The Explicator* 12, April 1954, item 36; George Knox, 'Donne's *Holy Sonnets*, XIV', *The Explicator* 15, Oct. 1956, item 2; A. L. Clements, 'Donne's Holy Sonnet XIV', *Modern Language Notes* 76, June 1961, 484–9; John E. Parish, 'No. 14 of Donne's *Holy Sonnets*', *College English*, Jan. 1963. The sequence may be followed in *John Donne's Poetry*, selected and edited by A. L. Clements (Norton Critical Edition, New York, 1966).

in those verbal triplets circling an apparently unspecific image, one guess seems as good as another.

In the absence of a finally satisfying metaphor to hold those explosives together, attention has subsequently been directed to the mannerism rather than the meaning. For some it is merely another more highly coloured version of 'Therfore that he may raise the Lord throws down' (Hymne to God my God, in my sicknesse); a violently emphatic expression of the paradox of the grain of wheat falling into the ground (to live, we must be destroyed); an enactment of the retribution and destruction which is the prerequisite for atonement. The *way* in which Donne here expresses this Christian commonplace has led to severe censure: Donne's penchant for drama can lead him, it is suggested, into 'the forced sensationalism of melodrama, especially when he gets his hands on an erotic conceit'.[3] So for some the opening quatrain of battering, rising and standing, being broken and blown, is an erotic conceit, a view developed by Wilbur Sanders who reads the end of the sonnet into its beginning and concludes that the 'vulgarity' in this poem 'springs' from a dangerously uncontrolled sensationalism'. Sanders wonders how the end of the poem, the 'sweet female passivity' (and one might wonder where he gets *that* from), is related to 'this invocation of violence at the beginning, to the desire to be battered and hammered, overthrown and bent, hurled about with exciting brutality . . . a hankering for *sexual* violence'. It is hardly surprising that such a reading of the poem should find that 'there's something hysterically out of control'.[4] It may appear to be out of control just because we can't find a stabilizing conceit to which those words can be attached and in terms of which they may be decoded. Uncertainty about what it might be, or the assumption that there isn't one, or aren't any, seems to have led Sanders to the extraordinary view that Donne is doing no more than hysterically exhibiting his masochistic sexual predilections.

A principle of control in terms of the *organization* of the quatrain is not hard to find, and has been much discussed. The 'three person'd God' works through three-fold verbs, the triplet sequence corresponding, in the view of some, 'to the respective members of the Trinity', God crushing the spirit as a prelude to the inspiration of the Holy Ghost and the warming benevolence of the Son/Sun.[5] Others had argued, notably A. L. Clements,[6] that the verbs knock, breathe, shine cannot be assigned exclusively to one each of the parts of the Trinity but imply all three in each verb, as do their counterparts, break, blow, burn. Whatever the subtleties of interpretation, the mechanics of Donne's organization are fairly clear; a Trinity working through trinities of verbs, and reflected in the sonnet as a whole in a trinity of metaphors. According to this mech-

3. Clay Hunt, *Donne's Poetry* (New Haven, 1954), 136.
4. Wilbur Sanders, *John Donne's Poetry* (Cambridge, 1971), 129–30.
5. Murray Roston, *The Soul of Wit* (Oxford, 1974), 172–3.
6. A. L. Clements, *supra;* see also Lucio P. Ruotalo, 'The Trinitarian Framework of Donne's Holy Sonnet XIV', *Journal of the History of Ideas* 27, 1966, 445.

anism (and it is still only a mechanism, still without any concrete metaphor around which its opening flourish centres) Donne appears to suggest that the normal biblical activities of three-personed God are going to be inadequate in his particular case. The door is open not only for accusations of sexual deviancy but also of a flamboyant egotism: as though Donne, in an ecstasy of guilt, is claiming that 'then can bee None of that kinde, of which he is, but hee', and God must adopt a novel approach.

The search for the implied conceit has thrown up an impressive array of suggestions. Some see no conceit at all, apart from the generalized one of the hardened human heart.[7] Many see it as an implied anticipation of the military image of the besieged town, and in it the heart is already being compared to a city wrongfully appropriated and helplessly possessed by God's enemy. The force of the verbs can thus become apparent only retrospectively. John E. Parish offered to tidy up the difficulties by interpreting the opening entirely in military terms. The conceit here is of a walled town, and Satan is inside. The King (God) knocks at the gate. But the King must burst the gates with a battering ram. 'The town must be destroyed and a new one *rise* in its place to *stand* for ever'. 'The verbs . . . suggest storming a citadel, and even 'blowe' may be intended to suggest the use of gunpowder to blow up the fortress or blow it into smithereens'.[8] Such a reading may be confirmed by others: 'bend/ Your force' may have siege connotations that suggest the bending of bows and catapults.[9] At all events we are asked to read the opening in terms of what follows, and not to worry too much if the whole sonnet *appears* to be articulated as a triplet, with three conceits, not two.

Other suggestions have involved allusion to Jacob wrestling with the angel, 'stand' and 'o'erthrow' being interpreted as wrestling terms: 'God is to overthrow the cowed wrestler, in order that the latter may raise [*sic*] and stand on his own feet'.[1] The technical wrestling argot which will accommodate 'breathe, and shine' and 'blowe, burn' is yet to be unearthed.

The curious thing about all these attempts to account for Donne's extraordinary language in the first quatrain is that the tentative observation made by Levenson that 'the various metaphors coherently suggest a single situation' was followed by the equally tentative suggestion that 'God is a tinker, Donne a pewter vessel in the hands of God the artisan'.[2] It seems to me by far the most useful suggestion, though it was promptly ruled out of court in the ensuing debate, George Herman even facetiously asking what the point was of shining pewter anyway. (Louthan, some two years before, had considered that Donne may have been 'a defective utensil', but the thought was not developed.) Levenson stoutly resisted criticism and asserted again that the stylistic obstacles to seeing any conceit at all in the first quatrain were overcome 'by the discovery of a single implied metaphor': 'the argument that Donne's neologism for

7. George Knox, *supra*.
8. John E. Parish, *supra*.
9. Doniphan Louthan, *The Poetry of John Dunne* (New York, 1951), 124.

1. Louthan, ibid.
2. J. C. Levenson, *The Explicator* 11, March 1953, item 31.

the potter-clay metaphor makes God here a worker in metals seems to me to hold'. However Levenson withdraws his use of the word 'tinker' since Donne's point is that tinkering is not enough.

Why God as a metal-worker should be thought of as a 'neologism' or 'a modern version of the potter-clay image' is difficult to understand, since the image is biblical ('And I will turn my hand upon thee, and purely purge away they dross, and take away all thy tin', Isaiah i.25) and lovers of Handel will know all about the refiner's fire. God as a gold-smith, or as a smith, occurs too in Ezekiel xx. 20–21, and Jeremiah, vi. 29, and was developed by Alanus de Insulis and Deguileville.[3] It is also of course used by Donne: 'Burne off my rusts, and my deformity,/ Restore thine Image' (*Good Friday, 1613. Riding Westward*). Such a conceit certainly brings those otherwise unattached verbs more sharply into focus: the tinkering which knocks (hammers), breathes (polishes) and shines (buffs up), and the remaking which breaks up, blows (in the furnace), burns, and 'makes new'.

Yet it seems unnecessary so readily to abandon the potter-clay image. Donne may well be suggesting both at once, and the crucial line, which underlines the dominant conceit here, is 'That I may rise, and stand, o'erthrow mee'. Unless we are happy enough to let Donne metamorphose his metal pot into a wrestler *protem*, and then return to it, there is for the metalwork image little *specific* sense in these particular and equally precise verbs, beyond the general sense of regeneration alluded to earlier. God as potter is of course a recurring biblical image of God's creativity. 'But now, O Lord, thou art our father; we are the clay, and thou our potter; and we all are the work of thy hand' (Isaiah lxiv. 8), or as an image of God's vengeance, 'And he shall break it as the breaking of the potter's vessel that is broken in pieces' (Isaiah xxx. 14). Donne uses the image, or plays variations on it, in his poetry (e.g. *Epitaph on Himselfe*, or *La Corona* 7, *Ascention*, in which 'this Sunne, and Sonne' has 'burnt your drossie clay'), and he employs it in *The Litanie* in a petitionary and verbal context which is very similar to the opening of the Holy Sonnet:

come
And re-create mee; now growne ruinous:
My heart is by dejection, clay,
And by selfe-murder, red.
From this red earth, O Father, purge away
All vicious tinctures, that new fashioned
I may rise up from death, before I'm dead.

What is usually glossed at this point is Donne's punning on the Hebrew *adam* (Adam) meaning 'red earth'; but what is relevant here is the prayer 're-create mee', the hearth-clay that must be 'new fashioned' ('make me

3. Alanus de Insulis, s.xiii; Deguileville, Deus . . . *tanquam mundi elegans architectus, tanquam aureae fabricae fater aurarius . . . etc.* P.L. CCX, 453.

new') so that 'I may rise up' ('that I may rise'). Donne doesn't *need* to mention clay specifically in the sonnet because it is, as it were, already there in this particular concatenation of words.

What difference might such a perception make to our comprehension of Donne's language? God the Father, Son and Holy Ghost knocks, breathes on, shines the defective clay pot—taps it to test its strength, breathes on it and shines it up to make it look all right superficially. But this is not enough: the pot must be broken, the bellows worked, the kiln fired again. Between these activities referring to technical processes are equally technical and punning verbs: 'That I may rise, and stand' certainly implies rising from eternal death, but more immediately it suggests the clay rising on the potter's wheel to 'stand'. 'O'erthrow' certainly implies being crushed and humbled, but again more immediately it suggests the punning over-throw or throwing over again of the vessel. The potter's wheel was sometimes known as the 'throwing-wheel', and *OED* certainly confirms such usage at this period, citing an account of 1604 'To the disshethrower, ix days throwing disshes and bassenes, iiis.'.

It may be objected that in this reading of the lines Donne appears to be asking for the pot (himself), which has already been thrown and fired, to be broken up, rethrown and fired again—a process which is not possible for reconstituted rubble. Donne of course knows this perfectly well, and may have chosen to ignore it, just as he knows perfectly well how porcelain is made but offers a quainter and more poetically useful version of it in his *Elegie on the Lady Markham* . . . ('As men of China, after an ages stay,/ Do take up Porcelane, where they buried Clay'). It is more likely however that Donne is thinking of two incompatible ideas at the same time (which is after all the rhetorical mode of the sonnet as a whole). One is the image of the vessel which, in the words of Jeremiah, 'he made of clay' and which was 'marred in the hands of the potter: so he made it again another vessel, as seemed good to the potter to make it' (Jeremiah xviii.4). The other is that the marring of the vessel is the result both of original sin and active, individual sin, and that for true regeneration he must become a new man 'in Christ' and hence analogically a new pot, the re-throwing representing the motions of grace. There is certainly no evidence in Jeremiah that the pot was marred in the firing or after; Jeremiah's lump of clay could be made again because things had gone wrong in the shaping 'upon the wheels'. There is an obvious theological difficulty in the passage from Jeremiah and the simile there is a loose one: God cannot logically be conceived of as having marred anything in the making; the marring must be symbolic of man's original sin. When God makes it 'again another vessel, as seemed good to the potter to make it' this can only be interpreted as the grace which regenerates marred and fallen men. In either case, whether marred in the making or marred after the firing, the basic material is nothing more than clay in God's hands. Donne's prayer is to be made in a similar way, and it is quite consistent with the hyperbole and paradox of the sonnet that he should ask God to perform a physically impossible feat. 'O'erthrow mee' out of rubble need be no more difficult to swallow than 'Nor ever chast, except you ravish mee'.

A further interest lies in this particular passage from Jeremiah (which Donne naturally knew) because it may be a clue to the creative process of the poet's mind as he forges a new image to follow the opening one. The prophet declares an analogy between the potter's vessel and the house of Israel: 'as the clay is in the potter's hand, so are ye in my hand'. Similarly a nation, or a kingdom, may be plucked up, pulled down, and destroyed. The following chapter pursues the same image of the 'potter's earthen bottle' which is to be shown to the people: 'And thou shalt say unto them, Thus saith the Lord of hosts; Even so will I break this people and this city, as one breaketh a potter's vessel, that cannot be made again' (Jeremiah xix. 10–11). Thus the connection is already made between the opening image of the poem and the 'usurpt towne', this city 'to another due' that follows.

It is possible then to see the opening quatrain of this sonnet as having as its subject an implied conceit of considerable specificity and a good deal of poetic muscle. It completes the trio of metaphors which may be thought of as assigned to the Father (the potter), the Holy Ghost whose inspiration releases captive reason, and the Son whose Bride Donne prays to become. It is not an uncontrolled outburst of whirling words, nor simply a verbal arithmetic of vaguely focused triplets, and though its imagery is rendered entirely through its verbs it is as clear and as consistent as the two subsequent extended metaphors.

RAYMOND-JEAN FRONTAIN: [Redemption Typology]†

In the seventeenth century, notes Barbara K. Lewalski, typological symbolism came to be considered as a way for the individual to explore one's own spiritual state and to discover "the workings of Divine Providence in one's own life."

> [T]he shift in emphasis in reformation theology from *quid agas* to God's activity in us made it possible to assimilate our lives to the typological design, recognizing the biblical stories and events, salvation history, not merely as exemplary to us but as actually recapitulated in our lives. These various impulses led to a new, primary focus upon the individual Christian, whose life is incorporated within, and in whom may be located, God's vast typological patterns of recapitulations and fulfillments operating throughout history.[1]

† Reprinted by permission from *Journal of the Rocky Mountain Medieval and Renaissance Association* 8 (1987): 163–76.

1. Barbara K. Lewalski, "Typological Symbolism and the 'Progress of the Soul' in Seventeenth-Century Literature," in *Literary Uses of Typology from the Late Middle Ages to the Present*, ed. Earl Miner (Princeton, N.J.: Princeton UP, 1977), pp. 81–82.

John Donne's Holy Sonnet XIV ("Batter my heart, three person'd God") is clearly the product of such interior exploration and discovery, a meditation upon what Donne calls elsewhere the "repeating againe in us, of that which God had done before to Israel."[2] For, in order to communicate to a Christian trinitarian god his readiness and complete desire for salvation, the speaker draws upon three images most often used in tandem by the Hebrew prophets to denounce sinful, apostate Israel: a vessel in need of repair, a usurped town under siege, and a woman trapped in a degrading sexual relationship. In Holy Sonnet XIV, the individual's life repeats a larger pattern, just as the larger pattern is only finally understood in terms of what it reveals about the Christian's spiritual state: the speaker of Holy Sonnet XIV must be broken, beaten, and divorced just as Israel was for having been unfaithful to the one true God, and the full significance to Israel's apostasy, punishment, and reclamation becomes clear only in the light of the Christian's sin against, and redemption by, a trinitarian god. Recognition of the poem's typological symbolism illuminates both the poem's significant prophetic dimensions and a rhetorical maneuver that it shares with other Holy Sonnets by which the speaker attempts to manipulate God in order to effect his own salvation.

For the reader's convenience, I reprint the sonnet here.

Batter my heart, three person'd God; for, you
As yet but knocke, breathe, shine, and seeke to mend;
That I may rise, and stand, o'erthrow mee, 'and bend
Your force, to breake, blowe, burn and make me new.
I, like an usurpt towne, to'another due,
Labour to'admit you, but Oh, to no end,
Reason your viceroy in mee, mee should defend,
But is captiv'd, and proves weake or untrue,
Yet dearely'I love you, and would be lov'd faine,
But am betroth'd unto your enemie,
Divorce mee, 'untie, or breake that knot againe,
Take mee to you, imprison mee, for I
Except you'enthrall mee, never shall be free,
Nor ever chast, except you ravish me.[3]

Prophetic Analogues

The specifically Christian resonance of the poem's language has been well analyzed by George Knox and A. L. Clements, among others.[4] In

2. Evelyn M. Simpson and George R. Potter, eds., *The Sermons of John Donne*, 10 vols. (Berkeley and Los Angeles: U of California P, 1953–62), 3: 313.
3. Helen Gardner, ed., *The Divine Poems of John Donne*, 2nd ed. (Oxford: Clarendeon Press, 1978), p. 11.
4. Explications by Knox and Clements, originally published in *The Explicator* (1956) and *Modern Language Notes* (1961), are conveniently reprinted in *John Donne's Poetry: A Norton Critical Edition*, ed. A. L. Clements (New York: Norton, 1966), pp. 246–59. Pagination cited parenthetically in my essay refers to this edition.
Further discussions of the Christian or Trinitarian elements of the poem include Lucio P. Ruotolo, "The Trinitarian Framework of John Donne's

1961, Clements qualified Knox's earlier insistence that "contemplation of the Trinity . . . determines the structure of the whole sonnet" (249), each of the three conceits in the poem describing the action of one of the Persons. Emphasizing the paradox of three-in-one, Clements demonstrated that Donne drew on rich biblical values and associations to implicate each of the Persons in the action of the other two, each set of commands (e.g., "breake, blowe, burn and make me new") listing verbs appropriate to each of the Persons and to the concerted action of the Trinity as well. So great is the speaker's desire to be roused from his extreme sinfulness, and so great is his need to be saved, that he calls upon all three members of the Trinity to act both as one and at once; he fears that the action of one alone at some later date will not be sufficient.

But while illuminating the deeply Christian language of the poem, such analysis has unfortunately distracted attention from the likewise deeply Hebraic resonance of the poem's three conceits.[5] The imperfect pot destroyed by the potter, the apostatized city about to be razed to the ground, and the unfaithful wife punished for her adultery are iterative images or situations in the Hebrew prophetic oracles; each has its basis in the covenant which Yahweh made with Israel in which the Israelites' undeviating worship of Yahweh as their one true god guaranteed them his protection as his chosen people. Thus, the potter image recalls the incident in Genesis in which the Lord creates man to his purposes by molding clay, as well as suggests the fragility of all human qualities in themselves apart from the protection of their maker. In Jeremiah 18 the Lord himself draws upon both of these qualities when he orders Jeremiah to go to the potter's house, where the prophet finds the mechanic working at his wheel. Jeremiah relates how

> Now and then a vessel he was making out of the clay would be spoilt in his hands, and then he would start again and mould it into another vessel to his liking. Then the word of the Lord came to me: Can I not deal with you, Israel, says the Lord, as the potter deals with his clay? You are clay in my hands like the clay in his, O house of Israel. At any moment I may threaten to uproot a nation or a kingdom, to pull it down and destroy it. . . . Go now and tell the men of Judah and the inhabitants of Jerusalem that these are the words of the Lord: I am the potter; I am preparing evil for you and perfecting my designs against you. Turn back, every one of you, from his evil course; mend your ways and your doings.[6]

Holy Sonnet XIV," *Journal of the History of Ideas* 27 (1966): 445–46; Charles E. Lloyd, "The Author of Peace and John Donne's Holy Sonnet XIV," *Journal of the History of Ideas* 30 (1969): 251–52; C. W. Moseley, "A Reading of John Donne's Holy Sonnet XIV," *Archiv für das Studium der neuven Sprachen und Literaturen* 217 (1980): 103–8; and Dennis R. Klinck, "John Donne's '*knottie Trinitie*' " *Renascence* 33 (1981): 240–55.

5. The exception is William R. Mueller, "Donne's Adulterous Female Town," *Modern Language Notes* 76 (1961): 312–14. Mueller's insistence that the speaker's comparison of himself with an adulterous female town be seen against "an Old Testament background" of similar images for the sinful community in the writings of the Hebrew prophets anticipates my thesis in part. However, Mueller failed to sound the depth of the resonance that the biblical conceits had for Donne, citing but three or four instances in Scripture (I have found over fifty), and ignoring the clay pot entirely.

6. Jeremiah 18:1–11. Scriptural passages are cited

Likewise, protecting as they did a small people from the threat of marauders and invading armies, the walls of the city symbolized the special protection that the Israelites were promised by Yahweh. The prophets insisted that attacks on Israelite cities were divinely directed punishment for the Jews' having broken the covenant. Indeed, the city walls risked becoming a symbol of the Jews' pride, so that destruction of the city was tantamount to smashing the sinful complacency which led the people to forget their Lord's commandments. Micah's warning can be taken as the general message of all eighth-century prophecy:

> Get behind your walls, you people of a walled city;
> the siege is pressed home against you[.]
>
> (Mich. 5:1)

In Lamentations, Jeremiah records the confidence of the people in their security:

> This no one believed, neither the kings of the earth
> nor anyone that dwelt in the world:
> that enemy or invader would enter
> the gates of Jerusalem.
>
> (Lam. 4:12)

Yet the enemy, Jeremiah warns his audience, "shall batter down the cities in which you trust, / walled though they are" (Jer. 5:17). Chapters 1–39 of Isaiah form a long, violent threat by the Lord against proud, idolatrous, walled Jerusalem. Chapter 52 of Jeremiah is an account of the fall of Jerusalem, while Lamentations is Jeremiah's dirge for the disaster, wept as he sat amidst the ruins of the once holy city.

As regards the third image, the Lord himself spoke in sexual terms of his special relationship with his chosen people. In Hosea 2:18–23, for example, the Lord "makes a covenant on behalf of Israel":

> I will betroth you to myself for ever, betroth you in lawful wedlock with unfailing devotion and love; I will betroth you to myself to have and to hold, and you shall know the Lord. . . . Israel shall be my new sowing in the land, and I will show love to Lo-ruhamah and say to Lo-ammi, "You are my people," and he will say, "Thou art my God."

In their pursuit of foreign gods, however, Israel and Judah were to be considered as harlots who leave their loving husband and go to sit "by the wayside to catch lovers":

---

in the translation of the *New English Bible with the Apocrypha* (New York: Oxford UP, 1972) because this is, for my purposes, the sharpest of the English translations linguistically. As Evelyn Simpson points out, Donne himself relied upon no particular vernacular translation, employing Coverdale, the Great Bible, the Geneva Bible, the Bishops' Bible, and the Authorized Version in his sermons, often comparing and correcting their offerings with his own translation of the original (*Sermons*, 10: 306–28).

Saint Paul continues the potter motif in Romans 9:21 and 2 Corinthians 4:7. On Reformantion uses of the motif, See M. A. Screech, *Rabelais* (Ithaca, N.Y.: Cornell UP, 1979), pp. 182–83; cf. pp. 63–64.

> In the reign of King Josiah, the Lord said to me, Do you see what apostate Israel did? She went up to every hill-top and under every spreading tree, and there she played the whore. Even after she had done all this, I said to her, Come back to me, but she would not. That faithless woman, her sister Judah, saw it all; she saw too that I had put apostate Israel away and given her a note of divorce because she had committed adultery. Yet that faithless woman, her sister Judah, was not afraid; she too has gone and played the whore. She defiled the land with her thoughtless harlotry and her adulterous worship of stone and wood. In spite of all this that faithless woman, her sister Judah, has not come back to me in good faith, but only in pretence.
>
> (Jer. 3:6–10)

The first three chapters of Hosea develop at length the analogy between the relationship of Hosea to his adulterous wife, Gomer, and that of Yahweh with sinful Israel; likewise, Ezekiel 16 repeats the Hosea story in miniature. The agony of the Lord as an unrequited lover refusing to throw off his adulterous wife, always willing to take her back, is one of the most powerful in Hebrew scriptures.

One may argue that other sources made these images or narrative situations potentially available to Donne and that, rather than meditating upon the significance of a biblical type to his own experience, he was imitating a literary or spiritual model. Spanish mystical writing, for example, saw the heart as an "interior castle" which might be besieged, and depicted spiritual rapture in terms of sexual ravishment.[7] But the frequency with which the pot, the city walls, and the unfaithful spouse are used in tandem in biblical prophetic texts, and the probability that the mystics themselves derived the images from Scripture, suggest the Bible as Donne's probable source. (Other considerations, I shall make clear below, reinforce the typological nature of the images' operation.)

The linguistic convention of referring to cities in the feminine makes the conflation of the besieged or disobedient city with the adulterous woman a natural one. "How the faithful city has played the whore," exclaims Isaiah (Isa. 1:21). Addressing Nineveh as

> . . . blood-stained city, steeped in deceit,
> full of pillage, never empty of prey [,]

the Lord swears through Nahum to

> . . . uncover your breasts to your disgrace
> and expose your naked body to every nation,
> to every kingdom your shame. . . .

7. The sonnet has been read as a document of mystical experience. See, for example, Giuseppe Conte, "Mistica e retorica: a propositio di un sonetto di John Donne," *Rivista di Storia e Letteratura Religiosa* 13 (1977): 127–33; John J. Pollock, "A Mystical Impulse in Donne's Devotional Poetry," *Studia Mystica* 2 (1979): 17–24; and Ralph Yarrow, "Admitting the Infinite: John Donne's Poem 'Batter My Heart,' " *Studies in Mystical Literature* 1 (1981): 210–17.

Then all who see you will shrink from you and
say, "Nineveh is laid waste; who will console her?"
(Nah. 3:1–7)

The demolished city, object of ridicule to its more powerful enemies, is often compared to a ravished woman, her nakedness exposed to strangers (see, for example, Isa. 3:16–26, 23:15–16; also, Jer. 50:14, 51:47). The most extended use of this analogy is made at the opening of Lamentations where the ruined, depopulated city speaks as a childless, grieving widow who admits that her having "wantonly rebelled" is the just cause of her punishment.

Likewise, the besieged city admits of conflation with the clay pot. In Jeremiah 19:11, for example, the Lord threatens to "shatter this people and this city as one shatters an earthen vessel so that it cannot be mended." All three images are implicit in Isaiah 54, where Yahweh promises the people redemption through the agency of the Suffering Servant, explaining how the "deserted wife" will be restored and the "storm-battered city" shall be mended and made invincible if only the people will return to the Lord. This particular passage moves abruptly to the conceit of God as smith or potter (54:16) from that of him as loving bridegroom ("for your husband is your maker"—54:5). So tightly interwoven are the prophet's images that, as in Donne's Holy Sonnet XIV, it is impossible at times to separate tenor and vehicle.

Provoking Salvation

Biblical Israel's historical drama of disobedience and chastisement, as delivered in her prophets' images of the imperfect pot, the besieged city, and the adulterous woman, clearly adumbrates the interior drama of the speaker of Holy Sonnet XIV, who hopes for divine action upon his sin-hardened heart. In the first quatrain, the speaker is partially imaged as a clay pot that is beyond simple repair; indeed, the damaged vessel must be completely broken or battered, as Yahweh threatened might happen in Jeremiah 18:1–11, and a new pot be blown and burned in the kiln, just as the speaker's old self must be destroyed for his spiritual self to be renewed. The conceit of the besieged town in the second quatrain suggests a medieval psychomachia in which the king's representative, Reason—that spark of divinity planted in man at the Creation, and so God's "viceroy" ruling every individual in virtuous action—has been impaired (generically by Adam's fall and individually by the speaker's own folly), and so is either too weak to defend the self/town from attack, or has been so treacherous ("untrue") as to betray the city to foreign occupation and the speaker into the captivity of sin.[8] And in the third conceit, sin is associated with the sullying that a woman feels when trapped in a degrading

8. Louis I. Bredvold discusses Donne's partial "dissatisfaction with the results of reason" in "The Religious Thought of Donne in Relation to Medieval and Later Traditions," in *Studies in Shakespeare, Milton and Donne by Members of the English Department of the University of Michigan* (New York: Haskell House, 1964), pp. 193–232.

relationship.[9] The final movement of the poem is the woman/speaker's paradoxical plea to be ravished by her true lover in order that she might feel chaste again, perversely enacting what Donne calls elsewhere the "amorousnesse of an harmonious Soule" ("Hymne to Christ," 16). In these three metaphors of Israel's salvation history, Donne has discovered a tangible way of expressing the invisible or intangible action of grace upon the heart of the sinner, while at the same time revealing the spiritual reality that lies beneath the "fleshly" form of the Old Testament texts. The external events of Israel anticipate the internal events of every Christian, the typological significance of the prophets' metaphors for Israel's history growing clearer as this is understood.

If the typological dimensions of Donne's three conceits are not immediately clear to the reader, this may be as much due to Donne's conflation of the images as to the modern reader's general ignorance of Scripture and of typological design. The debate which began in the 1950s over the integrity of the poem's conceits required several exchanges before the vehicles of the metaphors were clearly identified.[1] But as has been seen, in the Hebrew prophetic oracles, the three conceits function simultaneously, even at times interchangeably, as vehicles to the same implied tenor, and likewise the boundaries of Donne's conceits are not clearly defined but shift throughout the poem in a fluid, almost kaleidoscopic way. The battering which the speaker begs for in line 1 refers to the process of forcibly opening a city's gates, but is the same force applied to "breake, blowe, burn and make . . . new" the clay pot in line 4. "Labour to'admit you" (6) is military in its immediate context of the speaker's comparison of himself to "an usurpt towne" but is sexual as well in terms of the woman's forcing herself to submit to penetration by the holy rapist; either reading conveys the diseased will's struggle to submit to painful corrective action. Two of the conceits conspire in lines 5–10 to form a Spenserian allegorical romance in miniature, in which the heart, depicted as a woman engaged to a man against her will, is held captive in a city under siege. The woman's being repossessed by her rightful lover is equivalent to the usurped city's being liberated by its rightful lord; her paradoxically chastening rape includes a paradoxically freeing impris-

9. The rich sexual imagery of the Song of Solomon was taken to refer allegorically to the special relationship that existed between God and his chosen people and between Christ and the individual Christian's soul; see George L. Scheper, "Reformation Attitudes towards Allegory and the Song of Songs," *PMLA* 89 (1974): 551–62. Cf. Itrat Husain's discussion of Christ as Savior/Redeemer/Lover in Donne's religious thought in *The Dogmatic and Mistical Theology of John Donne* (1938; rpt. New York: Haskell House, 1971), pp. 137–40.

1. Debate over the integrity of the sonnet's conceits began in 1953 when J. C. Levenson argued that a single situation lies beneath the multiple metaphors and switching of verbs, that "God is a tinker, Donne a vessel in the hands of God the artisan." George Herman rejected this tinker metaphor to emphasize both the congruence and appropriateness of the language of triple activities as a three-personed God acts upon the woman–town. His objections caused Levenson to reconsider his original claim and to argue instead for Donne's employing three separate conceits: a metalworking one in the first quatrain, a military one in the second, and a sexual one in the third. Their articles, which originally appeared in *The Explicator* (1953–54), are reprinted in Clements, ed., *John Donne's Poetry*, pp. 246–59. Since then William W. Heist has argued that the unity of the poem is not of imagery but of theme, insisting that the images of the sonnet cannot be harmonized; see his "Donne on Divine Grace: Holy Sonnet No. XIV," *Papers of the Michigan Academy of Science, Arts, and Letters* 53 (1968): 311–20.

onment within the city walls (12–14).[2] Linguistically, Donne's Holy Sonnet XIV is a poem of conflations. Clements has shown that just as the individual members of the Trinity are conflated theologically into one "three-person'd God," so are the verb actions appropriate to one member in particular but applicable to the others as well. Likewise the terms of the three conceits substitute for and duplicate each other, as the dimensions of type and antitype are subsumed into an eternal drama in which the actors are both Israel and Yahweh, the individual Christian and the grace-giving Trinity.

There are two possible reasons for Donne's typological application of these three biblical conceits to himself. First, desire for such unity as is signified by the linguistic conflations involved in the biblical conceits is at the heart of Holy Sonnet XIV, in which a spiritually shattered speaker recognized that his only hope of reunion with God, and of being made whole again, paradoxically lies in being further battered and broken: recreation can come only after total destruction. The speaker of Holy Sonnet XIV is in effect imploring God to perform what the speaker of another Donne poem puts so simply: "Make all this All" ("Upon the Translation of the Psalms," 23). The speaker suffers the isolation of the soul when it is divorced from God by sin, and desires to be subsumed back into that creating power without which it is nothing. Spiritual peace and harmony can come only when the individual no longer acts apart from God but in concert with God's will. The passive posture of the ceramic pot in the hands of the potter, of the city before the besieging army, and of the bride before the holy rapist represents the speaker's relinquishment of his individual will before the Almighty in his desire to find his identity only in the All, no longer in himself.

But perhaps more significantly, the Hebraic types offer a possible solution to the dilemma which the speaker suffers. The speaker of Holy Sonnet XIV understands that no matter how ardent his desire may be to renounce sin, sheer human longing for salvation is insufficient to effect an individual's recreation. Only God can set in motion the process of salvation by granting that prevenient grace which would allow him to truly repent, and so make him worthy of yet further healing, strengthening grace. As Robert Shaw observes, the movement of thought not merely in Holy Sonnet XIV but in all the Holy Sonnets "is often like that of a squirrel in its cage." What Shaw calls "Donne's passive posture" (in Holy Sonnet XIV his wish to be violently acted upon) stems

> from a fear of taking any initiative which is not clearly urged upon him by Heaven. "Yet grace, if thou repent, thou canst not lacke," he reasons with himself [in 'Oh my blacke Soule!'], only to dash

2. Such kaleidoscopic concresence is mirrored by the very structure of the poem. In the first eight lines, the poem seems to be following the same plan as Shakespeare's Sonnet 73, each quatrain introducing a new image, but one to the same effect as the others, thus intensifying the speaker's statement. But after the conceit of the clay pot in lines 1–4 and that of the usurped town in lines 5–8, the conceit of the expected third quatrain spills over into what should be the final couplet, the language of sexual ravishment pertaining to the new conceit blending inextricably with that of military conquest from the second.

> this comforting thought to pieces in the next line: "But who shall give thee that grace to begin?" Although the *possibility* of such grace is held out as a hope . . . , it is not apparent anywhere in the sonnets that Donne has experienced it as a reality—has received justification, as theology would say.[3]

"Except thou rise and fight for me," the terrified speaker of "As due by many titles" reminds God, he is lost to Satan. Throughout the *Holy Sonnets*, Donne issues imperatives similar to those which characterize Holy Sonnet XIV:

> Impute me righteous ("This is my playes last
>   scene")
> Teach me how to repent ("At the round earths
>   imagin'd corners")
> repaire me now ("Thou hast made me")
> Batter my heart . . . o'erthrow mee . . . Divorce
>   mee . . . Take me to you, imprison
>   me . . . ("Batter my heart")

It is as though, linguistically, Donne would force God to begin the process of salvation by provoking God to begin finally to act on his behalf.

Under such circumstances, typology's peculiar ability to allow the spiritually attuned individual to understand his present circumstances, and in part even to prophesy his future, must have had particular appeal for Donne. For implicit in the biblical conceits employed in Holy Sonnet XIV is the very assurance of salvation that the speaker so ardently desires. The later prophets saw the demolished city as having been ordained from the beginning to be rebuilt; the restoration of Jerusalem was seen as proof of the Lord's ongoing care for, and protection of, his chosen people. Thus, in Isaiah 54:11 ff., the Lord addresses his "storm-battered city," promising complete restoration; chapters 60–66 of that scroll look forward to the reestablishment of Jerusalem, in keeping with the reinstitution of the covenant. Similarly Ezekiel and Zechariah experience visions of the city and temple restored (Ezek. 40–48; Zech. 12:1–14:21); Jeremiah even promised that once the city is rebuilt "it shall never be pulled down or demolished" again (Jer. 31:38–40). In Isaiah 49:16–19, the Lord promises that the widowed woman will be made a bride again, just as the city's walls will be restored:

> Your walls are always before my eyes . . . ,
> Those who are to rebuild you make better speed
>   than those who pulled you down. . . .
>   By my life I, the Lord, swear it,
> you shall wear [the people returning to inhabit you]

3. Robert B. Shaw, *The Call of God: The Theme of Vocation in the Poetry of Donne and Herbert* (Cambridge, Mass.: Cowley Publications, 1981), p. 51. Louis Martz speculates that the *Holy Sonnets* were written specifically out of Donne's struggle with the problem of election (*The Poetry of Mediation* [New Haven, Conn.: Yale UP, 1954], pp. 218–20).

proudly as your jewels,
and adorn yourself with them like a bride;
I did indeed make you waste and desolate,
I razed you to the ground,
but your boundaries shall now be too narrow
for your inhabitants
and those who laid you in ruins are far away.

Widowed Jerusalem, far from being permanently reduced to lamenting the loss of her children-inhabitants, will live to marvel at their numbers; the city-woman who was thrown down will be raised up in greater glory than before. God is brutal in his punishment of evil, but his punishment can be to purify as he exercises a paradoxically healing destruction. And this is the kind of chastening ravishment that the speaker of Holy Sonnet XIV would have directed toward himself.

Did Donne "discover" his own condition in that of apostate Israel? Or is the application of the biblical types to the speaker's situation a shrewd rhetorical gambit on Donne's part—an adroit maneuver, as it were, to remind God of what the outcome of the story *should* be? The terrible energy of Holy Sonnet XIV suggests no peace of mind on the speaker's part regarding his spiritual future, but at the same time the poem's lack of dramatic resolution leaves the question eternally open for readers. The poem's failure to specify God's response to the speaker's provocative imperatives only strengthens the dramatic tension which characterizes the sonnet.

The Prophet in the Poem

Recognition of the typological dimensions of Holy Sonnet XIV allows even further insight into other aspects of the poem. For Church Fathers, Doctors, and Reformers, typology possessed a close relation to prophecy, for as Karlfried Froehlich has pointed out, the only way that early Christians could lay claim to the Jewish scriptures was by deliberately shifting "the interpretive center of the Old Testament canon from the *Torah* (Law) to the *Nebiim* (the Prophets)," thereby reading "the events, persons, or institutions of the old dispensation . . . as 'types,' 'figures,' 'shadows,' of things to come or to be fulfilled in the time of Jesus and his Church,"[4] In stanza 8 of "A Litanie," Donne praises the prophets for just such a typological function when he addresses them as the

Churches Organs, and did sound
That harmony, which made of two
One law, and did unite, but not confound[.]

The prophets' inspired vision allowed them to speak secretly or mysteriously to later generations of the new dispensation even while speaking

4. Karlfried Froehlich, " 'Always to Keep the Literal Sense in Holy Scripture Means to Kill One's Soul': The State of Biblical Hermeneutics at the Beginning of the Fifteenth Century," in *Literary Uses of Typology*, pp. 20–21.

directly to the Israelites of the Mosaic law. They thus straddle the Old and New Testaments, harmonizing them without "confound[ing]" or blurring their discrete identities. In his ability to read his condition as a Christian in Old Testament texts, the speaker of Holy Sonnet XIV likewise functions as a prophet.[5]

Once this is acknowledged, the peculiar linguistic character of Holy Sonnet XIV becomes clearer. Hugh Richmond thinks that he has found in a sonnet by Pierre de Ronsard the source of Holy Sonnet XIV's vigorous opening, its "passionate, sexual intensity of . . . kinetic imagery," its "Hopkins-like massing of verbs," and its "alliterative verbal intensity."[6] Yet Holy Sonnet XIV's language is closer to Hebrew prophetic utterance, which Abraham Heschel describes as "urging, alarming, forcing onward," both "luminous and explosive, firm and contingent, harsh and compassionate, a fusion of contradictions."[7] Simultaneous to his sending their foes against the Israelites, the Lord sent his word forth against the tribes of Jacob through the prophet Isaiah (Isa. 9:8). This direct paralleling of armed men with prophetic speech suggests a similarity of purpose: the prophet's language must hammer and batter away at the sinful community's psychological defenses just as surely as the Aramean and Philistine armies will attack the city's physical defenses, its walls. Likewise, Ezekiel was ordered to perform an action emblematic of the prophet's use of language. "Man," the Lord said to him,

> take a tile and set it before you. Draw a city on it, the city of Jerusalem: lay siege to it, erect watch-towers against it, raise a siege-ramp, put mantelets in position, and bring battering-rams against it all around. Then take an iron girdle, and put it as a wall between you and the city. Keep your face turned towards the city; it will be the besieged and you the besieger. This will be a sign to the Israelites.
>
> (Ezek. 4:1–3)

The armed assaults on the city are really only emblematic. The city's actual besieger is the prophet, and his weapon of attack is his language—violent, frenzied, impassioned to the point of sounding irrational—much the same language employed by Donne's speaker in Holy Sonnet XIV.[8]

5. Typology, moral allegory, eschatology, and prophecy are so similar that it is often times difficult to separate them as interpretive modes, notes Earl Miner in his preface to *Literary Uses of Typology* (p. ix). Cf. the section on "Reading Prophecies into Texts" in the editors' introduction to *Poetic Prophecy in Western Literature*, ed. Jan Wojcik and Raymond-Jean Frontain (Rutherford, N.J.: Fairleigh Dickinson UP, 1984), pp. 17–20; and Paul J. Korshin's chapter on "Typology and Prophecy" in *Typologies in England 1650–1820* (Princeton, N.J.: Princeton UP, 1982), pp. 328–68.

6. Hugh Richmond, "Ronsard and the English Renaissance," *Comparative Literature* 7 (1970): 144.

7. Abraham J. Heschel, *The Prophets: An Introduction*, 2 vols. (New York: Harper Colophon Books, 1969), 2: 6–7.

8. In "The Uncertain Success of Isaiah's Prophecy: A Poetical Reading" (*Poetic Prophecy*, ed. Wojcik and Frontain, pp. 31–39), Jan Wojcik considers the nature and operation of biblical prophetic language. His observations concerning Isaiah's violent shifts in perspective bear upon the intentions of Donne's speaker switching, in a compressed fourteen lines, from a pottery conceit, to a military one, to a sexual one. For a parallel oper-

The figure that emerges from Holy Sonnet XIV, however, is a peculiarly Donnean sort of prophet, one who employs prophetic language to prophesy to God against himself! In the Old Testament the Lord employs the prophets to call the people's attention to their divergence from the law; the prophet's words are intended to shatter their sin-hardened hearts. But in Holy Sonnet XIV the speaker does not testify for God against a willful and disobedient people. Like Jeremiah, the speaker anticipates God's violently dashing the clay vessel of his own creation to the ground, but in Holy Sonnet XIV the vessel represents not the recalcitrant and idolatrous city Jerusalem but the speaker's own hardened heart. Like Hosea, he laments the unfaithfulness of the Lord's betrothed, but the woman who has played the whore this time is neither Judah nor Israel, but himself. And like Isaiah, Jeremiah, and Ezekiel, the speaker threatens the destruction of a proud and disloyal city, but ironically it is God's attention which he must first get, not that of the city's inhabitants, and the rebel city which he asks to be reduced to docility is, not Jerusalem, but his own helpless will. Rather than attacking the people's complacency and denouncing a sinful nation, the speaker storms God's ear to denounce himself, for unless God recognizes the speaker's contrition and acknowledges his desire to repent by offering him the gift of prevenient grace, the speaker is eternally lost. There is an extraordinary poignancy to the speaker's plight. So deep is his sense of sin that he must call upon all three persons of the Trinity in his meditation, and so extraordinary is his anxiety to receive some sign of election—even the seemingly negative one of healing destruction or of chastening rape—that he prophesies to God against himself. By describing his situation typologically, the speaker attempts to prod God into acting in the necessary way. For the desperate speaker—and the audacious poet—not even Scripture is exempt in the search to find ways to talk about the spiritual condition of the self.

ation in seventeenth-century poetry, see William Stull's analysis of Milton's use of "deliberately disjointed syntax" to create the "impression of prophetic speech" in the sonnet "Avenge O Lord thy slaughter'd Saints" in "Sacred Sonnets in Three Styles," *Studies in Philology* 79 (1982): 98.

A Critical Overview

JOHN R. ROBERTS

John Donne's Poetry: An Assessment of Modern Criticism †

In 1931, the tercentenary anniversary of Donne's death, T. S. Eliot announced in his essay "Donne in Our Time" that "Donne's poetry is a concern of the present and the recent past rather than of the future."[1] If, by his prophetic utterance of doom, Eliot intended to predict Donne's impending demise among scholars and critics, or if he thought that critical interest in Donne had reached its apex in 1931, then history has proved him quite mistaken. For during the past fifty years no fewer than 2,000 books, monographs, essays, and notes on Donne have appeared, and, as far as I can tell, there are no signs of diminishing interest in his poetry and prose among scholars and academic critics.

But, in all fairness, Eliot should not be judged too harshly for what may seem at first like a most unfortunate comment; for what he meant to express, I think, was that his own personal interest in Donne had faded by 1931 and that he had found new and more exciting models for his own poetry; he had found Dante. Thus, for Eliot himself, at least, his comment was completely accurate; for, although he refers to Donne occasionally in his later critical writings, the essay I have mentioned is his last sustained piece of Donne criticism. In fact, the longest and most detailed essay Eliot ever wrote on a single metaphysical poet was not on Donne at all but on George Herbert for the British Council's Writers and Their Works Series in 1962. And, although his interest in Donne waned, Eliot's appreciation for Herbert never did. In a short interview, entitled "Memories of T. S. Eliot" that appeared in *Esquire* in 1965, Igor Stravinsky reported that Eliot once told him that "Herbert is a great poet . . . and one of a few I can read again and again."[2]

But in addition to having lost interest in Donne as a major inspiration for his own poetry, by 1931 Eliot had other reasons as well for predicting

† Reprinted by permission from *John Donne Journal* 1 (1982): 55–67.

1. T. S. Eliot, "Donne in Our Time," in *A Garland for John Donne, 1631–1931*, ed. Theodore Spencer (Cambridge: Harvard Univ. Press, 1931), p. 5.

2. Igor Stravinsky, "Memories of T. S. Eliot," *Esquire* (August 1965), p. 92.

the end of the popular revival of interest in Donne that he had been so instrumental in generating both among critics and among practicing poets; for he was beginning to sense that his critical comments about Donne and the enthusiasm they had sparked were, perhaps, founded upon some rather important misconceptions or at least flawed concepts about Donne's art. Later, in the 1931 essay, Eliot confides: "It is impossible for us or for anyone else ever to disentangle how much [of Donne's modern popularity] was genuine affinity, genuine appreciation, and how much was just a *reading into* poets like Donne our own sensibilities, how much was 'subjective.' "[3] And years later, Eliot expressed his utter astonishment that his short review of Sir Herbert Grierson's *Metaphysical Lyrics and Poems of the Seventeenth Century*, which appeared in *TLS* in October of 1921, had caused such a critical stir; he had dropped the term "dissociation of sensibility," but he had no idea that literary history of the next twenty years or so would be rewritten to accommodate his suggestion. Thus, could it be that by 1931 Eliot himself recognized that if the success of the Donne revival depended upon what he had said about metaphysical poetry, then perhaps its days were indeed numbered?

Of course, it is possible that Eliot was not thinking of academic criticism and scholarship at all in his 1931 essay; he may have had a much more important audience in mind—the practicing poets of the day. Hence, if he meant to suggest that Donne's influence on poets was "a concern of the present and the recent past rather than of the future," then perhaps he was not entirely incorrect. In the 1930s and 1940s Donne was still a major catalyst in the poetry of several important poets: Elinor Wylie, Wallace Stevens, Herbert Read, William Empson, John Crowe Ransom, Allen Tate, Robert Penn Warren, Hart Crane, Edith Sitwell, Archibald MacLeish, and Yvor Winters, to name only a few. But I think I would be forced to agree with Denis Donoghue, who recently noted that "it would be hard to name any substantial poets now flourishing to whom Donne's poems speak with unusual force."[4] Certainly they do not seem to have the influence on practicing poets that they had in the not too distant past. And perhaps it is also worth noting that the truly exciting and most original periods of Donne criticism have been those in which major practicing poets, or at least creative writers, were numbered among his principal champions or even adversaries. The litany would begin with Ben Jonson, Thomas Carew, Dryden, and Pope; would perhaps include Dr. Johnson; would certainly include Coleridge, Hazlitt, DeQuincey, and Browning; and might conclude with Yeats and Eliot, in addition to the modern poets I have just enumerated. But who among the poets of the 1970s and 1980s would one choose to include? Therefore, although Donne continues to thrive and flourish in the halls of ivy and in library stacks from Texas to Tokyo and from Berkeley to Oxford, perhaps Eliot was not so terribly mistaken after all when he predicted

3. Eliot, p. 6.
4. Denis Donoghue, "Denis Donoghue Celebrates the Quatercentenary of John Donne," *Spectator*, 229 (November 18, 1972), 795.

nearly fifty years ago that Donne's reputation in the years ahead would be something quite different from what it was in 1931.

If Donne's poetry no longer commands the kind of attention and respect from practicing poets it once did, it continues, however, to engage and fascinate an ever-increasing number of scholars and critics. Even a most cursory glance at the seventeenth-century section of the annual MLA bibliography, which is, of course, far from comprehensive, will reveal that only Milton exceeds Donne in the number of yearly entries; that typically more items on Donne appear each year than on Herbert, Crashaw, and Vaughan combined; and that Donne entries far exceed those for Dryden and are roughly twice in number those listed in the Renaissance section for Sidney. In my efforts to update *John Donne: An Annotated Bibliography of Modern Criticism, 1912–1967* for the eleven-year period, 1968–78, I found that, generally speaking, approximately one hundred books, essays, and notes on Donne were published annually, excluding references, book reviews, and doctoral dissertations. In 1931, admittedly a big year for Donne studies, since it was the tercentenary anniversary of his death, only about fifty items were published, whereas in 1972, the 400th anniversary of Donne's birth, approximately 120 studies appeared. Quantity alone, of course, is finally rather meaningless, and I would be the first to admit that any number of books and essays that appear are minor efforts at best and that many are often repetitive, derivative, ill-conceived, and misleading. However, as I read and annotated the nearly 1300 entries in my bibliography for the years 1912–1967 and the more than 1,000 items that appear in my update for the years 1968–1978 I was struck again and again by the fact that Donne has engaged and continues to engage the interest of some of the best minds of the scholarly world and that any number of the studies produced during the past fifty years represent the major contributions to our understanding and knowledge not only of Donne but of the seventeenth century, of metaphysical poets as a whole, and even of the very nature of poetry itself. And I think it cannot be denied that nearly all serious students of literature now agree that Donne occupies a significant and permanent position in our understanding of the development of English poetry and that he is, in his own right, a major poet of continuing and lively interest.

Such a comment may seem painfully obvious, and it may be especially difficult for students, in particular, to recognize that this consensus did not always exist. At the beginning of this century, many critics were by no means willing to offer Donne a seat among the great poets of our language. In 1900, *The Oxford Book of English Verse* represented Donne with only eight pieces, two of which were actually not his and one of which was the first twenty lines of "The Extasie." A number of critics were, in fact, not only hostile to Donne's poetry but were quite scornful of those far from numerous admirers of his art. Edward Bliss Reed, for example, in his *Elizabethan Lyrical Poetry from Its Origins to the*

Present Time (1912) not only openly condemned Donne's poetry for its "unmusical moments," its "imperfect utterance," and its "morbid strain," but concluded his evaluation by remarking that "today Donne's poems are never imitated; they are not even widely read, for though he has a circle of devoted admirers, their number is small."[5] And, as late as 1917, five years after the publication of Sir Herbert Grierson's monumental two-volume edition of the poems and only four years before Eliot's endorsement, George Jackson announced in the *Expository Times*, apparently without fear of serious contradiction or general disagreement, that "it must be freely admitted that neither as poet, preacher, nor letter-writer is Donne ever likely to gain the suffrage of more than a few" and proceeded to characterize most of Donne's love poems as "fit only for the dunghill."[6] Fifty-five years later, in his preface to *John Donne: Essays in Celebration*, A. J. Smith observed that "As far as records tell this is the first time a centenary of his [Donne's] birth has been celebrated or as much as remarked" but assured his readers that "one can't conceive now that a time will come again when the names of Shakespeare, Milton, Wordsworth, Keats are known but the name of Donne is not."[7] Prophecy in literary criticism is a dangerous business at best, as we have seen, but Smith would seem to be on very solid ground in making his prediction.

Although we may be inclined to smile at the utter naiveté of some of our predecessors and may feel even comfortably liberated from their seemingly quaint moral and quixotic literary judgments, perhaps we should resist congratulating ourselves too uncritically and too hastily; for, although often rich and indeed exciting, the enormous body of scholarship and criticism that has been produced on Donne during the past fifty years has not necessarily moved us toward a general consensus about the precise qualities and merits of his poetry. Although we tend to agree that Donne is a major poet, we tend to disagree on exactly what accounts for his greatness or wherein his greatness lies. Therefore, what we have is a mass of criticism that continues to grow but often seems bewildering and even contradictory. Perhaps one example will illustrate my point.

Several years ago, Rosalie Colie, reviewing recent critical discussions of Donne's *Anniversaries*, observed that, although the poems have been interpreted by a number of highly respected scholars, "the various interpretations have seemed especially selective and difficult to modulate into a general understanding of the works."[8] After surveying the criticism of such eminent scholars as Marjorie Nicolson, Louis Martz, George Williamson, O. B. Hardison, Frank Manley, Northrop Frye, Earl Miner,

5. Edward Bliss Reed, *Elizabethan Lyrical Poetry from Its Origin to the Present Time* (New Haven: Yale Univ. Press, 1912), p. 233.

6. George Jackson, "The Bookshelf by the Fire: V. John Donne," *Expository Times*, 28 (1917), 217, 218.

7. A. J. Smith, Preface to *John Donne: Essays in Celebration* (London: Methuen, 1972), p. vii.

8. Rosalie Colie, " 'All in Peeces': Problems of Interpretation in Donne's Anniversary Poems," in *Just So Much Honor: Essays Commemorating the Four-Hundredth Anniversary of the Birth of John Donne*, ed. Peter Amadeus Fiore (University Park: Pennsylvania State Univ. Press, 1972), p. 189.

and others, all of whom, Colie points out, assist the reader by explaining aspects of the argument, imagery, philosophical doctrines, and structure of the poems, she then contends that all of these readings "conspicuously do not mesh with one another in mutually valuable contributions to interpretation."[9] Confronted by this array of bewildering and contradictory criticism, Colie finally concludes that perhaps the only way out of the labyrinth of critical confusion is to assume that "the poems' hospitality to multiple readings is not a function of the author's sloppiness so much as his rigorous inclusiveness" and then proceeds by attempting to show that in fact "the poems consciously exploit playfully and seriously a great many literary genres available to the Renaissance poet"[1] and that Donne simply fused together styles and themes that were normally held apart in separate poems. It would seem that the only way Colie can reconcile the strains of discordant criticism is to suggest that Donne "exploited various pieces of the Renaissance literary repertory" and "forced them beyond their own limits, towards a new coherence unspecified in the textbooks of mankind."[2] Colie goes so far as to conclude that it is precisely "this shiftiness that makes the *Anniversary Poems* so difficult for us to read, trained as we are to find unity of thought, structure, pattern, and tone in the 'good' poems we read."[3] Although this is not the occasion to explore in detail and perhaps to challenge certain of Colie's conclusions about the poems, it seems to me unfortunate that such an intelligent and sensitive critic as Rosalie Colie should be led to conclude from the existing conflicting criticism that the difficulty readers and critics experience in appreciating the *Anniversaries* stems from their unnatural expectation of finding unity in a work of art and that the only way around the mountain of contradictory criticism on the poems (especially when that criticism issues forth from such highly respected experts) is to conclude that Donne simply meant to accommodate all their differing points of view.

I should not want to be misunderstood on this point. I would not argue that the complexity and subtlety of Donne's poetry is ever likely to generate a highly harmonious chorus of uniformly held conclusions about the meaning of his poetry and about his way of achieving that meaning. Donne himself told us that "When thou hast done, thou hast not done, / For I have more," and he urges us in *Satyre III* to "doubt wisely." But still, I think it is not unreasonable for us to expect to find some generally acceptable overall conclusions and more dominating patterns emerging from the volume of critical writing that has been produced in recent years. Evaluations of the *Anniversaries*, however, as a case in point, do not seem to be moving in that direction, unless, of course, one wishes to endorse Rosalie Colie's thesis, which, I assume, most of us would agree perhaps "too much light breeds." In fact, I often feel that many books and essays on Donne tell me a great deal more about the critics

9. P. 192.
1. P. 193.
2. P. 214.
3. P. 193.

writing them than they do about Donne's poetry. It is the very nature of literary criticism, of course, to shift its perspectives from time to time and to invent new methods (which are frequently old methods refurbished) of exploring and understanding literary texts, which, it seems to me, is one guarantee we have that critics will not likely conclude soon that they have exhausted Donne's poetry. Each new generation of critics, with its own insights, concerns, sensitivity, newly acquired critical methodologies, and even its recognized and unrecognized biases, will continue to encounter Donne, more or less, on its own terms and will continue to provide us with fresh insights into his poetry. You will understand, then, that I am not advocating that we attempt to stifle critical debate, even if that were possible, nor am I recommending that we develop a set of rigid conclusions about Donne's poetry that we could carefully chisel into marble and preserve for all time.

On the other hand, with the vast accumulation of Donne criticism we have at our disposal, the time seems right to re-evaluate and reassess our notions about Donne, and perhaps about metaphysical poetry in general, to synthesize and then enunciate as best we can the major and even important minor discoveries and insights we have made about Donne and perhaps even to chart some possible new directions Donne scholarship might take in the future so that it will not only continue to proliferate but will thrive in such a way as to provide us with some genuinely new and fresh perspectives on his poetry. If you assume that in the remainder of this brief paper I am prepared to perform that desirable task magically by enunciating with clarity, elegance, economy, and admirable erudition all the major conflicting issues critics have raised during the past half century and then offer satisfactory resolutions to them, I regret to disappoint you. Clearly such an undertaking is far beyond the scope of this brief report and certainly beyond my own limited abilities. I shall, however, devote the remainder of my paper to a series of general observations about the present state of Donne scholarship that have become apparent to me as I have prepared my annotated bibliographies. My remarks are intended to create more questions than they provide answers for, and, if I am totally successful, they will spark a great deal of disagreement.

Before I proceed, however, I should like to call attention to and applaud the efforts of those who are currently engaged in preparing a detailed, scholarly variorum commentary on Donne's poems, a project which, when completed, will significantly contribute to the advancement of Donne scholarship and criticism. Having read through the vast amount of work produced on Donne in this century alone, I am painfully aware that the most important criticism is so hopelessly scattered throughout numerous journals and books, many of which are in foreign languages, that not even the more diligent and persistent scholar is ever likely to locate it all. Even though I should hope that recent annotated bibliographies have greatly assisted critics in this respect, I am convinced, nonetheless, that they do not perform adequately and fully the service that is needed. A variorum commentary will not only make Donne scholarship more readily accessible, but, in addition, it will allow us to make a general assessment of Donne criticism by synthesizing the most significant insights of critics and scholars during the past four centuries and will also perhaps serve as a solid guide for future research. But since we shall not have a variorum commentary for several years to come, we are left with nothing more satisfactory than general surveys of and general observations on Donne criticism, such as I propose to offer.

Surely the most disturbing fact about modern Donne criticism is that it concerns itself primarily with less than half of Donne's canon, confining itself narrowly to his secular love poems (a dozen or less of the poems in the *Songs and Sonets* and to a much lesser extent the *Elegies*), to his specifically religious poems (almost exclusively the *Holy Sonnets*, "Goodfriday, 1613," and the hymns), and more recently, to the *Anniversaries*. A recent check of items for 1968–1978 showed that criticism specifically on the verse epistles, for example, accounts for only approximately one percent of the total entries, even though the verse epistles themselves represent nearly a sixth of Donne's poetic canon—approximately the same as the religious poems. One possible conclusion, of course, is that the verse epistles are artistic failures and deserve no more attention than they have received. But if this conclusion is correct, and I, for one, would argue against it, then one would expect that that point would be made, defended, and demonstrated, but all one gets, in fact, is silent neglect. Perhaps it is even more surprising that Donne's *Satyres*, which are generally regarded as sophisticated examples of that important Renaissance genre, received only about three percent of the attention from critics during the 1968–1978 period. When we have two major critics, C. S. Lewis and Alvin Kernan, coming to almost diametrically opposed conclusions about the artistry of the *Satyres*, one would have expected a little more critical heat, if not light, to have been generated. Lewis condemned the *Satyres*, as you will recall, as shaggy and savage, unmetrical in versification, disgusting in diction, and obscure in thought, whereas Kernan, obviously reading the same poems, praised them precisely for being the least savage of the satires and for being, among other things, consistent and well-ordered. I do not mean to suggest that no serious work has been done on the epistles or on the satires (one has only to think of Milgate, for example), but the amount of attention given them is unquestionably slight in comparison to certain of Donne's love poems. And, as we might expect, the number of items on *The Progresse of the Soule*, the epigrams, the epithalamia, the funeral elegies, and even the religious poems, excluding the *Holy Sonnets*, "Goodfriday, 1613," and the hymns, is even more miniscule.

The most unfortunate result of centering attention almost exclusively on less than half of Donne's canon is that we have developed over the years what might be called a synecdochical understanding of and appreciation for Donne's total achievement as a poet: we have, in other words, substituted the part for the whole and then proceeded as if the part were, in fact, the whole. As a result, literary historians, critics, and teachers continue to repeat generalizations about Donne's poetry that although incomplete, partial, misleading, and sometimes incorrect, have about them almost the strength of established fact and the sacredness of a hallowed tradition. Admittedly the highly dramatic poems of the *Songs and Sonets* are characteristically colloquial, metrically rough and syntactically concentrated, witty and rhetorically ingenious, and psychologically complex and subtle in argument; but unfortunately Donne's other poems are often judged, and often slighted, because they do not have any or all of these so-called Donnean qualities. Even the *Holy Sonnets*, which on the whole have fared rather well, are often said to be lacking because they do not fully exploit the possibilities inherent in the *Songs and Sonets*, and the *Elegies* are praised because they show in an undeveloped and unsophisticated way some of the major features of Donne's poetry that will emerge clearly and emphatically in the *Songs and Sonets*.

Any number of fairly plausible speculations could be advanced, no doubt, that would at least partly account for the critics' neglect of a very sizeable part of Donne's canon, but I should like to restrict myself to only one that seems to me especially significant and from which we may learn an important lesson. It is well known that in the 1930s and 1940s the so-called "new critics" contributed more than their fair share to the revival of interest in Donne's poetry; for they discovered to their delight that in his love poems, in the *Holy Sonnets*, and in the hymns Donne had obligingly included all those very elements that for them constituted genuine poetry: ambiguity, paradox, tension, and so on. In other words, Donne's dramatic lyrics not only seemed to support and illustrate their own theories about the nature of good poetry, but, perhaps more importantly, the analytical methods and approaches that evolved from their theories were especially effective in interpreting Donne's dramatic lyrics. By the 1940s and 1950s and perhaps well into the 1960s the disciples of the "new critics" were teaching Donne in hundreds of colleges and universities throughout the country, and when they taught Donne they chose those poems that best lent themselves to close textual analysis: thus they were much more likely to choose "The Flea," "The Canonization," "The Extasie," or even "Batter my heart" or the "Hymne to God my God, in my sicknesse" than they were to select for intensive study and discussion, let us say, the verse epistles, *The Progresse of the Soule*, or even *La Corona* sequence. Thus, an implicit and often explicit notion of Donne's poetry was passed on to a later generation of critics, who, when confronted with the neglected half of Donne's canon, were predisposed to dismiss as inferior those poems that did not readily conform to the received notion of Donne's poetry. Also, since the neglected poems often did not fit neatly into established and well-wrought definitions of metaphysical poetry, or meditative poetry, or baroque poetry, they were simply passed over as being somehow not essential to an understanding of Donne's art.

Nearly a half-century ago Merritt Hughes warned his generation of the dangers of "kidnapping" Donne for its own purposes. In 1934, Hughes was primarily concerned that the efforts of critics such as Eliot and his followers to make Donne irresistibly modern and relevant not only were dangerously distorting historical reality but also were to a large degree distorting Donne's genuine originality and achievements. Hughes concluded that "As a matter of historical probability, we might surmise that Donne's outlook would be closer to that of Duns Scotus than to ours."[4] Hughes, of course, wanted to see Donne restored to his seventeenth-century context, but he recognized that any such attempts would be met with firm resistance. "To try to see him as he was," Hughes remarked, "is like removing fourteenth-century gilding from a Russian icon of the tenth century."[5] And he concludes, "Every audience makes its own experience of an artist's work, and when the artist is removed from his public by three hundred years, and when the modern conception of him has been interlaced with original and fructifying theories of poetry by at least one great poet, the recovery of the historic reality is an ungrateful task."[6]

Kenneth Burke, in an essay unfortunately entitled "On Covery, Re- and Dis-" that appeared in *Accent* in 1953, puts the case succinctly. Discussing modern approaches to Herbert in this instance, Burke comments on the position of Rosemond Tuve in her scholarly little book, *A Reading of George Herbert*, which had appeared the year before. Tuve claimed that in order to understand Herbert's poetry the reader must study and understand the cultural, linguistic, and religious traditions Herbert's poems reflect, especially the liturgical and iconographical contexts. Burke, while admiring much of Tuve's study, contrasts this emphasis on "re-covery" of the past, an approach Hughes would have applauded, with the tendency of many modern critics to engage in what he termed "dis-covery," that is, an attempt to find new things about the workings of a poet's mind and art by applying modern terms and techniques that would perhaps have been completely alien to the poet's own thinking, such as Empson delighted in doing by applying his particular brand of Freudian analysis to Herbert's "The Sacrifice," the poem which led in some ways to Tuve's book. In a response to Tuve's criticism, Empson, while agreeing with some of her conclusions, says that he could not feel "that the mass of erudition she brings down like a steam hammer really cracks any nuts"; and Tuve, while less blunt, makes it unmistakably clear that she holds in utter contempt Empson's kind of discovery. Empson and Tuve, I think, are fair representatives of the major split that continues to divide critics on Donne; the recoverers still regard with

4. Merritt Hughes, "Kidnapping Donne," *University of California Publications in English*, 4 (1934), 88.

5. P. 87.

6. P. 87.

suspicion the discoverers as dangerously clever, overly imaginative, unscholarly dilettantes, while the discoverers still dismiss with some contempt the recoverers as pedantic, literal-minded, harmless antiquarians who have nothing significant to contribute to the central, important issues of modern criticism. If forced to do so, I rather imagine I could divide the 1000 items in my updated bibliography roughly according to the two major approaches—re-covery and dis-covery.

In fact, one could probably obtain a reasonably good overview of the whole development of modern Donne criticism by simply following out, year by year and step by step, the debate that has been raging over the meaning of "The Extasie," a debate begun a half-century ago by Pierre Legouis, who, in *Donne the Craftsman*, challenged critical orthodoxy and argued that, for all its veneer of Platonism and scholastic erudition, the poem is fundamentally nothing more than a witty seduction poem, a kind of flea poem in a major key. Since then, every image, conceit, and allusion has been traced, discussed, and analyzed from any number of differing critical perspectives; and it has been suggested that Donne was influenced in his choice of theme, argument, and language by an ever-expanding circle of sources, including Giordano Bruno's *Candelaio*, Leone Ebreo's *Dialoghi d'Amore*, Antoine Héroët's *La Parfaict Amye*, possibly Shakespeare's *Venus and Adonis*, as well as the poetry and love philosophy of Dante, Guinizelli, Cavalcanti, Cino, and Benedetto Varchi, to say nothing of the works of Thomas Aquinas, Plotinus, Ficino, and others. Surely no other Donne poem has been so relentlessly run through various critical and scholarly sieves, and yet, try as they might, the critics simply cannot make the poem lie down quietly on their prefabricated Procrustean beds. And, if one were to follow out the critical debate on the poem, one might possibly conclude by agreeing, at least in part, with Empson, who, in 1972, reviewing Helen Gardner's edition of the love poems, argued that Donne desperately needs to be rescued (not kidnapped this time) from what he calls "the habitual mean mindedness of modern academic criticism, its moral emptiness combined with incessant moral nagging, and its scrubbed prison-like isolation."[7]

Although Empson's charge is characteristically too broad and too undiscriminating, I find his rescue plea attractive and perhaps even imperative if Donne criticism is to have much life in the future. No doubt Donne studies will continue to proliferate in the immediate years ahead. Critics will carry on, finding even more ingenious ways of testing their highly theoretical concepts on Donne's poems; and scholars, a hardy and not easily discouraged lot, will likely find even more wonderful and exotic sources for "The Extasie." But what concerns me most is that critics and scholars are increasingly talking only to themselves and to each other, not to a wider reading audience. The scholars have weighted down Donne's poems with such a burden of historical and philosophical

7. William Empson, "Rescuing Donne," in *Just So Much Honor*, p. 95.

speculation that even the sophisticated reader is made to feel inadequately prepared to cope with this staggering body of often irrelevant and esoteric information, while the critics, for their part, often speaking in a language that is unintelligible even to their professional colleagues, seem too exclusively concerned with demonstrating the range and complexity of their own critical sophistication or with dazzling their few readers with tricks of critical prestidigitation. Donne is often an occasion for critical debate, but the center of attention is frequently not Donne really but rather abstract, highly theoretical issues that are of little interest to anyone but their exponents. In a word, the critics this time, not the poets, have kidnapped Donne and have turned Donne studies into a self-perpetuating industry that nearly rivals the Milton industry. And in doing so, they have killed genuine interest in Donne's poetry. In many cases, Donne has been so successfully returned to his niche in the seventeenth century that many readers are quite content to leave him there, while they pay lip service to his greatness from a comfortable distance. In other instances, Donne has been explained in such complicated terms that even highly educated readers feel intimidated and put off. I am not suggesting, of course, that we abandon intellectually demanding and highly sophisticated literary approaches to Donne when those approaches are truly helpful in allowing us to appreciate and to understand better and more deeply his poetry, but I would argue for less specialized studies and for more comprehensive studies of his poetry that would enunciate in understandable English the major achievements of Donne's poetry. Donne is not a simple poet, nor is his art simple; but his poems were intended to communicate his particularly brilliant sense of reality to his readers, and I think that it is, therefore, the primary responsibility of critics to make clear, as best they can, what Donne is communicating. Often the books and articles I read on Donne are much more difficult to understand than are the poems about which they are supposedly written. For this reason as well as for others I have mentioned, I think a variorum commentary on Donne's poetry will be an important first step in sorting out, evaluating and enunciating the important discoveries and recoveries that have been made by any number of excellent critics and scholars. And perhaps, once a path has been cleared through the critical jungle, I should hope that more critics will give attention to the primary task of making Donne's poetry more, not less accessible to an even wider reading audience than he enjoys at the present time.

Selected Bibliography

This Selected Bibliography of this revised second edition updates the Selected Bibliography of the first edition of *John Donne's Poetry* (1966) mainly by adding major texts of poetry and prose, bibliographies and biographies, and a good number of the many textual studies, general studies, and criticisms of individual poems and groups of poems published in the past twenty-five years. Some of the general studies also include criticism of individual poems and of groups of poems. By consulting the bibliographies, especially John Roberts's annotated bibliographies, listed below, the student may find other relevant works. Helpful annual bibliographies are to be found in the *Publications of the Modern Language Association*, the Modern Humanities Research Association's *Annual Bibliography of English Language and Literature*, and the English Association's *The Year's Work in English Studies*, "a narrative and evaluative bibliography of scholarly writing." Students may also profitably consult the *John Donne Journal*, devoted to studies of Donne and related subjects, and published since 1982.

The important *Variorum Edition of the Poetry of John Donne* is being prepared by a number of scholars and will be published by the University of Missouri Press in the coming years.

H. C. Combs and Z. R. Sullens have published A *Concordance to the English Poems of John Donne*, Chicago, 1940; reprinted New York, 1970.

This Selected Bibliography is arranged largely in accord with the poetry and criticism contained in this edition: I. Poetry (texts of Donne's poetry; two also include some of his prose); II. Prose; III. Bibliography; IV. Biography; V. Textual Studies; VI. General Studies (a wide range of materials, including background, comprehensive, comparative, and so on); VII. Songs and Sonnets; VIII. Elegies; IX. Satires; X. Verse Letters; XI. Anniversaries; XII. Divine Poems; XIII. Holy Sonnet 10 (XIV) "Batter my heart." Selections of Criticism reprinted in this edition or referred to in the glosses on Donne's poetry are not included below.

I. POETRY

The Complete English Poems of John Donne. Ed. C. A. Patrides. London, 1985.

The Complete Poetry of John Donne. Ed. John T. Shawcross. Garden City, 1967.

John Donne: The Anniversaries. Ed. Frank Manley. Baltimore, 1963..

John Donne: The Complete English Poems. Ed. A. J. Smith. Harmondsworth, Middlesex. 1971.

John Donne: The Divine Poems. Ed. Helen Gardner. Oxford, 1952; 2nd ed., 1978.

John Donne: The Elegies and The Songs and Sonnets. Ed. Helen Gardner. Oxford, 1965.

John Donne: The Epithalamions, Anniversaries and Epicedes. Ed. W. Milgate. Oxford, 1978.

John Donne: Poetry and Prose. Ed. Frank J. Warnke. New York, 1967.

John Donne: Selections from Divine Poems, Sermons, Devotions, and Prayers. Ed. John Booty. New York, 1990. Most of the divine poems with a good selection of prose.

John Donne: The Satires, Epigrams and Verse Letters. Ed. W. Milgate. Oxford, 1967.

Poems. "By J. D. with Elegies on the Authors Death." Menston, Yorkshire, 1969. A facsimile of the first edition of 1633.
The Poems of John Donne. 2 vols. Ed. Herbert J. C. Grierson. Oxford, 1912.
The Songs and Sonets of John Donne. Ed. Theodore Redpath, 2nd ed. London, 1983.

II. PROSE

Biathanatos. Ed. Ernest W. Sullivan, II. Newark, Delaware, 1984.
Devotions upon Emergent Occasions. 2 vols. Ed. Elizabeth Savage. Salzburg, 1975.
Essays in Divinity. Ed. Evelyn M. Simpson. Oxford, 1952.
Ignatius his Conclave. Ed. T. S. Healy. Oxford, 1970.
Paradoxes and Problems. Ed. Helen Peters. Oxford, 1980.
Pseudo-Martyr. Facsimile. Introd. Francis Jacques Sypher. Delmar, N.Y., 1974.
Selected Prose. Chosen by Evelyn Simpson. Ed. Helen Gardner and Timothy Healy. Oxford, 1967.
The Sermons of John Donne. Ed. George R. Potter and Evelyn Simpson. 10 vols. Berkeley, 1953–62.
For selections of Donne's sermons arranged according to topics, with introductions by the editors, P. G. Stanwood and Heather Ross Asals, see *John Donne and the Theology of Language*, Columbia, Missouri, 1986. See also Donne's *Letters* listed under Biography, below, and Evelyn Simpson's *A Study of the Prose Works of John Donne*, 2nd ed., Oxford, 1948.

III. BIBLIOGRAPHY

Keynes, Sir Geoffrey. *A Bibliography of Dr. John Donne*. 4th ed. Oxford, 1973.
Roberts, John R. *John Donne: An Annotated Bibliography of Modern Criticism, 1912–1967*. Columbia, Missouri, 1973.
———. *John Donne: An Annotated Bibliography of Modern Criticism, 1968–1978*. Columbia, Missouri, 1982.

IV. BIOGRAPHY

The definitive biography of Donne is R. C. Bald's *John Donne: A Life*, Oxford, 1970 (reprinted with corrections, 1986). Other biographies and sources of biographical material include:
Bald, Robert Cecil. *Donne and the Drurys*. Cambridge, England, 1959.
Carey, John. *John Donne: Life, Mind and Art*. New York, 1981. A controversial biographical-critical study of Donne's imagination.
Donne, John. *Letters to Several Persons of Honour*. Ed. M. Thomas Hester. Delmar, N.Y., 1977. Facsimile of the 1651 edition of Donne's letters.
Fausset, Hugh I'Anson. *John Donne: A Study in Discord*. London, 1924.
Gosse, Sir Edmund. *The Life and Letters of John Donne*. 2 vols. London, 1899.
Hardy, Evelyn. *John Donne: A Spirit in Conflict*. London, 1942.
Le Comte, Edward. *Grace to a Witty Sinner: A Life of Donne*. New York, 1965.
Parker, Derek. *John Donne and His World*. London, 1975.
Walton, Izaak. *The Lives* . . . London, 1670. *Life of Donne* was first published with *LXXX Sermons*, 1640; it was enlarged and issued separately in 1658 and is available in various reprintings, such as *Life of Dr. John Donne*, edited by G. Saintsbury, Oxford, 1927.

V. TEXTUAL STUDIES

Empson, William. "Rescuing Donne." *Just So Much Honor*. Ed. Peter A. Fiore. University Park, Pennsylvania, 1972. 95–148.
Patrides, C. A. "John Donne Methodized: or, How to improve Donne's impossible text with the assistance of his several editors." *Modern Philology* 82 (1985): 365–73.
Pebworth, Ted-Larry. "Manuscript Poems and Print Assumptions: Donne and His Modern Editors." *John Donne Journal* 3 (1984): 1–21. Discusses difficulties in editing Donne.
Roberts, Mark. "If it were Donne when 'tis done . . ." *Essays in Criticism* 16 (1966): 309–29.
Shawcross, John T. "All Attest His Writs Canonical: The Texts, Meaning and Evaluation of Donne's Satires." *Just So Much Honor*. Ed. Peter A. Fiore. University Park, Pennsylvania, 1972. 245–72.
———. "A Text of John Donne's Poems: Unsatisfactory Compromise." *John Donne Journal* 2 (1983): 1–19.
———. "The Arrangement and Order of John Donne's Poems." *Poems in Their Place: The Inter-*

textuality and Order of Poetic Collections. Ed. Neil Freistat. Chapel Hill, 1986. 119–63.
———. "The Making of the Variorum Text of the *Anniversaries*." *John Donne Journal* 3 (1984): 63–72.
———. "The Text of John Donne and the Inadequacy of All Solutions." *John Donne Journal* 1 (1982): 55–67.
Sullivan, Ernest W., II. "Replicar Editing of John Donne's Texts." *John Donne Journal* 2 (1983): 21–29.
———, and David J. Murrah, eds. *The Donne Dalhousie Discovery*. Lubbock, Texas, 1987. Contains four essays on the text and editing of Donne, with special focus on the Dalhousie manuscripts and the forthcoming Variorum Edition.
Williamson, George. "Textual Difficulties in the Interpretation of Donne's Poetry." *Modern Philology* 38 (1940): 37–72.

VI. GENERAL STUDIES

Alvarez, A. *The School of Donne*. London, 1962.
Bennett, Joan. *Five Metaphysical Poets*. Rev. ed. Cambridge, England, 1963.
Bradbury, Malcolm, and David Palmer, eds. *Metaphysical Poetry*. Bloomington, 1971.
Bredvold, L. I. "The Naturalism of Donne in Relation to Some Renaissance Traditions." *Journal of English and Germanic Philology* 22 (1923): 471–502.
Bush, Douglas. *English Literature in the Earlier Seventeenth Century, 1600–1660*. 2nd ed. rev. Oxford, 1962.
Bush, Douglas. *Prefaces to Renaissance Literature*. Cambridge, Massachusetts, 1965.
Clements, Arthur L. *Poetry of Contemplation: John Donne, George Herbert, Henry Vaughan and the Modern Period*. Albany, 1990.
Coffin, Charles M. *John Donne and the New Philosophy*. 1937. New York, 1958.
Colie, Rosalie L. *Paradoxia Epidemica: The Renaissance Tradition of Paradox*. Princeton, 1966.
Datta, Kitty. "Love and Asceticism in Donne's Poetry: The Divine Analogy." *Critical Quarterly* 19 (1977) 2: 5–25.
Docherty, Thomas. *John Donne*, Undone. London, 1986.
Fiore, Peter A., ed. *Just So Much Honor*. University Park and London, 1972.
Gardner, Helen, ed. *John Donne: A Collection of Critical Essays*. Englewood Cliffs, N.J., 1962.
Gottlieb, Sidney. "Elegies Upon the Author: Defining, Defending, and Surviving Donne." *John Donne Journal* 2 (1983): 23–38. Discusses other writers' elegies on Donne published in the 1633 and 1635 editions of his poetry.
Halewood, William H. *The Poetry of Grace: Reformation Themes and Structures in English Seventeenth-Century Poetry*. New Haven, 1970.
Hughes, Richard E. *The Progress of the Soul: The Interior Career of John Donne*. New York, 1968.
Jackson, Robert S. *John Donne's Christian Vocation*. Evanston, 1970.
Jordan, Richard. *The Quiet Hero: Figures of Temperance in Spencer, Donne, Milton, and Joyce*. Washington, D.C., 1989.
Kermode, Frank, ed. *Discussions of John Donne*. Boston, 1962.
———, ed. *The Metaphysical Poets: Key Essays*. Greenwich, Connecticut, 1969.
———. *Shakespeare, Spenser, Donne: Renaissance Essays*. New York, 1971.
Larson, Deborah Aldrich. *John Donne and Twentieth-Century Criticism*. Rutherford, N.J., 1989.
Leishman, J. B. *The Metaphysical Poets: Donne, Herbert, Vaughan, Traherne*. Oxford, 1934.
Lewalski, Barbara K. *Protestant Poetics and the Seventeenth-Century Religious Lyric*. Princeton, 197.
Low, Anthony. 9 *Love's Architecture: Devotional Modes in Seventeenth-Century English Poetry*. New York, 1978.
McGrath, Lynette. "John Donne's Apology for Poetry." *Studies in English Literature* 20 (1980): 73–89.
Marotti, Arthur F. *John Donne, Coterie Poet*. Madison, 1986.
Martz, Louis L. "Donne and Herbert: Vehement Grief and Silent Tears." *John Donne Journal* 7 (1988): 21–34.
Martz, Louis L. *The Poem of the Mind*. New York, 1966.
———. *The Poetry of Meditation: A Study in English Religious Literature of the Seventeenth Century*. Rev. ed. New Haven, 1962.
———. *The Wit of Love*. Notre Dame, 1969.
Mazzaro, Jerome. *Transformations in the Renaissance English Lyric*. Ithaca, 1970.
Mazzeo, Joseph A. *Renaissance and Revolution: Backgrounds to Seventeenth-Century English Literature*. New York, 1965.
Miner, Earl. *The Metaphysical Mode from Donne to Cowley*. Princeton, 1969.
Mulder, John R. *The Temple of the Mind: Education and Literary Taste in Seventeenth-Century England*. New York, 1969.
Nicolson, Marjorie H. *The Breaking of the Circle: Studies in the Effect of the "New Science" Upon*

Seventeenth Century Poetry. Rev. ed. New York, 1960.
Norford, Don P. "Microcosm and Macrocosm in Seventeenth-Century Literature." *Journal of the History of Ideas* 38 (1977): 409–28.
Novarr, David. *The Disinterred Muse: Donne's Texts and Contexts*. Ithaca, 1980.
Parry, Graham. *Seventeenth-Century Poetry: The Social Context*. London, 1985.
———. *The Seventeenth-Century: The Intellectual Context of English Literature, 1603–1700*. White Plains, 1988.
Partridge, A. C. *John Donne: Language and Style*. London, 1978.
Patrides, C. A. *Premises and Motifs in Renaissance Thought and Literature*. Princeton, 1982.
———, and Raymond B. Waddington, eds. *The Age of Milton: Backgrounds to Seventeenth-Century Literature*. Manchester and New York, 1980.
———, and Joseph Wittreich, eds. *The Apocalypse in English Renaissance Thought and Literature*. Manchester and Ithaca, 1984.
Pepperdene, Margaret, ed. *That Subtile Wreath*. Atlanta, 1973.
Perry, T. Anthony. *Erotic Spirituality: The Integrative Tradition from Leone Ebreo to John Donne*. University, Alabama, 1980.
Praz, Mario. *Studies in Seventeenth-Century Imagery*. 2nd rev. ed. Rome, 1964.
Richards, Michael R. "The Romantic Critics and John Donne." *Bucknell Review* 25 (1980) 2: 40–51.
Roberts, John R., ed. *Essential Articles for the Study of John Donne's Poetry*. Hamden, Connecticut, 1975.
———, and Gary A. Stringer, eds. "A Special Issue: John Donne." *South Central Review* 4 (Summer 1987): 1–102. Contains various articles on Donne and his poetry, some of which are listed elsewhere in this bibliography.
Sellin, Paul R. *John Donne and "Calvinist" Views of Grace*. Amsterdam, 1983.
Sellin, Paul R. *So Doth, So Is Religion: John Donne and Diplomatic Contexts in the Reformed Netherlands, 1619–1620*. Columbia, Missouri, 1988.
Sharp, Robert L. *From Donne to Dryden: The Revolt Against Metaphysical Poetry*. Chapel Hill, 1940.
Shaw, Robert B. *The Call of God: The Theme of Vocation in the Poetry of Donne and Herbert*. Cambridge, Massachusetts, 1981.
Sherwood, Terry G. *Fulfilling the Circle: A Study of John Donne's Thought*. Toronto, 1984.
Slights, Camille Wells. *The Casiustical Tradition in Shakespeare, Donne, Herbert, and Milton*. Princeton, 1981.
Sloane, Thomas O. *Donne, Milton, and the End of Humanist Rhetoric*. Berkeley, 1985.
Sloane, Mary C. *The Visual in Metaphysical Poetry*. Atlantic Highlands, N.J., 1980.
Smith, A. J., ed. *John Donne: The Critical Heritage*. London, 1975.
———, ed. *John Donne: Essays in Celebration*. London, 1972.
———. *The Metaphysics of Love*. Cambridge, 1985.
Spencer, Theodore, ed. *A Garland for John Donne*. 1931. Gloucester, Massachusetts, 1958.
Stein, Arnold. *John Donne's Lyrics: The Eloquence of Action*. Minneapolis, 1962.
Stringer, Gary A., ed. *New Essays on Donne*. Salzburg, 1977.
Summers, Claude, J., and Ted-Larry Pebworth, eds. *"Bright Shootes of Everlastingnesse": The Seventeenth-Century Religious Lyric*. Columbia, Missouri, 1987.
———, and ———, eds. *The Eagle and the Dove: Reassessing John Donne*. Columbia, Missouri, 1986.
———, and ———, eds. *"The muses common-weale": Poetry and Politics in the Seventeenth Century*. Columbia, Missouri, 1988.
Tillyard, E. M. W. *The Elizabethan World Picture*. 1943. London, 1960.
Tuve, Rosemond. *Elizabethan and Metaphysical Imagery*. Chicago, 1947.
Warnke, Frank. *John Donne*. Boston, 1987.
White, Helen. *The Metaphysical Poets*. New York, 1936.
Williamson, George. *The Donne Tradition*. Cambridge, Massachusetts, 1930.
Zunder, William. *The Poetry of John Donne: Literature and Culture in the Elizabethan and Jacobean Period*. Totowa, N.J., 1982.

VII. SONGS AND SONNETS

Bell, Ilona. "The Role of the Lady in Donne's *Songs and Sonnets*." *Studies in English Literature* 23 (1983): 113–29.
Brodsky, Claudia. "Donne: The Imaging of the Logical Conceit." *ELH* 49 (1982): 829–48.
Brooks, Helen B. " 'Soules Language': Reading Donne's 'The Extasie.' " *John Donne Journal* 7 (1988): 47–63.
Carlson, Norman E. "The Drama of Donne's 'The Indifferent.' " *South Central Review* 4 (Summer 1987): 65–69.
Cathcart, Dwight. *Doubting Conscience: Donne and the Poetry of Moral Argument*. Ann Arbor,

1975. Discusses some other Donne works as well, but focuses on the Songs and Sonnets.
Chambers, A. B. "Glorified Bodies and the 'Valediction forbidding Mourning.' " *John Donne Journal* 1 (1982): 1–20.
Chambers, A. B. "The Fly in Donne's 'Canonization.' " *Journal of English and Germanic Philology* 65 (1966): 252–59.
Cirillo, Albert R. "The Fair Hermaphrodite: Love-Union in the Poetry of Donne and Spenser." *Studies in English Literature* 9 (1969): 81–95.
Clair, John A. "Donne's 'The Canonization.' " *PMLA* 80 (1965): 300–302.
Cognard, Roger A. "Donne's 'The Dampe.' " *Explicator* 36 (1978) 2: 19–20.
Collmer, Robert G. "Another Look at 'The Apparition.' " *Concerning Poetry* 7 (1974) 1: 34–40.
Cunnar, Eugene R. "Donne's 'Valediction: Forbidding Mourning' and the Golden Compasses of Alchemical Creation." *Literature and the Occult*. Ed. Luanne Frank. Arlington, Texas, 1977. 77–110.
Dean, John. "The Two Arguments of Donne's 'Air and Angels.' " *Massachusetts Studies in English* 3 (1972): 84–90.
Divine, Jay D. "Compass and Circle in Donne's 'A Valediction: Forbidding Mourning.' " *Papers on Language and Literature* 9 (1973): 78–80.
Edgecombe, Rodney. "An Enquiry into the Syntax of Donne's 'The Good-Morrow' and 'The Sunne Rising.' " *English Studies in Africa* 25 (1982): 29–38.
Estrin, Barbara L. "The Lady's Gestures and John Donne's Gestes." *Forum for Modern Language Studies* 24 (1988): 218–33. Includes "A Jet Ring Sent," "The Funeral," "The Dream."
Freccero, John. "Donne's 'Valediction: Forbidding Mourning.' " *ELH* 30 (1963): 335–376.
Gallant, Gerald, and A. L. Clements. "Harmonized Voices in Donne's *Songs and Sonets*: 'The Dampe.' " *Studies in English Literature* 15 (1975): 71–82.
Gardner, Helen. "The Argument about 'The Exstasy.' " *Elizabethan and Jacobean Studies*. Oxford, 1959. 279–306.
———. *The Business of Criticism*. Oxford, 1959. 62–75. On "Aire and Angels."
———. "A Nocturnal upon St. Lucy's Day." *Poetic Traditions of the English Renaissance*. Ed. Maynard Mack and George deF. Lord. New Haven, 1982. 181–201.
Graziani, Rene. "John Donne's 'The Extasie' and Exstasy." *Review of English Studies*, n.s., 19 (1968): 121–36.
Hamilton, R. W. "John Donne's Petrarchist Poems." *Renaissance and Modern Studies* 23 (1979): 45–62.
Haskin, Dayton. "Reading Donne's *Songs and Sonets* in the Nineteenth Century." *John Donne Journal* 4 (1985): 225–52.
Hughes, Merritt Y. "John Donne's 'Nocturnall upon S. Lucies Day': A Suggested Resolution." *Cithara* 4 (1965): 60–68.
Kronenfeld, Judy Z. "The Asymmetrical Arrangement of Donne's 'Love's Growth' as an Emblem of its Meaning." *Concerning Poetry* 9 (1976) 2: 53–58.
Lepage, John Louis. "Eagles and Doves in Donne and DuBartas: 'The Canonization.' " *Notes and Queries* 30 (October 1983): 428.
Lewalski, Barbara K. "A Donnean Perspective on 'The Extasie.' " *English Language Notes* 10 (1973): 258–62.
Lockwood, Deborah H. "Donne's Idea of Woman in the *Songs and Sonets*." *Essays in Literature* 14 (1987): 37–50.
Low, Anthony. "The Compleat Angler's 'Baite': or, The Subverter Subverted." *John Donne Journal* 4 (1985): 1–12.
Mann, Lindsay A. " 'The Extasie' and 'A Valediction: Forbidding Mourning': Body and Soul in Donne." *Familiar Colloquy*. Ed. Patricia Bruckmann. Toronto, 1978. 68–80.
Manning, John. "The Eagle and the Dove; Chapman and Donne's 'The Canonization.' " *Notes and Queries* 33 (September 1986): 347–48.
Marotti, Arthur F. "Donne and 'The Extasie.' " *The Rhetoric of Renaissance Poetry from Wyatt to Milton*. Ed. Thomas O. Sloan and Raymond B. Waddington. Berkeley, 1975. Ch. 7.
———. "Donne's 'Loves Progress,' ll. 37–38, and Renaissance Bawdry." *English Language Notes* 6 (1968): 24–25.
McKevlin, Dennis. *A Lecture in Love's Philosophy: Donne's Vision of the World of Human Love in the Songs and Sonnets*. Lanham, Maryland, 1984.
McLaughlin, Elizabeth. " 'The Extasie': Deceptive or Authentic?" *Bucknell Review* 18 (1971) 3: 55–78.
Mitchell, Charles. "Donne's 'The Extasie': Love's Sublime Knot." *Studies in English Literature* 8 (1968): 91–101.
Morillo, Marvin. "Donne's 'The Relique' as Satire." *Tulane Studies in English* 21 (1974): 47–58.
Mueller, Janel M. " 'The Dialogue of One': A Feminist Reading of Donne's 'Extasie.' " *ADE Bulletin* 81 (1985): 39–42.
Parish, John E. "The Parley in 'The Extasie.' " *Xavier University Studies* 4 (1965): 188–92.
Perrine, Laurence. "On Donne's 'The Apparition.' " *Concerning Poetry* 9 (1976) 1: 21–24.

Pinka, Patricia G. *This Dialogue of One: The Songs and Sonnets of John Donne*. University, Alabama, 1982.
Rajan, Tilottama. " 'Nothing Sooner Broke': Donne's *Songs and Sonets* as Self-Consuming Artifact." *ELH* 49 (1982): 805–28.
Rauber, D. F. "Donne's 'Farewell to Love': A Crux Revisited." *Concerning Poetry* 3 (1970) 2: 51–63.
Riemer, A. P. "A Pattern for Love: The Structure of Donne's 'The Canonization.' " *Sydney Studies in English* (1977): 19–31. On the numerological structure.
Rooney, William J. " 'The Canonization'—the Language of Paradox Reconsidered." *ELH* 23 (1956): 36–47.
Sheppeard, Sallye. "Eden and Agony in 'Twicknam Garden.' " *John Donne Journal* 7 (1988): 65–72.
Smith, A. J. *John Donne: The Songs and Sonets*. London, 1964.
Spenko, James L. "Circular Form in Two Donne Lyrics." *English Language Notes* 13 (1975): 103–7. On "The Undertaking" and "A Nocturnal."
Spitzer, Leo. "Three Poems on Exstasy: John Donne, St. John of the Cross, Richard Wagner." *Essays on English and American Literature*. Ed. Anna Hatcher. Princeton, 1962. Ch. 9.
Stewart, Jack F. "Irony in Donne's 'The Funeral,' " and "Image and Idea in Donne's 'The Good-Morrow.' " *Discourse* 12 (1969): 193–99, 465–76.
Stringer, Gary A. "Donne's 'The Primrose': Manna and Numerological Dalliance." *Explorations in Renaissance Culture* 1 (1974): 23–29.
Tate, Allen. "The Point of Dying: Donne's 'Virtuous Men.' " *Essays of Four Decades*. Chicago, 1969; 1970. 247–52. On "A Valediction: Forbidding Mourning."
Thomason, T. Katharine. "Plotinian Metaphysics and Donne's 'Extasie.' " *Studies in English Literature* 22 (1982): 91–105.
Vickers, Brian. "Donne's Eagle and Dove." *Notes and Queries* 32 (March 1985): 59–60.
Walker, Julia M. " 'Here you see mee': Donne's Autographed Valediction." *John Donne Journal* 4 (1985): 29–33.
———. "John Donne's 'The Extasie' as an Alchemical Process." *English Language Notes* 20 (1982): 1–8.
Warren, Austin. "Donne's 'Extasie.' " *Studies in Philology* 55 (1958): 472–80.
Welch, Dennis M. "The Meaning of Nothingness in Donne's 'Nocturnal upon S. Lucies Day.' " *Bucknell Review* 22 (1976) 1: 48–56.
Wiggins, Peter De Sa. " 'Aire and Angels': Incarnations of Love." *English Literary Renaissance* 12 (1982): 87–101.
Wilson, G. R., Jr., "The Interplay of Perception and Reflection: Mirror Imagery in Donne's Poetry." *Studies in English Literature* 9 (1969): 107–21.
Wilson, Scott W. "Process and Product: Reconstructing Donne's Personae." *Studies in English Literature* 20 (1980): 91–103.

VIII. ELEGIES

Allen, D. C. "A Note on Donne's Elegy VIII." *Modern Language Notes* 69 (1953): 238–39.
Armstrong, Alan. "The Apprenticeship of John Donne: Ovid and the *Elegies*." *ELH* 44 (1977): 419–42.
Deitz, Jonathan E. "Donne's 'To his Mistress Going to Bed,' 33–38." *Explicator* 32 (1974): 36.
Duncan-Jones, E. E. "The Barren Plane-Tree in Donne's 'The Autumnall' [ll. 29–32]." *Notes and Queries*, n.s., 7 (1960): 53.
Frontain, Raymond-Jean. "Donne's Erotic Spirituality: Ovidian Sexuality and the Language of Christian Revelation in Elegy XIX." *Ball State University Forum* 25 (1984): 41–54.
Gregory, E. R., Jr. "The Balance of Parts: Imagistic Unity in Donne's 'Elegie XIX.' " *University Review* 35 (1968): 51–54.
Greller, Mary A. "Donne's 'The Autumnall': An Analysis." *Literatur in Wissenschaft und Unterricht* 9 (1976): 1–8.
Hester, M. Thomas. "Donne's (Re)Annuniciation of the Virgin(ia Colony) in Elegy XIX." *South Central Review* 4 (Summer 1987): 49–64.
Hurley, C. Harold. " 'Covering' in Donne's Elegy XIX." *Concerning Poetry* 11 (1978) 2: 67–69.
Peacock, A. J. "Donne's Elegies and Roman Love Elegy." *Hermathena* 119 (1975): 20–29.
Rockett, William. "John Donne: The Ethical Argument of Elegy III." *Studies in English Literature* 15 (1975): 57–69.
Wiggins, Peter De Sa. "The Love Quadrangle: Tibullus 1.6 and Donne's 'lay Ideot.' " *Papers on Language and Literature* 16 (1980): 142–50.
Young, R. V. " 'O My America, My New-Found-Land': Pornography and Imperial Politics in Donne's *Elegies*." *South Central Review* 4 (Summer 1987): 35–48.

IX. SATIRES

Baumlin, James S. "Donne's 'Satyre IV': The Failure of Language and Genre." *Texas Studies in Literature and Language* 30 (1988): 363–87.

Bellette, A. F. "The Originality of Donne's Satires." *University of Toronto Quarterly* 44 (1975): 130–40.

Dubrow, Heather. " 'No man is an island': Donne's Satires and Satiric Traditions." *Studies in English Literature* 19 (1979): 71–83.

Eddy, Yvonne S., and Daniel P. Jaeckle. "Donne's *Satyre I*: The Influence of Persius's *Satire III*." *Studies in English Literature* 21 (1981): 111–22.

Elliott, Emory B., Jr. "The Narrative and Allusive Unity of Donne's *Satyres*." *Journal of English and Germanic Philology* 75 (1976): 105–16.

Geraldine, Sister M. "Donnes *Notitia*: The Evidence of the Satires." *University of Toronto Quarterly* 36 (1966): 24–36.

Hester, M. Thomas. *Kinde Pitty and Brave Scorn: John Donne's Satyres*. Durham, 1982.

Hutchinson, Alexander N. "Constant Company: John Donne and His Satiric Personae." *Discourse* 13 (1970): 354–63.

Koch, Walter A. "Linguistic Analysis of a Satire." *Linguistics* 33 (1967): 68–81. On *Satire II*.

Lein, Clayton D. "Theme and Structure in Donne's *Satyre II*." *Comparative Literature* 32 (1980): 130–50.

Miller, Clarence H., and Caryl K. Berrey. "The Structure of Integrity: The Cardinal Virtues in Donne's *Satyre III*." *Costerus*, n.s., 1 (1974): 27–45.

Moore, Thomas V. "Donne's Use of Uncertainty as a Vital Force in *Satyre III*." *Modern Philology* 67 (1969): 41–49.

Newton, Richard C. "Donne the Satirist." *Texas Studies in Literature and Language* 16 (1974): 427–45.

Parker, Barbara L., and J. Max Patrick. "Two Hollow Men: The Pretentious Wooer and the Wayward Bridegroom of Donne's *Satyre I*." *Seventeenth Century News* 33 (1975): 10–14.

Roberts, John R. "Donne's Satyre III Reconsidered." *College Language Association Journal* 12 (1968): 105–15.

Sellin, Paul R. "The Proper Dating of John Donne's *Satyre III*." *Huntington Library Quarterly* 43 (1980): 275–312. Dates it in 1620.

Zivley, Sherry. "Imagery in John Donne's *Satyres*." *Studies in English Literature* 6 (1966): 87–95.

X. VERSE LETTERS

Byard, Margaret M. "The Trade of Courtiership: The Countess of Bedford and the Bedford Memorials—A Family History from 1585 to 1607." *History Today* (1979): 20–28.

Cameron, Allen B. "Donne's Deliberative Verse Epistles." *English Literary Renaissance* 6 (1976): 369–403.

Lein, Clayton D. "Donne's 'The Storme': The Poem and the Tradition." *English Literary Renaissance* 4 (1974): 137–63.

Mauer, Margaret. "John Donne's Verse Letters." *Modern Language Quarterly* 37 (1976): 234–59.

Mizejewski, Linda. "Darkness and Disproportion: A Study of Donne's 'Storme' and 'Calme.' " *Journal of English and Germanic Philology* 76 (1977): 217–30.

Nellist, B. F. "Donne's 'Storm' and 'Calm' and the Descriptive Tradition." *Modern Language Review* 59 (1964): 511–15.

Pebworth, T. L., and C. J. Summers. ". . . The Exchange of Verse Letters between Donne and Henry Wotton." *Modern Philology* 81 (1984): 361–77.

Sackton, Alexander. "Donne and the Privacy of Verse." *Studies in English Literature* 7 (1967): 67–82.

Storhoff, Gary. "Metaphors of Despair in Donne's 'The Storme' and 'The Calme.' " *Concerning Poetry* 9 (1976) 2: 41–45.

Thomson, Patricia. "Donne and the Poetry of Patronage: The Verse Letters." *John Donne: Essays in Celebration*. Ed. A. J. Smith. London, 1972. Ch. 11.

XI. ANNIVERSARIES

Bath, Michael. "Donne's *Anatomy of the World* and the Legend of the Oldest Animals." *Review of English Studies* 32 (1981): 302–8.

Bellette, Antony F. "Art and Imitation in Donne's *Anniversaries*." *Studies in English Literature* 15 (1975): 83–96.

Clark, Ira. " 'How witty's ruine': The Difficulties of Donne's 'Idea of a Woman' in the First of his *Anniversaries*." *South Atlantic Review* 53 (1988): 19–26.

Elliott, Emory B., Jr. "Persona and Parody in Donne's *The Anniversaries*." *Quarterly Journal of Speech* 58 (1972): 48–57.

Fox, Ruth A. "Donne's *Anniversaries* and the Art of Living." *ELH* 38 (1972): 528–41.

Hughes, Richard E. "The Woman in Donne's *Anniversaries*." *ELH* 34 (1967): 307–26.

Kreps, Barbara I. "The Serpent and Christian Paradox in Donne's *First Anniversary*." *Rivista di letterature moderne e comparate* 24 (1971): 198–207.

Lebans, W. M. "Donne's *Anniversaries*" and the Tradition of Funeral Elegy." *ELH* 39 (1972): 545–59.

Lewalski, Barbara K. *Donne's "Anniversaries' and the Poetry of Praise: The Creation of a Symbolic Mode*. Princeton, 1973.

Love, Harold. "The Argument of Donne's *First Anniversary*." *Essential Articles for the Study of John Donne's Poetry*. Ed. John R. Roberts. Hamden, Connecticut, 1975. 355–62.

Low, Anthony. "The 'Turning Wheele': Carew, Jonson, Donne and the First Law of Motion." *John Donne Journal* 1 (1982): 69–80.

Maud, Ralph. "Donne's *First Anniversary*." *Boston University Studies in English* 2 (1956): 218–25.

Parrish, Paul A. "Donne's *The First Anniversarie*." *Explicator* 33 (1975): 64.

Willard, Thomas. "Donne's Anatomy Lesson: Vesalian or Paracelsian?" *John Donne Journal* 3 (1984): 35–61.

Williamson, George. "The Design of Donne's *Anniversaries*." *Modern Philology* 60 (1963): 183–91.

XII. DIVINE POEMS

Anderson, Donald K., Jr. "Donne's 'Hymne to God my God, in my Sicknesse' and the T-in-O Maps." *South Atlantic Quarterly* 71 (1972): 465–72.

Asals, Heather. "John Donne and the Grammar of Redemption." *English Studies in Canada* 5 (1979): 125–39.

Baumgaertner, Jill. " 'Harmony' in Donne's 'La Corona' and 'Upon the Translation of the Psalms.' " *John Donne Journal* 3 (1984): 141–56.

Bellette, Anthony F. " 'Little Worlds Made Cunningly': Significant Form in Donne's *Holy Sonnets* and 'Goodfriday, 1613,' " *Studies in Philology* 72 (1975): 322–47.

Blanch, Robert J. "Fear and Despair in Donne's *Holy Sonnets*." *American Benedictine Review* 25 (1974): 476–84.

Bloomer, Peggy A. "A Re-Examination of Donne's *La Corona*." *Essays in Arts and Sciences* 7 (1978): 37–44.

Chambers, A. B. " 'Goodfriday, 1613. Riding Westward': Looking Back." *John Donne Journal* 6 (1987): 186–201.

Chambers, A. B. " 'Goodfriday, 1613. Riding Westward': The Poem and the Tradition." *ELH* 28 (1961): 31–53.

Clark, Ira. "Explicating the Heart and Dramatizing the Poet: Seventeenth-Century Innovations by English Emblematists and Donne." *Christ Revealed*. Gainsville, Florida, 1982. Ch. 3.

Dubinski, R. R. "Donne's *La Corona* and Christ's Mediatorial Office." *Renaissance and Reformation* 4 (1980): 203–8.

Duncan, Joseph E. "Donne's 'Hymne to God my God, in my sicknesse' and Iconographic Tradition." *John Donne Journal* 3 (1984): 157–80.

Evans, Gillian R. "John Donne and the Augustinian Paradox of Sin." *Review of English Studies*, n.s., 33 (1982): 1–22.

Flynn, Dennis. " 'Awry and Squint': The Dating of Donne's Holy Sonnets." *John Donne Journal* 7 (1988): 35–46.

French, A. L. "The Psychopathology of Donne's Holy Sonnets." *Critical Review* 13 (1970): 111–24.

Friedman, Donald M. "Memory and the Art of Salvation in Donne's Good Friday Poem." *English Literary Renaissance* 3 (1973): 418–42.

Handscombe, Richard. "Donne's Holy Sonnet VI: A Problem of Plainness." *Language and Style* 13 (1980) 2: 98–108.

Leigh, David J. "Donne's 'A Hymne to God the Father': New Dimensions." *Studies in Philology* 75 (1978): 84–92.

Malpezzi, Frances M. "The Weightlessness of Sin: Donne's 'Thou hast made me' and the Psychostatic Tradition." *South Central Review* 4 (Summer 1987): 71–77.

Maurer, Margaret. "The Circular Argument of Donne's *La Corona*." *Studies in English Literature* 22 (1982): 51–68.

Nania, John, and P. J. Klemp. "John Donne's *La Corona*: A Second Structure." *Renaissance and Reformation*, n.s., 2 (1978): 49–54.

O'Connell, Patrick F. " 'Restore Thine Image': Structure and Theme in Donne's 'Goodfriday.' " *John Donne Journal* 4 (1985): 13–28.
———. "The Successive Arrangements of Donne's *Holy Sonnets*." *Philological Quarterly* 60 (1981): 323–42.
Pollock, John J. "A Mystical Impulse in Donne's Devotional Poetry." *Studia Mystica*, 2 (1979): 17–24. On "A Hymn to Christ, . . ."
Pritchard, Allan. "Donne's Mr. Tilman." *Review of English Studies*, n.s., 24 (1973): 38–42.
Ricks, Don M. "The Westmoreland Manuscript and the Order of Donne's *Holy Sonnets*." *Studies in Philology* 63 (1966): 187–95.
Stachniewski, John. "John Donne: The Despair of the *Holy Sonnets*." *ELH* 48 (1982): 677–705.
Stull, William L. " 'Why are not Sonnets made of thee?': A New Context for the *Holy Sonnets* of Donne, Herbert, and Milton." *Modern Philology* 80 (1982): 129–35.
Sullivan, David M. "Riders to the West: 'Goodfriday, 1613.' " *John Donne Journal* 6 (1987): 1–8.
Walker, Julia. "The Religious Lyric as Genre." *English Language Notes* 25 (1987): 39–45. On "La Corona," compared to other poems.
Wall, John N., Jr. "Donne's Wit of Redemption: The Drama of Prayer in the *Holy Sonnets*." *Studies in Philology* 73 (1976): 189–203.
Zitner, S. P. "Rhetoric and Doctrine in Donne's Holy Sonnet IV." *Renaissance and Reformation*, n.s., 3 (1979): 66–76.

XIII. HOLY SONNET 10 (XIV) "Batter my heart"

Ching, Marvin K. L. "The Relationship Among the Diverse Senses of a Pun." *The SECOL Bulletin* 2 (1978): 1–8.
Clements, Arthur L. *Poetry of Contemplation*. Albany, 1990. 69–75, 260–62. First published in *Modern Language Notes* 76 (1961): 484–89.
Cornelius, David K. "Donne's Holy Sonnet XIV." *Explicator* 24 (1965): 25.
Graham, Desmond. *Introduction to Poetry*. London, 1968. 29–30, 63–66.
Gregory, Michael. "A Theory for Stylists—Exemplified: Donne's 'Holy Sonnet XIV.' " *Language and Style* 7 (1974): 108–18.
Hagopian, John. "John Donne: Batter My Heart." *Insight III*. Frankfurt, 1969, 86–96.
Heist, William W. "Donne on Divine Grace: Holy Sonnet No. XIV." *Papers of the Michigan Academy of Science, Arts and Letters* 53 (1968): 311–20.
Kerrigan, William. "The Fearful Accommodations of John Donne." *English Literary Renaissance* 4 (1974): 337–63. 351–56 on Holy Sonnet 10 (XIV).
Klinck, Dennis R. "John Donne's 'knottie Trinitie.' " *Renascence* 33 (1981): 240–55. 248–50 on Holy Sonnet 10 (XIV).
Lloyd, Charles E. "The Author of Peace and John Donne's Holy Sonnet XIV." *Journal of the History of Ideas* 30 (1969): 251–52.
McCormick, Frank. "Donne, the Pope, and 'Holy Sonnets XIV.' " *CEA Critic* 45 (1983): 23–24.
Moorhem, Joan. "Two Explications—John Donne's Holy Sonnet XIV and Gerald Manley Hopkins' Sonnet 69." *Insight* 3 (1971): 62–71.
Moseley, C. W. R. D. "A Reading of John Donne's Holy Sonnet XIV." *Archiv für das Studium der neuven Sprachen und Literaturen* 217 (1980): 103–8.
Mueller, William R. "Donne's Adulterous Female Town." *Modern Language Notes* 76 (1961): 312–14.
Newton, Willoughby. "A Study of John Donne's Sonnet XIV." *Anglican Theological Review* 41 (1959): 10–12.
Romein, Tunis. "Donne's 'Holy Sonnet XIV.' " *Explicator* 42 (1984): 12–14.
Ruotolo, Lucio P. "The Trinitarian Framework of Donne's Holy Sonnet XIV." *Journal of the History of Ideas* 60 (1966): 445–46.
Sherwood, Terry G. *Fulfilling the Circle: A Study of John Donne's Thought*. Toronto, 1984. 151–54.
Steele, Thomas J.S.J. "Donne's Holy Sonnets, XIV." *Explicator* 29 (1971): 74.
Steig, Michael. "Donne's Divine Rapist: Unconscious Fantasy in Holy Sonnet XIV." *University of Hartford Studies in Literature* 4 (1972): 52–58.
Tsur, Reuven. "Poem, Prayer, and Meditation: An Exercise in Literary Semantics." *Style* 8 (1974): 404–24.
Wanninger, Mary. "Donne's Holy Sonnets, XIV." *Explicator* 28 (1969/70): 37.
Winny, James. *A Preface to Donne*. Rev. ed. London, 1981. 160–64.
Yarrow, Ralph. "Admitting the Infinite: John Donne's Poem 'Batter My Heart.' " *Studies in Mystical Literature* 1 (1981): 210–17.

Index of Titles

Index of First Lines